Locke's defence of toleration is increasingly recognized as a topic not only of historical interest but also of importance for contemporary political theory, and politics. John Tate has written a book that reflects close understanding of Locke's texts and circumstances and of the sophisticated scholarship that has been devoted to them. This is a thorough and engaging book on a major topic.

Richard Vernon, *University of Western Ontario, Canada*

In this bold and important new book John Tate seeks to rescue Locke from the claims of the historians of contemporary irrelevance and the charges of illiberalism of some liberal political philosophers. Through a careful and sensitive discussion of the development of his ideas about toleration, and in particular close attention to the protracted debate with Jonas Proast, Tate seeks to re-establish Locke's credentials as a founder of the liberal tradition of continuing relevance to liberal theorising.

John Horton, *Professor Emeritus of Political Philosophy, Keele University, UK*

Liberty, Toleration and Equality

The seventeenth century English philosopher John Locke is widely recognized as one of the seminal sources of the modern liberal tradition. *Liberty, Toleration and Equality* examines the development of Locke's ideas on toleration, from their beginnings, to the culmination of this development in Locke's fifteen-year debate with his great antagonist, the Anglican clergyman Jonas Proast. Locke, like Proast, was a sincere Christian but, unlike Proast, Locke was able to develop, over time, a perspective on toleration which allowed him to concede liberty to competing views which he, personally, perceived to be "false and absurd". In this respect, Locke sought to affirm what has since become the basic liberal principle that liberty and toleration are most significant when they are accorded to views to which we ourselves are profoundly at odds.

John William Tate seeks to show how Locke was able to develop this position on toleration over a long intellectual career. Tate also challenges some of the most prominent contemporary perspectives on Locke, within the academic literature, contending that these fall short of perceiving what is essential to Locke's position.

John William Tate is Senior Lecturer in Politics at the University of Newcastle, Australia. His primary research interest is in the area of political philosophy and history of political thought.

Routledge Studies in Social and Political Thought

103 **Authenticity, Autonomy and Multiculturalism**
Geoffrey Brahm Levey

104 **Marxism, Religion and Ideology**
Themes from David McLellan
Edited by David Bates, Iain MacKenzie and Sean Sayers

105 **Distributive Justice Debates in Political and Social Thought**
Perspectives on Finding a Fair Share
Edited by Camilla Boisen and Matthew C. Murray

106 **Re-Grounding Cosmopolitanism**
Towards a Post-Foundational Cosmopolitanism
Edited by Tamara Caraus and Elena Paris

107 **Panarchy**
Political Theories of Non-Territorial States
Edited by Aviezer Tucker and Gian Piero de Bellis

108 **Gramsci's Critique of Civil Society**
Towards a New Concept of Hegemony
Marco Fonseca

109 **Deconstructing Happiness**
Critical Sociology and the Good Life
Jordan McKenzie

110 **Novels and the Sociology of the Contemporary**
Arpad Szakolczai

111 **Liberty, Toleration and Equality**
John Locke, Jonas Proast and the *Letters Concerning Toleration*
John William Tate

112 **Jürgen Habermas and the European Economic Crisis**
Cosmopolitanism Reconsidered
Edited by Gaspare M. Genna, Thomas O. Haakenson, and Ian W. Wilson

Liberty, Toleration and Equality

John Locke, Jonas Proast and the *Letters Concerning Toleration*

John William Tate

NEW YORK AND LONDON

First published 2016
by Routledge
711 Third Avenue, New York, NY 10017

and by Routledge
2 Park Square, Milton Park, Abingdon, Oxon, OX14 4RN

First issued in paperback 2018

Routledge is an imprint of the Taylor & Francis Group, an informa business

© 2016 Taylor & Francis

The right of John William Tate to be identified as author of this work has been asserted by him in accordance with sections 77 and 78 of the Copyright, Designs and Patents Act 1988.

All rights reserved. No part of this book may be reprinted or reproduced or utilized in any form or by any electronic, mechanical, or other means, now known or hereafter invented, including photocopying and recording, or in any information storage or retrieval system, without permission in writing from the publishers.

Trademark notice: Product or corporate names may be trademarks or registered trademarks, and are used only for identification and explanation without intent to infringe.

Library of Congress Cataloging in Publication Data
Names: Tate, John William, author.
Title: Liberty, toleration and equality : John Locke, Jonas Proast and the letters concerning toleration / John William Tate.
Description: New York, NY : Routledge, 2016. | Series: Routledge studies in social and political thought ; 111 | Includes bibliographical references and index.
Identifiers: LCCN 2015045827| ISBN 9781138647800 (hbk) | ISBN 9781315626864 (ebk)
Subjects: LCSH: Toleration–Early works to 1800. | Liberty–Early works to 1800. | Locke, John, 1632-1704. Epistola de tolerantia. | Proast, Jonas.
Classification: LCC BR1610 .T28 2016 | DDC 323.44/2–dc23
LC record available at http://lccn.loc.gov/2015045827

ISBN 13: 978-1-138-59966-6 (pbk)
ISBN 13: 978-1-138-64780-0 (hbk)

Typeset in Sabon
by Wearset Ltd, Boldon, Tyne and Wear

For Gina and Maurie Tate

"The horrid cruelties that in all ages, and of late in our view, have been committed under the name, and upon the account of religion, give so just an offence and abhorrence to all who have any remains, not only of religion, but humanity left, that the world is ashamed to own it".
(John Locke, "A Third Letter for Toleration", in J. Locke, *The Works of John Locke*, Vol. VI, Aalen: Scientia Verlag, 1963, p. 262)

Contents

Preface   xiii
Acknowledgements   xvi

Introduction   1
Locke and the Liberal Tradition 2
Theological Foundations 4
The Limits of Theology 5
"Civil Concerns" 6
Locke and the History of Toleration 7
The Focus 8
Tensions 9
The Wider Literature 10
Inside and Outside 11
Summary of Chapters 13

1 Locke, Liberty and Governance   21
The Normative and Practical Justification of Toleration 24
Categorical Distinction 25
Varieties of Toleration 28
Separation of Church and State 28
Consent, Legitimacy and Obligation 31
Consent, Legitimacy and Toleration 34
Realpolitik 37

2 From Conformity to Toleration – Matters of Influence   47
Two Tracts on Government 49
Wider Events 52
Locke's Early Rejection of Toleration 53
Locke, Liberty and the Two Tracts 55
Outcomes 57
Locke's Shift 57

      Quantitative vs. Qualitative 59
      Matters of Influence 61
      An Alternative View 65
      "A Black Hole" 67

3 **From Conformity to Toleration – Matters of Argument**   75
      Locke's Transition 75
      Locke's Practical Reassessment 76
      Normative Dimension 78
      Competing Imperatives 79
      Locke's Normative Reassessment 80
      From the Two Tracts *to* An Essay Concerning Toleration 81
      Premise (ii) 83
      Realpolitik Revisited 88
      Premise (i) 89
      Premise (iii) 92

4 **Locke in the Dock**   101
      The Practical *Discourse of the* Letter 101
      The Normative *Discourse of the* Letter 102
      Locke and Rights 106
      The Two Treatises *and the* Letter 107
      Locke as Anti-Liberal 108
      Waldron's Reading of the Letter 110
      Waldron's Locke 110
      Waldron, Locke and the State 113
      Waldron, Locke and Legitimacy 115
      Waldron, Locke and Liberalism 117

5 **Three "Considerations" for Toleration**   125
      Locke and the "Modal" Account of the State 125
      The Truth Argument 127
      The "Truth Argument" Considered 129
      Pitfalls of the "Truth Argument" 131
      "Truth" vs. "Rationality" 132
      The Rationality Argument 135
      The Consent Argument 136
      The "Three Considerations" 138

6 **Locke vs. Proast**   143
      The Revolution of 1688 144
      Locke and Proast 147

Pitfalls 148
"Indirectly *and* At a Distance" 150
Proast and Restoration England 152
Waldron, Goldie and Dunn 153
"*Third Sort or Degree of Perswasion*" 157
Goldie Revisited 159

7 Proast's Response: "True Religion and the Salvation of Souls"   167
Proast and the Letter 167
The Truth Argument 168
Proast and "True Religion" 172
"*Begging the Question*" 173
"*Non-Neutral Principles*" 175
"*Geneva" and the "Indies*" 176
Proast and Religious Diversity 180
Proast and the Consent Argument I 181
Proast and the Consent Argument II 184
Proast's Appeal to God 186
Proast, Berlin and Mill 188
The Rationality Argument 190

8 Locke's Reply: "That Which Without Impiety Cannot be Said"   195
"*Penalties*" 196
"*Proportion" and "Design*" 196
Punishment and Conversion 201
Locke, Proast and Consent 204
Locke, Proast and God 206
God, Man and Commonwealths 207
Locke's Response to Proast's Appeal to God 209
Christian History 211
Proast and the Will of God 215
Proast's Contradiction 216
Proast Agonistes 218

9 Locke, Scepticism and Consent   225
Locke and Scepticism I 226
(a) and (b) 228
Locke and Scepticism II 232
Toleration and Moral Choice 240
Ultimate Conditions of Possibility I 242

xii *Contents*

Ultimate Conditions of Possibility II 244
Locke, Truth and Diversity 245

10 Locke's "Civil Perspective"   251
The Civil Perspective 251
Public Agreement 253
Locke and the "Legislative Point of View" 255
Locke's Legacy: John Rawls and Political Liberalism *256*
Rawls and Locke 259

11 Conclusion   266

Index   269

Preface

On 7 January 2015, at 11.30 a.m., two brothers, Chérif and Saïd Kouachi, carrying Kalashnikov assault rifles, arrived at the Paris headquarters of the *Charlie Hebdo* magazine, located on the Rue Nicolas-Appert. Encountering Corinne Rey, one of the cartoonists for the magazine, and her young daughter outside the building, they forced her to grant them key-code access to the premises. Upon entering the ground floor they shot dead the caretaker of the building, Frédéric Boisseau, before making their way to the second floor where an editorial meeting for the magazine was taking place. There they entered and shot dead the editor's police body-guard, Franck Brinsolaro, before calling for the editor of the magazine, and four of its cartoonists, by name, killing each of them also. These were Stéphane Charbonnier, Jean Cabut, Bernard Verlhac, Philippe Honoré and Georges Wolinski. As they killed these individuals the gunmen were heard to yell, in Arabic, "God is great" and "We have avenged the Prophet Muhammad". They also killed three other editorial staff present in the room, Bernard Maris, Mustapha Ourrad and Elsa Cayat, as well as a guest, Michel Renaud, who was attending the meeting that day. Upon leaving the building, the gunmen killed a police officer, Ahmed Merabet, shooting him twice on the pavement outside.[1]

This tragic event, in which so many lives were lost, is part of a much longer history. This is the history of the three-hundred-year struggle of what we now know as the liberal tradition to advance the frontiers of freedom of speech, thought and inquiry against the certitudes and, at times, violent dogmatism of religion. Those involved with *Charlie Hebdo* died in this struggle just as much as their earlier counterparts who perished at the hands of church and state in defence of similar principles. This will no doubt sound pompous and melodramatic to the wry and sardonic individuals who write and draw for *Charlie Hebdo*. But it is true nevertheless.

The latter part of this book focuses on one of the seminal episodes in this history – the late-seventeenth-century debate between the English philosopher John Locke and the Anglican clergyman Jonas Proast. The topic of Locke and Proast's engagement was "toleration", not least the extent to which individuals are entitled to arrive at their own beliefs and practices concerning religion independent of church or state authority, thereby exercising their individual liberty in these areas. Locke, like Proast, was a sincere Christian but, unlike Proast, Locke was able to develop, over time, a perspective on toleration which allowed him to concede to individuals a liberty concerning religious belief and practice even when he, personally, believed such beliefs and practices to be "false and absurd". In this respect, Locke sought to affirm what has since become the basic liberal principle that liberty and toleration are most significant when they are accorded to views to which we ourselves are profoundly at odds.

Given the fundamental importance of religion within late-seventeenth-century English society, and the extent to which church and state were entwined on this matter, to consider the question of religious toleration at this time meant raising profound issues concerning the scope of individual liberty and its relation to the prevailing political and religious authorities. It was these late-seventeenth-century questions concerning individual liberty, freedom of conscience and religious toleration which, in the eighteenth century, animated much of the European Enlightenment, in its engagement with these same authorities of church and state, and have helped provide the continuing impetus for the liberal tradition as it developed in the nineteenth, twentieth and twenty-first centuries.

Charlie Hebdo and its staff are on the side of the liberal tradition, with its emphasis on the entitlement of individuals to engage in freedom of thought, inquiry and expression on any topic to which they put their mind. Certainly many who work at *Charlie Hebdo* are left-wing in orientation, and so would be critical of other elements of the liberal tradition, not least its belief that individual liberty is expanded when economic outcomes are determined by free markets rather than the state. But in regard to the liberal principle that freedom of thought, inquiry and expression are fundamental to individual liberty, and to a free society itself, *Charlie Hebdo* and the liberal tradition are at one.[2]

We shall see that some Locke scholars have sought to distance Locke from this liberal tradition, emphasizing his own connections to religion and the obligations associated with it. Yet it is Locke's vital links to the liberal tradition, and his continuing relevance to it, which this book seeks to show, and does so by tracing the evolution of Locke's ideas on toleration as these developed throughout his intellectual career. Magazines such as *Charlie Hebdo*, on the other hand, and the recent tragic fate of some of its most prominent staff, demonstrate the continuing importance and relevance of this tradition itself.

Notes

1 BBC (2015); Walt (2015).
2 It is the liberal, rather than the democratic, tradition which has an overwhelming commitment to individual liberty, and therefore to the freedom of conscience, expression and inquiry that is a necessary part of this liberty. As Will Kymlicka tells us: "The basic principles of liberalism, of course, are principles of individual freedom" (Kymlicka 1995: 75). The democratic tradition, by contrast, has an

overwhelming commitment to the "collective" (generally understood as the political "majority"). From the perspective of the liberal tradition, it is often the intrusion of the "collective" that has to be resisted if individual liberty (particularly the liberty of individuals belonging to unpopular minorities or expressing unpopular views) is to be protected within polities. This is one of the dominant themes of John Stuart Mill's essay, *On Liberty*, published in 1859 (Mill 1971). The *Charlie Hebdo* affair, on the other hand, shows that individual liberty must also be protected from militant minorities seeking to inflict physical (as distinct from verbal) retribution on those whose views they find abhorrent. Most Western polities are "liberal democracies", meaning that both the liberal and the democratic traditions, along with their very different values and priorities, must be negotiated within them.

References

BBC (2015) "Charlie Hebdo Attack: Three Days of Terror", *News Europe*. Available at www.bbc.co.uk/news/world-europe-30708237 (last accessed 1 September 2015).

Kymlicka, W. (1995) *Multicultural Citizenship. A Liberal Theory of Minority Rights*. Oxford: Oxford University Press.

Mill, J. S. (1971) "On Liberty". In: J. S. Mill, *Utilitarianism, Liberty, Representative Government*. London: Dent.

Walt, V. (2015) "Meet the Woman the Paris Gunmen Spared", *Time*, 9 January 2015. Available at http://time.com/3661222/charlie-hebdo-women-gunmen-spared/.

Acknowledgements

I would like to thank my parents, Gina and Maurie Tate, without whose encouragement and support I would never have made it through university, let alone other aspects of life. I would also like to thank my birth mother, Dianne Harvey, who, in inauspicious and difficult circumstances, made the decision to bring me into the world in the first place. I would also like to thank my sister Carolyn Tate.

I would like to thank Natalja Mortensen and Lillian Rand, at Routledge, along with Hannah Riley at Wearset and Liz Hunter at Humbie Editorial, for their assistance and support in getting this book to print.

I also wish to thank Professor Richard Vernon of Western University, Canada and Associate Professor Greg Melleuish of the University of Wollongong, Australia, for taking the time and effort to read and evaluate this text, and for their positive and encouraging comments in regard to it.

I would like to thank the Faculty of Business and Law (within which the Politics discipline is located) at the University of Newcastle, Australia, for the generous material support they provide in order to encourage research among academic staff, as well as the academic staff themselves for making the Faculty a collegiate and friendly environment within which to work.

I would like to thank the Morrell Centre for Toleration, located in the Politics Department at the University of York, UK, and in particular its Director, Professor Matt Matravers, where I was "Visiting Scholar" for part of 2012 and where some of the research and writing for this book was undertaken. In 2012 and 2015, I presented papers at the Morrell Centre on the topic of toleration and therefore involving subject matter related to the topic of this book. I would like to thank the staff and students at York who attended the papers and whose discussion and advice (as well as disagreement) were so valuable in helping me to clarify my own ideas. I would also like to thank the staff and students at the "Political Theory Workshop" at Nuffield College, Oxford, and the School of Politics and International Relations at Queen Mary, University of London, where I presented papers in 2015 on the topic of toleration, and whose rigorous discussion also helped me to advance my own ideas.

Finally, and most importantly, I would like to thank my wife, Josie, and my two daughters, Jasmine and Jade, for their love and affection, for making every day worthwhile and for putting up with all the hours I spend in my office at home with the door closed.

Permission has been granted by the relevant publishers to quote excerpts from the following sources:

Maurice Cranston, "The Politics of John Locke", *History Today*, 2 (9) 1952. Copyright © 1952 *History Today*. Reprinted with permission of the publisher.

Philip Abrams, "Introduction", to John Locke, *Two Tracts on Government*, ed. Philip Abrams (Cambridge: Cambridge University Press, 1967). Copyright © 1967 Cambridge University Press. Reprinted with the permission of Cambridge University Press.

James Tully, "Introduction", in John Locke, *A Letter Concerning Toleration*, ed. James Tully (Indianapolis. IN: Hackett Publishing Co., 1983). Copyright © 1983. Hackett Publishing Company. Reprinted with permission of the publisher.

Jeremy Waldron, "Locke: Toleration and the Rationality of Persecution", in Susan Mendus (ed) *Justifying Toleration. Conceptual and Historical Perspectives* (Cambridge: Cambridge University Press, 1988). Copyright © 1988 Cambridge University Press. Reprinted with the permission of Cambridge University Press.

John Rawls, *Political Liberalism*. Exp. ed. (New York: Columbia University Press, 2005). Copyright © 2005 Columbia University Press. Reprinted with the permission of the publisher.

Introduction

This book traces the development of John Locke's ideas on toleration, from their origins when Locke was a Student at Christ Church, Oxford, to his debate with the Anglican clergyman Jonas Proast in the last fourteen years of Locke's life. This debate was the final act in Locke's engagement with toleration, his last *Letter* to Proast ending in mid-sentence in the year of his death, 1704. In taking this longer perspective, the book differs from most other accounts of the Locke/Proast debate, which tend to focus primarily on the debate itself. I believe the longer perspective is justified because Locke, in this debate, drew upon decades of involvement with the subject of toleration and also encountered, in Proast, a critic sufficiently tenacious to make him justify, often in new ways, positions he might have thought had been substantiated long before. Old positions were buttressed, in some cases discarded, and new ones developed by Locke, as he sought to respond to Proast's vigorous defence of religious conformity within England and the use of force, on the part of governments, necessary to sustain this. The debate therefore provides revealing insights into Locke and his conception of toleration which are not available elsewhere.

As will become apparent in the chapters that follow, this book also differs, in other ways, from the most prominent accounts of this topic within the secondary literature. These competing perspectives provide a useful set of contrasts against which the book seeks to develop its own ideas and interpretations. However the primary focus of analysis is centred, not on the secondary literature, but on Locke's works themselves, seeking to explain how they, and the thoughts on toleration that they express, developed over time, and how Locke, who arrived late within European toleration debates, advanced the basic propositions, perspectives and values which would eventually help form the basis of what we now know as the liberal tradition.

The American scholar Stanley Fish declared in 1997:

> The modern contours of the debate concerning the relationship between church and state were established in 1689 by Locke in *A Letter Concerning Toleration*, and discussion of the issue has not advanced one millimetre beyond Locke's treatment even though over three hundred years have passed.[1]

2   Introduction

While containing a significant element of hyperbole, this statement nevertheless does show the immense influence wielded by Locke, and in particular his *Letter Concerning Toleration*, on subsequent debates within the liberal tradition. The development of Locke's thought on toleration is often believed to culminate in *A Letter Concerning Toleration*, first published in 1689, with his subsequent engagement with Jonas Proast being conducted, as Mark Goldie tells us, "on an apparently narrow front", with "no general theory of toleration ... at issue".[2] Yet this book will show that Locke's engagement with Proast was conducted on a much broader front, involving much more significant debate concerning toleration, than either Professor Goldie or other Locke scholars such as Jeremy Waldron or John Dunn have recognized. Not least, Locke, in his engagement with Proast, significantly expanded his discussion and his defence of toleration, beyond that which he offered in the *Letter*, as well as discarding some of the positions which he had advanced in the *Letter* itself. For all these reasons, Locke's debate with Proast, as well as the development of Locke's thoughts on toleration leading up to this debate, are well worth renewed consideration. It is such consideration which the subsequent chapters seek to provide.

This introduction will point to some of the basic features of Locke's political philosophy, beginning with Locke's relationship to the liberal tradition. It will then explain the approach which the book adopts for engaging with his political philosophy and investigating the development of his ideas on toleration over time. Finally, it will provide a brief description of the content of each chapter and how each contributes to the overall argument of the book and the conclusions it seeks to reach.

Locke and the Liberal Tradition

In 1859, only eleven years after the publication of the first volumes of Thomas Babington Macaulay's *History of England*, John Stuart Mill sounded a note of scepticism concerning any Whig optimism about the advance of religious liberty in Europe and the religious toleration exercised by European states that made this possible. The triumph of religious liberty, Mill argued, had little to do with the intrinsic worth of the principle of liberty itself, or the rigour of argument in favour of toleration, and instead much to do with the material realities of political power. As Mill put it in his essay *On Liberty*:

> [T]he dictum that truth always triumphs over persecution is one of those pleasant falsehoods which men repeat after one another till they pass into commonplaces, but which all experience refutes. History teems with instances of truth put down by persecution. If not suppressed forever, it may be thrown back for centuries. To speak only of religious opinions: the Reformation broke out at least twenty times before Luther, and was put down. Arnold of Brescia was put down.

Fra Dolcino was put down. Savonarola was put down. The Albigeois were put down. The Vaudois were put down. The Lollards were put down. The Hussites were put down. Even after the era of Luther, wherever persecution was persisted in, it was successful. In Spain, Italy, Flanders, the Austrian Empire, Protestantism was rooted out; and, most likely, would have been so in England, had Queen Mary lived, or Queen Elizabeth died. Persecution has always succeeded, save where the heretics were too strong a party to be effectually persecuted.... It is a piece of idle sentimentality that truth, merely as truth, has any inherent power denied to error of prevailing against the dungeon and the stake.[3]

And yet, Mill's pessimism notwithstanding, the history of liberal political thought and practice is strewn with concerted attempts, on the part of its adherents, to defend religious liberty as a principle, along with the state policy of toleration which they believe makes such liberty possible. Indeed, for many liberals, freedom of conscience, when it comes to matters such as religion, is just as foundational an expression of individual liberty as freedom of speech. In fact, for liberals such as Mill, the two were "practically inseparable".[4]

John Locke died more than a century before Mill made his first appearance in the world but, like Mill, Locke is widely recognized as an inaugural figure within the liberal tradition.[5] Certainly it is anachronistic to call Locke himself a "liberal" for, as Maurice Cranston tells us, "No one spoke of 'liberals' until after Waterloo".[6] Indeed, as Quentin Skinner points out, we must also be careful in identifying Locke *entirely* with the liberal tradition, given that he began his intellectual career advancing a set of authoritarian concerns in no way consistent with this later doctrine.[7] Nevertheless, as we shall see in Chapters 2 and 3, by the time of *An Essay Concerning Toleration*, composed in 1667, Locke had established a set of ideas and a framework for understanding political practice which were quite distinct from his earlier authoritarian outlook and which would exercise a seminal influence upon what would eventually come to be known as the "liberal tradition".[8]

Needless to say, Locke himself was not aware of this. It is only in retrospect that a "tradition" is conceived as existing, let alone as existing in cohesive terms, thereby giving a sense of continuity to the whole. As Zygmunt Bauman tells us, "tradition lives only by being recapitulated, by being construed as a *heritage* ... it appears, if at all, only at the end, never at the beginning, of agreement".[9] It is in these retrospective terms, therefore, that Locke's foundational status for the liberal tradition can be recognized.[10]

Locke's conception of toleration is one feature of his political philosophy which would resonate widely with later liberals. This ideal of toleration is linked to other themes within Locke's political philosophy and, as we shall see, ultimately arose from his foundational commitments to individual liberty and equality. It is these commitments to liberty and equality which, therefore, provide the normative basis for Locke's commitment to toleration, and, for this reason, this book's title combines all three terms together. For Locke, toleration is ultimately justified, in normative terms, because it gives expression to individual liberty and the *equal* entitlement of individuals to this liberty.

However from the time of *An Essay Concerning Toleration*, in 1667, Locke also advances a set of *practical* justifications for toleration, quite separate from these normative concerns. One of these is his insistence that toleration is justified, as state policy, because it is the most effective means for states, in a context of religious difference and diversity, to secure practical political ends, not least civil peace, and the effective state governance necessary to achieve this. Such matters are quite distinct from any concern with individual liberty or individuals' equal entitlement to this liberty. As we shall see, this normative/practical divide in Locke's justification of toleration runs right throughout his political philosophy.

Theological Foundations

Locke's foundational commitments to individual liberty and equality, which form the normative basis of his justification of toleration, ultimately arose from his theological convictions – not least his belief in the inherently equal worth of each individual. In his most mature political work, the *Two Treatises of Government*, published in 1689, Locke, in two early passages within the second *Treatise*, makes clear that, in his view, this inherently equal worth, and the individual entitlement to liberty and equality which arises from it, are due to our equal status as God's "Creatures" (though some feminist theorists have questioned whether Locke intended this liberty and equality to apply equally, in every respect, to men and women).[11] Both passages in the *Two Treatises* therefore make clear that the ultimate normative foundation of Locke's political philosophy, centred on individual entitlements to liberty and equality, arises from theological sources.

The first of these two passages in the *Two Treatises* refers to the natural state of "liberty" and "equality" that Locke believes individuals occupy in a pre-political "state of nature" – a liberty and equality which, he says, arise from the fact that we are all "Creatures of the same species and rank promiscuously born to all the same advantages of Nature, and the use of the same faculties", with the result that we "should also be equal one amongst another without Subordination or Subjection".[12]

The second passage, in making reference to natural law, explicitly refers to the theological source of this liberty and equality. Locke identifies natural law, as it exists within the state of nature and civil society, with the will of God, and also with human reason.[13] He insists that it is this natural law which provides the prescriptive basis for individual relations within the state of nature and upholds the ideal that individuals enjoy a liberty and equality in relation to each other.[14] Further, he argues that this natural law gives rise to natural rights which each individual possesses – not least natural rights to this liberty and equality – some of which are so fundamental that, short of individuals being guilty of an unjust act of war, such rights are not able to be surrendered to another.[15] Once again, Locke insists, all of this arises from our equal status as God's "Creatures":

> The *State of Nature* has a Law of Nature to govern it, which obliges every one: And Reason, which is that Law, teaches all Mankind, who will but consult it, that being all equal and independent, no one ought to harm another in his Life, Health, Liberty, or Possessions. For Men being all the Workmanship of one Omnipotent, and infinitely wise Maker; All the Servants of one Sovereign Master, sent into the World by his order and about his business, they are his Property, whose Workmanship they are, made to last during his, not one anothers Pleasure. And being furnished with like Faculties, sharing all in one Community of nature, there cannot be supposed any such *Subordination* among us, that may Authorize us to destroy one another, as if we were made for one anothers uses, as the inferior ranks of Creatures are for ours.[16]

The Limits of Theology

We see, therefore, that the key normative ideals of Locke's political philosophy, centred on individual liberty and equality, have theological foundations. However this does not mean that we can reduce Locke's political philosophy entirely to this theology, as some Locke scholars have sought to do. On the contrary, as I have argued elsewhere, Locke made a concerted effort, within his political philosophy, to widen its ambit beyond these theological foundations, not least because he knew the conclusions of this philosophy needed to convince a wide audience (including, among others, "pagans", "Mahometans" and "Jews") often profoundly divided by faith.[17]

Similarly, when it came to the justification and practice of toleration, Locke sought to separate it from theological concerns. For instance, we shall see that he insisted that the theological "truth" of particular beliefs or practices was not a relevant consideration in determining whether these ought to be tolerated or proscribed within civil society. Rather, we shall see that such outcomes were dependent on how these beliefs and practices impacted on "civil" concerns – not least whether they were "prejudicial to other men's rights" or broke "the public peace of societies" – considerations which are inherently practical and have no relation to theology at all.[18]

"Civil Concerns"

Locke's interest in such "civil" concerns, with their practical intent, arose from his desire, to ensure civil peace and effective state governance within individual polities. These commitments are evident from the very beginnings of his political philosophy and arose, in part, from the fact that Locke's early life was dominated by the absence of such peace and governance, coinciding as it did with the upheaval of the English Civil Wars and the closing years of the Cromwellian Protectorate.[19]

The reason why civil concerns such as civil peace and effective state governance are relevant to Locke's conception of toleration is due to the political context within which Locke knew his ideals of toleration would have to be applied. Above all, this context was defined, within the England of Locke's time, by the immutable fact of religious disagreement and division and the conflict to which this could give rise. As Locke puts it: "in this great variety of ways that men follow, it is still doubted which is this right one".[20] Given this religious division, opinion was divided, in Locke's time, as to whether the most effective means to secure civil peace and effective state governance was for state authorities to engage in a process of toleration, allowing each individual to pursue their religious liberty in their own way or adopt a policy of enforced religious conformity where all individuals, on matters of religion, submitted, in terms of their outward behaviour, to the magistrate's command. Locke distinguishes between these two options, as alternative policies for states dealing with religious diversity, in the opening paragraph of *An Essay Concerning Toleration*:

> In the question of liberty of conscience, which has for some years been so much bandied amongst us, one thing that hath chiefly perplexed the question, kept up the dispute, and increased the animosity hath been, I conceive, this: that both parties have with equal zeal and mistake too much enlarged their pretensions, whilst one side preach up absolute obedience, and the other claim universal liberty in matters of conscience, without assigning what those things are which have a title to liberty, or showing the boundaries of imposition and obedience.[21]

In this passage, Locke sets out his basic purpose, which characterizes all his subsequent writing on toleration. This is to determine those "things" which have a "title to liberty" and therefore should be left to individuals' own choice and judgment, and those others which, falling within "the boundaries of imposition and obedience", are a matter of "civil" concern and so ought to be subject to the magistrate's command. This balance or boundary between toleration, on the one hand, and "imposition and obedience", on the other, is a perennial concern for Locke and represents a continual tension within his writings on toleration. After all, the scope of the liberty that toleration makes possible cannot be determined unless the limits upon that liberty are also identified. Indeed, for Locke, the two are inseparable, for liberty without limit is what Locke calls "license", which, in its capacity to undermine political authority and civil order, he sees as ultimately a threat to liberty itself.[22] Liberty, in order to be meaningful, must therefore have limits, imposed for the sake of civil peace and upheld by effective state governance. The result is a continual tension in Locke's writing on toleration between the normative concerns of individual liberty and the practical concerns of civil peace and effective state governance. The demarcation that Locke prescribes between the two will shift throughout his intellectual career – from the excessive concern with effective state governance in his early *Two Tracts on Government*, to his willingness, by the time of the *Two Treatises of Government*, to sacrifice governance entirely to the imperative of liberty in those instances where he upholds an individual right of resistance to government. Locke insists that individuals, in such circumstances, determine when that right ought to be exercised, at those points where they believe their fundamental liberties are most threatened.[23] In all such cases, Locke is negotiating the boundary between liberty and governance and therefore between the normative and practical dimensions of his political philosophy, this being most apparent in his discussion of toleration, where both the scope of individual liberty, and the limits imposed upon it, must be determined.

Locke and the History of Toleration

It is important to note that while Locke was a seminal influence upon what subsequently came to be known as the liberal tradition, nevertheless, in terms of the wider toleration debates in Europe within Locke's time, his contribution came rather late. This debate had its origins in the sixteenth century, in the wake of a Reformation that had divided Europe into hostile, at times warring parties, and had forced upon state leaders the practical problem of ensuring civil peace within their borders between individuals fundamentally divided by religious faith. As J. W. Allen tells us:

> It was absolutely impossible in the sixteenth century that the question of how governments should, or had best, deal with ... "heresy", should not be widely debated and from many different points of view. It was a question which, however put, directly and acutely affected the lives of multitudes of men and women all over Western Europe. Every government had to make up its mind at least as to practical action; and that in face of all manner of difficulties and complications.[24]

Professor Allen points to how the discussion of toleration, arising from these origins, sought to address these practical concerns, centred on how the state was to ensure effective governance and civil peace in a context of religious diversity. But the discussion of toleration also sought to address normative concerns, centred on individual liberty. Professor Allen tells us that, on the question of these normative and practical issues, opinion in Europe was divided from the start:

To the question as a practical one put in general terms, every possible answer ... was given. It was maintained that under some circumstances it was expedient, under others inexpedient, to "persecute", and that the ruler had a right to judge and to act at his discretion. It was also maintained that he had no choice about the matter. It was asserted that he was bound to endeavour to stamp out false religion by force, if force was necessary; it was maintained, on the contrary, that he was bound, morally, to allow people to preach and worship as they pleased, so long as they did not break the peace or incite to breach of it.... "Toleration" as a practical solution of intolerable difficulties and "toleration" as a general principle of action in relation to religious differences, both appear quite early in the sixteenth century.[25]

John Locke thought and wrote in the wake of these toleration debates in England and Europe, but also within the midst of the religious controversies of his own time. Locke's *A Letter Concerning Toleration*, composed in 1685 while Locke was a political exile in Holland, was not only a reflection upon developments within the English polity, but also, in part, a response to developments in France, where the Edict of Nantes, which had hitherto accorded a measure of toleration to French Huguenots, had been revoked by Louis XIV in that year.[26] Consequently, while the subsequent chapters of this book will focus specifically on the development of Locke's thought on toleration and will situate this within the wider context of his political philosophy as a whole, it is important to remember that Locke was not writing on toleration in isolation, but was part of a much wider debate, both in England and upon the European continent, stretching back more than a century.

The Focus

This book seeks to trace the development of John Locke's ideas on toleration, from their antediluvian beginnings in the *Two Tracts on Government* (1660–62) to their robust development in *An Essay Concerning Toleration* (1667), *A Letter Concerning Toleration* (1689) and Locke's subsequent exchange with the Anglican clergyman Jonas Proast, which was the sequel to the *Letter*, and which occurred throughout the 1690s and beyond. Locke wrote all of these texts in English, with the exception of *A Letter Concerning Toleration*, which he wrote in Latin. However, as will be explained in the next chapter, the *Letter* was translated into English by Locke's friend William Popple, in the same year as its Latin publication. As it was the English translation that Locke went on to defend, almost line by line, in his engagement with Proast, we can accept this translation as an accurate representation of his views.

At various points in the discussion, I shall situate Locke's conception of toleration within the broader context of his political philosophy as a whole. This is because Locke's conception of toleration occupies an integral place within that broader philosophy, drawing upon it for its meaning, justification and purpose. This often requires a close reading of the relevant texts and, therefore, at times, the use of quotations from these texts. The meaning and content of Locke's arguments for toleration are explored in this context and his intentions in advancing these arguments are examined.

In the chapters that follow, I will endeavour to show that Locke's conception of toleration, as it emerged over time, developed a definite structure and coherence, centred on his normative commitment to individual liberty and his practical commitment to civil peace and effective state governance. We can see the roots of this structure in Locke's earliest engagement with the subject of toleration in his *Two Tracts on Government* (1660–62). Although Locke, in this text, opposed toleration as state policy, nevertheless, as we shall see in Chapter 3, he advanced specific premises within this text which, when he subsequently re-evaluated them at a later date, were important for his affirmation of toleration in *An Essay Concerning Toleration* (1667), *A Letter Concerning Toleration* (1689) and his engagement with Jonas Proast in the second, third and fourth *Letters Concerning Toleration* (1690, 1692 and 1704).[27]

Tensions

Yet we shall also see that there were tensions in the development of Locke's thought on toleration, not least between the normative and practical commitments referred to above. Both the normative imperative of individual liberty, and the practical imperative of civil peace and effective state governance, were necessary to the development of Locke's thought on toleration, but we shall see that both are also potentially at odds.

In terms of Locke's major writings, the tension between these normative and practical imperatives is first apparent in *An Essay Concerning Toleration*. It is in this text that Locke first seeks to accompany his practical concerns, centred on civil peace and effective state governance, which had dominated his discourse in the *Two Tracts on Government*, with a normative commitment to individual liberty which extends beyond inner conscience to outward religious worship. In other words, Locke seeks, in the *Essay*, to justify a policy of toleration not only as the best means to ensure civil peace and the effective state governance necessary to achieve this, but also as the best means of ensuring liberty for individuals in their religious concerns.

Each imperative is therefore advanced, in the *Essay*, in support of toleration. Yet the tension between these imperatives arises because, at times, the advancement of one can only take place at the expense of the other. The normative imperative of liberty, for instance, may be threatened by an excess of governance, advanced for the sake of civil peace, while civil peace and effective state governance are themselves threatened by an excess of liberty, or what Locke refers to above as "license". Throughout Locke's writing on toleration, therefore, this tension between these competing imperatives is continually negotiated. Indeed, it is inescapable, because, as explained above, both imperatives are equally necessary to Locke's conception of toleration, but are also potentially at odds.

For this reason, the development of Locke's ideas on toleration are not a simple linear or evolutionary process – moving from "law and civil authority", in the *Two Tracts*, to "individual rights and liberty" in his later writings, as Wolfgang von Leyden has suggested.[28] Rather, the development is uneven, as Locke must continually negotiate the tension between the two entities to which von Leyden refers, centred on his normative and practical imperatives. The advancement of one, we have seen, may involve the diminishment of the other and yet both are necessary if Locke is to reconcile the wider commitment to individual liberty, which he embraces in the wake of the *Two Tracts*, with the concern for civil peace and effective state governance which dominates the *Two Tracts* itself. Locke may have moved in what will later be understood as a "liberal" direction in the wake of the *Two Tracts*, embracing the ideal of toleration which he had repudiated in this earlier text, but he in no way left behind the practical concerns of civil peace and effective state governance which are so prominent in these early political writings. He continues, in his later writings, to search for the appropriate limits of individual liberty, in the face of government authority, just as he seeks, in converse fashion, to determine the limits of that authority necessary to secure this liberty. Only in this way is he able to realize both of his imperatives referred to above.

The Wider Literature

In adopting such an approach, I recognize the relevance of Quentin Skinner's injunctions concerning how the study of the history of political thought ought to be conducted. Skinner argues that any work of political thought is a specific intervention in a range of debates and concerns occupying a specific author, and his or her society, at a particular point in time.[29] It is a *purposeful* intervention, designed to answer a series of specific questions uppermost in the author's mind – questions that themselves arise from circumstances and events specific to his or her environment.[30]

It is in terms of precisely such a wider set of circumstances, and the issues to which they give rise, that I seek, in Chapter 2, to explain Locke's engagement with the subject of toleration, not least why the issue was of such perennial concern to him that he continued to wrestle with it throughout his intellectual career. Locke's own upbringing during the English Civil War and the upheavals he experienced at this time provide one such set of circumstances, while we shall see in Chapter 6 that his engagement with Jonas Proast, late in his career, can at least partly be explained by the aftermath of the Revolution of 1688 and the divisions between contending church parties to which this gave rise.

I do not claim any originality for these reflections on the background circumstances of Locke's thinking on toleration. Others have supplied such background in far greater detail, and with far greater precision and expertise, than I, and I acknowledge them here and in later chapters accordingly.[31]

Any claims to originality in this book, such as they are, must reside elsewhere. To be specific, I believe they reside in my account of the development of Locke's ideas on toleration, where I seek to explain these in terms of his re-evaluation of key premises that first emerged in his *Two Tracts on Government* (Chapter 3) and the continual negotiation of his normative and practical imperatives that this re-evaluation involved. They also reside in the challenges which this account provides to some of the dominant interpretations of Locke within the existing literature. For instance, in Chapters 4 and 5, I engage with Jeremy Waldron's interpretation of *A Letter Concerning Toleration*, particularly his claim that Locke, within this text, identified with the interests of "persecutors" at the expense of their victims. David Wootton has declared that "[t]he most influential critique of the argument of the *Letter* written by a contemporary philosopher is that by Jeremy Waldron".[32] Similarly, Paul Bou-Habib points out that Waldron "has influenced much of the secondary literature on the *Letter*".[33] Finally, Alex Tuckness has pointed to Waldron as one of two thinkers (the other being John Dunn) who have provided the "dominant view" of Locke on toleration.[34] It is precisely this "dominant view", as advanced by Waldron, that I seek to show is fundamentally flawed, not least because it is based on a thorough misreading of Locke's *Letter Concerning Toleration*, as well as the later letters which Locke wrote in response to Proast. We shall see that even Waldron's more recent writing on Locke, in which he seeks to situate Locke's political philosophy in a theological context, still repeats his earlier errors concerning Locke's *Letter Concerning Toleration*.

In Chapter 6, I challenge Jeremy Waldron, Mark Goldie and John Dunn's interpretation of the Locke/Proast debate, not least the primary issues which they believe to be at stake within it. In Chapter 9, I consider competing accounts concerning the role that scepticism plays in Locke's account of toleration, as advanced by Peter Nicholson, Adam Wolfson and Richard Vernon. My own position, articulated in that chapter, is that, while scepticism plays an important role for Locke, it is his normative commitment to individual liberty which provides what I call the "ultimate conditions of possibility" for his defence of toleration. In these respects, this book does seek to move beyond the existing scholarship concerning Locke and toleration and, in doing so, builds, in part, on some of my previous publications.[35]

Inside and Outside

Quentin Skinner insists that we can never hope to attain an understanding of any major work of political thought "simply by reading the text itself 'over and over again' in the way that some commentators have urged".[36] On the contrary, referring to Locke as his example, he states:

> It is only if and when we have mapped out all the prevailing conventions of political discussion that we can begin to observe the points at which, and the extent to which, Locke may be concerned to breach or repudiate them.[37]

As evidence for this, Skinner point to the fact that Locke omits any reference to the "ancient constitution" in his *Two Treatises of Government*, despite the fact that this was a widely used concept, among Englishmen of his time, to critically evaluate existing political affairs.[38] Given that Locke does not mention this concept, such an omission would not be apparent without having "mapped out all the prevailing conventions of political discussion" that surrounded his own authorship of the *Two Treatises*.

Mark Goldie has also pointed to a lacuna in Locke's account of toleration which, as with Skinner's "ancient constitution" above, would not be discernible simply by a focus on the texts themselves. Goldie points out that, in Locke's toleration texts, Locke does not seek to engage with, or refute, St. Augustine, the foremost patristic authority for persecution, who advocated the forcible inclusion of some of those outside the established church of his own time, and who was much cited by Anglican divines to justify coercion of Dissenters in the seventeenth century.[39] By contrast, French toleration theorists such as Pierre Bayle did engage with Augustine.[40] Once again, what is *present* in a text does not necessarily tell us what is *absent* from it, and an exclusive focus on Locke's writings on toleration would not alert us to the omission of Augustine.

There are other insights into Locke on toleration which would not be available unless we adopted Skinner's injunction and "mapped out all the prevailing conventions of political discussion" within Locke's own time. John Marshall declares that, from the time of *An Essay Concerning Toleration* onwards, Locke's ideas on toleration were quite radical relative to others being advanced within the England of his day. Marshall points out that most Independents in England at this time, despite their dissident status (situated as they were outside the Anglican and Presbyterian churches), still believed the state ought not to tolerate what they perceived to be "false" religions, for which, they reasoned, liberty of conscience could not be claimed.[41] As we shall see, Locke, by contrast, eschewed all notions of "truth" and "falsity" as a criterion for determining which faiths ought and ought not to be tolerated, instead insisting that the magistrate ought only to interfere with religion for "civil" reasons, centred on public safety and other material concerns, for which the state had jurisdiction and responsibility.[42] As Marshall points out, in 1667, the year Locke composed *An Essay Concerning Toleration*, only "a few radical Independents such as William Walwyn and Roger Williams" advanced views of this nature.[43] The result, Marshall says, is that "[f]ew Independents … would have been happy with the breadth of opinions that Locke desired to be tolerated in 1667".[44] Locke's radical status, relative to the other religionists of his time, would once again not have been evident simply from a focus on Locke's tolerationist texts themselves.

However, there are two strong countervailing considerations why I have not adopted such a Skinnerian approach in these pages. The first of these concerns the level of misunderstanding that I believe to exist within the secondary literature concerning Locke's ideas on toleration. I have made reference to this above, when I indicated that this book will break significantly from some of the dominant interpretations within this field. This misunderstanding occurs at the level of the content of Locke's texts themselves. It does not occur outside those texts, in the "prevailing conventions of political discussion" that Skinner refers to. Engagement with this alleged misunderstanding therefore requires a close analysis of Locke's texts and their place in the context of Locke's political philosophy, not the process of broad interpretive dispersal that characterizes Skinner's attempt to excavate all the "prevailing conventions" that surround a text in order to elucidate its internal meaning.

The second issue is one of word length. Skinnerian approaches begin wide and run long. I cannot situate Locke's texts within the wider "conventions of political discussion" in his own time *and* provide the level of textual analysis and interpretation that is necessary to engage with the misinterpretations that I believe to exist within some of the most prominent analyses in the secondary literature. A choice therefore has to be made and, although I have drawn widely on sources outside Locke's texts to explain Locke's motives and intentions in writing about toleration, I have focused primarily on those texts and their context within Locke's wider political philosophy, in order to understand Locke's account of toleration itself. This is not to deny the added insights into these texts provided by Skinner's method. It is simply to acknowledge the limits imposed by space and purpose. Ultimately it is up to the reader to decide whether, in terms of the content and conclusions of this book, such a choice is justified.

Summary of Chapters

Chapter 1 begins with a discussion of Locke's *A Letter Concerning Toleration* – this being Locke's most commonly recognized account of toleration. The chapter shows how the ideal of toleration that Locke advances in this text (as well as in his earlier *Essay Concerning Toleration*) is linked to wider elements of his political philosophy, such as his conception of individual consent and his ideal of a separation of church and state. The chapter also shows how Locke's justification of toleration, as advanced within these texts, is divided between normative and practical imperatives and explains the categorical difference between the two.

This first chapter would appear to be an anticipation of much later discussion in the book, given that the chapter which follows reverts to Locke's earliest known political composition, the *Two Tracts on Government*. Yet this wide overview in the first chapter is a necessary preliminary to the later discussion as it identifies the place of toleration within Locke's wider political philosophy and so provides an important formative background for the discussion to come.

The second and third chapters focus, in different ways, on Locke's composition of the *Two Tracts on Government* and *An Essay Concerning Toleration*. Both are important preludes to Locke's composition of *A Letter Concerning Toleration* and show how this later text had important antecedents in Locke's earlier writings. However, what is significant for our purposes is that between the *Two Tracts* and the *Essay*, Locke actually reverses his position on toleration. From being opposed to toleration in the *Two Tracts*, Locke becomes its open advocate in *An Essay Concerning Toleration*. Chapters 2 and 3 seek to provide an explanation of this very important shift in Locke's political thought, but in very different ways. Chapter 2 focuses on the wider influences in Locke's own life, outside his texts, that might have led him to alter his position in this way. Chapter 3 focuses on the actual intellectual shifts that took place within and between these two texts themselves, which made such a discursive transition possible.

Chapter 4, entitled "Locke in the Dock", focuses on what, as we saw above, is "[t]he most influential critique of the argument of the *Letter* written by a contemporary philosopher" – that of Jeremy Waldron. In particular, it focuses on Waldron's indictment of Locke, in which he claims that Locke, in the *Letter*, identified with the interests of persecutors rather than their victims, declaring that Locke was concerned to ensure that these persecutors adopted methods of persecution which were "rational" for their purposes, and so capable of achieving their ends. The immense influence of Waldron's interpretation of the *Letter*, as well as the extraordinary nature of his claims, so at odds, as they are, with our received notions of Locke, demand that such claims be addressed. Waldron's later book on Locke, which shifts to a theological framework for understanding Locke's political thought, does not include an explicit retraction of this earlier interpretation.[45] Indeed, we shall see that this later work compounds some of the earlier errors which led Waldron to arrive at such excoriating conclusions in the first place.

Chapter 5 focuses on the content of the *A Letter Concerning Toleration*. Locke makes clear in the *Letter* that he offers three "considerations" for toleration – which I have identified, respectively, as the "truth argument", the "rationality argument" and the "consent argument".[46] We shall see that these "three considerations" also form the basis of Locke's engagement with Proast, with Proast seeking to refute each of these. These "three considerations" therefore closely link Locke's engagement with Proast to the content of the original *Letter* itself.

It is therefore on the basis of a comprehensive reading of the *Letter* that we then confront the Locke/Proast debate. Chapter 6 introduces this debate by providing an account of its background in the context of England's Revolution of 1688 and its immediate aftermath. Drawing strongly on the work of Mark Goldie, we see that Locke and Proast belonged to different and competing church parties in the wake of this Revolution.

Once again, however, this chapter points to shortcomings within the wider Locke literature. It shows that Jeremy Waldron, John Dunn and Mark Goldie all provide a truncated account of the Locke/Proast debate, failing to perceive the full scope of the arguments for and against toleration that both Locke and Proast advance within it. This leads to Goldie's associated failure to perceive the normative role that liberty, and the epistemological role that scepticism, play within Locke's defence of toleration – a lacuna that enables Goldie to mistakenly ascribe to Locke a strategy of religious convergence, Goldie insisting that Locke believed the role of toleration was to "bring people to true religion".[47]

Chapters 7 and 8 focus on the substance of the Locke/Proast debate in detail – considering Locke and Proast's responses to each other in turn. What these chapters show is that the issues traversed by Locke and Proast in their debate are far broader than either Waldron, Goldie or Dunn concede. Locke and Proast engage on all three of Locke's "considerations" for toleration present in the original *Letter*, and, while Locke effectively abandons the "rationality argument" (i.e. the sole argument that Waldron, Goldie and Dunn identify[48]), admitting that the conditions upon which it relies as a defence of toleration are unlikely to apply in practice, he deepens his defence of both the "truth argument" and the "consent argument" and the case they make for toleration. Whereas Waldron is of the view that Locke's defence of toleration ultimately fails against Proast, and Dunn is of the view that Locke's response to Proast is "feeble", I seek to show that Locke's response is sufficiently robust to maintain as strong a case for toleration in the face of Proast's criticisms as he advanced in the original *Letter*.[49] As we shall see in Chapter 8, it is ultimately Proast's position that falters, due to the difficulties Proast encounters on theological matters, not least concerning the "grace" of God.

Chapter 9 seeks to investigate more closely the role that scepticism plays in Locke's account of toleration. Word limits prevent a wider comparative approach, seeking to compare Locke to other theorists who also resorted to particular types of scepticism to ground their case for toleration, such as his French contemporary Pierre Bayle. The result is that the main focus of the chapter remains on the role which scepticism plays in Locke's own arguments for toleration. In particular, the chapter identifies the moral challenge that toleration posed for both Locke and Proast and how Locke's scepticism, concerning all claims to "true religion" allowed him to overcome this challenge in ways that Proast could not. However, this chapter will also show that, although scepticism assists Locke in overcoming the moral challenge of toleration, it is not scepticism that provides the ultimate conditions of possibility for Locke's ideal of toleration. Rather it is his normative commitment to individual liberty that provides this condition. Of Locke's "three considerations" for toleration, initially advanced in the *Letter*, it is the "consent argument" which upholds this normative commitment to individual liberty. For this reason, it will be shown that, among Locke's three "considerations", it is the "consent argument" which has a greater priority than either the "truth" or "rationality argument" as a basis for Locke's justification of toleration.

Chapter 10 seeks to link Locke's account of toleration with later developments within the liberal tradition. It explains how Locke adopts what one might call a "civil perspective" on all matters of religion within civil society. It is this "civil perspective" which, in its contrast to Proast's "theological perspective", helps explain why Locke and Proast, who shared a sincere Christianity, could nevertheless arrive at such fundamentally different positions concerning toleration and the way in which the English state should respond to the religious diversity within its midst. It is Locke's "civil perspective" which also links Locke quite closely to later developments in the liberal tradition, not least the prominent late-twentieth-century liberalism of John Rawls. In this way, Chapter 10 seeks to provide some credence to the claim that Locke played a seminal role in the development of the liberal tradition – a view which has been strongly criticized of late.[50]

In all these ways, this book seeks to challenge some of the dominant interpretations of Locke within the literature and advances a perspective that seeks to show that it is Locke's normative commitment to liberty and equality, and his practical commitment to civil peace and effective state governance, which makes his commitment to toleration possible. We live in a world that, despite its technological sophistication and societal secularization, still witnesses religious conflict of a ferocity reminiscent of the sixteenth and seventeenth centuries in Europe. We have therefore yet to arrive at a world in which Locke's fixation with toleration is an irrelevant or redundant concern.

Note: From the time of the *Two Tracts on Government*, Locke uses the term "magistrate" as a shorthand identification for those exercising political authority within a polity.[51] I use the terms "magistrate", "government" and "state" largely synonymously in the following pages.

Notes

1 Fish 1997: 2255.
2 Goldie 1999: 24.
3 Mill 1971: 89–90.
4 Ibid.: 75.
5 See Macpherson 1962: 262; Laslett 1965: 103; Seliger 1968: 45; Plamenatz 1972: 252.
6 Cranston 1952: 619. See also Skinner 2002: 74.
7 Ibid.: 69. On Locke's early "authoritarian" position, see Ch. 2 below.
8 There are those who challenge this association between Locke and liberalism. See the opening remarks of John Dunn and Mark Goldie in Stanton 2012. See also Ch. 10 (note 1). For a contrary view, identifying Locke's links with the subsequent liberal tradition, see Ch. 10 below.
9 Bauman 1991: 250.

10 On this recognition, see note 5 above.
11 Locke 1965: II § 4, 6. On natural liberty, see ibid.: II § 22, 87, 190. On natural equality, see ibid.: II, § 54. Locke concedes that there are some variations between individuals within the context of this aggregate equality, arising from "Age or Virtue", or "Excellency of Parts and Merit", which may give some a "just Precedency" and place them "above the Common Level" (ibid.: II § 54). But all of this, he insists, is consistent with "the *Equality*, which all Men are in, in respect of Jurisdiction or Dominion one over another … being that *equal Right* that every Man hath, *to his Natural Freedom*, without being subjected to the Will or Authority of any other Man" (ibid.: II § 54). For an evaluation of Locke from a distinctly feminist perspective, questioning whether Locke's norms of liberty and equality were intended by him to apply, at all instances, equally to men and women, see Pateman 1995: 3, 21–3, 91–4.
12 Locke 1965: II § 4.
13 On Locke's identification of natural law with the will of God, see ibid.: II § 6, 8, 135, 142, 195. On Locke's identification of natural law with human reason, see ibid.: II § 8, 10, 11, 12, 96. Locke's identification of natural law with human reason is not a claim that natural law is "innate" to the human mind but rather "something that we being ignorant of may attain to the knowledge of, by the use and due application of our natural Faculties" (Locke 1979: Bk. I, ch. 3, § 13, p. 75). On Locke's claim that natural law still has a moral authority within civil society, see Locke 1965: II § 134, 135, 142, 171, 195.
14 See ibid.: II, § 6–13, 57, 87, 128.
15 On natural rights being derived from natural law, see ibid.: II § 4, 6, 22, 87, 128. On some of these rights being so fundamental that individuals are not entitled to surrender them to another, see ibid.: II § 23, 24, 135, 149, 164, 168, 171, 172, 179. On an unjust act of war being an exception to this, see ibid.: II § 16–17, 19, 23, 172, 178, 180, 181, 207, 232, 242.
16 Ibid.: II § 6. Indeed, the other of the two passages of the *Two Treatises* referred to also makes reference to natural law – see ibid.: II § 4.
17 For Locke's references to "pagans", "Mahometans" and "Jews", see Locke 1993a: 431. Concerning my contention that, contrary to the views of Locke scholars such as Jeremy Waldron, John Dunn, Ian Harris and Timothy Stanton, Locke sought to separate the conclusions of his political philosophy from their theological foundations, see Tate 2010a: 141–7; 2010b: 958–64; 2012, 2013, 2015.
18 See Ch. 1 (notes 32, 43–8); Ch. 3 (note 71); Ch. 9 (notes 73–4).
19 See Locke 1967a: 119–20. See also Ch. 2 (notes 25–6).
20 Locke 1993a: 407. See also Ch. 4 (note 67).
21 Locke 1993b: 186. Locke refers to these same competing claims between proponents of toleration and conformity in the *Two Tracts* – see Locke 1967a: 140, 166–7; 1967b: 210–11.
22 On Locke's distinction between "liberty" and "license", see Locke 1965: II § 6, 22, 57.
23 On Locke's right of resistance see Ch. 1 (notes 90–3).
24 Allen 1960: 73.
25 Ibid.: 73–4.
26 See Vernon 1997: 6–9; Wootton 1993: 95–6; Marshall 1996: 357. Indeed, in his later debate with Jonas Proast, Locke frequently depicted France and "King Louis" as synonymous with religious intolerance and state persecution. See Locke 1963a: 64, 69, 72, 87, 151, 152–3; 1963b: 283, 285, 286, 409, 413, 530.
27 Locke also wrote a number of minor notes and pieces on toleration between these major texts. These have been collected by Mark Goldie in the Cambridge University Press edition of Locke's political writings and have been identified

under the headings of "Toleration A (c. 1675)", "Toleration B (1676)", "Toleration C (1678)", and "Toleration D (1679)". See Locke 2004a, 2004b, 2004c, 2004d.
28 Von Leyden 1958: 15.
29 See Skinner 1988a: 102, 104–5; 2002: 86–9.
30 See ibid.
31 See in particular Dunn 1969; Ashcraft 1986; Harris 1995; Marshall 1996; 2009; Goldie 1991; 2002; Vernon 1997.
32 Wootton 1993: 97.
33 Bou-Habib 2003: 611.
34 Tuckness 2002: 289.
35 See Tate 2009, 2010a, 2010b, 2010c, 2012, 2013, 2015. Although my engagement with Mark Goldie and John Dunn on the Locke/Proast debate, and Peter Nicholson, Richard Vernon and Adam Wolfson on Locke and scepticism, is exclusive to this book, I have challenged Jeremy Waldron and John Dunn's interpretation of Locke elsewhere. For Waldron, see Tate 2009 and 2010c. For Waldron and Dunn, see Tate 2013.
36 Skinner 1988a: 105. An earlier version of Skinner's "Meaning and Understanding" article contains a similar point concerning Locke's *Two Treatises*. See Skinner 1988b: 62.
37 Skinner 1988a: 106.
38 Ibid.: 105.
39 Goldie 1991: 339.
40 Ibid.: 339.
41 Marshall 1996: 59–60.
42 On Locke's rejection of "truth" as a criterion of toleration, see Ch. 3 (note 71). On his insistence that the magistrate only interfere with religions for "civil" reasons, see note 18 above.
43 Marshall 1996: 60–1.
44 Ibid.: 61.
45 See Tate 2009: 774–5; 2010c: 1004–5, 1008 (note 41).
46 I have identified all three arguments in these terms in previous publications – see Tate 2009: 767–9; 2010c: 991–3. Since publishing these articles I have discovered that Adam Wolfson also refers to what I have called the "consent argument" by the same name – see Wolfson 2010: xiv.
47 See Ch. 6 (notes 85 and 94).
48 See Ch. 4 ("Waldron's Reading of the Letter" and "Waldron's Locke"); Ch. 6 (notes 65, 66, 69, 70).
49 For Waldron and Dunn's view, see Ch. 6 (notes 55–62) and Ch. 6 (note 66) respectively.
50 See note 8 above.
51 See Locke 1967a: 125; 1967b: 212–13.

References

Allen, J. W. (1960) *A History of Political Thought in the Sixteenth Century*. London: Methuen.
Ashcraft, R. (1986) *Revolutionary Politics & Locke's Two Treatises of Government*. Princeton, NJ: Princeton University Press.
Bauman, Z. (1991) *Modernity and Ambivalence*. Cambridge: Polity Press.
Bou-Habib, P. (2003) "Locke, Sincerity and the Rationality of Persecution", *Political Studies*, 51 (4): 611–26.
Cranston, M. (1952) "The Politics of John Locke", *History Today*, 2 (9): 619–22.

Dunn, J. (1969) *The Political Thought of John Locke. An Historical Account of the Argument of the 'Two Treatises of Government'*. Cambridge: Cambridge University Press.

Fish, S. (1997) "Mission Impossible: Settling the Just Bounds Between Church and State", *Columbia Law Review*, 97 (8): 2255–333.

Goldie, M. (1991) "The Theory of Religious Intolerance in Restoration England". In: Ole Peter Grell, Jonathan I. Israel and Nicholas Tyacke (eds) *From Persecution to Toleration. The Glorious Revolution and Religion in England*. Oxford: Clarendon Press, pp. 331–68.

Goldie, M. (1999) "Introduction to Jonas Proast, 'The argument of the Letter Concerning Toleration briefly consider'd and answer'd'". In: M. Goldie (ed.) *The Reception of Locke's Politics. Vol. 5. The Church, Dissent and Religious Toleration, 1689–1773*. London: Pickering & Chatto, p. 24.

Goldie, M. (2002) "John Locke, Jonas Proast and Religious Toleration 1688–1692". In: J. Walsh, C. Haydon and S. Taylor (eds) *The Church of England c.1689–c.1833. From Toleration to Tractarianism*. Cambridge: Cambridge University Press, pp. 143–71.

Harris, I. (1995) *The Mind of John Locke: A Study of Political Theory in its Intellectual Setting*. Cambridge: Cambridge University Press.

Laslett, P. (1965) "Introduction". In: J. Locke *Two Treatises of Government*. Peter Laslett (ed.). New York: New American Library, pp. 15–148.

Locke, J. (1963a) "A Second Letter Concerning Toleration". In: J. Locke *The Works of John Locke*. Vol. VI. Aalen: Scientia Verlag, pp. 61–137.

Locke, J. (1963b) "A Third Letter for Toleration". In: J. Locke *The Works of John Locke*. Vol. VI. Aalen: Scientia Verlag, pp. 141–546.

Locke, J. (1965) *Two Treatises of Government*. Peter Laslett (ed.). New York: New American Library.

Locke, J. (1967a) "The First Tract on Government". In: J. Locke *Two Tracts on Government*. P. Abrams (ed.). Cambridge: Cambridge University Press, pp. 117–81.

Locke, J. (1967b) "The Second Tract on Government: Translation". In: J. Locke *Two Tracts on Government*. P. Abrams (ed.). Cambridge: Cambridge University Press, pp. 210–41.

Locke, J. (1979) *An Essay Concerning Human Understanding*. Peter H. Nidditch (ed.). Oxford: Clarendon Press.

Locke, J. (1993a) "A Letter Concerning Toleration". In: J. Locke *Political Writings*. David Wootton (ed.). London: Penguin, pp. 390–436.

Locke, J. (1993b) "An Essay Concerning Toleration". In: J. Locke *Political Writings*. David Wootton (ed.). London: Penguin, pp. 186–210.

Locke, J. (2004a) "Toleration A". In: J. Locke *Political Essays*. M. Goldie (ed.). Cambridge: Cambridge University Press, pp. 230–5.

Locke, J. (2004b) "Toleration B". In: J. Locke *Political Essays*. M. Goldie (ed.). Cambridge: Cambridge University Press, pp. 246–8.

Locke, J. (2004c) "Toleration C". In: J. Locke *Political Essays*. M. Goldie (ed.). Cambridge: Cambridge University Press, p. 269.

Locke, J. (2004d) "Toleration D". In: J. Locke *Political Essays*. M. Goldie (ed.). Cambridge: Cambridge University Press, pp. 276–7.

Macpherson, C. B. (1962) *The Political Theory of Possessive Individualism: Hobbes to Locke*. Oxford: Clarendon Press.

Marshall, J. (1996) *Resistance, Religion and Responsibility*. Cambridge: Cambridge University Press.

Marshall, J. (2009) *John Locke, Toleration and Early Enlightenment Culture*. Cambridge: Cambridge University Press.
Mill, J. S. (1971) "On Liberty". In: J. S. Mill *Utilitarianism, Liberty, Representative Government*. London: Dent, pp. 61–170.
Pateman, C. (1995) *The Sexual Contract*. Cambridge: Polity.
Plamenatz, J. (1972) *Man and Society*. Vol. 1. London: Longman.
Seliger, M. (1968) *The Liberal Politics of John Locke*. London: Allen and Unwin.
Skinner, Q. (1988a) "Some Problems in the Analysis of Political Thought and Action". In: J. Tully (ed.) *Meaning and Context. Quentin Skinner and His Critics*. Cambridge: Polity Press, pp. 97–118.
Skinner, Q. (1988b) "Meaning and Understanding in the History of Ideas". In: J. Tully (ed.) *Meaning and Context. Quentin Skinner and His Critics*. Cambridge: Polity Press.
Skinner, Q. (2002) "Meaning and Understanding in the History of Ideas". In: Q. Skinner *Visions of Politics. Vol. 1: Regarding Method*. Cambridge: Cambridge University Press, pp. 57–89.
Stanton, T. (2012) "Locke and the Fable of Liberalism". *The Third Balzan-Skinner Lecture in Modern Intellectual History*. University of Cambridge, 5 October 2012. Available at: www.sms.cam.ac.uk/media/1327380 (accessed 10 October 2013).
Tate, J. W. (2009) "Locke and Toleration: Defending Locke's Liberal Credentials", *Philosophy and Social Criticism*, 35 (7): 761–91.
Tate, J. W. (2010a) "Toleration, Neutrality and Historical Illiteracy", *Journal of European Studies*, 40 (2): 129–57.
Tate, J. W. (2010b) "A Sententious Divide: Erasing the Two Faces of Liberalism", *Philosophy and Social Criticism*, 36 (8): 953–80.
Tate, J. W. (2010c) "Locke, Rationality and Persecution", *Political Studies*, 58 (5): 988–1008.
Tate, J. W. (2012) "Locke, God and Civil Society: Response to Stanton", *Political Theory*, 40 (2): 222–8.
Tate, J. W. (2013) "Dividing Locke from God: The Limits of Theology in Locke's Political Philosophy", *Philosophy and Social Criticism*, 39 (2): 133–64.
Tate, J. W. (2015) "Locke, Toleration and Natural Law: A Reassessment", *European Journal of Political Theory*, published on the journal's "early view" website in "Online First" on 8 November 2015. DOI: 10.1177/1474885115609739. Available at: http://ept.sagepub.com/content/early/2015/11/04/1474885115609739.abstract.
Tuckness, A. (2002) "Rethinking the Intolerant Locke", *American Journal of Political Science*, 46 (2): 288–98.
Vernon, R. (1997) *The Career of Toleration: John Locke, Jonas Proast and After*. Quebec: McGill Queens University Press.
Von Leyden, W. (1958) "Introduction". In: J. Locke *Essays on the Law of Nature*. W. von Leyden (ed.). Oxford: Clarendon Press.
Wolfson, A. (2010) *Persecution or Toleration. An Explication of the Locke–Proast Quarrel, 1689–1704*. Lanham, MD: Lexington Books.
Wootton, D. (1993) "Introduction". In: J. Locke *Political Writings*. London: Penguin, pp. 7–122.

1 Locke, Liberty and Governance

John Locke's *A Letter Concerning Toleration* is one of the foundational documents of the liberal tradition. It was published anonymously, in Latin, in 1689 and translated into English the same year by Locke's friend, William Popple. It was re-published again that year, but still the identity of its author remained unknown. This anonymity was characteristic of Locke. Even though the political culture of late-seventeenth-century England had changed much after 1688, with the overthrow of James II and the accession of William of Orange and his wife Mary to the English throne, Locke was nothing if not circumspect and, at all times, cautious. Despite his close association with the new ruling authorities – he had arrived in England from Holland in February 1689 as part of the same maritime convoy as the Princess Mary – he still thought it necessary to hide his authorship of the *Letter*.[1] He wrote it in 1685, during his self-imposed political exile in Holland, where he had fled in 1683, seeking to escape retribution for his participation in the Whig opposition to Charles II and his brother James. This opposition was led by Locke's patron, Anthony Ashley Cooper, the first Earl of Shaftesbury, and culminated in the Rye House Plot.[2] Events during Locke's period of exile, such as Louis XIV's revocation of the Edict of Nantes in 1685, which had hitherto granted a measure of toleration to Huguenots in France, as well as the history of Anglican intolerance towards Dissenters in England, were no doubt much on his mind when he composed the *Letter*. James Tully, in his introduction to a 1983 edition of the *Letter*, explains the genesis of the text in these terms:

> *A Letter Concerning Toleration* is a translation of the *Epistola de Tolerantia*, a letter written in Latin by John Locke to his close friend Philip van Limborch, a Dutch Arminian, during the winter months of 1685. At the time Locke was a political exile in Amsterdam, living underground in the home of Dr. Egbert Veen under an assumed name in order to elude extradition and persecution for his part in the revolutionary activity for toleration in England in 1679–83. The *Epistola de Tolerantia* was first published anonymously and without Locke's knowledge in May, 1689, in Gouda, after Locke had returned to England in the wake of William of Orange's conquest of the English

throne in the winter of 1688. William Popple, a fellow radical Whig and religious dissenter, translated the *Epistola de Tolerantia* into English, wrote a preface ... and had it published by the Whig publisher, Awnsham Churchill, anonymously, yet with Locke's knowledge, as *A Letter Concerning Toleration* in October 1689. A second corrected edition appeared in March, 1690.[3]

Gouda, Holland, was an appropriate place for the publication of the original Latin version of the *A Letter Concerning Toleration*. This is because, in addition to impressive cheese, it had a history of religious toleration.[4] By the time of this publication, in May 1689, Locke had already arrived in England and was sent some advanced copies by his friend Philip van Limborch, who was Professor of Divinity at the Arminian, or Remonstrant, Church at Amsterdam. As Tully points out in the passage above, Limborch was also the addressee of the *Letter* itself.[5]

The *Letter*, when it appeared, aroused admiration among those circles in Holland committed to toleration and religious dissent. Speculation arose immediately as to the identity of its author. As Raymond Klibansky tells us, van Limborch was the only person at the time to know the author's identity, and he wrote to Locke informing him of the inquiries to which the publication of the *Letter* had given rise, maintaining the fiction, within his note, that neither of them knew who the author was:

> Many people here are curious to know who the author is. However, he hides himself and nobody is able to detect him. At the request of Mr. Le Clerc I asked the printer who the author was, but he replied that the *Epistola* had been sent to him, joined to a short covering letter, which was unsigned and addressed in an unknown hand. Hence he could not even make a good guess from where it had come. From the subject matter and from the way it is argued some people infer that the treatise issued from the workshop of the Arminians. However, when we consider the cast of mind and the style of each single member of our community, we do not find anyone to whom we could ascribe a text so learned and so elegantly written. That a Calvinist should have fathered so moderate a text is in no way credible unless, perhaps, some erudite man who is in sympathy with the moderation of us Arminians conceals himself in that vast community. That there are many such sympathisers among them is certain; yet there are few who could have produced an Epistle of this kind. Therefore I cannot give you any information about the author.[6]

As time passed, and speculation continued, the *A Letter Concerning Toleration* was attributed increasingly to Locke. However Locke's caution remained. He persisted in denying authorship. Indeed, he was alarmed when, in April 1690, a friend in Amsterdam, Peter Guenellon, wrote to him suggesting that he was the author of the *Letter*. Locke immediately wrote to Limborch, "demanding to know whether he had given away the secret".⁷ Limborch replied that he had, on the grounds that

> he could not have told a lie when their mutual friend Guenellon pointedly asked whether Locke was the author of the *Epistola*; and that ... the fact, being now generally known in England, could hardly be long concealed from Guenellon and [Dr Egbert] Veen, Locke's closest friends in Holland. He insisted that no harm had been done and that, on the contrary, Locke's name would attract even more readers and confer even greater prestige on the treatise.⁸

Locke, however, would not be consoled and replied to Limborch in terms of both apprehension and admonishment:

> I am surprised, I must confess, by your readiness to talk and by the fact that some inquisitive men here, who are none too well-disposed toward me, were able to fish out of you a confidence which I hoped was safe in your keeping. For as long as the rumours, spread by these same people, were disseminated without their source being known, they did not trouble me since they were bound to die down soon.... But now through your admission they have acquired authority. I only want to say that if you had confided such a secret to me I should never have divulged it, neither to any relative nor to any friend nor to any human being at all, under any circumstances whatever. You do not know in what a situation you have landed me.... All that now remains for you to do is to try your best to induce these two others to join you in keeping the secret which you could not keep by yourself.⁹

Peter Laslett, referring to the inordinate lengths to which Locke went in order to conceal his authorship of another text, the *Two Treatises of Government*, published in the same year as the *Letter*, has declared that such "exasperating attempts" at concealment "can only be called abnormal, obsessive" and suggest "a peculiarity in Locke's personality as a man and in his personality as an author".¹⁰ However, Laslett also tells us that Locke's Whig associate, Algernon Sidney, had had his *Discourses Concerning Government* brought against him as evidence in his trial for treason in the wake of his involvement in the Rye House Plot – Sidney ultimately suffering execution.¹¹ Locke was associated with those involved in this plot, and his *Two Treatises of Government* was, like Sidney's *Discourses*, an argument against the royalist views of Sir Robert Filmer. Given these circumstances, perhaps Locke's caution was not as "peculiar" as first seems. After all, after decades as Ashley's close associate, Locke himself would have been fully aware of the fickle winds of political fortune. Even the revolutionary settlement of 1688 may not, to Locke's cautious eyes, have appeared permanent or irreversible and he may have wanted to conceal his past in order not to incriminate his future.¹²

Gordon Schochet also provides a reason why Locke might have wanted to conceal his authorship of the *A Letter Concerning Toleration*. The *Letter*, after all, advocated a separation of church and state, which, in political terms, meant the disestablishment of the Church of England as the official state church.[13] Schochet suggests that these circumstances may explain Locke's desire to avoid acknowledgement of his authorship of the *Letter*:

> That denial [of authorship] and [Locke's] continuing membership in the church may have been signs of Locke's appreciation of the radical nature of his argument. Throughout the 1690s he moved in Anglican circles that would have been closed to an enemy of the establishment and held government positions that he might have been denied had his true beliefs been known.[14]

Raymond Klibansky tells us that it was only at the end of Locke's life, in 1704, in a codicil to his will written a month before his death, that Locke, in donating the manuscripts of his *Letters Concerning Toleration* to the "Library of the University of Oxford", finally admitted authorship of these texts, adding that the original *Letter* was "translated into English without my privity".[15] It was also in this codicil that Peter Laslett tells us Locke finally acknowledged authorship of the *Two Treatises of Government*, the manuscripts of which he was also donating to the library. As Laslett puts it: "Without this final, almost accidental afterthought we should have no direct proof that he wrote the book at all."[16]

The Normative and Practical Justification of Toleration

But what was this ideal of toleration, and the various arguments in support of it, which Locke desired to advance but the authorship of which he wished to conceal? The introduction discussed how Locke, from the time of *An Essay Concerning Toleration* onwards, provided two distinct justifications for his ideal of toleration. One was a *practical* justification and the other a *normative* justification. Locke's practical justification of toleration presented toleration as a desirable policy for governments to adopt should governments wish to achieve, within their jurisdiction, specific political ends. These ends were civil peace between individuals thoroughly divided by faith and the effective state governance necessary to achieve this. But, as we shall see in Chapter 3, it might also include the security of the state itself in the face of otherwise hostile religious dissidents.

These were not solely state concerns. After all, Locke tells us in the *Two Treatises of Government* that individuals left the state of nature and sought the security of stable political authority precisely to achieve an environment of effective governance and civil peace.[17] But these practical ends, shared by individuals within civil society, are also wholly endorsed by the state, and are consistent with state purposes.

On the other hand, we saw that Locke also sought to advance a distinctly *normative* justification of toleration. This normative justification was articulated quite independently of any practical ends of government, and, as we saw, referred to the capacity of toleration to advance the specific norm of individual religious liberty and the equal entitlement of individuals to that liberty.

The following will discuss the categorical distinction between Locke's normative and practical justifications of toleration. It will leave the discussion of Locke's actual resort to these justifications to Chapter 3.

Categorical Distinction

Locke's practical justification of toleration is inherently instrumental and consequentialist in nature. Toleration is justified, in this context, not as an end in itself, but rather as the most effective *means* to achieve some other end, such as state security or civil peace. The capacity of governments to achieve these ends via a policy of toleration is of course affected by any number of empirical circumstances. The result is that the justification of toleration, in such practical terms, is vulnerable to a shift in these circumstances (or people's perceptions of them) which might make toleration, as a policy, less able to achieve these ends, or less likely to be perceived as having this capacity, relative to other means available. The relation between toleration, as a means of achieving these ends, and these ends themselves, is therefore contingent rather than necessary – dependent on shifting empirical circumstances, and governments' capacity to respond to or control these. Given a change in these circumstances, other policies may have a greater capacity to achieve the end in question, thereby becoming a more effective *means* for this purpose, and so displace toleration as the preferred policy of government. Such an outcome would weaken any justification of toleration in *practical* terms.

In regard to Locke's *normative* justification of toleration, toleration is justified as the best means to achieve a particular norm (as distinct from a practical end of government) – this norm being individual liberty, and individuals' equal entitlement to that liberty. Locke perceives individual liberty as a norm not because it is a desired end of government. Rather, liberty is a norm because it is desired as an end in itself. This is evident in Locke's declaration, in the *Two Treatises of Government*, that each individual is one of God's "Creatures", with natural rights to liberty, and an equal entitlement to this liberty, in relation to other individuals.[18] We shall see in a later chapter that Locke links this liberty to human dignity.[19] Toleration is justified, in normative terms, as the best means to secure this liberty because, in seeking to limit the capacity of government to intrude on the lives of individuals, a policy of toleration helps provide the material circumstances that make such liberty possible.

Of course, this normative justification of toleration is still instrumental and consequentialist. This is because the justification of toleration is still dependent on its achieving some other end – in this case, the end of individual liberty.[20] But in other respects, the normative and practical justifications of toleration are categorically distinct from each other. In the first place, the norm underwriting the normative justification of toleration (individual liberty) arises from the natural rights of individuals, not (as in the case of civil peace or effective state governance) from the commitments of government or the practical concerns of its citizens for peace and security.[21] Indeed, the "natural" status of such rights to liberty means that they *precede* government, arising, Locke insists, from a "state of nature", and ultimately, we saw, from natural law.[22] Indeed, so fundamental are these natural rights to liberty that Locke insists that governments, when created by those emerging from a state of nature, are limited in terms of them, with individuals giving up some of the liberties they possessed in the state of nature (such as the right to enforce the law of nature) to provide government with the material capacity to protect their other, more fundamental liberties, in turn.[23] This is discussed further below.[24] The fact that the normative justification of toleration has its foundations in such natural rights means that, unlike the practical justification of toleration, the normative justification is not necessarily coextensive with government interests or subordinate to government purposes. Rather, by seeking to limit the capacity of government to intrude on the lives of individuals, particularly when it does so for ends unrelated to the purposes of government, the normative justification of toleration seeks to act as a limit upon government itself.

By contrast, because toleration, in its practical justification, is coextensive with government purposes, it is only justified to the extent that it is capable of aiding government in the achievement of these purposes. Although we have seen that these purposes might also be consistent with the interests of individuals subject to government authority, not least their concern for peace and security, nevertheless it is government purposes that are the necessary and sufficient justification of toleration in this practical context because it is for the sake of such purposes that governments adopt a policy of toleration in the first place.

We see, therefore, that the structure of justification of toleration is very different within the normative and practical examples above. This is due to the fact that each draws on quite distinct sources to underwrite this justification, one independent of government purposes and the other coextensive with them. In this respect, we see once again the categorical difference between the two.

One other categorical difference between the normative and practical justification of toleration concerns the relationship between toleration and the ends it seeks to achieve. We saw that in the practical justification of toleration, this relation was a contingent one, since toleration may be rendered less effective as a means to achieve these ends, relative to other means available, due to changes in empirical circumstance. In the case of the normative justification of toleration, on the other hand, this relation between toleration and its end is not contingent but, rather, necessary. This is because toleration is an indispensable means to the achievement of the end in question – this end being individual liberty. After all, it is only if toleration, as state policy, places limits on the entitlement of the state to intrude upon the lives of individuals that the material conditions for such liberty is ensured. The relationship is not, therefore, dependent on shifting empirical circumstances.

We can see this necessary relationship between toleration and liberty in terms of the way in which Locke seeks to define the two. To take religious liberty as an example, Locke defines this as an individual's entitlement to be left alone to decide their own faith, and being allowed a space within civil society to practise that faith uncoerced by either the state, other churches or other individuals. As Locke tells us: "the care of each man's salvation belongs only to himself".[25] Toleration, on the other hand, is defined by Locke as this process of "leaving alone". As Locke puts it: "Force, you allow, is improper to convert men to any religion. Toleration is but the removing that force".[26] Thus Locke defines the parameters of toleration, and the liberty it makes possible in matters of religion, as follows:

> Concerning outward worship, I say ... that the magistrate has no power to enforce by law, either in his own Church, or much less in another, the use of any rites or ceremonies whatsoever in the worship of God.... Speculative opinions ... and articles of faith ... which are required only to be believed, cannot be imposed on any Church by the law of the land.... Further, the magistrate ought not to forbid the preaching or professing of any speculative opinions in any Church, because they have no manner of relation to the civil rights of the subjects.[27]

In this respect, we see the *necessary* relationship between toleration and liberty within Locke's framework, where one is the indispensable means to the achievement of the other. In the case of religious liberty, Locke insists that such liberty is consistent with the entitlement of individuals (or indeed the magistrate as a private individual) to persuade, exhort and admonish others regarding their religious beliefs and practices.[28] But this gives rise to no obligations of obedience on the part of these others, Locke insisting that, on such matters, each individual "has the supreme and absolute authority of judging for himself".[29] A state policy of toleration, by limiting the authority of others (either exhortative individuals or institutions such as churches or states) to impinge upon individuals in a coercive way, in regard to their religious beliefs or practices, ensures this liberty of judging for ourselves.[30]

Varieties of Toleration

In the *A Letter Concerning Toleration*, Locke distinguishes between three varieties of toleration. He refers to toleration as practised by churches, by the magistrate and by individuals. He insists that churches (and individuals) are not entitled to use the political power reserved to the magistrate (what Locke calls the "sword") to invade the civil rights of anyone, be they a member of their own congregation or any other, and all church attendance on the part of individuals is to be entirely voluntary.[31] Equally, the magistrate, as the sole possessor of the "sword", is not entitled to use that power for purposes of religion. Rather, religion is only subject to his or her authority if it interferes with the civil purposes for which that authority was first created and to which it is solely directed.[32] In such cases, the magistrate is required to treat religion as a "thing indifferent" and therefore open to his or her regulation only for the sake of civil purposes.[33] This will be discussed further below.

Locke also refers to toleration as practised by individuals within civil society towards each other, Locke insisting (as explained above) that these individuals have every right to entreat, persuade, admonish or exhort each other on matters of religion, but at no point are they entitled to physically interfere with, intimidate or coerce each other on these matters.[34] In each case therefore, the state, the churches and individuals are limited by state laws in their capacity to intrude upon or interfere with the beliefs and practices of others, so in each case they are required to tolerate that which they are not entitled to alter or expunge.[35] As Locke puts it:

> Nobody therefore, in fine, neither single persons, nor Churches, nay, nor even commonwealths, have any just title to invade the civil rights and worldly goods of each other, upon pretence of religion.[36]

Separation of Church and State

Toleration, within Locke's schema, is therefore based on limits – limits on the capacity and entitlement of the state, the churches or individuals to impinge on the liberties of others. One of the primary ways in which Locke conceives of limits upon the state is in terms of its separation from the church. Locke's *Letter Concerning Toleration* continually reiterates this separation.[37] The state, Locke insists, is limited to the civil purposes for which it was established, the church to spiritual ones. As explained above, there may be times when the state must impinge on spiritual purposes for civil reasons – for instance because a particular religious belief or practice threatens what the state conceives as the public interest – but on the whole, Locke writes,

> if each of them would contain itself within its own bounds, the one attending to the worldly welfare of the commonwealth, the other to

the salvation of souls, it is impossible that any discord should ever have happened between them.[38]

It is therefore "civil" purposes, not spiritual ones, which constitute the legitimate realm of state authority. Locke makes this point as early as *An Essay Concerning Toleration* (1667):

> The magistrate, as magistrate, hath nothing to do with the good of men's souls or their concernments in another life, but is ordained and entrusted with his power only for the quiet and comfortable living of men in society, one with another, as hath been already sufficiently proved.[39]

Locke makes the same point, over twenty years later, in *A Letter Concerning Toleration*:

> For the political society is instituted for no other end but only to secure every man's possession of the things of this life. The care of each man's soul, and of the things of heaven, which neither does belong to the commonwealth nor can be subjected to it, is left entirely to every man's self. Thus the safeguard of men's lives, and of the things that belong unto this life, is the business of the commonwealth; and the preserving of those things unto their owners is the duty of the magistrate.[40]

In this respect, we see how Locke clearly seeks to separate the jurisdiction of the state, centred on civil concerns, from matters of religion. This ideal of separation of church and state would later resonate deeply with the liberal tradition. Yet, like toleration, this ideal has a long ancestry, which precedes Locke and stretches back to at least the time in which it first became an urgent political issue – when the Christian church and the imperial Roman state first came into close proximity with the elevation of Constantine as the first Christian Roman Emperor in 306 AD. Hosius, Bishop of Cordova, expressed such an ideal of separation in a letter he wrote to Constantine's son, Constantius, in 355 AD:

> Do not interfere in matters ecclesiastical, nor give us orders on such questions, but learn about them from us. For into your hands God has put the kingdom; the affairs of the Church He has committed to us.... "Render unto Caesar the things that are Caesar's and unto God the things that are God's." We are not permitted to exercise an earthly rule; and you, Sire, are not authorized to burn incense.[41]

This ideal of separation has resonated throughout the Christian centuries but (to misapply Shakespeare) has been honoured far more in the breach than in the observance. It was only in the wake of the Reformation that it again emerged onto the political agenda in a significant form, to be espoused by some but not by others, and Locke takes it up as an abiding principle. As he puts it in the *Letter*:

> I esteem it above all things necessary to distinguish exactly the business of civil government from that of religion, and to settle the just bounds that lie between the one and the other. If this be not done there can be no end put to the controversies that will be always arising between those that have, or at least pretend to have, on the one side, a concernment for the interest of men's souls, and, on the other side, a care of the commonwealth.[42]

For Locke, separation of church and state is understood primarily in terms of the limitations discussed above, where each institution, in terms of its specific jurisdiction, provides a boundary to that of the other. As we have seen, this does not mean that religion is always outside the state's purview, since the state may seek to regulate religion for "civil" purposes. An example Locke provides in the *Letter* concerns animal sacrifice. As a religious practice, Locke insists that magistrates are not entitled to proscribe animal sacrifice, no matter how "sinful" they personally find it, because they are not entitled to use their authority for religious purposes. But they are entitled to proscribe it if it affects civil concerns such as public food supplies.[43] Another example is when churches preach doctrines contrary to civil peace or state security, such as that "faith is not to be kept with heretics" or "kings excommunicated forfeit their crowns and kingdoms".[44] In each instance, Locke insists, magistrates are entitled to proscribe such doctrines because they have an adverse impact on the civil matters that fall within their jurisdiction.[45]

But the magistrate is not entitled to impinge on religious doctrines or practices, however "sinful" he or she may find them, when these have no such civil consequences – for instance, where they are "not prejudicial to other men's rights, nor ... break the public peace of societies".[46] We saw Locke impose the same limits at note 27 above when he declared that "the magistrate ought not to forbid the preaching or professing of any speculative opinions in any Church, because they have no manner of relation to the civil rights of the subjects". In each case, if the religious belief or practice in question does not impinge on the magistrate's sphere of authority, confined as this is to civil matters, it is left to the liberty of the individual.

In this way, the entitlement of the state to impinge on matters of religion is, according to Locke, entirely governed by the purposes underwriting such impingement. Only when matters of religion impede the civil concerns for which, Locke tells us, the state has responsibility is the state entitled to intrude. In such instances, the state treats religious matters as "things indifferent", of concern to the state not in terms of their intrinsic religious qualities but only in terms of their external (civil) consequences.[47] But, in so doing, the state does not transgress the limits of church and state. Rather, because only the external (civil) consequences of religious matters are at stake, what were once religious issues now become, from the state's perspective, civil issues, falling within its legitimate jurisdiction. For instance, in the case of animal sacrifice referred to above, Locke tells us that, in such circumstances where public food supplies are at stake, this becomes an issue, not of animal "sacrifice", but of animal "slaughter", and therefore a legitimate concern for the state: "Only 'tis to be observed that in this case the law is not made about a religious but a political matter; nor is the sacrifice but the slaughter of calves thereby prohibited."[48]

Whereas the state is not entitled to impinge on religion, except for civil purposes, Locke insists that the church is not entitled to impinge on the state, or its sphere of authority, for *any* purpose. So, for instance, we have seen that Locke demands that churches not use those means of force exclusively reserved to the state (the "sword") to impinge on the civil rights of their congregations, or confiscate their property, for the sake of imposing church discipline, instead limiting such discipline to the penalty of excommunication.[49] This is because "to give laws, receive obedience, and compel with the sword, belongs to none but the magistrate".[50] Further, Locke insists that individuals or churches ought not, on the pretext of religion, to claim specific rights or jurisdiction at the expense of the state or other citizens, such as when they insist that "dominion is founded in grace" or otherwise "arrogate to themselves, and to those of their own sect, some peculiar prerogative, covered over with a specious show of deceitful words, but in effect opposite to the civil right of the community".[51] In each of these instances, Locke insists, individuals or churches are seeking to regulate "civil" matters in the name of religion and so are again transgressing the separation that Locke seeks to establish between church and state.

In this manner, both the church and the state are each assigned specific purposes, and therefore limited jurisdictions. It is the limits imposed upon both that underwrites the process of toleration, since such limits, when applied, allow individuals the liberty and discretion to make their own choices in matters of religion, without coercive interference from others, consistent with the wider parameters of civil peace and effective state governance which, Locke tells us, are necessary for the preservation of liberty as a whole. Of course, in practice, as the section entitled "Realpolitik" below will make clear, the relative jurisdiction of church and state is liable to be open to dispute and, at times, conflict. But, in principle, Locke insists upon such a separation, each institution exercising their authority within their respective jurisdictions, and both underwriting Locke's ideal of toleration.

Consent, Legitimacy and Obligation

We have seen how toleration is linked to one central feature of Locke's broader political philosophy – his ideal of a separation of church and state. But it is also linked to another, that being Locke's conception of individual consent. Consent plays a central role in Locke's political philosophy. It is consent which, Locke insists, underwrites the legitimacy of government, the limits imposed upon it, and our obligation to obey government authority when that authority, falling within these limits, is considered legitimate.[52] Consent makes possible this link between legitimacy, obligation and authority, through what Locke calls a process of "compact" (or what liberals today call "contract").[53] This "compact" is a process of agreement, based on mutual consent, which Locke perceives as arising between individuals within a state of nature and is the basis upon which both civil society and government is inaugurated, as individuals agree with each other to create these entities in order to escape what they perceive to be the inconveniences of the state of nature.[54] Locke believes that this process of "compact" represents the actual origins of civil societies and governments.[55] However he admits that any evidence for these origins would be lost in the mists of time.[56] It is individual consent which provides the moral currency underwriting this contractual process because, as an expression of individual liberty, freely given or withheld, Locke believes consent gives rise to obligations on the part of individuals, not least an obligation to obey the political authority that such consent has both inaugurated and legitimated.[57] In this way, Locke seeks to reconcile, within this contractual process, the liberty of individuals (expressed through consent) with the obligations of obedience necessary for effective state governance and civil peace.[58]

We saw in the introduction that Locke, in the *Two Treatises*, identified individuals as having natural rights to liberty and equality, given their equal status as God's "Creatures". "Consent" is very much the political expression of this natural liberty and equality. Consent is an expression of individual liberty because individuals can choose whether or not to bestow it in particular circumstances.[59] It is an expression of individual equality because each adult individual has an equal entitlement to bestow such consent and so is in an equal relationship to others when it comes to processes in which consent is a source of legitimacy, such as the process of "compact" which inaugurates government.[60] The moral and political authority of consent – i.e. its status as a source of political legitimacy and individual obligation – arises precisely because it is an expression of this liberty and equality of individuals. But clearly such authority is only possible if consent is exercised by individuals in their adulthood and when possessed of sound minds. Indeed, Locke's conception of individual liberty and equality presumes, in its fullest measure, such adulthood and such sanity (though we have seen that some feminists have questioned whether Locke perceived such liberty and equality as applying equally, in all respects, to men and women).[61]

It is in the process of "compact" that the moral and political authority of consent becomes most apparent. The process involved in the "compact" is one wherein individuals decide what natural rights, exercisable in the state of nature, they should surrender to make civil society and government possible, in return for what securities and guarantees governments will provide for their remaining liberties.⁶² Natural rights are understood by Locke as liberties exercisable by individuals within the state of nature.⁶³ In order to create civil society and government, individuals give up, for instance, their right within the state of nature to act as judge and executioner of the law of nature, ceding that authority to government which now acts as a common "umpire", adjudicating disputes between individuals within civil society.⁶⁴ However, Locke insists that individuals only give up these rights in return for government guaranteeing their other natural rights, some of which, we saw, were so fundamental that Locke believed they could not be surrendered by any individual except when guilty of an unjust act of war.⁶⁵ Such inalienable rights would include, for instance, each individual's right to their own self-preservation – Locke declaring that "no Man, or Society of Men, having a Power to deliver up their *Preservation*, or consequently the means of it, to the Absolute Will and arbitrary Dominion of another".⁶⁶

It is on the basis of this process of "compact", therefore, that consent becomes a fundamental source of both legitimacy and authority in civil society, since it is the mutual consent, bestowed by individuals, which makes the "compact", and therefore the civil society and government that arises upon it, possible:

> Men being, as has been said, by Nature, all free, equal and independent, no one can be put out of this Estate, and subjected to the Political Power of another, without his own *Consent*. The only way whereby any one devests himself of his Natural Liberty, and *puts on the bonds of Civil Society* is by agreeing with other Men to joyn and unite into a Community, for their comfortable, safe, and peaceable living one amongst another, in a secure Enjoyment of their Properties, and a greater Security against any that are not of it. This any number of Men may do, because it injures not the Freedom of the rest; they are left as they were in the Liberty of the State of Nature. When any number of Men have so *consented to make one Community* or Government, they are thereby presently incorporated, and make *one Body Politick*, wherein the *Majority* have a Right to act and conclude the rest.⁶⁷

The status of consent within Locke's political philosophy has been a matter of some debate. Some deny it has very much significance at all.⁶⁸ Others argue that its significance is very much less than what had previously been thought.⁶⁹ But I think, as the above passage and the preceding discussion indicates, that Locke himself perceived it as playing a pivotal role in his political philosophy. Locke also distinguishes between "express" and "tacit" consent, insisting that, although those involved in the original "compact" will give their "express" consent to the inauguration of civil society and government, thereby giving rise to direct obligations of political obedience, others born into civil society, in the wake of this "compact", can be assumed to have given their "tacit" consent to both it and government if they "hath any Possession, or Enjoyment, of any part of the Dominions of any Government".[70] In other words, Locke insists that individuals are obligated to obey government, even if they have not given their *express* consent to it, if they are beneficiaries of the authority and security that government provides. In this way, Locke believes he has reconciled the authority of government (and the obligations of obedience this authority requires) with the liberty of individuals.[71]

Consent, Legitimacy and Toleration

But what is the link between this account of the origins of government, centred on "compact" and consent, and Locke's conception of toleration? The answer lies in the process whereby these origins, and the consent that makes these origins possible, ultimately limit the authority of government and so limit government's entitlement to impinge on the liberty of individuals. As Locke insists, these origins, centred on "compact", ensure that only those purposes of government to which individuals have consented are purposes governments are legitimately entitled to pursue, and it is only when the actions of government fall within these legitimate purposes that individuals are obligated to obey.[72] Those purposes which fall outside this framework, and to which individuals have not consented, are not, Locke insists, legitimate purposes of government (governments having no "commission" to pursue them[73]) and therefore do not give rise to obligations of obedience. As Locke puts it:

> But if the law indeed be concerning things that lie not within the verge of the magistrate's authority ... men are not in these cases obliged by that law, against their consciences.[74]

Of course, much conflict of opinion is likely to surround the question of whether a particular action of government does or does not fall within the scope of its legitimate purposes. Further, even in those instances where individuals believe governments are acting outside the scope of these purposes and are therefore exercising power illegitimately, such individuals may choose not to resist government, believing such resistance may not have much likelihood of success. We will discuss both of these matters in the section "Realpolitik" below. But the connection between "compact" and consent, on the one hand, and toleration, on the other, arises from the limits imposed on government by "compact" and consent. To take the case of religious toleration, Locke's assumption is that, as individuals could never be presumed to have consented to governments exercising an authority over something so intimate and crucial to their interests as their religious beliefs and practices, governments cannot be perceived as legitimately exercising authority for that purpose.[75] Such matters therefore fall outside the "commission", and therefore jurisdiction, of governments, with the result that they are left to the liberty of individuals. Locke refers to this process, in which the scope of government authority is determined by the original purposes for which government is established, and the limits this places on governments' entitlement to impinge upon religion, as follows:

> [I]n all societies instituted by man, the ends of them can be no other than what the institutors appointed; which I am sure could not be their spiritual and eternal interest. For they could not stipulate about these one with another, nor submit this interest to the power of the society, or any sovereign they should set over it.... [A]ll your saying, "doubtless commonwealths are instituted for the attaining of all the benefits which they can yield", will not give authority to any one or more, in such a society, by political government or force, to procure directly or indirectly other benefits than that for which it was instituted.[76]

One of the first instances in which we see Locke making this link, on the basis of "compact", between the origins of government, the purposes for which it was established and the limits this imposes on its authority, is in his early text, the *Two Tracts on Government*. But at that time he insisted he was only making this link in a hypothetical manner, for polemical purposes – as this was the contractual model of authority usually adopted by advocates of toleration, and he wanted to show that arguments for toleration did not apply even when based on the premises advanced by their proponents.[77] Elsewhere in the *Two Tracts*, Locke makes clear that he actually perceives the authority of government as deriving from Scripture, and therefore the will of God.[78]

It is in *An Essay Concerning Toleration* that Locke initiates his significant departure from the *Two Tracts*. Locke begins the *Essay* by referring to different opinions concerning the origins of government prevalent in the England of his time. In the first instance, he refers to those who believe that the origins of government arise "iure divino" (i.e. by a law of God), with the result that the limits of government authority (and indeed its legitimacy) are seen to derive from this divine law.[79] Locke is sceptical of such claims. He suggests that those who advance such a view in England to justify "absolute monarchy" do so in ways at odds with "Magna Carta", and those who advance it to justify a "limited monarchy" ought to be made to show the "charter from heaven" from whence these limits derive.[80] He then identifies a different basis for the origin, limits and legitimacy of government, referring to those who believe that these are "granted" by the "consent" of the "people".[81] To this view he appears much more favourably disposed, and immediately links such an origin to the question of legitimacy by insisting (as at note 76 above) that this "grant", and the authority it bestows on government, ought not to exceed the purposes for which it was given (which do not include religion):

> There are others who affirm that all the power and authority the magistrate hath is derived from the grant and consent of the people, and to

> those I say it cannot be supposed the people should give any one or more of their fellow men an authority over them for any other purpose than their own preservation or extend the limits of their jurisdiction beyond the limits of this life.[82]

Elsewhere in the *Essay* Locke distances himself from such a contractual position, insisting that although the scope of the magistrate's authority is limited to the purposes for which it is established, these purposes are determined by God, not the "people", the magistrate not being "accountable to any tribunal here".[83] Yet, while acknowledging God as the source of the magistrate's authority, Locke continues to insist on the same principle he expounds above – that whatever the ultimate origins of its authority, government ought to be limited in its authority to the purposes for which it is established and that these purposes are entirely "civil" in nature, in no way extending to the religious interests of individuals:

> God hath appointed the magistrate his vicegerent in this world with power to command, but 'tis but like other deputies, to command only in the affairs of that place where he is vicegerent. Whoever meddle in the concernments of the other world have no other power but to entreat and persuade. The magistrate, as magistrate, hath nothing to do with the good of men's souls or their concernments in another life, but is ordained and entrusted with his power only for the quiet and comfortable living of men in society, one with another, as hath been already sufficiently proved.[84]

By the time of the *Two Treatises of Government* and *A Letter Concerning Toleration*, Locke is willing to affirm contractual origins for government, premised on individual consent (as distinct from the will of God) and, as per the *Essay* above, again confines the magistrate's jurisdiction to "civil" concerns (excluding religion) by linking the origins of government with the purposes for which it was established and the limits this places on its authority:

> These things being thus explained, it is easy to understand to what end the legislative power ought to be directed, and by what measures regulated; and that is the temporal good and outward prosperity of the society; which is the sole reason of men's entering into society, and the only thing they seek and aim at in it.[85]

By limiting government to a specified set of purposes, centred on civil concerns (the things of "this life"[86]) and insisting that governments lack legitimacy if their authority extends beyond these purposes, Locke's conception of "compact" ensures that key aspects of individuals' lives, such as religion, reside outside the framework of government altogether. Of course, in the *Two Tracts*, Locke also declared that government authority ought to be directed to the purposes for which it was established and that these purposes are primarily "civil" in nature.[87] It is not, therefore, the identification of government authority with "civil" purposes that distinguishes Locke's later writings from the *Two Tracts*. Rather, what does distinguish the later writings is the origin of the limits upon government, confining its authority to such "civil" concerns – these origins arising (by the time of the *Two Treatises* and *Letter*) from a "compact" emanating from the consent of the people and not the will of God to which Locke refers at notes 78 and 83 above. Also, what distinguishes the later writings is the series of normative and practical judgments that Locke makes in the wake of the *Two Tracts*, discussed in Chapters 2 and 3, which result in a position where, although Locke is still willing (as in the *Two Tracts*) to use state power to limit outward religious expression when it impinges on "civil" purposes, he is able to allow a far greater individual liberty when it comes to religion than he was willing to concede in that earlier text. It is toleration, exercised by government, that makes such liberty politically possible.

Locke's conception of "compact" and the consent which makes it possible, therefore, underwrites Locke's policy of toleration, since, by limiting government in this way, it ensures (at least in principle) that individuals are left alone to exercise their own liberty within specific areas of their lives. But "compact", in overcoming the inconveniences of the state of nature, still ensures states a capacity for governance and therefore a capacity to ensure civil peace, not least (Locke tells us) by transferring to government the executive capacity which individuals had exercised in the state of nature to enforce natural law.[88] In this way, Locke's conception of "compact" helps to reconcile, on the one hand, the normative imperative of individual liberty, and, on the other, the practical imperatives of civil peace and effective state governance, present throughout his political writings.

Realpolitik

Of course, the account I have provided above is one that ignores the practical realities of realpolitik. Governments, after all, are often capable, in practice, of exceeding the limits of their authority, particularly if these limits are designated by normative ideals rather than by legal or practical enforcement. Often opinion will differ as to whether these norms have in fact been transgressed at all.

Locke himself did not ignore these realities. Indeed, as Richard Ashcraft has pointed out at length, Locke's own personal involvement in the political struggles of his patron, Anthony Ashley Cooper, against the authority of Charles II, forced upon him a recognition that liberty is often a matter of political contestation, arising from competing perspectives and conflicting interests.[89] In this respect, Locke was fully aware of the fact that, irrespective of the purposes governments declare they are pursuing, and the claims to legitimacy they make on this basis, from the perspective of some individuals subject to this authority, individual liberties may still be transgressed and the natural rights for whose protection (Locke believed) these individuals (or their predecessors) first created government may be undermined. It is for this reason that Locke, in his mature political philosophy, accorded to individuals a right of resistance against government should they believe government to be acting in ways that transgress what they perceive to be their fundamental liberties. As Locke put it:

> For all *Power given with trust* for the attaining an *end*, being limited by that end, whenever that *end* is manifestly neglected, or opposed, the *trust* must necessarily be *forfeited*, and the Power devolve into the hands of those that gave it, who may place it anew where they shall think best for their safety and security. And thus the *Community* perpetually *retains a Supream Power* of saving themselves from the attempts and designs of any Body, even of their Legislators, whenever they shall be so foolish, or so wicked, as to lay and carry on designs against the Liberties and Properties of the Subject.[90]

For Locke, the normative source of this right of resistance was, again, those natural rights to liberty and equality which, deriving from our equal status as God's creatures, and ultimately from natural law and the will of God, no individual had the authority to surrender to another except, Locke says, when they are guilty of an "unjust" act of war.[91] We saw that, for Locke, these natural rights included a right of self-preservation and it is this right to which Locke refers as ultimately justifying resistance to government:

> For no Man, or Society of Men, having a Power to deliver up their *Preservation*, or consequently the means of it, to the Absolute Will and arbitrary Dominion of another; whenever any one shall go about to bring them into such a Slavish Condition, they will always have a right to preserve what they have not a Power to part with; and to rid themselves of those who invade this Fundamental, Sacred, and unalterable Law of *Self-Preservation*, for which they enter'd into Society. And thus the *Community* may be said in this respect to be *always the Supream Power*, but not as considered under any Form of Government, because this Power of the People can never take place till the Government be dissolved.[92]

Locke allows individuals themselves to choose whether they will exercise this right of resistance and the time and circumstance in which they will exercise it.[93] However, he cautions (once again in the name of realpolitik) that, if they do seek to resist government, they should have the "greater part" of the "people" on their side, for if their grievance:

> reach no farther than some private Mens Cases, though they have a right to defend themselves, and to recover by force, what by unlawful

force is taken from them; yet the Right to do so, will not easily ingage them in a Contest, wherein they are sure to perish; it being as impossible for one or a few oppressed Men to *disturb the Government*, where the Body of the People do not think themselves concerned in it, as for a raving mad Man, or heady Male-content to overturn a well-settled State; the People being as little apt to follow the one, as the other.[94]

The exercise of such a right of resistance amounts, in effect, to revolution, since, in such circumstances, dissidents do not accord any legitimacy to government. The result, Locke says, is a state of war between dissidents and government, there being no earthly arbiter between them, with the result, Locke says, that the "appeal is to Heaven" – a reference to the fact that the dispute, involving a state of war, therefore involves the clash of force, with the result that the outcome, being contingent on this, cannot be determined in advance.[95]

Yet Locke also refers to a form of resistance which stops short of such a state of war. Within contemporary liberal parlance, such resistance is referred to as "conscientious objection". The key difference of this to the right of resistance above is that such a process involves dissidents refusing to obey laws contrary to their conscience, but nevertheless accepting the state's penalty for such disobedience. In such way, their consciences are preserved and the authority and legitimacy of the state respected. Locke describes such a process in his early work, *An Essay Concerning Toleration*:

> [I]f the magistrate ... by laws and impositions, endeavour to restrain or compel men contrary to the sincere persuasions of their own consciences, they ought to do what their consciences require of them, as far as without violence they can; but withal are bound at the same time quietly to submit to the penalty the law inflicts on such disobedience, for by this means they secure to themselves their grand concernment in another world, and disturb not the peace of this, offend not against their allegiance either to God or the king, but give both their due, the interests of the magistrate and their own being both safe.[96]

In conclusion, therefore, although Locke in his political philosophy sought to place normative limits on the authority of government, by grounding the legitimacy of that authority in the consent of individuals, his own political experience would have forced upon him the (*realpolitik*) recognition that in practice it is the *practical* limits on government – the limits which governments believe they cannot transgress without provoking the successful resistance of those subject to their command – which would often determine the *actual* scope of government jurisdiction. This will be particularly evident in Chapter 3 when we discuss the *practical* arguments that Locke advanced in favour of toleration, where Locke insists that toleration is often the best means for magistrates to secure civil peace if they confront dissidents of equal or greater force or strength than themselves and therefore likely to successfully resist any attempt by government to impose conformity in matters of religion.

Notes

1 Locke's close association with the new ruling authorities is evident in the fact that he says he had been asked by Viscount Mordaunt to "take care of his wife on her passage with the Princess [Mary] from The Hague, and I could not do less than accept the office" (Locke to Limborch, 5 February 1689, Amsterdam: Remonstrants' MSS. Ba. 256h: Latin, quoted in Cranston 1957: 307).
2 See Laslett 1965: 44–5; Ashcraft 1986: ch. 8.
3 Tully 1983: 1. See also Klibansky 1968: ix, xvi–xvii, xix–xxiii. However see Ch. 2 (note 1).
4 Klibansky 1968: xix.
5 As Limborch has written: "In that winter (1685–86), in the house of Mr. Veen, he wrote, unbeknown to anybody but myself, that excellent *Epistola de tolerantia* which he addressed to me" (Philip Van Limborch, "Letter to Lady Masham", 24 March 1705, Amsterdam: University Library, MS. III D 16, f.54, in Klibansky 1968: ix).
6 Philip van Limborch, "Bodl. MS. Locke c.14, f.24", in Klibansky 1968: xx.
7 Ibid.: xxii–xxiii.
8 Ibid.: xxiii.
9 Locke, "22 Apr/2 May 1690, MS Locke c.24, f.155", in ibid.: xxiii–xxiv.
10 Laslett 1965: 18.
11 Ibid.: 45.
12 Peter Nicholson has made this point:

> The Toleration Act had now been passed (May 1689) ... Locke surely would have regarded the degree of toleration established as precarious, after his lifetime's experience of political upheaval and reversal (it is only with hindsight that the revolutionary settlement can be viewed as inaugurating stability).
>
> (Nicholson 1991: 171)

13 On Locke's advocacy of separation, see Locke 1993a: 393, 403, 433.
14 Schochet 1992: 148. My addition.
15 Klibansky 1968: xxv–xxvi.
16 Laslett 1965: 17.
17 See Locke 1965: II § 13, 21, 90, 94, 95, 123, 127, 136, 137, 171. See also Locke 1993a: 422–3.
18 See Introduction (notes 11, 12 and 16).
19 See Ch. 3 (note 65).
20 Indeed, Locke makes clear in *An Essay Concerning Toleration* that the "liberty" in question extends beyond religious liberty, to include "practical principles or opinions by which men think themselves obliged to regulate their actions with one another" (Locke 1993b: 191).
21 On natural rights to liberty, see Locke 1965: II § 22, 87, 91, 123, 128, 149. See also Introduction (notes 12–16).
22 See ibid. (notes 12, 15 and 16).
23 See Locke 1965: II § 88, 128–30, 131, 134–8, 171, 222. See also Ch. 1 (note 62). On some of these liberties being so fundamental that, short of individuals being guilty of an unjust act of war, they cannot be surrendered to another (including government) see Introduction (note 15). On government being limited in terms of these individual liberties, see Locke 1965: II 131, 135–40, 142, 149, 171–2, 222.

24 See notes 62–6 below.
25 Locke 1993a: 421. See also ibid.: II 393, 394, 396, 403, 405, 405–6, 411, 412, 422–3, 423.
26 Locke 1963: 62.
27 Locke 1993a: 411, 420.
28 Ibid.: 395, 399, 405, 421–2; Locke 1993b: 195. See also note 84 below.
29 Locke 1993a: 422.
30 On Locke's claim that neither the church nor the state is entitled to engage in such coercion by imposing civil penalties for religious beliefs, see ibid.: 399, 400, 400–1, 403, 403–4, 405, 417, 423–4. At most, the ultimate penalty that can be imposed for religious beliefs or behaviour is excommunication by the church, which involves no impact on one's material well-being, but only banishment from the church – see ibid.: 399–400.
31 Locke defines a church as "a voluntary society of men, joining themselves together of their own accord in order to the public worshipping of God, in such a manner as they judge acceptable to him, and effectual to the salvation of their souls" (ibid.: 396. See also ibid.: 399–405). On the non-entitlement of the church to impose civil penalties, see note 30 above. On its non-entitlement to confiscate property, see Locke 1993a: 399, 400, 403–4. On the exercise of the "sword" (the punitive authority capable of impinging on the liberty of individuals) being the sole possession of the magistrate, see ibid.: 395, 399, 400, 401 and note 50 below.
32 Ibid.: 393–6, 405–10, 411–17, 420–6, 430–1. See also Locke 1993b: 186, 187, 191, 192, 193, 195, 196.
33 On the need for the magistrate to treat all religious matters as "things indifferent", see Locke 1993a: 411. See also Locke 1993b: 192–5.
34 As Locke puts it: "[N]o private person has any right, in any manner, to prejudice another person in his civil enjoyments because he is of another Church or religion" (Locke 1993a: 400). On the right to persuade, exhort and admonish, see note 28 above.
35 In this respect, Locke's conception of toleration, being based on *limits* to authority and power, is quite distinct from those definitions of toleration which insist upon a tolerator's capacity to proscribe or expunge an activity, toleration arising from their voluntary choice not to – see Raphael 1988: 139; Horton 1996: 28; Galeotti 2002: 22; Cohen 2004: 69.
36 Locke 1993a: 403. As early as the *Two Tracts on Government*, Locke had presented such non-interference as an ideal, and one which alone made toleration of a variety of religions possible (see Ch. 2 note 38 and Ch. 3 note 51). However as his "leeks" and "onions" quote makes clear, he believed that, given circumstances as they existed in England in his time, such non-interference in matters of religion was unlikely, and therefore toleration was unworkable. See Ch. 2 (note 34); see also Ch. 2 (notes 39, 40, and 59).
37 See note 13 above.
38 Locke 1993a: 433. On the state proscribing religious beliefs or practices for civil reasons, see ibid.: 415, 424–6.
39 Locke 1993b: 195. Indeed Locke makes the same point even earlier in the *Two Tracts* – see Locke 1967a: 137, 145; 1967b: 219–20, 237.
40 Locke 1993a: 423. See also ibid.: 393–4.
41 "A Letter from Hosius, Bishop of Cordova (296–357), to Constantius", Athanasius, *Hist. Ar.* 44, in Henry Bettenson (ed.) *Documents of the Christian Church* (Oxford: Oxford University Press, 1954), p. 27, cited in Davis 1966: 19–20.
42 Locke 1993a: 393. See also ibid.: 403.
43 See ibid.: 415.
44 Ibid.: 425. See also Locke 1993b: 201.
45 Locke 1993a: 425.

46 Ibid.: 417. See also Ch. 9 (note 72).
47 See note 33 above.
48 Locke 1993a: 415.
49 See notes 30 and 31 above.
50 Locke 1993a: 395. See also note 31 above.
51 Locke 1993a: 425. See also Locke 1993b: 189–90.
52 See Locke 1965: II § 15, 22, 83, 94, 95, 99, 112, 117, 119, 121, 122–4, 131, 134–5, 137–40, 149, 171, 175, 186, 192, 193, 195, 198, 212, 216, 222, 227. For my rejection of Timothy Stanton's claim that "consent" does not play a central role in Locke's political philosophy, see Ch. 5 (notes 46 and 47).
53 On Locke's references to "compact" and "original Agreement", see Locke 1965: II § 14, 97, 99, 122, 171, and ibid.: II § 211, 243 respectively. See also Locke 1993a: 422–3, where Locke describes such a process of "compact" as a basis for government without referring to it by name.
54 On the reasons why Locke believes individuals seek to leave the state of nature and form civil society and government, see note 17 above. See also Locke 1965: II § 87, 124, 131, 134, 192, 222.
55 See ibid.: II § 14, 99, 101, 104, 106, 112.
56 Ibid.: II § 101.
57 See note 52 above. On the limits of such obligations of obedience, expressed in Locke's right of resistance to government, see notes 90 and 92 below.
58 On such reconciliation, see Locke 1965: II § 22, 94, 95, 117, 119, 131, 134, 192.
59 See ibid.: II § 95. On Locke's discussion of "tacit consent", which applies to those already born within civil society, and subject to government, see note 70 below and Ch. 5 (note 63).
60 On how Locke perceives all individuals in an equal relationship when it comes to determining the "compact", giving up equal liberties for equal guarantees of their remaining liberties in return, see Locke 1965: II § 130, 135, 171, 211. Of course, there was much discussion in the 1960s and 1970s as to whether Locke indeed perceived the entire population as "equal" in terms of consent, or only the "political population", thereby reflecting the restricted voting franchise of his time. The key text which initiated much of this debate is Macpherson 1962.
61 Locke's identification of individual liberty with "adulthood" and "sanity" is most evident in those passages in the *Two Treatises* where he depicts individual reason as a necessary precondition of individual liberty (and so denies such liberty to children and individuals of unsound mind). As Locke states:

> The *Freedom* then of Man and Liberty of acting according to his own Will, is *grounded on* his having *Reason*, which is able to instruct him in that Law he is to govern himself by, and make him know how far he is left to the freedom of his own will. To turn him loose to an unrestrain'd Liberty, before he has Reason to guide him, is not the allowing him the privilege of his Nature, to be free; but to thrust him out amongst Brutes, and abandon him to a state as wretched, and as much beneath that of a Man, as theirs. This is that which puts the *Authority* into the *Parents* hands to govern the *Minority* of their Children.
>
> (Locke 1965: II § 63)

On the same grounds, Locke says that "*Lunaticks* and *Ideots* are never set free from the Government of their Parents" (Locke 1965: II § 60). On the feminist analysis of Locke's *Two Treatises*, see Introduction (note 11).
62 On the idea that individuals give up some natural liberties in return for guarantees from civil society and government concerning their others, see Locke 1965: II § 88, 123–4, 129–31, 134–8, 171, 211, 222. See also note 23 above.
63 See Locke 1965: II § 4, 22, 87, 91, 127, 128. See also note 21 above and Introduction (notes 14 and 15).

64 See Locke 1965: II § 128–30. On government as "umpire", see ibid.: II § 87, 90, 127, 212.
65 See Introduction (note 15).
66 Locke 1965: II § 149. See also ibid.: II § 23.
67 Ibid.: II § 95. For Locke's other references to "consent", see note 52 above.
68 See, for instance, Timothy Stanton at Ch. 5 (note 46). For my response to Stanton, see Ch. 5 (note 47).
69 See, for instance, John Dunn at Ch. 5 (note 45).
70 Locke 1965: II § 119.
71 See note 58 above.
72 On government limited to the purposes for which it was established, see Locke 1993b: 186, 192, 193, 195; 1993a: 422–3; 1963: 119, 121; 1965: II § 83, 123, 124, 131, 134–40. On obedience limited to these terms, see ibid.: II § 135, 149, 171, 222.
73 On Locke's references to "commission", see Ch. 5 (notes 8 and 9).
74 Locke 1993a: 423.
75 See ibid.: 422–3; 1963: 119, 121. Indeed, Locke makes this point as early as the *Two Tracts* (see Locke 1967a: 129–30), but at that time only inward matters of conscience were perceived by Locke as being encompassed by the realm of individual liberty, and therefore it was only these that were perceived as falling outside the magistrate's command – see Ch. 2 ("Locke, Liberty and the *Two Tracts*").
76 Locke 1963: 121. See also ibid.: 119. For a further discussion of the reasons why Locke believed that religion was not a matter on which individuals, engaged in the process of "compact", "could not stipulate about ... one with another, nor submit ... to the power of the society", see Ch. 8 (notes 47–51). The standard conception of toleration assumes that individuals who tolerate have the capacity (or at least a *belief* that they have the capacity) to reverse this toleration and engage in proscription, if they wish; otherwise, if they are powerless to reverse this process, they are not engaging in "toleration" but rather enduring that which they are unable to alter (Raphael 1988: 139; Cohen 2004: 93, 94; Jones 2007: 384–5; 2012: 266–7; Balint 2014: 267). Consequently, the idea, advanced by Locke, that the scope of toleration (the realm within which individuals are free from government intrusion) is established by *limits* imposed on government by "compact" and consent is, at least to some extent, at odds with such a view. While governments could always transgress these limits, and engage in proscription, intruding upon that with which they are not entitled to interfere, the fact that in doing so they would be acting *illegitimately* distances Locke's account of toleration from the standard account above. We see elsewhere how Locke's conception of toleration differs from the standard account in other ways (see note 35 above; Ch. 4 note 28).
77 Locke 1967a: 122–3, 128–9, 174–5.
78 Locke 1967b: 223, 226–8. See also Locke 1967a: 124. However see Locke 1967a: 122–3, 174–5; 1967b: 230 where Locke seeks to reserve judgment on the origin of political authority altogether.
79 Locke 1993b: 186–7.
80 Ibid.: 186–7. Conversely, in the *Two Tracts*, it is the "people" whom Locke challenges to show the "charter" of their own liberty and the limits it places on government – Locke 1967a: 123.
81 Locke 1993b: 187.
82 Ibid.: 187. See also Locke 1967a: 129.
83 Locke 1993b: 193, 195. Locke again distances himself from such a contractual model of authority when he refers, in the *Essay*, to "the bounds that God hath set to the power of the magistrate and the obedience of the subject" (ibid.: 201).
84 Ibid.: 195. For similar limits on the magistrate's command, see ibid.: 186, 187, 188, 191, 192, 193, 196, 200.

85 Locke 1993a: 423. On Locke's reference to "compact" in the *Two Treatises of Government*, see note 53 above.
86 As Locke declares at note 40 above: "For the political society is instituted for no other end but only to secure every man's possession of the things of this life". See also Ch. 5 (note 54).
87 As Locke states:

> [I]t is not lawful for [the magistrate] to bind all free and indifferent things and enclose them within the boundaries of the laws and impose them on the people, since in truth a magistrate is set above a people and governs them for this reason, that he may provide for the common good and the general welfare; he holds the helm so that he may guide the ship into harbour and not on to the rocks. The measure of this power is to be taken from the end or intention of the legislator; that is to say, the magistrate can impose whatever he judges to serve the well-being of the community but, on the other hand, he cannot – without sin, that is – impose that which he does not consider to serve or be subordinate to this end.
> (Locke 1967b: 219–20)

However the difference from Locke's later writings can be detected in the very next paragraph of Locke's text where, the "limits" referred to above notwithstanding, Locke declares that those subject to the magistrate's command have an absolute obligation of obedience, even in those instances where the magistrate exceeds these limits and so "sins" by engaging in "unlawful" action (ibid.: 220. See also Ch. 2 note 20).

88 See note 64 above.
89 Of all Locke scholars, Peter Laslett and Richard Ashcraft have done most to link Locke's political philosophy to his practical political activity, arguing that Locke's later political philosophy, culminating in the *Two Treatises of Government* (1689), was written for the purpose of opposing the executive government of Charles II which, Locke believed, threatened the established constitutional liberties of the English. See Laslett 1965: 60, 74–9; Ashcraft 1980: 431, 436, 438–7, 449, 451, 466, 468, 474–5; 1986: 9–13.
90 Locke 1965: II § 149. See also ibid.: II § 131, 135, 168, 171, 222. On Locke's defence of a right of resistance in the *A Letter Concerning* Toleration, see Ch. 4 (note 32).
91 See Introduction (note 15).
92 Locke 1965: II § 149.
93 See ibid.: II § 21, 168, 212, 241, 242.
94 Ibid.: II § 208. See also ibid.: § 230.
95 On Locke's reference to an "appeal to heaven", see ibid.: II § 20, 21, 168, 176, 241, 242. On Locke's conception of a "state of war", see ibid.: II § 16–20, 155, 172, 181, 196, 207, 222, 227, 232, 242. It is the removal of an authoritative "umpire", able to decide between antagonists, which Locke perceives as a primary feature of the state of war – ibid.: II § 21, 212, 227, 242. Some scholars have missed the full dimension of this element of Locke's political philosophy. For instance, pointing to the conflict between governments, on the one hand, and dissidents resisting government authority, on the other, J. W. Gough declares that, if governments remain within the limits Locke has prescribed for them and only impinge on individual liberties when "civil" interests are at stake, "recalcitrants have no valid grounds for complaint" (Gough 1991: 69). But the very point of the element of realpolitik in Locke's political philosophy (evident, I believe, in his phrase "appeal to Heaven") is his recognition that the question of whether government has indeed transgressed its authorized limits, and so exercised power illegitimately, or whether it has remained within these limits and so dealt appropriately with "recalcitrants" is one of the issues open

to contestation within any possible conflict. Because the conflict is characterized by a "state of war" between competing sides possessing competing perspectives, and there is, within the temporal sphere, no neutral or authoritative "umpire" to decide between them, such questions concerning who has "valid" grounds for "complaint" cannot be determined in advance. Indeed Locke, at one point, says it can only be determined, by "God alone", on the final Day of Judgment – Locke 1993a: 424. It is such contingent realities, at least within the temporal sphere, that Locke's realpolitik perspective acknowledges and Gough's statement above does not.

96 Locke 1993b: 193–4. See also Locke 1993a: 423. See also Ch. 3 (note 14) for how Locke, in the *Essay*, although advancing a right of conscientious objection, does not yet accord to individuals a right of resistance against government.

References

Ashcraft, R. (1980) "Revolutionary Politics and Locke's *Two Treatises of Government*: Radicalism and Lockean Political Theory", *Political Theory*, 8 (4): 429–86.

Ashcraft, R. (1986) *Revolutionary Politics and Locke's Two Treatises of Government*. Princeton, NJ: Princeton University Press.

Balint, P. (2014) "Acts of Tolerance: A Political and Descriptive Account", *European Journal of Political Theory*, 13 (3): 264–81.

Cohen, A. J. (2004) "What Toleration Is", *Ethics*, 115 (1): 68–95.

Cranston, M. (1957) *John Locke. A Biography*. London: Longmans, Green and Co.

Davis, R. H. C. (1966) *A History of Medieval Europe. From Constantine to St. Louis*. London: Longmans, Green and Co.

Galeotti, A. E. (2002) *Toleration as Recognition*. Cambridge: Cambridge University Press.

Gough, J. W. (1991) "The Development of Locke's Belief in Toleration". In: John Horton and Susan Mendus (eds) *John Locke. A Letter Concerning Toleration in Focus*. London: Routledge, pp. 57–77.

Horton, J. (1996) "Toleration as a Virtue". In: D. Heyd (ed.) *Toleration. An Elusive Virtue*. Princeton, NJ: Princeton University Press, pp. 28–43.

Jones, P. (2007) "Making Sense of Political Toleration", *British Journal of Political Science*, 37 (3): 383–402.

Jones, P. (2012) "Legalising Toleration: A Reply to Balint", *Res Publica*, 18 (3): 265–70.

Klibansky, R. (1968) "Preface". In: J. Locke *Epistola de Tolerantia. A Letter on Toleration*. Trans. J. W. Gough. Oxford: Clarendon Press, pp. vii–xliv.

Laslett, P. (1965) "Introduction". In: J. Locke *Two Treatises of Government*. Peter Laslett (ed.). New York: New American Library, pp. 15–148.

Locke, J. (1963) "A Second Letter Concerning Toleration". In: J. Locke *The Works of John Locke*. Vol. VI. Aalen: Scientia Verlag, pp. 61–137.

Locke, J. (1965) *Two Treatises of Government*. Peter Laslett (ed.). New York: New American Library.

Locke, J. (1967a) "First Tract on Government". In: J. Locke *Two Tracts on Government*. P. Abrams (ed.). Cambridge: Cambridge University Press, pp. 117–81.

Locke, J. (1967b) "Second Tract on Government: Translation". In: J. Locke *Two Tracts on Government*. P. Abrams (ed.). Cambridge: Cambridge University Press, pp. 210–41.

Locke, J. (1993a) "A Letter Concerning Toleration". In: J. Locke *Political Writings*. David Wootton (ed.). London: Penguin, pp. 390–436.

Locke, J. (1993b) "An Essay Concerning Toleration". In: J. Locke *Political Writings*. David Wootton (ed.). London: Penguin, pp. 186–210.

Macpherson, C. B. (1962) *The Political Theory of Possessive Individualism: Hobbes to Locke*. Oxford: Oxford University Press.

Nicholson, P. (1991) "John Locke's Later Letters on Toleration". In: J. Horton and S. Mendus (eds) *John Locke. A Letter Concerning Toleration in Focus*. London: Routledge, pp. 163–87.

Raphael, D. D. (1988) "The Intolerable". In: S. Mendus (ed.) *Justifying Toleration. Conceptual and Historical Perspectives*. Cambridge: Cambridge University Press, pp. 137–53.

Schochet, G. J. (1992) "John Locke and Religious Toleration". In: L. G. Schwoerer (ed.) *The Revolution of 1688–1689*. Cambridge: Cambridge University Press, pp. 147–64.

Tully, J. (1983) "Introduction". In: J. Locke *A Letter Concerning Toleration*. J. Tully (ed.). Indianapolis, IN: Hackett Publishing Co.

2 From Conformity to Toleration – Matters of Influence

We have seen that Locke spent much of the 1680s in hiding in Holland, seeking to escape prosecution for his involvement in the Whig opposition to Charles II. During this time he no doubt ruminated upon the circumstances of his own exile and the dark shadows of religious persecution spreading across Europe. It was during this period, as we know, that Locke composed *A Letter Concerning Toleration*.

At the beginning of Chapter 1, James Tully provided an account of the historical circumstances behind the composition of the *Letter*. Richard Ashcraft, in the following passage, provides a more specific account of the textual circumstances of this composition, suggesting, among other things, that the composition extended well beyond 1685:

> According to Limborch, Locke wrote the *Epistola de tolerantia* during the winter of 1685–1686. Thus it appears that a draft of the *Epistola* was in existence by the end of January 1686. The work was dedicated and written in the form of a letter to Locke's friend Limborch. Yet, curiously, we have no evidence that the manuscript was actually delivered to Limborch until just prior to its publication, which he arranged, three years later.... A draft of the *Epistola*, then, certainly existed in 1686, but the extent to which Locke worked on and revised its arguments prior to his departure from Holland is much more difficult to determine. There are good reasons to assume that Locke did make such revisions – none of his major works, with the possible exception of *The Reasonableness of Christianity*, seems to have escaped the process of extended revising – but we do not have for the *Letter* a record of Locke's reading and notes accompanying its composition, as we do for the *Two Treatises* or the *Essay Concerning Human Understanding*.[1]

What is certainly apparent is that the *Letter* and its content did not simply spring to Locke's mind, *ex nihilo*, as he contemplated the ominous issues of the day. Rather, Locke's arguments for toleration, as present in the *Letter*, build upon his earlier writings on toleration, stretching back a quarter of a century. His minor essays, collected in a recent edition by

Mark Goldie, show the frequency with which Locke returned to the subject of toleration throughout his intellectual career.[2] *A Letter Concerning Toleration* was therefore the culmination of much previous reflection on Locke's part. As Locke's biographer, Maurice Cranston, puts it:

> [Locke's] renown as a theorist of toleration is based on the *Letters for Toleration* and other political works which he published during the reign of William III; but most of the principles he set forth in those *Letters* were already contained in the manuscript essay [known as *An Essay Concerning Toleration*] of 1667.[3]

A Letter Concerning Toleration appeared in translation in England in 1689 and, among other things, addressed an important practical question: how to ensure civil peace within polities between inhabitants fundamentally divided by religious faith. This concern had enormous longevity for Locke. Indeed, it was this very matter which had inspired his first major political work, the *Two Tracts on Government*, which Locke wrote between 1660 and 1662 while he was a Student at Christ Church, Oxford.[4] It was also the primary impetus behind *An Essay Concerning Toleration*, written in 1667 while Locke was located at Exeter House as a member of the household of Anthony Ashley Cooper, later the first Earl of Shaftesbury.

This chapter and the next will focus on both the *Two Tracts on Government* and *An Essay Concerning Toleration*. Both are important preludes to Locke's composition of the *A Letter Concerning Toleration*, which will be discussed in Chapters 4 and 5. What is significant for our purposes is that, between the *Two Tracts on Government*, composed in 1660–62, and *An Essay Concerning Toleration*, composed in 1667, Locke's views on toleration underwent a fundamental transformation. From being opposed, in the *Two Tracts*, to states adopting toleration as an appropriate response to religious diversity within their borders, Locke, by the time of the *Essay*, had become an open advocate of such a policy.

Why was Locke able to shift from being a vocal opponent of toleration, insisting, in the *Two Tracts*, that it was a threat to civil peace, to seeing toleration, in the *Essay*, as an important component of that peace and arguing that political authorities ought to adopt this policy in order to ensure civil coexistence between individuals fundamentally divided by faith? What were the considerations that informed Locke's assessment of toleration, and the circumstances in which it would be applied, that allowed him to alter his views in this way? It is these questions that the rest of this chapter and the next seek to answer.

Each of these chapters will seek to answer these questions in a different way. This chapter will do so by focusing on the wider influences within Locke's life that might have led him to alter his position on toleration. The next chapter will focus on the *Two Tracts* and the *Essay* themselves, identifying the discursive shifts both within and between these texts which made such an alteration in Locke's position possible.

Two Tracts on Government

In 1947, the Bodleian Library acquired, from the Earl of Lovelace, a collection of Locke manuscripts. The collection contained "some 2,700 letters and about 1,000 miscellaneous items including notebooks, journals, accounts, academic exercises and drafts of several of Locke's published works".[5] Within it was also included "John Locke's earliest writings on politics" – one treatise in English and the other in Latin.[6] The editor of these works, Philip Abrams, has referred to them as "Locke's first attempt at sustained political and ethical argument."[7] Neither treatise had a title. As Abrams writes:

> Locke gave no title to his papers.... Their only heading is a statement of the problem to be discussed. Some convenient short title was required and I have named them Locke's *Tracts on Government*. Their polemical character, their similarity of form with the *Two Treatises*, and their underlying concern with questions of law and obligation will, I hope, justify this choice.[8]

The *Two Tracts on Government* are in fact two quite different documents. The first, written in English, and in the year 1660, is Locke's response to Edward Bagshaw who, like Locke, was a Student of Christ Church, Oxford, but who, unlike Locke, actively campaigned within the college for toleration in matters of religion and was eventually deprived of his Studentship in the college for this reason.[9] Bagshaw had written a pamphlet, *The Great Question Concerning Things Indifferent in Religious Worship*, which he published in 1660, the year of Charles II's Restoration.[10] "Things Indifferent" referred to those matters which were neither commanded nor forbidden by Scripture and so thought by many to be open to the discretion of secular authorities or, indeed, individuals' conscience.[11] They were also referred to in Latin as "adiaphora", which is a term arising from ancient Stoic philosophy meaning things outside the moral law, and therefore neither commanded nor forbidden by it.[12] "Things indifferent" raised the question of toleration, because, not being commanded by divine law, they left open the question of whether these matters could be left to the free choices of individuals, rather than the authority of the state.[13]

The second *Tract* was written in Latin. Although it dealt with similar issues, Philip Abrams believes it was written some time later than the first *Tract*, around 1661–62, and for a very different purpose.[14] He cites evidence suggesting it was written as a "formal academic oration" upon Locke's "own appointment as Rhetor (Praelector Rhetoricus) in Christ Church on Christmas Eve 1662".[15]

The key issue for Locke in both *Tracts* was the issue raised by Bagshaw. This concerned whether governments ought to regulate and govern "indifferent things" in matters of religion or adopt a policy of toleration towards them, leaving these to the free choice of individuals or church congregations. Certainly many matters in civil affairs were "indifferent" because they were not subject to the command of Scripture, and in those instances where the magistrate had not decided to regulate them, these were left to the liberty and judgment of individuals. In Locke's time, the sticking point concerned whether this should apply to matters of religion, such as church dress, ceremony and other details of religious worship not determined by Scripture. If these were "indifferent", could the magistrate safely consign them to the discretion of individuals or church congregations, without risk of schism or public disorder, or should the state intervene to prescribe precisely what form these religious observances should take?

As Peter Abrams points out, the debate itself was very well established by the time Locke wrote upon it and had for a long time animated many of the members of his college.[16] It was a question of fundamental importance because it concerned the limits of individual liberty, in relation to government, upon a matter of profound (and perhaps eternal) importance to many individuals – the manner and conduct of the worship of God. It was for this reason that the debate over "indifferent" things in religious worship aroused so much passion, rancour and intensity. As Abrams states:

> The political problem which the debate on indifferent things was meant to solve was a real, troublesome and long-standing one. As [Edward] Stillingfleet wrote: "If any controversy hath been an increaser and fomenter of heart-burnings and divisions among us, it hath been about the determination of indifferent things".... The argument Locke produced in 1660 was not an original one. Rather, it was a late statement of an old orthodoxy. The case on both sides had been rehearsed many times in the century before Locke wrote.[17]

Bagshaw, in his contribution to the debate, insists that the state ought to allow individuals and congregations a free discretion when it comes to "indifferent" matters of religious worship.[18] He insists that such matters should ultimately be left to individual conscience, rather than the state, so that individuals ought to have liberty to decide upon them as they please.[19] In other words, Bagshaw was insisting that, when it came to "indifferent" matters of religion, the state should practise *toleration* – refraining from interfering in such concerns and leaving these instead to the personal choice of individuals or church congregations.

The Locke who responded to Bagshaw in 1660 was a very different intellectual figure to the Locke who is remembered as a seminal influence upon the liberal tradition. As we shall see, at this early stage of his intellectual career, Locke rejected any suggestion that the state should accord toleration to "things indifferent" in religion. On the contrary, he insisted that not only did the state (or what Locke called the "magistrate") have an authority to legislate on "things indifferent", whether civil or religious, but those individuals subject to state authority had an absolute and unconditional obligation to obey that authority, irrespective of whether its injunctions were just or unjust. As Locke put it:

> As to the obligation of subjects, it must be understood that the power of the magistrate is on the one hand regulatory and on the other coercive, to which corresponds a double obligation, (i) the obligation to act, (ii) the obligation, if I may put it thus, to suffer; or as it is commonly put, an active and a passive obedience. On which premises I hold ... [t]hat the subject is bound to a passive obedience under any decree of the magistrate whatever, whether just or unjust, nor, on any ground whatsoever may a private citizen oppose the magistrate's decrees by force of arms, though indeed if the matter is unlawful the magistrate sins in commanding.[20]

Such unconditional demands for obedience contrast sharply to the later Locke of the *Two Treatises*, and his defence of an individual right of resistance against the unjust intrusions of government, discussed in the previous chapter.[21] Peter Laslett says of Locke's demands for total obedience in the *Two Tracts* that "no sharper conflict could be found with the doctrine of *Two Treatises of Government*".[22] The only exception to this demand for total obedience concerns, as we shall see, laws that impinge on individuals' inward liberty of conscience, or what Locke calls their "judgment".[23] As will be explained below, in regard to these, Locke is willing, in the *Two Tracts*, to grant an (inner) liberty of conscience. But in terms of outward behaviour, Locke insists, in the passage above, that individuals' obligation of obedience to the magistrate is both unconditional and absolute.

The result, therefore, is a significant difference between Locke and Bagshaw, both in terms of their basic assumptions and the conclusions they reach concerning "things indifferent". Peter Abrams has summarized the differences that emerged between them as follows:

> Like Locke, Bagshaw upholds an extensive and authoritarian competence of magistracy in all civil affairs; he claims liberty only in respect of religious ceremonial. But here their agreement ends. The settlements they urge on the King are incompatible. The political and moral theories on which they ground their appeals to his discretion conflict at every point. Bagshaw maintains that neither the magistrate nor any Christian may determine the use of any indifferent thing of a religious character for any other Christian. Locke replies that the magistrate, and he alone, can and must determine the use of any or all indifferent things at his own discretion. Bagshaw's argument starts from the theological assumption that a sense of spiritual integrity rooted in conscience is essential to the devout Christian and not to be violated at any cost.... Locke's problem was thus to make a case for civil law which would allow its authority to be interposed between the revealed will of God which left ceremonies indifferent and the conscience of

each and every individual.... [He believed] to permit individual freedom in the use of all indifferent things is to open the door to chaos and disorder. It follows as a condition of order that all indifferent things ought to be susceptible to civil law.[24]

Wider Events

Why is Locke so willing, at this early stage of his intellectual career, to insist upon an unconditional obligation on the part of individuals to obey the magistrate in all matters? The answer lies in Locke's biography. Locke is composing the *Two Tracts* in conscious reflection on the recent events of English political history – the Civil Wars of the 1640s, the Interregnum of Oliver Cromwell, the upheavals and uncertainties that followed upon Cromwell's death and the recent Restoration of Charles II. John Marshall had pointed to how closely enmeshed was Locke's own life with these events:

> Locke had been ten when the Civil War broke out, sixteen when the King was executed next to his school [at Westminster], and twenty-six when Oliver Cromwell's death in 1658 plunged England back into political turmoil for two years until the Restoration of Charles II.[25]

Locke himself acknowledged the traumatic impact these events had upon him, suggesting in the passage below that his early existence was characterized by upheaval and disorder. As he explains in this passage, it is this experience that now inscribed within him a desire for the security and stability which, he hoped, obedience to the new Restoration authorities might bring:

> I no sooner perceived myself in the *world* but I found myself in a storm, which hath lasted almost hitherto, and therefore cannot but entertain the approaches of a calm with the greatest joy and satisfaction; and this methinks obliges me, both in *duty* and gratitude to be chary of such a blessing, and what lies in me to endeavour its continuance, by disposing men's minds to obedience to that government which hath brought with it that quiet and settlement which our own *giddy folly* had put beyond the reach, not only of our *contrivance*, but *hopes*.[26]

It is this desire for political stability and security which, it seems, above all other things, informs Locke's opposition to Edward Bagshaw. Bagshaw's plea for a toleration regarding "things indifferent" in matters of religion is perceived by Locke as a threat to the political stability so recently re-established by the restoration of Charles II, auguring a possible return to the upheaval of the past, seeking, as it does, to limit the King's authority, and that of Parliament, for the sake of a freedom of individual conscience:

All the *freedom* I can wish my country or myself is to enjoy the *protection* of those *laws* which the prudence and providence of our ancestors established and the happy return of his Majesty hath restored: a body of laws so well composed, that whilst this nation would be content only to be under them they were always sure to be above their neighbours.... 'Tis therefore in defence of the *authority* of these laws that against many reasons I am drawn to appear in public, the preservation whereof as the only security I can yet find of this nation's *settlement*.[27]

Consequently, at this early stage of his intellectual career, Locke, unlike Bagshaw, was a model of Restoration orthodoxy.[28] In contrast to his later political writings, there is nothing in his defence of established authority, within the *Two Tracts*, that seeks to weaken or dilute that authority in the name of an outward liberty for individuals or a policy of toleration.

Locke's Early Rejection of Toleration

It was Edward Bagshaw, therefore, not Locke, who was the dissident figure in 1660. Bagshaw's plea for toleration of "things indifferent" in matters of religion was nothing less than a demand for the limitation of state authority over individuals when it came to matters of religious worship not prescribed by Scripture. In coming years, it would be the English Parliament, rather than the King, who would be most insistent on denying such toleration and imposing punitive sanctions on those (known as "Dissenters") unable to conform to the beliefs and ceremonies of the Church of England. Parliament's vigour in this regard would soon issue, between 1661 and 1665, in the series of statutes known to posterity as the Clarendon Code.[29] Mark Goldie has described the punitive attitude of the English parliamentary and Anglican authorities towards religious dissent at this time as follows:

> Restoration England was a persecuting society. It was the last period in English history when the ecclesiastical and civil powers endeavoured systematically to secure religious uniformity by coercive means. Those who set about this task were not silent about their reasons.... Many an assize sermon became a fruitful occasion for rhetorically yoking priest and magistrate together in a godly cause, the sword of the latter animated by the spiritual admonition of the former. When heretics pervert the church's doctrine, when schismatics disrupt its order, when libertines scandalize its purity, then a bishop "must betake himself unto his rod and his keys" and summon the magistrate to undertake "the pious use of the sword".[30]

It was precisely this coercive reality that Bagshaw sought, in a limited way, to oppose, prior to the Clarendon Codes, with his plea for a toleration of "things indifferent" in matters of religion. Locke's opposition to even this mild form of toleration was total. This opposition needs to be explained and understood not only in terms of Locke's own experience of political upheaval, in the years prior to Charles II's return, but also in terms of what he believed was the source of that upheaval. That source, for Locke, was the English populace itself, and what he perceived as its propensity for disorder, particularly when it came to matters of religion.[31] Locke, at this time, possessed an almost "Hobbesian" vision of the "multitude" as inherently unruly and liable to break the bounds of restraint: "Who knows but that since the multitude is always craving, never satisfied, that there can be nothing set over them which they will not always be reaching at and endeavouring to pull down."[32]

Locke's opposition to toleration in the *Two Tracts*, therefore, arises from practical rather than normative sources. He believes that, in allowing for the open expression of religious differences, toleration provides the space for disagreement, and, given the nature of the English populace, this therefore provides the circumstances for upheaval and disorder to ensue.[33] This places toleration at odds with the imperatives of civil peace and effective state governance which, we have seen, Locke valued so highly in the wake of the "storm" of his formative years. He insists that even the most seemingly innocuous matters of religion could produce this conflict, taking on the most vociferous significance, given that, in such disputes, many believed their eternal salvation, or the salvation of others, to be at stake:

> And he must confess himself a stranger to England that thinks that *meats* and *habits*, that *places* and *times* of worship etc., would not be as sufficient occasion of hatred and quarrels amongst us, as *leeks* and *onions* and other *trifles* described in that satire by Juvenal was amongst them, and be distinctions able to keep us always at a distance, and eagerly ready for like violence and cruelty as often as the *teachers* should alarm the *consciences* of their zealous votaries and direct them against the adverse party.[34]

Religion is therefore a volatile source of conflict, in Locke's opinion, precisely because, in the minds of the individuals concerned, their eternal interests are at stake.[35] Further, as he suggests in the passage above, the religious scruples of some individuals are vulnerable to being appropriated by those with ulterior motives, so that religion itself becomes a cloak for more earthly ambitions.[36] It is all these aspects of religion which, Locke believes, renders it a source of upheaval and disorder. And it is the free expression of religious differences that toleration makes possible which, in Locke's opinion, provides a space for such outcomes. As he puts it: "Grant the people once free and unlimited in the exercise of their religion and where will they stop, where will they themselves bound it, and will it not be religion to destroy all that are not of their profession?"[37]

Locke admits that not all Christians would abuse the liberty that toleration provides in this way so that, if these more moderate individuals held sway, toleration might be consistent with civil peace and security.[38] But his point is that we have no means to distinguish, ahead of time, those that will make such sober use of the liberty that toleration allows from those who will not, and, given that both will be able to access the same toleration, but for contrary ends, toleration in any guise becomes a dangerous policy for the state to adopt:

> I cannot deny but that the sincere and tender-hearted Christians should be gently dealt with and much might be indulged them, but who shall be able to distinguish them, and if a toleration be allowed as their right who shall hinder others who shall be ready enough to lay hold on the same plea?[39]

Locke insists, therefore, that the toleration for which Bagshaw is asking, in allowing a liberty for the expression of religious differences, is likely to produce its opposite, undermining liberty and producing a religious tyranny, wherein peaceful coexistence will become an impossibility. As he puts it:

> I find that a *general freedom* is but a *general bondage*, that the popular asserters of public liberty are the greatest engrossers of it too ... and I know not whether experience (if it may be credited) would not give us some reason to think that were this part of *freedom* contended for here by our *author* generally indulged in *England* it would prove only a *liberty* for *contention, censure* and *persecution* and turn us loose to the *tyranny* of a *religious rage*.[40]

Even as late as the *A Letter Concerning Toleration*, Locke recognised that there were religious views and practices that had the potential to produce such upheaval and so threaten civil peace and state security.[41] As such, he was always aware that toleration, if it was to be consistent with civil peace, required limits, outside of which some religious views and practices were to be proscribed. But what makes the *Two Tracts* so different from Locke's later writings is that these limits, and the proscription that they apply, are potentially *total*, so that complete outward conformity to the magistrate's command, on all religious matters, is possible, should the magistrate decree it, and toleration, with the small exception of the liberty of individual conscience referred to at note 23 above, is not rendered possible at all.[42] It is to this small exception, centred on conscience, that we now turn.

Locke, Liberty and the *Two Tracts*

We have seen that, in the *Two Tracts*, Locke was willing to sacrifice the normative imperative of individual liberty almost entirely to the practical imperative of civil peace and effective state governance. The only liberty that Locke conceded to individuals, in this early text, was a purely inward liberty of conscience, and this not because individuals had a freedom of will in this area, but precisely the opposite – Locke declaring that their incapacity to alter their beliefs at will meant they could not do so at the behest of the magistrate, with the result that the coercive capacity of the latter could not reach to this area of their lives.[43]

Locke insisted that this inward liberty of conscience was entirely consistent with an outward obedience to the magistrate's command and in no way diminished by it. He based this claim on a distinction, which he advanced within the *Two Tracts*, between a "liberty of the judgment" and a "liberty of the will". "Liberty of the judgment" refers to the inward assent of the individual, and it is here, Locke tells us, that "the whole liberty of the conscience" resides.[44] "Liberty of the will", on the other hand, is related to outward behaviour. It is only the "liberty of the will", Locke insists, that is impacted upon when the magistrate seeks to impose his or her command upon "things indifferent" in matters of religion.[45] This is because, unlike matters of Scripture, these "things indifferent" are not intrinsically "necessary" (i.e. they do not arise "by virtue of the force of the divine law") and so they do not oblige the individual conscience in "material" terms, by demanding an inward assent to their "necessity" at the level of "judgment". Rather, they only oblige the individual in "formal" terms, at the level of "will", involving an outward obedience of behaviour to the magistrate's command.[46] In such matters, the magistrate's command can therefore be obeyed at the level of the "will", without impinging on the inward liberty of "judgment".[47] In constraining outward behaviour ("liberty of the will") in this way, but not "liberty of judgment", Locke insists that that the inner conscience of the individual remains as free as before.[48]

It is only those laws which the magistrate insists are "necessary" rather than "indifferent", because commanded by God, when in fact they are not, that Locke insists impinge unjustly upon the consciences of individuals, since such laws demand, on the part of individuals, an inward ("material") judgment concerning their "necessity", when in fact there is no such "necessity" at all.[49] In such cases, Locke says, the magistrate, by imposing such laws, "ensnares the liberty of conscience and sins in commanding it"[50] – though as Locke points out at note 20 above, such "sin" does not absolve those subject to the magistrate's command from their outward obligation of obedience. On the other hand, if the magistrate insists that a law is "necessary", because commanded by God, and this is in fact the case, Locke insists that such an injunction, although limiting the liberty of judgment, is a justified limitation, since it imposes no greater imposition by the magistrate than that imposed by God Himself.[51]

Abrams points out that there was nothing innovative in Locke's articulation of this relationship between individual conscience and the magistrate's command. Rather, he insists, the reconciliation that Locke effects between the two, by claiming that an inward liberty of conscience is consistent with a complete outward obedience to political authority, was an orthodox one within Anglican circles of his time. As Abrams declares: "Locke follows the Anglican orthodoxy in reserving the freedom of judgment to the individual and thus holding that freedom of conscience is possible even while we obey the magistrate in all our actions."[52]

Outcomes

Locke never published his response to Bagshaw.[53] Nevertheless, the outcomes of the dispute for each of these Students of Christ Church could not have been more different. Edward Bagshaw was expelled from Christ Church for his pamphlet, *The Great Question Concerning Things Indifferent in Religious Worship*, and was eventually imprisoned for his religious opinions, dying while he was on bail from Newgate a few years later.[54] Locke, by contrast, prospered, retaining his Studentship at Christ Church and being appointed lecturer in Greek at the college in the same year as he wrote his reply to Bagshaw (1660).[55] Later he was appointed Lecturer in Rhetoric, Censor of Moral Philosophy and eventually was given one of two medical studentships at Christ Church.[56] It was only when Locke was involved in the political opposition to Charles II, led by the Earl of Shaftesbury, that culminated in the Rye House Plot, and was put under clerical surveillance, that he was expelled from Christ Church just prior to his flight into exile to Holland in 1683.[57] By contrast, in this earlier period, as his own academic advancement makes clear, Locke was seen as no threat to the established political and religious order. Indeed, quite the contrary – he was a model of religious and political orthodoxy. As Richard Ashcraft has written:

> [W]hat the recently discovered writings on politics and morality demonstrate is that Locke's thinking on these subjects began well within accepted orthodoxy. How deeply committed Locke was to the beliefs and practices of Anglican royalism is open to question, but it is safe to say that he was a de facto supporter of the dominant political and intellectual assumptions that structured the social consciousness of the inhabitants of Restoration England.[58]

Locke's Shift

Yet, despite this orthodoxy, by 1667, Locke's position on these matters had altered profoundly. The evidence for this resides in Locke's authorship of *An Essay Concerning Toleration* in that year. Within this text, Locke is still concerned with the same practical political problems that he confronted in the *Two Tracts on Government*. He is still concerned to ensure civil peace and security within a polity whose inhabitants are fundamentally divided on matters of religion. But the *means* by which he believes state authorities are best able to achieve this outcome have altered significantly. Locke, in the *Two Tracts*, had refused to countenance religious toleration as a means of ensuring this peace and security, believing toleration undermined this end. As he put it: "a liberty for tender consciences was the first inlet to all those confusions and unheard of and destructive opinions that overspread this nation", with the result that a "general freedom" is likely to produce a "general bondage".[59] Consequently, far from advocating toleration in the *Two Tracts*, we saw that Locke instead insisted upon an outward conformity to the magistrate's command, declaring that in these circumstances, "there is no other help but in eagerness to obey".[60]

By 1667, Locke's position had shifted. Far from confining religious liberty to the private and innocuous realm of individual conscience, as he had done in the *Two Tracts*, Locke was now of a very different view. At the beginning of the *Essay* he distinguishes between three types of "opinions and actions of men": those that are "such opinions and actions as in themselves concern not government or society at all, and such are all purely speculative opinions and divine worship"; those that "are such as in the[ir] own nature are neither good nor bad, but yet concern society and men's conversations one with another, and these are all practical opinions and actions in matters of indifferency"; and those that "are such too as concern society, but are also good or bad in their own nature, and these are moral virtues or vices".[61] Of these he says "that the first sort only (viz. speculative opinions and divine worship) are those things alone which have an absolute and universal right to toleration".[62]

With this conclusion, Locke breaks fundamentally from his previous position in the *Two Tracts*. "Opinions" and "worship", in order to be meaningful, must be outwardly expressed. Consequently, far from insisting that all outward behaviour is governable by the rules and regulations of the magistrate, Locke, with his reference to "an absolute and universal right to toleration", is insisting, in the *Essay*, that some aspects of individuals' outward behaviour ("speculative opinion and divine worship") "concern not government or society at all", and therefore government authority ought to be limited in relation to them. No longer is Locke of the view, as he was in the *Two Tracts*, that all "indifferent" matters (i.e. those matters not determined by divine law) are potentially subject to the magistrate's command.[63] Instead, his new position is that some matters, such as "speculative opinion", although "indifferent" (i.e. falling outside of divine law) nevertheless (like "divine worship") also fall outside the magistrate's command and so require limits upon it. Further, Locke argues in the *Essay* that when individuals are of the view that God has decreed that certain "indifferent" matters ought to be part of divine worship, then for the individuals concerned, these wholly cease to be "indifferent", instead becoming "necessary" – and so binding on the individual conscience – with the result that, if they do not impinge on civil concerns, these matters also ought to fall outside the scope of the magistrate's command (a conclusion wholly at odds with the *Two Tracts*).[64] This shift from things "indifferent" to "necessary" and its impact on the magistrate's command will be discussed further in Chapter 4.

In all these ways, a sphere of individual liberty, extending beyond individual conscience to outward opinion and behaviour, is thereby prescribed in the *Essay*, and this liberty, in order to outwardly express itself, requires limitations on the magistrate's authority and his or her entitlement to intrude upon specific areas of individuals' lives. It is a policy of toleration that seeks to enforce these limitations.

We see, therefore, the immense shift that occurs between the *Two Tracts* and the *Essay*. As the above makes clear, such a shift involves an alteration in the relationship between individuals and government, so that, far from the magistrate having a potential authority over all "indifferent" things and therefore over the outward behaviour of the individual, his or her authority is limited in a number of ways. First, as discussed in Chapter 1, Locke makes very clear in the *Essay* that the magistrate's authority is limited to "civil" matters, with all other matters that fall outside this "civil" realm being left to the liberty of the individual.[65] As Chapter 1 made clear, this, in and of itself, does not thoroughly distinguish the *Essay* from the *Two Tracts* as Locke had also sought, in that earlier text, to confine the magistrate's authority to "civil" matters, limiting the magistrate's authority to only those "indifferent things" that concern the "common good and the general welfare".[66] But we saw the immense scope that Locke, in the *Two Tracts*, believed this gave the magistrate over individuals lives, excluding only individual conscience. The *Essay*, by contrast, in *its* emphasis on limiting the magistrate's command to "civil" matters, clearly perceives a more rigorous limitation, since it perceives this limitation as giving rise to a wider realm of individual liberty, extending well beyond individual conscience to what Locke calls the "private" realm of the individual.[67] It is this process, along with the attempt by Locke, in the *Essay*, to exclude entirely from the magistrate's command some matters ("speculative opinion and divine worship"), even if "indifferent", as well as those matters which individuals, on the basis of their conscience, decide are "necessary" for religious worship, which places significant limits on that command, and so constitutes a significant departure from the *Two Tracts*.

Quantitative vs. Qualitative

One might argue that Locke's expansion of the realm of individual liberty, from the inner conscience of the *Two Tracts* to the outward realm of "speculative opinion and divine worship" in the *Essay*, is a *quantitative* increase, simply expanding the size of the area within which the magistrate is not entitled to interfere. At one level this is true. But the narrowing of the magistrate's jurisdiction that this process entails also involves the beginnings of a *qualitative* shift, since it initiates a process which, in Locke's later writings, will involve an entirely new ("contractual") way of determining the limits of the magistrate's authority, based, in turn, on a fundamentally different understanding of the relationship between government and the individual.

Concerning the quantitative increase, this change is one from inward to outward liberty – Locke declaring in the *Essay* that:

> in speculations and religious worship every man hath a perfect, uncontrollable liberty which he may freely use, *without, or contrary to the magistrate's command*, without any guilt or sin at all; provided always that it be all done sincerely and out of conscience to God, according to the best of his knowledge and persuasion.[68]

Once liberty extends, in this way, to outward actions, such as religious worship, this requires a limitation on the authority of the magistrate and his or her entitlement to interfere with such matters. In the *Two Tracts* we saw that intrusions by the magistrate on outward religious practice were considered compatible with an inner liberty of conscience. This is no longer the case when the entitlements of such conscience extend to outward practice (i.e. where individuals have conceived such outward practice as "necessary" to worship), since there must be a free space for such practice to occur if liberty of conscience is not to be impinged upon. Consequently, once conscience extends to outward practice, Locke conceives of individual liberty imposing *limits* on the magistrate's authority.

But the shift from the *Two Tracts* to the *Essay* also involves the beginnings of a *qualitative* change in how the scope of the magistrate's authority is understood. This is because such a process, when it reaches its fruition in Locke's later writings, will presuppose a fundamentally different relationship between government and the individual. Rather than the "vertical" relationship that Locke upheld in the *Two Tracts*, in which the individual is subject to a hierarchy of power stemming from God and the magistrate, we shall see in Chapter 4 that, by the time of Locke's *Two Treatises of Government* and *Letter Concerning Toleration*, the model of the magistrate's power that Locke employs involves a more "horizontal" relationship between the individual and government, arising from the process of "compact" (discussed in Chapter 1), in which the liberty of the individual places *limits* on the magistrate's authority. It is in this context that concepts arising in Locke's later writings, such as an individual right of resistance to the magistrate's command, acquire their meaning, in a way that would not be possible in the context of the more "hierarchical" discourse of the *Two Tracts*.[69] It is the beginnings of this qualitative shift which accompanies the quantitative increase in individual liberty from the *Two Tracts* to the *Essay*.[70]

But these are wider issues that take us beyond our present concerns. For the moment we are confronted with two basic questions of interpretation. The first of these is, *why* did Locke's transition between the *Two Tracts* and the *Essay*, involving all of the changes referred to above, take place?

In other words, what motives and influences inspired Locke to shift his position in this way, with very significant implications for his views on toleration? And second, *how* did this transition take place? In other words, in what way did Locke alter the content of his intellectual discourse and the arguments contained within it so as to abandon the political authoritarianism of the *Two Tracts* and advance a very different position in the *Essay*? We shall deal with the first question in the current chapter, referring to it in terms of "matters of influence". We shall deal with the second question in the next chapter, referring to it as "matters of argument".

Matters of Influence

An Essay Concerning Toleration remained unpublished during Locke's lifetime. It was written by Locke while he was a member of the household of his new patron Anthony Ashley Cooper, later the first Earl of Shaftesbury.[71] Locke had first met Ashley when Ashley had arrived in Oxford, in July 1666, to visit his 14-year-old son, then an undergraduate at Trinity College.[72] He had also come to Oxford to drink some of the waters of Astrop as a means to help him recover from a recurrent liver complaint, arising from a hydatid disease.[73] The physician at Oxford with whom Ashley was in contact, Dr Thomas, was unable to deliver the waters and sent Locke in his stead, and that is how Locke's friendship with Ashley began.[74]

At the time of their meeting, Locke was engaged in medical studies at the university and, upon his later arrival at Exeter House, in 1667, not only acted as Ashley's physician but also supervised an operation to remove an abscess that had formed on Ashley's liver, inserting a silver (later gold) pipe "through the stomach wall as a drain to prevent another abscess from forming. Ashley wore the pipe for the rest of his life."[75] Indeed, on the basis of this operation, "Ashley was convinced ... that he owed his life to Locke".[76] Peter Laslett points out that "more recent medical opinion" suggests that "the drainage pipe was useless, but that the operation did save Shaftesbury's life and its success was almost miraculous".[77]

Once established at Exeter House, Locke's intellectual and personal relationship with Ashley soon became a close one. As Ashley's grandson the third Earl of Shaftesbury has written:

> Mr Locke grew so much in esteem with my grandfather that, as great a man as he had experienced him in physic, he looked upon this but as his least part. He encouraged him to turn his thoughts another way.... He put him upon the study of the religious and civil affairs of the nation with whatsoever related to the business of a minister of state, in which he was so successful that my grandfather began soon to use him as a friend and consult with him on all occasions of that kind.... When my grandfather quitted the Court and began to be in danger

from it, Mr Locke now shared with him in dangers as before in honours and advantages. He entrusted him with his secretest negotiations, and made use of his assistant pen in matters that nearly concerned the state, and were fit to be made public, to raise that spirit in the nation which was necessary against the prevailing Popish party.[78]

The political life at Exeter House would therefore have provided Locke with the stimulus and the purpose for the development of his political thought, as well as his many other talents. Maurice Cranston has made this point as follows:

> It was Ashley who discovered and helped Locke to discover his own true genius. Before he went to Exeter House, Locke was a minor Oxford scholar, an ex-diplomatist of small experience, an amateur scientist, an unpublished writer and unqualified physician. In Ashley's home he blossomed into a philosopher, an economist and a medical *virtuoso*.[79]

An Essay Concerning Toleration was composed by Locke in his first year at Exeter House. It has been suggested that the text was written by Locke to aid Ashley in his attempt, as one of the King's ministers, to persuade Charles II to provide some relief to Dissenters, subject to persecution under the series of parliamentary statutes known as the Clarendon Code. Such relief could arise by Charles resorting to the royal prerogative to suspend imposition of the Code, thereby bypassing Parliament and adopting a policy of toleration towards Dissenters by royal command. David Wootton is one Locke scholar who suggests that the *Essay* was written for this purpose.[80] Others include Maurice Cranston. As Cranston writes, the *Essay* did not "differ in much except length from the memorial presented by Shaftesbury to Charles II in 1669 begging for 'Indulgence to Dissenters'".[81] On these grounds, Cranston argues that the four extant drafts of *An Essay Concerning Toleration* can be conceived as a "a series of memoranda" which Locke prepared for Ashley's purpose.[82] Indeed Cranston goes so far as to claim that these drafts can "be read as an exercise in 'speech writing' done by Locke for Shaftesbury's use: and parts may even have been dictated by Shaftesbury".[83]

Certainly Ashley himself possessed all the credentials to act as a significant influence on Locke and the development of his ideas on toleration. Ashley's support, within Parliament, for the principle of toleration, based on his opposition to the Clarendon Code, had been vigorous. As Cranston writes:

> In the Cavalier Parliament of 1661, [Ashley] opposed the Corporation Act, which compelled all holders of municipal offices to take the Anglican sacraments; in 1662, he opposed the Act of Uniformity, which enforced episcopal ordination and other measures distasteful to many clergymen; in 1663, he supported a Bill to allow the King to dispense

with the Act of Uniformity; in 1665, he opposed the Five Mile Act, which curbed the movements of Dissenting preachers; and when this measure was passed, he busied himself with another Bill to allow the King to suspend all such measures against the Non-conformists.[84]

In this respect, Cranston refers to Ashley, during his parliamentary career in the 1660s, as "the most ardent opponent of the [Clarendon] Code, the most eloquent champion of toleration".[85] It is on this basis that Cranston concludes that there is strong circumstantial evidence that Ashley had a significant impact on the political views of John Locke:

> I have searched in vain for evidence of Locke's holding liberal views before his introduction to Lord Shaftesbury in 1666. There is much to show that Locke held such views soon afterwards; and I cannot help wondering if he learned them from Shaftesbury. For it is certainly not the case, as I have seen it sometimes suggested, that Shaftesbury learned his liberalism from Locke. Shaftesbury had been famous since before the Restoration for his advocacy of toleration.... However, if Locke did learn the principle of religious toleration from Shaftesbury, he was a quick and ready pupil. Within a year of their meeting, and before he had installed himself in Shaftesbury's home as a domestic physician and philosopher, Locke was writing the first of several essays on toleration.[86]

Like Cranston, Peter Laslett argues that Locke's composition of *An Essay Concerning Toleration* was for Ashley's purpose – a process which, he says, reflects Locke's role in Ashley's household. As Laslett puts it:

> These publications indicate one of the ways in which [Locke] acted as "assistant pen" to his master in the first period of their association, before he left for France in 1675. He would also draft official papers, record conversations and negotiations, even prompt his master from behind his chair, as he is supposed to have done when Lord Chancellor Shaftesbury delivered the famous speech *Delenda est Carthago* against the Dutch enemy in 1673. But his important literary function was to write out for Shaftesbury's use an account of this or that political or social problem, telling him what had been thought or written about it, what arguments were likely to convince intelligent people of the correctness of a certain attitude to it. The successive drafts on toleration, economics, even perhaps on education and philosophy fit into this context, as well as being records of Locke's own intellectual development. They are supplemented by what he wrote in his diaries, his letters and his commonplace books.[87]

Peter Laslett was responsible, as editor, for the first critical edition of the *Two Treatises of Government*, published by Cambridge University Press in

1960. David Wootton has pointed to the seminal importance of Laslett's achievement for modern Locke scholarship as follows:

> Two events mark the beginning of modern Locke scholarship: Eric Stokes's discovery, in 1944 or 1945, in the library of Christ's College, Cambridge, of a revised text of the *Two Treatises of Government*, prepared by Locke for the printer ... and the purchase of the Earl of Lovelace's collection of Locke manuscripts by the Bodleian Library in 1947.... The first event gave rise to Peter Laslett's brilliant edition of the *Two Treatises* (1960).... The second led to the Clarendon Edition of Locke's works, which is still in progress.[88]

Yet irrespective of Laslett's authority, the editors of the most recent critical edition of *An Essay Concerning Toleration*, J. R. and Philip Milton, have criticized the account which Laslett provides at note 87 above, challenging Laslett's attempt to situate and explain Locke's composition of the *Essay* in terms of his wider role within Ashley's household:

> Laslett saw the *Essay* as the first of a succession of works written by Locke for his patron.... This is not a very accurate characterization of any of Locke's writings, and certainly not of the *Essay concerning Toleration*: far from telling the reader what had been thought or written about toleration, the *Essay* is wholly silent about the contemporary debate. One cannot rule out the possibility that Locke was asked by Ashley to prepare a summary of the works written for and against toleration in 1667–8, but if he did, no evidence whatever has survived.[89]

However, in support of the Laslett thesis that the *Essay* was written for Ashley's purposes, the Miltons do acknowledge that the *Essay* is addressed to the reader in the second person – referring to "your people", "your subjects", etc. This, they claim, suggests "on the face of it" that the addressee of the *Essay* may have been Charles II.[90] Yet they also point out that the *Essay* lacks sufficient deference in tone, and is too restrictive in its account of the royal prerogative, for it ever to have been intended by Locke or Ashley that the King would actually read it in the form in which it is written.[91] They do concede, however, that it might have been intended to be read by others with some influence on government policy, although they point out that "even this is far from certain".[92] Consequently, the Miltons counsel caution regarding any attempt to attribute *An Essay Concerning Toleration* to Ashley's political purposes and Locke's part in advancing them. They concede that this might be the *Essay's* purpose, but in the absence of further evidence it is not something they can definitely affirm:

> There can be little doubt that Locke began writing the *Essay* after he joined Ashley's household in May 1667. The intellectual atmosphere he encountered there would have been very unlike the one he had

known at Christ Church. Although outwardly a conforming Anglican, Ashley's private opinions seem to have been far from orthodox.... He was certainly a supporter of toleration for dissenting Protestants, and perhaps even for Catholics.... It is not easy to say what part if any he had in the genesis of the *Essay*. He may have suggested to Locke that he should write something on the subject of toleration, but in the absence of further evidence this is not something about which it is possible to be certain.[93]

John Marshall has provided a broader framework for the interpretation of the *Essay*. He acknowledges that the *Essay* would have most likely had its genesis in Locke's discussions with Ashley on the subject of toleration, given Ashley's interest in the subject and Locke's position within Ashley's household. But he also suggests that the *Essay* might have had a different provenance altogether:

> In 1667 or early 1668 Locke wrote an "Essay on Toleration". It is extremely likely that consultations with Ashley were part of the context in which Locke first composed this "Essay on Toleration". A discussion of religious toleration would have been exactly the kind of issue that Ashley, with his own firm commitment to ecclesiastical liberty, would have requested of Locke.... It is also possible, however, that the "Essay on Toleration" began simply as some form of discussion document involving a group of friends. It went through four drafts, at least two of which were not in Locke's hand. One version was signed by Locke as "Atticus", a pseudonym that he used with various of his Oxford friends. The first two *Drafts* of the *Essay Concerning Human Understanding* were the result of a group that met at Exeter House in about 1670 or 1671 which probably included some of Locke's Oxford friends. The influence of such a group might help to explain some of the contradictions and tensions between the four drafts [of the "Essay on Toleration"] and even within single drafts.[94]

An Alternative View

Like Marshall, not all have been willing to endorse a trajectory of influence flowing directly from Ashley to Locke as an explanation for the development of Locke's views on toleration. Some have argued that this development arose from sources quite separate from and independent of Ashley and Exeter House. Esmond de Beer, for instance, points to Locke's experience of religious toleration at Cleves as an important source of his views. Locke travelled to Cleves in 1665, prior to his association with Ashley, having been appointed secretary to a diplomatic mission sent by Charles II to the Elector of Brandenburg.[95] In particular, de Beer points to Locke's correspondence with Robert Boyle while Locke was in Cleves, in which Locke expresses astonishment at the religious pluralism evident there and the toleration which (the proscription of Anabaptists notwithstanding) made this possible. In particular, he expresses admiration that such toleration appears to be consistent with civil peace. Locke writes:

> The town is little, and not very strong or handsome; the buildings and streets irregular; nor is there a greater uniformity in their religion, three professions being publicly allowed: the Calvinists are more than the Lutherans, and the Catholics more than both (but no papist bears any office), besides some few Anabaptists, who are not publicly tolerated. But yet this distance in their Churches gets not into their houses. They quietly permit one another to choose their way to heaven; for I cannot observe any quarrels or animosities amongst them upon the account of religion. This good correspondence is owing partly to the power of the magistrate, and partly to the prudence and good nature of the people, who (as I find by inquiry) entertain different opinions without any secret hatred or rancour.[96]

Such a letter suggests that Locke perceived toleration not merely as a possibility, but a desirability, depending on the "power of the magistrate" and the "prudence and good nature of the people" and that he did so prior to any meeting with Ashley.[97] Indeed, even in the *Two Tracts*, we saw that, Locke considered toleration as a possibility, if only those divided by religion "could be content ... [to] use no other weapons to conquer each other's opinions but pity and persuasion".[98] He merely denied this possibility "among a people", such as those in the England of his time, who "are ready to conclude God dishonoured upon every small deviation from that way of his worship which either education or interest hath made sacred to them".[99]

Yet Locke's realization that toleration was a plausible possibility did not begin at Cleves or in the *Two Tracts*. In 1659, prior to both, Locke had acknowledged this possibility, the only question being, he insisted, its practicability given current English circumstances. The occasion was a letter he wrote to Henry Stubbe, another fellow at Christ Church, replying to a pamphlet Stubbe had written advocating toleration, entitled *An Essay in Defence of the Good Old Cause; or a Discourse Concerning the Rise and Extent of the Power of the Civil Magistrate in Reference to Spiritual Affairs*.[100] In his correspondence with Stubbe, Locke questions whether toleration can be extended to Catholics, largely for the reason (further developed eight years later in *An Essay Concerning Toleration*) that they owe their allegiance to a foreign power (the Pope), who is capable of authorizing them to dispense with their oaths and commitments in a Protestant country.[101] But as to Stubbe's broader plea for toleration, Locke finds no problem in principle, simply questioning where it is "practicable" given present English circumstances.[102]

There are two significant aspects of Locke's letter to Stubbe, written a year or two prior to the *Two Tracts*, that we should note here. The first is that it appears to show that, from the earliest period of his intellectual career, Locke had no objection to toleration in principle. Rather, it makes apparent that his primary reservation concerned whether it was applicable to particular societies, given their present circumstances, in practice.[103]

If such prudential concerns regarding present circumstances were all that were preventing Locke from endorsing a policy of toleration, then presumably, as Locke's assessment of those circumstances altered, so too would his opinion concerning the possibility of toleration. It is precisely this proposition which is advanced in the following chapter as the practical (as distinct from normative) means by which Locke shifted his position on toleration from the *Two Tracts* to the *Essay*. In other words, it will be suggested that Locke's practical reassessment of the material circumstances in which toleration would be applied was one means by which he moved from an opposition to an avowed commitment to this policy.

The second significant aspect of Locke's letter to Stubbe is that it shows the evolutionary nature of Locke's thoughts on toleration. As early as 1659 Locke is conceiving of toleration as a possibility, and not dismissing it entirely. Even in the *Two Tracts*, we saw, he considers toleration as a possibility if rival religious groups were willing to act differently towards each other. He rejects this possibility in the *Two Tracts* but, his visit to Cleves intervening, embraces it in *An Essay Concerning Toleration*. Consequently, given this history, any attempt to present these shifts in Locke's position as due solely to the influence of Ashley truncates the evolution of Locke's thought. Locke's letter to Stubbe, his *Two Tracts on Government* and his visit to Cleves precede his association with Ashley. In each of these, Locke showed himself willing to consider the possibility of toleration, and even, in the case of Cleves, admire it in practice.

As such, once these circumstances are taken into account, it seems misleading to explain Locke's conversion to toleration solely in terms of his relationship to a single individual, however influential upon him. Ashley may have provided the final impetus for Locke's political development, pushing him, as a result of political circumstances in which Ashley himself was involved, towards an open avowal of a policy of toleration, but this was a position that Locke had already considered in principle well before his association with Ashley.

"A Black Hole"

At various points in the discussion above, a number of Locke scholars have pointed to an inability to confirm the exact contours of Locke's relationship with Ashley – in particular, the specific lines of influence informing the development of Locke's thoughts on toleration – due to a lack of sufficient corroborating evidence. Indeed, this absence of evidence extends well beyond the subject of toleration. Much of the information concerning Locke's relationship with Ashley is missing, and deliberately so. In 1683, both Locke and Ashley (who by this time was the first Earl of Shaftesbury) were implicated in the Rye House Plot against Charles II, and forced to flee abroad, covering their tracks as they went. The result was that "some of Locke's letters and papers, as well as virtually all of the important Shaftesbury papers and correspondence, were burnt and destroyed".[104] In the words of Richard Ashcraft, this means that "there is a large, black hole in the center of the Locke–Shaftesbury relationship, which is there precisely because of their political relationship and because of the dangerous situation in which the two men found themselves in the 1680s".[105]

As a result of this paucity of evidence, which might otherwise allow us to establish the lines of intellectual influence that tie Ashley to Locke or Locke to Ashley, with a greater degree of precision than we presently possess, one Locke scholar, John Dunn, has reserved judgment on the whole question of Ashley's influence upon Locke:

> Why then did [Locke] join the Shaftesbury entourage and why did he change his opinions? Was the first a consequence of the second or the second a consequence of the first?... This is a startlingly crude question, involving the most profound issues of continuity and authenticity in Locke's intellectual life. It is raised here in this simple-minded form because we do not at the moment apparently (and may never) know the answer to it.[106]

Concerning Locke's wider intellectual trajectory leading from the *Two Tracts* to *An Essay Concerning Toleration*, Dunn therefore concludes:

> The precise balance of causality and rationality remains obscure.... To have an explanation of this transition, it is necessary to make claims within the severely causal domain of psychology. Since such an explanation, at least at the moment, seems inaccessible, we must insist that we have no adequate and established explanation of why Locke should have become the particular sort of liberal that he did become.[107]

We see, therefore, that there is a wide range of opinion within the Locke literature concerning the significance of Locke's association with Ashley, as well as the nature of that relationship itself and its associated lines of influence. Some see the relationship as seminal to Locke's subsequent development. Others identify a less progenitive association, pointing to alternative influences upon Locke. Still others, such as John Dunn, reserve judgment altogether. What is clear, however, is that, by the time of *An Essay Concerning Toleration*, Locke was advancing views on toleration concerning liberty of opinion and worship which extended well beyond those he had put forward in the *Two Tracts* and, as we have seen above, were quite contrary to them.[108] The following chapter will focus in more detail on how Locke was able to articulate, at the level of his discourse, such a profound transformation in his political and intellectual outlook, as well as justify the shift involved. In other words, whereas the present chapter has looked at this transition in terms of matters of influence, the next will look at it in terms of matters of argument.

Notes

1 Ashcraft 1986: 475–6.
2 See Introduction (note 27).
3 Cranston 1957: 111. My addition.
4 As Peter Laslett points out, in Locke's time a "Student" at Christ Church was equivalent to a "Fellow" at other Oxford colleges, and so should not be confused with the term "student" (i.e. undergraduate) in the modern sense of the word (Laslett 1965: 31).
5 Abrams 1967a: 3.
6 Abrams 1967b: ix.
7 Abrams 1967a: 3.
8 Abrams 1967b: ix.
9 "Bagshaw was expelled, in his own view, 'for no reason at all that I know of unless for the impartial and unbiased discovery of my judgment about indifferent or rather doubtful things in religious worship'" (Abrams 1967a: 13).
10 See Cranston 1957: 59.
11 See Locke 1967a: 221.
12 See Marshall 1996: 11.
13 See Locke 1967a: 221–9.
14 As Abrams states:

> The fact that the draft version of the Latin *Tract* is found at the beginning of a notebook which contains drafts of the *Essays on the Law of Nature* suggests that it was penned at about the same time as the first of [Locke's] natural law writings was begun, in 1661–62.
>
> (1967a: 16. My addition.)

15 Ibid.
16 As Abrams states:

> Locke and Bagshaw were both Students of Christ Church at the time of their dispute. Indeed, Locke's *Tracts* could be read as referring exclusively to the domestic politics of his college and university. Indifferent things, surplices in particular, had been an explosive issue in Christ Church long before 1660.
>
> (1967c: 30)

The "surplice" was a loose fitting white liturgical vestment worn over a cassock by clergy, and, in the mid-seventeenth century, was particularly associated with ceremonies of the Church of England in the period when William Laud was Archbishop of Canterbury (1633–45). It was opposed by those with Puritan sympathies who wished to rid the Church of such liturgical symbols, associated as they were, in their minds, with the customs of the Roman Catholic Church. As Abrams states:

> Bagshaw and his friends ... refused to wear surplice or gown and inveighed publicly against both the imposing of indifferent things and the indifferent practices [upon church worship].... In January [1661] Bagshaw's party in Christ Church stole as many of the offending surplices as they could find and buried them in the college sewers.
>
> (Ibid.: 34, 36. My addition.)

17 Ibid.: 36.

18 See Abrams 1967a: 4–5, 18.
19 Ibid.
20 Locke 1967a: 220. Locke also insists on such obligations of absolute obedience elsewhere – see ibid.: 212, 226, 227, 238, 239; Locke 1967b: 119–23, 129, 130, 143, 144, 152, 159. On the magistrate's authority to legislate on all "things indifferent", civil as well as religious, see ibid.: 122–23, 125, 129, 146, 164, 168, 172, 175; Locke 1967a: 213, 216, 218, 223, 229, 232, 237.
21 See Ch. 1 (notes 90 and 92).
22 Laslett 1965: 32.
23 See Locke 1967a: 238–9.
24 Abrams 1967a: 18–19, 20–1. My addition.
25 Marshall 1996: 8. My addition.
26 Locke 1967b: 119–20.
27 Ibid.: 121.
28 See Richard Ashcraft's comment on this at Ch. 2 (note 58).
29 See Milton and Milton 2010: 12–13; Ashcraft 1986: 22; Trevelyan 1956: 24, 26–7.
30 Goldie 1991: 331.
31 See Locke 1967b: 149, 154, 158, 158–9, 160–1, 161–2, 169–70.
32 Ibid.: 158–9.
33 See ibid.: 118, 120–1, 160–1.
34 Ibid.: 121.
35 See ibid.: 120–1, 160–1.
36 See ibid.: 160. As late as the *A Letter Concerning Toleration*, Locke was still pointing to the fact that religion is often used for ulterior motives, to advance highly profane interests, and that this explains much of the conflict that occurs in the name of religion – Locke 1993a: 402–3, 405, 417, 431–2, 432–3.
37 Locke 1967b: 159.
38 See ibid.: 159–60. As Locke states in the first *Tract*:

> [I]f the believer and unbeliever could be content as Paul advises to live together, and use no other weapons to conquer each other's opinions but pity and persuasion, if men would suffer one another to go to heaven every one his one way, and not out of a fond conceit of themselves pretend to greater knowledge and care of another's soul and eternal concernments than he himself, how much I say if such a temper and tenderness were wrought in the hearts of men our author's doctrine of toleration might promote a quiet in the world, and at last bring those glorious days that men have a great while sought after the wrong way, I shall leave everyone to judge.
> (Ibid.: 161; see also Ch. 1 (note 36) and Ch. 3 (note 51))

39 Locke 1967b: 160.
40 Ibid.: 120.
41 Locke 1993a: 424–6. See also Ch. 1 (notes 44, 45 and 51).
42 See notes 20 and 23 above. Given that Locke declares, at note 20 above, that "the subject is bound to a passive obedience under any decree of the magistrate whatever, whether just or unjust", this means that the subject's obligations of obedience to the magistrate extend beyond merely "indifferent" matters (whether civil or religious). If the magistrate seeks to regulate beyond this realm, although this might be an illegitimate extension of the magistrate's authority, and therefore "unjust", the subject, according to Locke at note 20 above, is still obligated to obey. It is in this respect that the magistrate's authority in the *Two Tracts*, underwritten by the subject's unconditional obligations of obedience, are potentially total.
43 Locke 1967b: 127, 129–30. See also Ch. 3 (notes 24–6); Ch. 4 (note 50) and Ch. 5 (notes 34–6).

44 Ibid.: 238.
45 Ibid.: 239.
46 Ibid. On "necessity", see Locke 1967b: 150–51; Locke 1967a: 223, 226, 228.
47 Ibid.: 238–9.
48 Ibid.
49 Ibid.: 239.
50 Ibid.
51 Ibid.
52 Abrams 1967d: 77.
53 See Cranston 1957: 61, 63–4; Abrams 1967a: 12–15.
54 See Cranston 1957: 64. Abrams points out that Bagshaw was "deprived of his Studentship" at Christchurch at the end of 1661 and in May 1662 he appealed to the Lord Chancellor, the Earl of Clarendon, "against charges of disloyalty" (Abrams 1967c: 31). "On 30 December [1662] a warrant was issued for his arrest and in January he and his books were seized and he was thrown into prison" (Locke 1967c: 31).
55 Cranston 1957: 69.
56 Ibid.: 73, 78, 160.
57 Goldie 2002: 155.
58 Ashcraft 1987: 17–18.
59 Locke 1967b: 120, 160. See also note 40 above.
60 Locke 1967a: 212.
61 Locke 1993b: 187.
62 Ibid. See also ibid.: 190–1, 201.
63 See note 20 above.
64 See Locke 1993b: 190. See also ibid.: 188; 2004a: 232–3; 2004b: 276–7.
65 See Ch. 1 (notes 32 and 84).
66 See Ch. 1 (note 87).
67 On Locke's conception of the "private", see Ch. 7 (note 88). On "civil" purposes see Ch. 1 (notes 32 and 84).
68 Locke 1993b: 190–1. Emphasis added.
69 On this right of resistance in the *Two Treatises*, see Ch. 1 (notes 90 and 92). On the right of resistance in the *A Letter Concerning Toleration*, see Ch. 4 (note 32). Concerning the more "hierarchical" discourse of the *Two Tracts*, in which the individual is subject to a "vertical" relationship of power "stemming from God and the magistrate", see Ch. 4 (note 12).
70 It is this qualitative shift, and therefore the categorical distinction between Locke's *Two Tracts* and the *Essay* which, I believe, is missed by Robert Kraynak in his attempt to present religious conformity (*Two Tracts*) and toleration (*Essay*) as simply two different "strategies" that Locke adopts for dealing with the same problem of ensuring civil peace in a context of religious diversity (Kraynak 1980: 55, 68). It is on this basis that Kraynak declares that "absolutism and toleration are the same in principle despite their great difference in practice", and concludes that "absolutism is the original form of liberalism" (ibid.: 53, 55). The extent of Kraynak's error can be seen in the fact that he does not believe Locke defends toleration in the *Essay* in terms of an individual entitlement to liberty at all (the basis of Locke's "qualitative shift"), instead declaring that Locke, in that text, perceived toleration solely as a means of "managing religion" for the sake of civil peace (ibid.: 60. See also ibid.: 62). Contrary to Kraynak, we shall see in Chapter 3 that Locke defends toleration in the *Essay* on *both* normative grounds (centred on individual liberty) and practical grounds (centred on civil peace). Kraynak is therefore mistaken to believe that Locke's discourse on toleration in the *Essay* can be wholly reduced to the latter imperative.
71 I refer to Locke's patron as "Ashley", rather than "Shaftesbury", as he did

not attain his earldom from Charles II until 1672, well after the events described here.
72 Milton and Milton 2010: 1.
73 Laslett 1965: 37–8.
74 See Cranston 1957: 94; Laslett 1965: 38.
75 Ibid. See also Cranston 1957: 113.
76 Laslett 1965: 38.
77 Ibid.: 38n.
78 This extract is quoted by Peter Laslett in ibid.: 39. Laslett gives the source as a letter written by the third Earl of Shaftesbury to Jean Leclerc in February 1705 (ibid.: 39n.). Leclerc was one of Locke's "closest friends in Holland" and editor of the periodical *La Bibliothèque Universelle*, to which Locke contributed and in which Leclerc published, in 1691, "a summary of the whole of *Two Treatises* ... from the English original" (ibid.: 25). The reference to "physic" in the passage is of course an allusion to Locke's role as Ashley's medical practitioner.
79 Cranston 1957: 113.
80 Wootton 1993a: 18. See also Marshall 1996: 69.
81 Cranston 1952: 621.
82 Cranston 1987: 103.
83 Ibid.: 103n. See also Laslett 1965: 41–2.
84 Cranston 1952: 620.
85 Cranston 1957: 107.
86 Cranston 1952: 620. Richard Ashcraft is critical of Cranston's suggestion, in the passage above, that Locke acquired his political views from Ashley. Ashcraft responds:

> This states the point perhaps too crudely, since what is at issue is not so much a direct transmission of political values from Shaftesbury to Locke as the contention that Shaftesbury gave Locke the opportunity and the responsibility of thinking through the major political problems of the day.
> (1987: 21)

At one point in his biography of Locke, Cranston is more circumspect concerning the alleged causal influence running from Ashley to Locke that he traces above (see Cranston 1957: 111).
87 Laslett 1965: 43. See also ibid.: 41–2.
88 Wootton 1993b: 1.
89 Milton and Milton 2010: 49.
90 Ibid.: 49. See also Marshall 1996: 49.
91 See Milton and Milton 2010: 49–52.
92 Ibid.: 50, 52.
93 Ibid.: 27.
94 Marshall 1996: 49. My addition.
95 De Beer 1969: 36. See also Cranston 1957: 82–3.
96 Locke 1993c: 184.
97 Indeed on the basis of Locke's letter to Boyle, written from Cleves, Locke's biographer Maurice Cranston contrasted it to the earlier *Two Tracts* and declared: "Clearly Locke was already moving away from his Hobbesian views of 1661" (Cranston 1957: 82).
98 See notes 38 and 39 above. See also Locke 1967b: 170 concerning the propensity of "underling and tolerated" faiths to be "quiet" and not "troublesome to the magistrate".
99 Ibid.: 161. See also ibid.: 160.
100 See Cranston 1957: 44. David Wootton, as editor of Locke's *Political Writings*, dates Locke's letter to Stubbe to the year 1659 (Wootton 1993a: 35).

101 Locke 1993d: 138. For Locke's similar position on Catholics in *An Essay Concerning Toleration*, see Ch. 3 (notes 28–35). For Jeremy Waldron's claim that Locke was willing, by the time of the *A Letter Concerning Toleration*, to tolerate Catholics, see Ch. 3 (note 68).
102 Locke 1993d: 138.
103 See Wootton 1993a: 35–36. John Marshall, however, has counselled caution in any attempt to read into Locke's letter to Stubbe a support, on Locke's part, for toleration. Rather, he points out that Locke may have simply been providing a diplomatic response to a tract written by a more senior fellow in his college at an uncertain moment in college, university and national politics (Marshall 1996: 7).
104 Ashcraft 1980: 461.
105 Ibid.
106 Dunn 1969: 28.
107 Ibid.: 29–30, 30.
108 See the sections "Locke's Shift" and "Quantitative vs. Qualitative" above.

References

Abrams, P. (1967a) "John Locke as a Conservative". In: J. Locke *Two Tracts on Government*. P. Abrams (ed.). Cambridge: Cambridge University Press, pp. 3–29.

Abrams, P. (1967b) "Foreword". In: J. Locke *Two Tracts on Government*. P. Abrams (ed.). Cambridge: Cambridge University Press, pp. ix–x.

Abrams, P. (1967c) "The Context of Conservatism: John Locke in 1660". In: J. Locke *Two Tracts on Government*. P. Abrams (ed.). Cambridge: Cambridge University Press, pp. 30–62.

Abrams, P. (1967d) "The Politics of Conservatism: The Besieged City". In: J. Locke *Two Tracts on Government*. P. Abrams (ed.). Cambridge: Cambridge University Press, pp. 63–83.

Ashcraft, R. (1980) "Revolutionary Politics and Locke's *Two Treatises of Government*: Radicalism and Lockean Political Theory", *Political Theory*, 8 (4): 429–86.

Ashcraft, R. (1986) *Revolutionary Politics and Locke's Two Treatises of Government*. Princeton, NJ: Princeton University Press.

Ashcraft, R. (1987) *Locke's Two Treatises of Government*. London: Allen and Unwin.

Cranston, M. (1952) "The Politics of John Locke", *History Today*, 2 (9): 619–22.

Cranston, M. (1957) *John Locke. A Biography*. London: Longmans, Green and Co.

Cranston, M. (1987) "John Locke and the Case for Toleration". In: Susan Mendus and David Edwards (eds) *On Toleration*. Oxford: Clarendon Press, pp. 101–21.

De Beer, E. (1969) "Locke and English Liberalism: The *Second Treatise of Government* in its Contemporary Setting". In: John Yolton (ed.) *John Locke; Problems and Perspectives*. Cambridge: Cambridge University Press, pp. 34–44.

Dunn, J. (1969) *The Political Thought of John Locke. An Historical Account of the Argument of the 'Two Treatises of Government'*. Cambridge: Cambridge University Press.

Goldie, M. (1991) "The Theory of Religious Intolerance in Restoration England". In: Ole Peter Grell, Jonathan I. Israel and Nicholas Tyacke (eds) *From Persecution* to Toleration. *The Glorious Revolution and Religion in England*. Oxford: Clarendon Press, pp. 331–68.

Goldie, M. (2002) "John Locke, Jonas Proast and Religious Toleration 1688–1692". In: J. Walsh, C. Haydon and S. Taylor (eds) *The Church of England c.1689–c.1833. From Toleration to Tractarianism*. Cambridge: Cambridge University Press, pp. 143–71.

Kraynak, R. P. (1980) "John Locke: From Absolutism to Toleration", *The American Political Science Review*, 74 (1): 53–69.

Laslett, P. (1965) "Introduction". In: J. Locke *Two Treatises of Government*. Peter Laslett (ed.). New York: New American Library, pp. 15–148.

Locke, J. (1967a) "Second Tract on Government: Translation". In: J. Locke *Two Tracts on Government*. P. Abrams (ed.). Cambridge: Cambridge University Press, pp. 210–41.

Locke, J. (1967b) "First Tract on Government". In: J. Locke, *Two Tracts on Government*. P. Abrams (ed.). Cambridge: Cambridge University Press, pp. 117–81.

Locke, J. (1993a) "A Letter Concerning Toleration". In: J. Locke *Political Writings*. David Wootton (ed.). London: Penguin, pp. 390–436.

Locke, J. (1993b) "An Essay Concerning Toleration". In: J. Locke *Political Writings*. David Wootton (ed.). London: Penguin, pp. 186–210.

Locke, J. (1993c) "Letter to the Hon. Robert Boyle (12/22 December 1665)". In: J. Locke, *Political Writings*. David Wootton (ed.). London: Penguin, pp. 184–5.

Locke, J. (1993d) "Letter to S.H. [Henry Stubbe]". In: J. Locke *Political Writings*. David Wootton (ed.). London: Penguin, pp. 137–9.

Locke, J. (2004a) "Toleration A". In: J. Locke *Political Essays*. M. Goldie (ed.). Cambridge: Cambridge University Press, pp. 230–5.

Locke, J. (2004b) "Toleration D". In: J. Locke *Political Essays*. M. Goldie (ed.). Cambridge: Cambridge University Press, pp. 276–7.

Marshall, J. (1996) *Resistance, Religion and Responsibility*. Cambridge: Cambridge University Press.

Milton, J. R. and Milton, P. (2010) "General Introduction". In: J. Locke *An Essay Concerning Toleration and Other Writings on Law and Politics, 1667–1683*. J. R. Milton and P. Milton (eds). Oxford: Clarendon Press, pp. 1–161.

Trevelyan, G. M. (1956) *The English Revolution 1688–1689*. London: Oxford University Press.

Wootton, D. (1993a) "Introduction". In: J. Locke *Political Writings*. D. Wootton (ed.). London: Penguin, pp. 7–122.

Wootton, D. (1993b) "Preface". In: J. Locke *Political Writings*. D. Wootton (ed.). London: Penguin, pp. 1–4.

3 From Conformity to Toleration – Matters of Argument

Our discussion in the previous chapter tried to provide some account of the motive and intent behind John Locke's composition of *An Essay Concerning Toleration* in 1667, not least why Locke was willing, in this text, to break so fundamentally from his previous views on toleration advanced in the *Two Tracts on Government* only a few years before. The present chapter will focus on the content of both the *Two Tracts* and the *Essay* to explain how, in terms of the actual arguments Locke advances in these texts, this transition was achieved. Was the relationship between the earlier and later text one of radical disjunction and rupture, as is so widely believed, or were there continuities between the discourses present in each text? Did Locke, at this stage in his career, undergo an intellectual metamorphosis, entirely repudiating his earlier views and donning new ones, or is there a greater element of consistency between his two positions than is commonly thought?

Of course, the fact that each text arrives at opposite conclusions concerning the worth of toleration suggests that "disjuncture" rather than "continuity" would more accurately describe their relationship, although continuities will be identified as well. However, at the most immediate level, the basic differences between the two texts are palpable. These differences reside, primarily, at the normative and practical level. In Chapter 1, we discussed how Locke's arguments for toleration can be characterized in either normative or practical terms. We found that each type of argument is categorically distinct from the other. Locke's shift from the *Two Tracts* to the *Essay*, and the transformation in his attitude to toleration that this involved, was made possible, at the level of argument, by the changes he made to both the normative and practical elements of his discourse.

Locke's Transition

Both the *Two Tracts* and the *Essay* contain *practical* arguments either for or against toleration. We saw in Chapter 1 how such arguments rely on empirical assumptions. This means that they are vulnerable to any shift in the material circumstances upon which these empirical assumptions are based or any alteration in Locke's assessment of these. We shall see that one of the ways in which Locke was able to transform his position on toleration, from the *Two Tracts* to the *Essay*, was precisely by such a reassessment of these material circumstances, leading to changes in empirical assumptions. This reassessment centred around two key empirical premises – what I have called premises (i) and (ii) – which we shall discuss below.

Concerning the normative elements within these two texts, we saw that Locke offered only a very limited defence of individual liberty within the *Two Tracts*, confining such liberty to the inner realm of individual conscience, and the judgments it makes. He insisted that such inner liberty was entirely consistent with an outward obedience to the magistrate's command. By the time of *An Essay Concerning Toleration*, however, we saw in the previous chapter that Locke had expanded the realm of individual liberty to include the outward realm of religious expression and religious worship, insisting that, in "speculative opinions and divine worship", individuals have "an absolute and universal right to toleration".[1] Consequently, in addition to the alteration in Locke's empirical assumptions, referred to above, we saw in the previous chapter that one other means by which Locke shifted his position from the *Two Tracts* to the *Essay* was by a quantitative (and qualitative) transformation of his normative conception of individual liberty and its relationship to the magistrate's command.[2] These normative elements are encapsulated in terms of a third premise – what I call premise (iii) – also discussed below.

In this way, we see how the shift in Locke's position from the *Two Tracts* to the *Essay*, and the alteration in his commitment to the policy of toleration that this involved, was based on a fundamental reassessment of the normative and practical elements of his discourse. We shall present this reassessment in terms of the framework provided by the three premises above. Only by engaging in this reassessment was Locke able to advance an argument in the *Essay* that, in breaking from his old one in the *Two Tracts*, allowed him to articulate an entirely new position on toleration. We shall consider Locke's reassessment of the practical elements of his discourse first, before going on to consider his normative reassessment.

Locke's Practical Reassessment

As we saw in the previous chapter, the arguments which underwrote Locke's conclusions in the *Two Tracts*, directed against toleration and in favour of obedience to the magistrate's command, were primarily *practical* in nature. That is, they were directed to the achievement of specific material ends. Toleration was opposed, and outward conformity to the magistrate's command affirmed, because this was believed by Locke to be the best means to ensure the practical ends of civil peace and effective state governance. Locke was able to arrive at this conclusion on the basis of two fundamental empirical assumptions. The first assumption was that the English populace, if allowed to openly express their religious differences, would ultimately produce upheaval and disorder. Locke sought to advance this point with his "leeks" and "onions" statement in the preceding chapter, and made reference to what he saw as the English populace's propensity for disorder by declaring that the "multitude" are "as impatient of restraint as the sea", and are "always craving, never satisfied, that there can be nothing set over them which they will not always be reaching at and endeavouring to pull down".[3] His second empirical assumption – an important one, given his advocacy of outward religious conformity as a means to ensure civil peace – was that the state had the requisite material capacity to effectively impose this conformity, eradicating, where necessary, visible religious differences, and the disagreement and conflict arising from them, so as to avoid this upheaval and disorder.

We shall refer to each of these assumptions as empirical premise (i) and empirical premise (ii). Each of these assumptions, both implicit and, at times, explicit, in Locke's discourse within the *Two Tracts*, were necessary, underwriting his argument for outward religious conformity in this text, and providing the means by which such an argument could be cogently sustained. This is because empirical premise (i), in referring to the propensity of religious differences, openly expressed, to produce upheaval and disorder, gives rise to the need for outward religious conformity, imposed by the magistrate's command, in order to avoid such outcomes. Empirical premise (ii), on the other hand, in supposing the magistrate has the material capacity to effectively impose this conformity, presumes that his or her command can be enforced in ways that ensure such outcomes are avoided. In this way, each of these empirical premises reinforce the other, and underwrite the content, and uphold the plausibility, of Locke's discourse in the *Two Tracts*. We shall set them out in schematic form as follows:

(i) Religious differences, openly expressed, will, as a matter of fact, produce the sort of disagreement which will ultimately degenerate into conflict, upheaval and disorder within civil society.
(ii) The state has the material capacity to effectively impose outward conformity in matters of religion, by eradicating, where necessary, the visible expression of religious difference and to do so without producing more disorder than such a policy is intended to avoid.

It was Locke's reassessment of these two empirical premises that, in part, made possible the shift in his position from the *Two Tracts* to the *Essay*. To be more specific, between the *Two Tracts* and the *Essay*, Locke adopts (a) a very different assessment concerning the extent to which religious differences, openly expressed, will, as a matter of fact, produce the sort of disagreement which will ultimately degenerate into conflict, upheaval and disorder within civil society (thereby reassessing premise (i)); and (b) a very different assessment of the material capacity of the state to effectively impose outward religious conformity in ways that do not produce more disorder than such a policy is intended to avoid (thereby reassessing premise (ii)). In this way, the two premises, and their subsequent reassessment, provide a framework within which we can, at least in part, understand Locke's departure from his position on toleration in the *Two Tracts* and his affirmation of a very different position in the *Essay*.

Both premise (i) and premise (ii) implicitly endorse civil peace as a desirable end. The first, in presenting upheaval and disorder as an undesirable outcome, and the second, in insisting on the state's material capacity to prevent this disorder, both implicitly affirm civil peace in this way. At a practical level, therefore, what divides Locke's *Two Tracts* and his *Essay* is not the end of civil peace itself, but rather whether toleration of religious differences, or outward conformity to the magistrate's command, is the better policy for the state to adopt, in a context of religious diversity, in order to achieve this end. As with all such practical questions, the answer is affected by empirical circumstances. Which of these policies better achieves civil peace will depend on Locke's assessment of the material conditions present within the England of his time and how these impinge on his two premises above.

Normative Dimension

Yet the transformation in Locke's position that occurs between the *Two Tracts* and the *Essay* is due not only to a shift in the practical elements of Locke's discourse or a reassessment of the empirical conditions underwriting these. It is also due to a shift in its normative elements. As we saw in Chapter 1, normative arguments are distinct from practical arguments because, at least in the context we are discussing, they advance a *necessary* relation between means and ends rather than a contingent one, and therefore a relation which is not vulnerable to alterations in empirical circumstance. In this respect, we saw in Chapter 1 that toleration is presented, in this normative context, as a *necessary* means to the achievement of the end of individual religious liberty, because such liberty would not be possible without toleration.[4] After all, individual liberty, in matters of religion, is inconsistent with the magistrate's use of force in religious affairs, and, as Locke explains in Chapter 1, "[t]oleration is but the removing that force".[5] In regard to toleration and individual liberty, therefore, one becomes the necessary means to the other, and, unlike the practical argument for toleration, this necessity is not affected by shifts in empirical circumstance.

Consequently, Locke's normative argument for toleration is not affected by the two empirical premises listed above because an alteration in either does not affect the necessary relationship between toleration and individual liberty that this normative argument supposes. In this respect, it is only when Locke is advancing his *practical* arguments for toleration that he has to refute the two empirical premises (premise (i) and (ii)) above, these being the premises that underwrote his contrary position in the *Two Tracts*.

Competing Imperatives

But the fact that Locke's normative argument for toleration may safely ignore the two empirical premises above means that there may be a tension between the normative and practical elements of his discourse when it comes to his overall justification of toleration. The significance of the two empirical premises is related to the practical imperative of civil peace and the effective state governance that makes this peace possible. Each premise acquires its meaning and significance on the assumption that civil peace is an imperative that ought to be achieved. The first premise identifies the absence of such peace as something to be avoided, while the second premise affirms the state's capacity for the effective governance that makes such peace possible. We saw that the imperative of civil peace was consistent both with government purposes and the purposes of those individuals in civil society who seek stability and security. But it is government that enforces either the toleration or conformity which is a means to this peace. Consequently, any practical argument for toleration is only going to have validity if it assists government in achieving this peace. To this extent, such practical arguments for toleration are dependent on the effective maintenance of the magistrate's command. This is the case even though the toleration advanced, if effective, imposes limits on this command. After all, if toleration is justifiable, in the practical terms identified above, such limits will be the most effective means of maintaining that command, because they will be the most effective means of ensuring civil peace and effective state governance.

On the other hand, a normative argument for toleration, based on the imperative of individual liberty, can potentially challenge the magistrate's command, because this imperative possesses a rationale which is quite independent of the magistrate and the effective maintenance of his or her authority. Within Locke's framework, we have seen that the imperative of individual liberty ultimately arises from our equal status as God's creatures, and the natural rights to liberty associated with this status – all of which, at a conceptual level, precede government.[6] There is therefore no necessary fit between this normative imperative, arising from such sources, and the maintenance of the magistrate's command, centred on the practical imperative of effective state governance and civil peace. In fact, we saw that, in the case of Locke's right of resistance, upheld in the *Two Treatises of Government* and the *Letter Concerning Toleration*, these competing imperatives can be at odds – the normative imperative of liberty challenging, in this instance, the magistrate's command in ways detrimental to civil peace.[7] Locke suggests this potential for conflict as early as *An Essay Concerning Toleration*, where, as quoted in Chapter 2, he refers to "speculations and religious worship" which are "perfect" and "uncontrollable", and can be exercised "without, or *contrary* to the magistrate's command" (though such "contrariness" does not extend, at this early stage, to a right of resistance).[8]

Consequently, whereas Locke's practical arguments for toleration are consistent with, or even subordinate to, the purposes of the magistrate, this is not the case with his normative argument for toleration. The very different imperative upon which this normative argument is based may mean that it can, at times, challenge the magistrate's command, in ways not consistent with effective state governance and civil peace. The result is a tension between Locke's normative and practical arguments for toleration, arising from these competing imperatives. In practice, we shall see that Locke tries to balance these competing imperatives throughout his discussion of toleration, either by seeking to impose limits on governance, for the sake of individual liberty, or limits on liberty, for the sake of effective governance. The latter is achieved, for instance, when Locke proscribes certain religious beliefs and practices when these threaten civil peace.[9] Or else Locke seeks to reconcile individual liberty with effective state governance by the processes of contract and consent discussed in previous chapters.[10] But the tensions nevertheless remain. This is inevitable once Locke extends the scope of individual liberty beyond the realm of inner conscience, upheld in the *Two Tracts*, to the outward realm of "religious worship", affirmed in the *Essay*, because as we saw in Chapter 2, this then confronts the magistrate's command with demands for limits upon it, limits whose purported justification reside in the normative imperative of individual liberty.[11]

The result, once again, is a categorical distinction between Locke's normative and practical justifications of toleration. Both may lead to the same policy of toleration, and therefore endorse the same state commitments to that policy, but each is based on fundamentally different imperatives and purposes, and each therefore seeks to affirm toleration for the sake of very different ends. Further, the fact that neither of the imperatives underwriting these arguments for toleration can be advanced without placing potential limits on the other means that conflict between them is possible, so that the respective boundaries of each must be continually negotiated within Locke's political philosophy.

We will now consider the normative reassessment in which Locke engaged within his discourse in order to shift his position on toleration from one of opposition, as advanced in the *Two Tracts*, to the positive endorsement of the *Essay*. It is this discursive shift which, along with the wider processes of influence discussed in the previous chapter, helps make Locke's transition to toleration possible.

Locke's Normative Reassessment

With his reference to "a perfect, uncontrollable liberty" in "speculations and religious worship", exercised "without, or contrary to the magistrate's command", we see Locke, in *An Essay Concerning Toleration*, advancing a fundamental entitlement, on the part of each individual, to liberty, and an *equal* entitlement to that liberty, which extends to outward behaviour and is quite independent of the magistrate's command. This is evident in the fact that individuals, in exercising such liberty, are entitled to act "without or contrary" to this command. This, as we saw, moves Locke well beyond his position in the *Two Tracts*, where liberty was confined to inward conscience. Locke's advancement of this broader entitlement to liberty introduces into his political philosophy a third premise, quite distinct from the first two above, which we can articulate as follows:

(iii) There is a fundamental entitlement, on the part of individuals, to liberty, where this liberty (and each person's *equal* entitlement to this liberty) includes not only an inward liberty of conscience, but also an outward liberty of religious expression, in the form of "speculations and religious worship", with all the limits this presupposes on the authority and jurisdiction of the magistrate's command.

It is this premise, which we shall refer to as premise (iii), and the imperative of individual liberty which it represents, which gives Locke's normative argument for toleration in the *Essay* its moral weight. We saw in the previous chapter that there were elements of this premise in the *Two Tracts*, where Locke defended the sanctity of each individual's inward liberty of conscience, and the judgments arising from it.[12] But the crucial difference to the *Essay* is that Locke, in the *Two Tracts*, considers this inward liberty to be entirely consistent with an outward obedience to the magistrate's command, even in those instances where the magistrate acts "unjustly" (i.e. beyond the scope of his or her authority).[13] Locke's reference in the *Essay* to an entitlement of individuals to act "without, or contrary to the magistrate's command" suggests a significant departure from this earlier position, although we saw that Locke does not, in the *Essay*, go on to articulate the full right of resistance to the magistrate's command that he advances in the *Two Treatises* or the *Letter*, instead advancing the right of conscientious objection referred to in Chapter 1.[14] Nevertheless, it is the imperative of individual liberty which underwrites both conscientious objection and resistance, in each case entitling an individual to act in ways at odds with the magistrate – something that Locke could never have countenanced in the *Two Tracts*. It is this imperative which is represented by premise (iii).

Given the very different origins, and purpose, of premise (iii), and the imperative it represents, compared to the first two premises articulated above, Locke's normative argument for toleration is likely to retain its moral weight even when its advancement is considered contrary to the practical imperative of effective state governance and civil peace. It is for this reason, once again, that Locke's normative and practical imperatives, although both equally necessary to his case for toleration, are also potentially at odds.

From the *Two Tracts* to *An Essay Concerning Toleration*

If we interpret Locke's *Essay* in terms of its departure from the *Two Tracts*, then it is possible to explain this departure in terms of the three premises above. It is Locke's re-evaluation and refutation of the (empirical) premises (i) and (ii), and his advancement of the (normative) premise (iii), which defines this departure, and allows Locke to arrive, in the *Essay*, at a position concerning toleration entirely at odds to the one that he upheld in the *Two Tracts*.[15]

The following will consider each of these premises in turn. We shall consider premise (ii) first. This premise affirms the material capacity of the magistrate to effectively impose outward religious conformity upon individuals for the sake of civil peace. The magistrate's capacity in this regard means that a policy of outward religious conformity will not give rise to more resistance, and therefore more civil disorder, than such a policy is intended to avoid, and so is an effective means of ensuring civil peace. Toleration, on the other hand, was presented in the *Two Tracts* as producing more disorder than it was intended to avoid, and so, relative to outward conformity, was *not* an effective means of ensuring civil peace.[16] In this way, therefore, premise (ii) helped underwrite Locke's practical argument *against* toleration, and in *favour* of conformity, as presented in the *Two Tracts*. We shall see below how Locke's refutation of this premise constitutes an important part of his practical argument *in favour* of toleration in the *Essay*.

Premise (i) was the other empirical premise crucial to Locke's practical argument against toleration in the *Two Tracts*. This is the premise which claims that "religious differences, openly expressed, will, as a matter of fact, produce the sort of disagreement which will ultimately degenerate into conflict, upheaval and disorder within civil society". So long as Locke assumes such outcomes are likely, toleration, which allows for the open expression of such differences, will *not* be an effective means of ensuring civil peace. Just as with premise (ii), therefore, premise (i) is fundamental to Locke's case *against* toleration in the *Two Tracts*. Indeed, it is an even more fundamental premise in this respect than premise (ii). This is because premise (ii) only has worth if there is a *need* to impose state conformity in matters of religion. It does not justify that conformity, or produce that need itself, only referring to the magistrate's capacity to meet this need if necessary. It is premise (i) which, in referring to upheaval and disorder arising when religious differences are openly expressed, produces that need, and so justifies a policy of religious conformity. Only in the context of premise (i), therefore, is the state's material capacity to effectively impose outward conformity in matters of religion (premise (ii)) likely to be of significance.

Consequently, Locke must refute premise (i) far more than premise (ii) if he is to establish a practical (as distinct from normative) justification for toleration. After all, if premise (ii) were refuted, and premise (i) remained intact, this would not establish the case for toleration, since toleration would still allow for the open expression of religious differences, with all the "conflict, upheaval and disorder" that premise (i) describes. The threat to civil peace would therefore remain. Consequently, it is premise (i) which is the primary premise which Locke must refute if a practical case for toleration is to be established. If Locke cannot do this, then all he has is a normative justification of toleration, centred on premise (iii). And, because premise (i) remains intact, this normative justification of toleration would be directly at odds with Locke's practical imperative of civil peace and effective state governance. Consequently, in order to establish his case for toleration, Locke must establish this case on both normative *and* practical grounds, involving not simply the advancement of premise (iii), but the empirical re-evaluation, and ultimate refutation, of premise (i) and (to a lesser extent) premise (ii). We shall now consider Locke's engagement with premise (ii), premise (i) and premise (iii) – each in that order.

Premise (ii)

Two Tracts

We saw that Locke, in the *Two Tracts*, perceived the outward expression of religious differences, however seemingly innocuous, as liable to degenerate into "conflict, upheaval and disorder". As mentioned earlier, his reference to Juvenal's satire, with its conflict over "leeks" and "onions", and his insistence that religious conflict in England was equally capable of arising over such "trifles", was meant to convey this point.[17] So was his insistence, at the end of the *Two Tracts*, that "in the nature of things there is nothing so utterly perfect and harmless that from it no evil can, or is accustomed to, derive, or at least be feared".[18] Toleration, he insisted, merely provides the space and the opportunity for such upheaval and disorder to arise, since it allows for the open expression of religious differences, from which, he believed, disorder would almost inevitably follow.[19] All of these assumptions are embodied in premise (i).

Given such assumptions, a state policy of outward religious conformity, eradicating, where necessary, the visible expression of individual religious differences by demanding outward obedience to the magistrate's command, appears a far more prudent policy for the state to adopt than toleration, because it removes the source of disorder and so provides a means by which civil peace might be achieved. Locke tells us in the *Two Tracts* that such outward conformity is his preferred policy, being "all that is here required".[20]

Throughout the *Two Tracts*, Locke assumes that the magistrate has the material capacity to impose this conformity in ways that will not give rise to more disorder than such a policy is intended to avoid (premise (ii)). However Locke did acknowledge that prudence in the exercise of the magistrate's command was an important element in this capacity. As Locke put it:

> The magistrate's concernments will always teach him to use no more rigour than the temper of the people and the necessity of the age shall call for, knowing that too great checks as well as too loose a rein may make this untamed beast to cast his rider.[21]

Indeed, Locke declares that "outward violence" is "never to be applied but when there is hopes it may bend the dissenter to a submission and compliance".[22] In this respect, the exercise of prudence by the magistrate, in the application of force is, according to Locke, an important means of ensuring the success of such force in achieving its ends, thereby ensuring that premise (ii) is affirmed.

Locke refers in the *Two Tracts* to one other element of prudence. This concerns the need for the magistrate to ensure that he or she does not seek to apply force in those circumstances in which it can have no effect at all and which, in rendering it futile, lays it open to disrepute.[23] Locke points out in the *Two Tracts*, just as he does in the *Essay* and *Letter Concerning Toleration*, that force can have no impact on the inner belief of the individual, because belief is a product, not of the will, but of "understanding and assent", which is "not to be wrought upon by force".[24] To apply force in such circumstances renders force futile, because "rigour.... cannot work an internal persuasion".[25] Rather, it can only have an impact on the external actions of the individual, since these are subject to the will.[26] The result is that force is capable, in such circumstances, of only producing an "outward conformity" to the magistrate's command, rather than an inward assent – an outcome which, Locke tells us at note 20 above, is "all that is here required" (and therefore all that premise (ii) assumes).

So whereas Locke's first account of prudence in the *Two Tracts* above concerns the application of force, and the degree to which it should be applied if it is to achieve its ends, his second account concerns the objects to which force should be directed, and the need to avoid directing it to those objects upon which it can have no effect. He insists that, to lack prudence of the second type, so as to impose the magistrate's force "upon impossibilities where they are sure to be ineffectual", is to "discredit and abuse punishments, the great instruments of government and remedies of disorders", and "make enemies rather than proselytes".[27] Premise (ii), therefore, is only capable of being affirmed if magistrates exercise prudence of both types in their application of force in matters of religion.

Re-Evaluation

If premise (i) and (ii) hold true, then the state's imposition of outward religious conformity upon individuals inwardly divided by religion will indeed be both a necessary and an effective means to ensure civil peace and effective state governance. However, what explains the shift between the *Two Tracts* and the *Essay*, at the level of Locke's practical (as distinct from normative) discourse, is that, by the time of the *Essay*, Locke no longer believed that, with the exception of specific groups such as "papists" and atheists, *either* of these premises *did* hold true.

In other words, Locke's shift from the *Two Tracts* to the *Essay*, and the transformation of his position on toleration that this involved, entailed nothing less than a fundamental re-evaluation and refutation of premises

(i) and (ii), and therefore of the empirical assumptions that underwrote these. We shall now consider this re-evaluation of premise (i) and (ii) in relation to "papists" and "fanatics". We shall engage further in consideration of Locke's re-evaluation of premise (i) further below.

"Papists"

Locke identifies in *An Essay Concerning Toleration* two religious groups in English society which reside outside the established bounds of the Church of England – those he calls "papists" and those he calls "fanatics". Each was therefore a candidate for the state's imposition of either toleration or enforced outward conformity. Locke refers to these two options, and these two religious groups, as follows:

> To consider, therefore, the state of England at present, there is but this one question in the whole matter, and that is whether toleration or imposition be the readiest way to secure the safety and peace, and promote the welfare, of this kingdom.... What influence toleration hath ... cannot be well seen without considering the different parties now among us, which may well be comprehended under these two: papists and fanatics.[28]

"Papists" are, of course, Catholics who, from the time of Henry VIII and his break from the Church of Rome, had been excluded from the state religion in England. Locke, in the *Essay*, denies toleration to Catholics on a number of grounds. The first of these is that they owe their primary allegiance to a foreign power (the Pope in Rome) who, Locke says, "hath the keys of their consciences tied to his girdle and can upon occasion dispense with all their oaths, promises, and the obligations they have to their prince", whom they perceive a "heretic", "and arm them to the disturbance of the government".[29] In this respect, Locke perceives Catholics as a risk to state security, and therefore to effective state governance, because they "mix with their religious worship and speculative opinions other doctrines absolutely destructive to the society wherein they live".[30]

The second reason Locke denies toleration to Catholics is because, he insists, Catholics, when they have the power, deny this toleration to others.[31] This is an early example of what I will call in later chapters Locke's "criterion of reciprocity", in which Locke insists that rights or entitlements accorded to one party within civil society ought to be accorded to others.[32] Richard Vernon has referred to how Locke applies such "reciprocity" in his later debate with Jonas Proast.[33] We shall see that this "criterion of reciprocity" is fundamental to Locke's case against Proast, and Proast's attempt to justify a state policy of conformity upon those outside the Church of England.

In this respect, the presence of Catholics in the English polity, and the threat Locke believes they constitute to that polity, confirms, in their case, premise (i). The question then arises (under the terms of premise (ii)), whether, in denying toleration to Catholics, and instead "imposing" on their religion, the magistrate is capable of effectively enforcing this policy without producing more disorder than the policy is intended to avoid.[34]

Locke gives no indication in the *Essay* that he believes the magistrate lacks the material capacity to successfully impose such policies on Catholics. Indeed, quite the contrary. Locke provides a number of reasons why he believes such imposition, in regard to Catholics, is likely to be successful, diminishing the number of Catholics overall and so reducing their threat to the state. These reasons include Locke's claim that, unlike "fanatics" (Protestant non-conformists), penalties imposed on Catholics are not likely to make them unite with others, at greater threat to the state; or encourage others, through sympathy for their sufferings, to unite with them; but rather is likely to unite all Protestants within the realm against a "common enemy".[35] In offering these reasons in the *Essay*, Locke is directly addressing what we have called premise (ii) – providing explanations of why, in the case of Catholics, persecution is likely to be successful in ensuring civil peace by not giving rise to more conflict, upheaval and disorder than such a policy is intended to avoid.

"Fanatics"

The situation is very different regarding the other religious group to whom Locke refers in the *Essay* as residing outside the Church of England – these being Protestant non-conformists or "Dissenters", all of whom, Locke tells us, "come under the opprobrious name of fanatics".[36] Indeed, Locke cautions against such a label, since, although "factious" and divided, nevertheless "by giving one common name to different parties" it is possible to "teach those to unite" whom the state is concerned "to divide and keep at a distance one among another".[37]

Dissenters are Protestants who, from the time of the restoration of the Church of England as the established church in 1662, were unable, for reasons of conscience or some other concern, to conform to the Church of England.[38] They emerged from a far broader group in the pre-Civil War era known as "Puritans". John Spurr has explained the relationship between Puritanism and Dissent as follows:

> Seventeenth-century puritans were not one group, but many. The varieties of Elizabethan and Jacobean puritanism were succeeded by a host of rival denominations and sects unleashed by the apparent religious anarchy of the civil wars. After the restoration of the monarchy in 1660 and the Church of England in 1662, the various denominations now classified as nonconformists or dissenters seemed to have little in common and often followed their own paths.[39]

It is to this division and disunity among Dissenters that Locke refers when he describes the "fanatics" as "crumbled into different parties amongst themselves" and "shattered into different factions", their "principles and worship and tempers" being "so utterly inconsistent".[40] Indeed, from a practical perspective (i.e. one oriented to effective state governance and civil peace), this is one reason why Locke is willing, in the *Essay*, to accord toleration to "fanatics" in a way that he is not to Catholics. Such "divisions", Locke believes, made it less likely that "fanatics", if tolerated, would produce the sort of upheaval and disorder referred to by premise (i). Indeed, he argues that, in such circumstances, it is in the state's interest to tolerate "fanatics", since their divisions in relation to each other are likely to bind them more strongly to the state, should the state concede toleration to them, and so vitiate any threat they might pose to it. Addressing himself directly to the magistrate, Locke makes this point as follows:

> For the fanatics taken all together being numerous, and possibly more than the hearty friends to the state religion, are yet crumbled into different parties amongst themselves, and are at as much distance one from another as from you, if you drive them not further off by the ill-treatment they receive from you, for their bare opinions are as inconsistent one with another as with the Church of England. People, therefore, that are so shattered into different factions are best secured by toleration, since being in as good a condition under you as they can hope for under any, 'tis not like[ly] they should join to set up any other, whom they cannot be certain will use them so well. But if you persecute them you make them all of one party and interest against you, tempt them to shake off your yoke and venture for a new government, wherein everyone has hopes to get the dominion themselves or better usage under others.[41]

In this statement, we see that Locke is insisting that "fanatics", if tolerated, will *not* produce the upheaval associated with premise (i). This is a significant re-evaluation of the position he upheld in the *Two Tracts*, wherein he had argued that the open expression of *any* religious difference was liable to produce disorder, with the result that toleration, in allowing for such expression, was the "first inlet to all those confusions and unheard of and destructive opinions that overspread this nation".[42] As we shall see in the further discussion of premise (i) below, Locke, in relation to "fanatics", is able to arrive at the contrary conclusion because he no longer believes that the religious differences of "fanatics", openly expressed, will, as a matter of fact, necessarily produce such disorder at all. In other words, Locke's toleration of "fanatics" in the *Essay* is upheld by a fundamental re-evaluation of premise (i) and the empirical assumptions upon which it relies.

Another reason why Locke thinks the state should tolerate "fanatics" is that, unlike the situation with Catholics, he believes it is less likely that the state, through the use of force, will have the ability either to reduce the number of "fanatics" or to successfully impose conformity upon them. In other words, in relation to this group, Locke believes the state may lack the material capacities that we have associated with premise (ii), with the result that any attempt to impose religious conformity upon "fanatics" will result in more disorder than such a policy is intended to avoid. So for instance, because "force and harsh usage will not only increase the animosity but number of enemies". Locke refers to the "hazard" involved in any "attempt" by the magistrate to forcibly compel Dissenters in England to conformity with the magistrate's religion, because " 'twas never known that men lay down quietly under the oppression, and submitted their backs to the blows of others when they thought they had strength enough to defend themselves."[43] In this way, by invoking the possibility of resistance (perhaps successful resistance) on the part of "fanatics", premise (ii) is, in these circumstances, refuted.

We see, therefore, that Locke arrives in the Essay at a position entirely at odds with the Two Tracts, perceiving the forcible imposition of religious conformity upon at least some religious groups in England ("fanatics") as a threat to civil peace, and toleration its favourable alternative. Such a conclusion could only be arrived at by a thorough re-evaluation and refutation of premise (i) and (ii).

Realpolitik Revisited

By invoking the possibility of resistance, in the discussion above, Locke's advocacy of toleration for "fanatics" is based on a recognition of the exigencies of realpolitik, discussed at the end of Chapter 1. This recognition is even more apparent in the following passage from the *Essay* in which Locke invokes the respective balance of forces between the magistrate and religious dissidents as a relevant consideration for the magistrate in any decision concerning toleration or conformity in relation to the latter. Thus, again addressing himself directly to the magistrate, Locke states:

> But if you think the different parties are already grown to a consistency and formed into one body and interest against you, whether it were the hardships they suffered under you made them unite or no, when they are so many as to equal or exceed you in number, as perhaps they do in England, force will be but an ill and hazardous way to bring them to submission.[44]

Indeed, Locke insists that even if the magistrate is apparently successful in imposing religious conformity upon "fanatics", thereby fulfilling the material conditions of premise (ii), this leads to no greater security, since such success only drives resistance underground, where it is less visible – and so more dangerous to the state – resulting in what Locke calls "a false, secret, but exasperated enemy, rather than a fair, open adversary".[45] Once again, on the basis of this analysis, Locke distinguishes "fanatics" from "Catholics", concluding that, unlike the latter, a policy of enforced conformity imposed upon "fanatics" is likely to produce more disorder than it is intended to avoid, with the result that, once more, premise (ii) cannot be sustained.

Further, because "no consideration could be sufficient to force a man from or to that which he was fully persuaded was the way to infinite happiness or infinite misery",[46] Locke insists that a policy of enforced conformity demands of "fanatics" precisely that which they are not able to concede – a resignation of the outward profession of those beliefs upon which they believe their eternal salvation to depend. Given such an obstacle, and the resistance to which it is likely to give rise, Locke insists that the only hope for the magistrate in seeking to deal with "fanatics" by force, is likely to be the "extirpation" of "fanatics" altogether, with all the upheaval and disorder that would follow. As Locke puts it:

> What efficacy force and severity hath to alter the opinions of mankind ... history be full of examples, and there is scarce an instance to be found of any opinion driven out of the world by persecution, but where the violence of it at once swept away all the professors too.... If, therefore, violence be to settle uniformity, 'tis in vain to mince the matter: that severity which must produce it cannot stop short of the total destruction and extirpation of all dissenters at once.[47]

The idea that religious conformity could only be successfully imposed if those dissidents to whom it is applied were destroyed shows the extent to which Locke now believes that such a policy of conformity produces more disorder than it is intended to avoid, thereby again overturning premise (ii). Toleration once again becomes a viable alternative.

What the above discussion shows is that Locke's re-evaluation of the empirical assumptions underlying premise (i) and (ii) has allowed him to refute both premises, at least in relation to "fanatics", and so move beyond the position of the *Two Tracts*. The outward imposition of religious conformity, which was presented in the *Two Tracts* as the means to civil peace, is now depicted (at least in relation to this religious group) as yielding the contrary outcome. Such a revision would not have been plausible without the refutation of premises (i) and (ii) in which Locke engages in the *Essay*. Toleration, by contrast, is presented throughout the *Essay* as the best means to "secure" people who are "shattered into different factions", thereby avoiding disorder and ensuring civil peace.[48]

In this way, by re-evaluating and refuting premise (i) and (ii), Locke advanced, in the *Essay*, a *practical* argument for toleration of "fanatics". We shall see further below in our discussion of premise (iii) that, unlike Catholics, Locke also advances a *normative* argument for tolerating this religious group. In this respect, we see the extent to which Locke has moved beyond the parameters and assumptions of the *Two Tracts*.

Premise (i)

Premise (i) concerned Locke's belief that religious differences, if allowed to become visible within civil society by being openly expressed, would lead to disagreement between rival religious adherents and ultimately degenerate into conflict, upheaval and disorder, thereby undermining civil peace. In the *Two Tracts*, Locke made clear that, in arriving at this conclusion, he felt he had history on his side. As we saw, he believed that one of the causes of the English Civil Wars and their aftermath was the "liberty" granted to "tender consciences".[49] He declared that, irrespective of Charles II's Restoration, "[t]he same hearts are still in men as liable to zealous mistakes and religious furies" and "there wants but leave for crafty men to inspirit and fire them with such doctrines".[50] Locke did acknowledge, in the *Two Tracts*, that toleration was a desirable ideal and one that might be possible if "religion were banished the camp and forbid to take arms, at least to use no other sword, but that of the word and spirit".[51] He just believed that, given the circumstances that existed within England in his time, such outcomes were unlikely, given the propensity of religion to become an object of contestation, with the result that "a general freedom" in matters of religion will be but a "general bondage", because "the popular asserters of public liberty are the greatest engrossers of it too".[52]

Such propositions in the *Two Tracts* support the empirical veracity of premise (i). Toleration, in such a context, is presented as a sure path to upheaval and disorder. In order to establish a practical argument for toleration in the *Essay*, Locke needed to refute the empirical assumptions underwriting premise (i), by demonstrating that religious differences, openly expressed, will have no such effects and that toleration, which allows for such expression, will produce no such consequences.

Locke does not assume, in the *Essay*, that all forms of religion and religious observance are benign. Just as in the *Letter Concerning Toleration*, over twenty years later, Locke is aware that "experience vouches the practice" that "men are not all saints that pretend conscience".[53] In this respect, toleration, as espoused by Locke throughout his intellectual career, always had limits, outside of which certain religious beliefs and practices, being of sufficient threat to civil peace or effective state governance, were proscribed (such as atheists).[54] But if Locke was to move beyond the anti-toleration position of the *Two Tracts*, he needed to argue that, *within* these limits, the open expression of religious differences, made possible by toleration, would not produce upheaval and disorder. He therefore needed to refute premise (i).

It is in the second half of the *Essay* that Locke advances the evidence with which to do so. This involves, firstly, a straightforward empirical claim that the visible expression of religious differences will *not* produce the conflict, upheaval or disorder that he had supposed in the *Two Tracts* and to which premise (i) refers. To this end, and in direct contradiction to his "leeks" and "onions" passage in the *Two Tracts*, Locke states:

> For the praying to God in this or that posture does no more make men factious or at enmity one with another, nor ought otherwise to be

treated, than the wearing of hats or turbans, which yet either of them may do.[55]

Yet although Locke attempts in this manner to distance himself from the empirical assumptions of premise (i), insisting that the open expression of at least some religious differences is consistent with civil peace, he does admit that religion, just as easily as "hats" or "turbans", may become a mark of distinction among groups of individuals, allowing them to separate themselves from the rest of society, thereby providing the conditions for "factiousness" and "turbulency" and so justifying their proscription.[56] But, in making this admission, Locke concedes nothing to premise (i), insisting that such "factiousness" does not arise from anything intrinsic to religion. Rather, he declares, religion (like "hats" or "turbans") is simply an extrinsic mark, or "badge", made convenient use of by groups who would have otherwise still been at odds with each other or the state – "religion, i.e. this or that form of worship, being the cause of their union and correspondence, not of their factiousness and turbulency".[57]

On this basis, Locke, in the *Essay*, insists that dissenting sects are not a danger to the state or civil society, because "for the most part the matters of controversy and distinction between sects are no parts or very inconsiderable ones and appendices of true religion".[58] If Locke was still of the view, as he was in the "leeks" and "onions" passage in the *Two Tracts*, that differences in religion, however innocuous, are "distinctions able to keep us always at a distance, and eagerly ready for like violence and cruelty", he could not have made this claim. Indeed Locke suggests in the *Essay* that, far from anything intrinsic to religion rendering it a source of upheaval and disorder, it is the state's persecution of religion that does so:

> [I]f the example of old Rome (where so many different opinions, gods, and ways of worship were promiscuously tolerated) be of any weight, we have reason to imagine that no religion can become suspected to the state of ill-intention to it till the government first by a partial usage of them different from the rest of the subjects declare its ill-intentions to its professors, and so make a state business of it.[59]

In this way, Locke, in the *Essay*, seeks to reconcile the empirical fact that, at times, religion has been a mark of "factiousness" and "turbulency" within England, with his equal insistence that, contrary to premise (i), there is nothing intrinsic to religion, or the open expression of religious differences, which produces such upheaval and disorder. We see, therefore, the distance which Locke has travelled, from the empirical assumptions of the *Two Tracts*, wherein he had insisted that the source of such upheaval and disorder resided with religion itself, with the result that the open expression of its differences was "only a *liberty* for *contention, censure* and *persecution*" which would "turn us loose to the *tyranny* of a *religious rage*".[60]

Of course, Locke cannot *guarantee* that religious differences will *never* produce such upheaval or disorder, and this because "men are not all saints that pretend conscience".[61] As such, Locke cannot guarantee that a state policy of toleration, allowing for the open expression of such differences, will always be conducive to effective state governance and civil peace. The most Locke can do, once he has recommended the proscription of those religions he believes at odds with civil peace and so imposed the limits on toleration referred to above, is to insist that a policy of toleration is *less* likely to produce such adverse outcomes than the policy of outward conformity that he advocated in the *Two Tracts*, because *less* likely to produce resistance and upheaval.[62] All this Locke seeks to achieve with his re-evaluation of premise (i) and premise (ii).

Premise (iii)

We saw that the normative argument for toleration that Locke introduces in the *Essay* is directed towards a very different objective than his practical arguments, oriented, as the latter are, to civil peace and effective state governance. The normative argument has as its objective an end which is essentially prescriptive in nature – the advancement of individual liberty. Based as it is on premise (iii), the normative argument for toleration is not dependent on the empirical conditions relating either to the propensity of religious differences to produce conflict and disorder (premise (i)) or the material capacity of the state to prevent this (premise (ii)). Consequently, unlike his practical arguments for toleration, Locke, in order to advance his normative argument, has no need to overturn either premise (i) or (ii) by refuting the empirical assumptions underwriting these.[63]

It is with Locke's references to individual liberty within the *Essay* that the shift towards premise (iii), and its independence from premise (ii), is most evident. Premise (ii), with its emphasis on effective state governance as a means of avoiding civil disorder, assumes the primacy of the magistrate's command. Locke's references to individual liberty in the *Essay*, by contrast, seek to impose limits on this command. This is evident in Locke's primary reference to liberty in the *Essay*, quoted at note 8 above, which, far from being subordinate to the magistrate's command, is a liberty, Locke tells us, that can be exercised "without or contrary" to it.

Similarly, Locke imposes in the *Essay* a categorical distinction between individual liberty and the magistrate's command when he refers to "liberty of conscience" as "being the great privilege of the subject", which he then contrasts to the "right of imposing", which, he tells us, is the "great prerogative of the magistrate".[64] He makes the same distinction again when (in proto-Kantian fashion) he identifies individual liberty as a condition of human dignity, distinguishing it from the process of "imposing", referred to above, by declaring that "so chary is human nature to preserve the liberty of that part wherein lies the dignity of a man, which could it be imposed on would make him but little different from a beast".[65]

In this way, we see how Locke's advancement of a normative discourse in the *Essay* is categorically distinct from the practical discourse present elsewhere in that text and pervasively present in the *Two Tracts*. Locke's practical discourse is centred on the concern to maintain civil peace, and the effective state governance necessary to achieve this. His *Two Tracts* and *Essay* differ only as to whether toleration or outward conformity is the best means to achieve these ends. In each case, we saw, such ends are consistent with state interests.

Individual liberty, on the other hand, falls outside these practical concerns, and is presented by Locke, in the *Essay*, as quite independent of them, both in terms of its origins and its aims. Indeed, we saw that once Locke extends his ideal of individual liberty in the *Essay* beyond the realm of inner conscience to the outward realm of "speculations" and "religious worship" (premise (iii)), such liberty is capable of coming into conflict with these practical concerns centred on civil peace and effective state governance. We saw that Locke, throughout his career, adopted various mechanisms to avoid this conflict, but once he advances in the *Two Treatises* a much more explicit imperative of individual liberty, represented by an individual's "Lives, Liberties and Estates", which has as its ultimate defence an individual right of resistance to government, exercisable at an individual's discretion, such conflict becomes manifest.[66] In all these ways, therefore, we see how Locke's normative discourse is categorically distinct from his practical discourse throughout his political philosophy.

What is important to recognize, therefore, is that "civil peace" becomes a much wider and more complex goal to achieve once Locke, in advancing premise (iii), introduces into his political philosophy a normative ideal of liberty extending beyond the realm of inner conscience, whose free expression requires limits on the magistrate's command. Once this occurs, "civil peace", in order to be achieved, must reconcile the imperative of individual liberty *and* the imperative of effective state governance, since the existence of one now requires limits on the other. This is in contrast to the *Two Tracts* where no such reconciliation was necessary, liberty being consistent with a complete outward conformity to the magistrate's command.

We have seen that the one important denominational exception that Locke makes regarding his normative argument for toleration is Catholics, Locke denying them, in the *Essay*, the entitlements to liberty associated with premise (iii).[67] Jeremy Waldron insists that this is no longer the case by the time Locke composes the *Letter Concerning Toleration*, almost twenty years later. Waldron cites evidence in that text which, he insists, shows that Locke, by that time, was willing to tolerate Catholics within the English polity.[68]

Where Locke does not shift between the *Essay* and the *Letter* is in his refusal to tolerate atheists. As with Catholics and those engaged in animal sacrifice (discussed in Chapter 1), Locke refuses toleration to atheists solely as a result of the civil consequences of their beliefs, in terms of their impact on the material interests of society. This is evident when Locke insists that atheists are "incapable of all society" because, belief in God being "the foundation of all morality", they cannot be trusted to act "morally", and therefore cannot be trusted to abide by their "promises, covenants and oaths".[69]

Locke's proscription of atheists solely for the external (civil) consequences of their beliefs and their material impact on society, not the intrinsic content of those beliefs themselves, arises from Locke's insistence, discussed in Chapter 1, that the magistrate's authority is exercised solely for "civil" purposes.[70] The absence of religious "truth" that the magistrate, as an individual, might perceive in Catholicism or atheism is irrelevant to this proscription because "the business of laws is not to provide for the truth of opinions, but for the safety and security of the commonwealth, and of every particular man's goods and person".[71] To proscribe atheists for intrinsic reasons – because, for instance, the magistrate perceives their absence of belief to be "unholy", "profane" – or an abomination in the eyes of God – would involve the magistrate exercising authority for religious reasons, which, we have seen, is at odds with the limitation of that authority to "civil purposes", referred to above, as well as being at odds with Locke's ideal of a separation of church and state.[72] Indeed we saw that Locke insists that the magistrate treat all matters of religion, insofar as they are an object of his or her authority, as a "thing indifferent", and therefore, once again, as subject to his or her command only insofar as they impact on the "civil" matters over which she or he exercises jurisdiction.[73]

We see, therefore, how the limits on the magistrate's command are an important basis for Locke's normative discourse of toleration, centred on individual liberty, since it is these limits which, in leaving all other matters to the voluntary choices and actions of individuals, make such liberty possible. But equally, we see that in relation to Catholics, atheists and others to whom Locke denies toleration, the limits on toleration are understood by Locke as ensuring the practical ends of effective state governance and civil peace, since without such limits liberty (at least from Locke's perspective) threatens to degenerate into "license".[74] Once again, therefore, Locke's normative and practical discourses, and their competing imperatives, are coupled throughout his political philosophy, each pursuing different, but equally necessary ends, centred on individual liberty and effective state governance, and each thereby acting as a potential limit (but also a potential source of conflict with) the other.

Notes

1 Locke 1993a: 187. See also Ch. 2 (notes 62 and 68).
2 See Ch. 2 ("Quantitative vs. Qualitative").
3 Locke 1967a: 158. See also Ch. 2 (note 32). On "leeks" and "onions", see Ch.2 (note 34).
4 See Ch. 1 ("Categorical Distinction").
5 See Ch. 1 (note 26).
6 See Introduction ("Theological Foundations").
7 See the discussion at the end of Introduction ("Civil Concerns").
8 On "without or contrary to the magistrate's command", see Ch. 2 (note 68). On this stopping short of a right of resistance, see Ch. 1 (note 96).

9 See Ch. 1 (notes 44 and 51) and Ch. 2 (note 41). See also the discussion of the proscription of atheists and Catholics in the sections "Papists" and "Premise (iii)" below.
10 On the role of contract and consent in seeking such reconciliation, see Ch. 1 ("Consent, Legitimacy and Obligation" and "Consent, Legitimacy and Toleration").
11 See Ch. 2 ("Locke's Shift").
12 See Ch. 2 (note 43).
13 See Ch. 2 (note 20).
14 See Ch. 1 (note 96). The fact that Locke does not extend his position in the *Essay* to a full right of resistance is evident in his claim that the magistrate "is not accountable to any tribunal here" (Locke 1993a: 193) – the implication being that the magistrate is accountable only to God.
15 Chapter 4 will add to this explanation by showing how, from the *Two Tracts* to the *Essay*, Locke shifted from a "vertical" to a "horizontal" conception of the relation between liberty and governance.
16 See Ch. 2 (notes 33, 34, 37, 39, 40).
17 See Ch. 2 (note 34).
18 Locke 1967b: 240.
19 See Ch. 2 (notes 31–7, 40, 59).
20 Locke 1967a: 128.
21 Ibid.: 158.
22 Ibid.: 127.
23 See ibid.: 127, 128, 129.
24 Ibid 127. See ibid 128–30, 165, 167; Locke 1967b: 214, 238–39. See also Locke 1993a: 188–89. As Locke puts it in the *Letter*: "For it is absurd that things should be enjoined by laws which are not in men's power to perform. And to believe this or that to be true, does not depend upon our will" (Locke 1993b: 420). We shall see that Locke ultimately shifts position on the inviolability of belief, in the face of force, in his debate with Jonas Proast, to the detriment of what we shall call Locke's "rationality argument" for toleration (see Ch. 5 note 33).
25 Locke 1967a: 128. See also Ch. 2 (note 43); Ch. 4 (note 50); Ch. 5 (notes 34 and 36).
26 See Locke 1967a: 127–30, 165, 167. So, in *An Essay Concerning Toleration*, Locke pointed out that as force "cannot alter men's minds" in matters of religion, but can only produce outward conformity at the level of the external actions of the individual, the resentment this arouses, whereby individuals are forced to "lie for their errors", professing religious "truths" in which they do not believe, makes those upon whom such force is applied "very much more" the "enemy" of those that apply it (Locke 1993a: 192-3. See also ibid.: 204–5, 207). The result, Locke says, is that force, in being unable to alter belief in such circumstances, "cannot produce any real effect to that purpose for which it is designed" (ibid.: 192).
27 Locke 1967a: 127, 128. Locke makes the same point in the *Essay* – see note 26 above.
28 Locke 1993a: 201-2.
29 Ibid.: 202-3. Locke makes a similar point in Locke 1993c: 138-9.
30 Locke 1993a: 197.
31 Ibid.: 202.
32 Of course, I have lifted the term "criterion of reciprocity" from John Rawls who places it at the centre of his idea of public reason. In defining my criterion as one where "rights or entitlements accorded to one party within civil society ought to be accorded to others", I am departing from Rawls's own definition, which concerns the rules of public dialogue when such dialogue is oriented to agreement:

> The criterion of reciprocity requires that, when...terms are proposed as the most reasonable terms of fair cooperation, those proposing them must also think it at least reasonable for others to accept them, as free and equal citizens, and not as dominated or manipulated, or under the pressure of an inferior political or social position.
>
> (Rawls 2005: 446)

33 Vernon 2013: 217–18.
34 When describing the policies to be applied to Catholics, Locke refers to "suppression", "restraint", and "punishment" (Locke 1993a: 202–4).
35 Ibid.: 202–3, 203–4.
36 Ibid.: 204.
37 Ibid.
38 See Miller 1983: 45–6. Coffey 2000: 36.
39 Spurr 1998: 3.
40 Locke 1993a: 203, 207.
41 Locke 1993a: 207. See also Locke 1993b: 429. Locke makes the same point, earlier in the *Essay*, declaring: "[T]he minds of men are so various in matters of religion, and so nice and scrupulous in in things of an eternal concernment, that where men are indifferently tolerated and persecution and force does not drive them together, they are apt to divide and subdivide into so many little bodies, and always with the greatest enmity to those they last parted from or stand nearest to, that they are a guard one upon another, and the public can have no apprehensions of them as long as they have their equal share of common justice and protection" (Locke 1993a: 197–198).
42 See Ch. 2 (notes 59). See also note 18 above.
43 See Locke 1993a: 205, 207.
44 Locke 1993a: 207. Locke makes the same point elsewhere in the *Essay*, declaring: "But if the magistrate chance to find the dissenters so numerous as to be in a condition to cope with him, I see not what he can gain by force and severity when he thereby gives them the fairer pretence to embody and arm, and make them all unite the firmer against him" (Locke 1993a: 200). See also Locke 1993b: 432.
45 Locke 1993a: 206.
46 Ibid.: 189.
47 Locke 1993a: 204, 208. Locke does not apply the same reasoning, centered on "extirpation", to Catholics. Perhaps this is because he believes that "popery", being sustained by "artifice" and "force", "is the most likely of any religion to decay where the secular power handles [it] severely" (ibid. 203).
48 See note 41 above.
49 See Ch. 2 (note 59).
50 Locke 1967a: 160.
51 Ibid.: 161. See also Ch. 1 (note 36) and Ch. 2 (note 38).
52 Ch. 2 (note 40). See also Ch. 2 (notes 34, 37, and 59).
53 Locke 1993a: 198. Concerning a similar recognition in the *Letter*, see Locke 1993b; 424–26.
54 On the limits of toleration, see the end of the section "Civil Concerns" in the Introduction and the last paragraph of Ch. 3. On proscribed beliefs and practices, see Ch. 1 (note 43-45, 48 and 51) and Ch. 4 (note 5). On Locke's proscription of "atheists", see note 69 below.
55 Locke 1993a: 199. Locke makes the same point concerning the benign consequences of religious worship in the first half of the *Essay* – see ibid: 189. On Locke's "leeks" and "onions" passage, see Ch. 2 (note 34).
56 Locke 1993a: 198–9. In the *Essay*, Locke declares that the magistrate is entitled to suppress such "factions", of whatever type, on the grounds that "such a number, of any opinion whatsoever, who dissented would be dangerous" (ibid.:

199. See also ibid.: 198). By the time of the *Letter*, however, Locke has moved in a much more permissive direction, and so further away from premise (i), insisting that no group, simply on the basis of its separatism, is a danger to the state. Rather, he insists, it is only the magistrate's persecution that makes them so: "there is only one thing which gathers people into seditious commotions and that is oppression" (Locke 1993b: 429. See also Locke 1993b: 428, 428–429, 431, 432). For similar claims in the *Essay Concerning Toleration*, see note 59 below.

57 Locke 1993a: 199. See also ibid.: 189–90 where Locke makes a similar point.
58 Ibid.: 209.
59 Ibid.: 198. Similarly, Locke, in the *Letter*, insists that there is nothing "peculiar unto the genius" of dissenting "assemblies" that makes them "nurseries of factions and seditions", such upheaval emanating from "the unhappy circumstances of an oppressed or ill-settled liberty", where this oppression is produced by state persecution (Locke 1993b: 427. See also ibid.: 428–9 and note 56 above). Of course, we have seen that, in contrast to Dissenters, Locke, in *An Essay Concerning Toleration*, does not perceive in state persecution the source of Catholicism's danger to state and society, but rather its solution. Yet even here it seems it is not anything intrinsic to the Catholic religion which produces this danger, but rather, according to Locke, the "doctrines" and "opinions" that Catholics "mix" and "blend" with it, as well as the fact that they owe their allegiance to "a foreign enemy prince" (Locke 1993a: 197, 203. See also ibid.: 189–90). Indeed Milton and Milton argue that in the first draft of the *Essay*, Locke is quite explicit on this point (Milton and Milton 2010: 28 and 40).
60 See Ch. 2 (note 40).
61 See Ch. 3 (note 53). Indeed, from the *Two Tracts* to the *Letter Concerning Toleration*, Locke insisted that Christianity, although blameless in itself, is continually used for ulterior ends by those with profane and ambitious motives – Locke 1967a: 160–1; 1993b: 402–3, 405, 417, 431–2, 432–3. See also Ch. 2 (note 36).
62 See Locke 1993a: 207; 1993b: 428–9.
63 See the section "Normative Dimension" above.
64 Locke 1993a: 194.
65 Locke 1993a: 204. See also Locke 1967a: 120. It was Kant, of course, who, almost a century after Locke, insisted that it was the "autonomy" of individuals (i.e. their free capacity to act as a law unto themselves) that made possible, not only their moral responsibility, but also their dignity, since it was this which, in making them self-determining, distinguished them from nature (Kant 1949: IV 435, 435–6, 446; 1991: 226, 227). As Kant puts it: "Autonomy is thus the basis of the dignity of both human nature and every rational nature" (Kant 1949: IV 436. See also ibid.: IV 435). Kant's "autonomy" is, however, quite distinct from Locke's "liberty". Kant identified "autonomy" with "reason" and "morality", so that "autonomous" choices were also "rational" and "moral" ones (ibid.: IV 412, 446, 452). Locke identified "liberty" with a rational capacity to make our own choices (see Ch. 1 note 61) free from the "arbitrary" interference of others (Locke 1965: II § 22, 57, 190), but this included a capacity to make "irrational" choices. See Ch. 7 ("Proast, Berlin and Mill").
66 Concerning this conflict see the end of the section "Civil Concerns" in the Introduction. See also Ch. 1 ("Realpolitik") and Ch. 3 ("Competing Imperatives"). On "Lives, Liberties and Estates", see Locke 1965: II § 123.
67 See notes 29 to 31 above.
68 See Waldron 2002: 218–23. One of Locke's two key statements in the *Letter* implying that he accords toleration to Catholics is quoted at ch. 4 (note 26) below. The other is when Locke declares, in the *Letter*, that "[i]f a Roman Catholic believe that to be really the body of Christ which another man calls bread, he does no injury thereby to his neighbour." (Locke 1993b: 420). Yet

what casts some doubt that such statements in the Letter are an admission of toleration for Catholics is that in *An Essay Concerning Toleration*, where Locke, at specific points, clearly denies such toleration (Locke 1993a: 197, 202-03), he nevertheless, at one point, appears (just like the *Letter*) to concede such toleration: "[W]hether I worship God in the various and pompous ceremonies of the papist or in the plainer way of the Calvinists, I see nothing in any of these, if they be done sincerely and out of conscience, that can of itself make me either the worse subject to my prince, or worse neighbour to my fellow-subject" (Locke 1993a: 189). We have seen that John Marshall has suggested that that the Essay may have been written by more than one hand (see ch. 2 note 94) which might explain some of these inconsistences.

69 Locke 1993a: 188; 1993b: 426. For further discussion of Locke and atheists, see Tate 2010a: 998-9; 2010b: 961; 2013: 154-5. For this reason I believe Timothy Stanton is in error when he tells us that Locke's willingness to proscribe atheists confirms that, from Locke's perspective, "God's purposes" were not "absent from politics" (Stanton 2012: 232). "God's purposes" were precisely what needed to be "absent" from politics if the magistrate was to treat all matters of religion, including the proscription of atheists, as "things indifferent", falling within the magistrate's jurisdiction only insofar as they impacted on "civil matters", for which the latter had authority (see Ch. 1 note 33 and 47). For the magistrate to act according to "God's purposes" was *not* to treat such matters as "things indifferent" at all. Equally, and for the same reason, I believe Ian Harris is mistaken in his insistence that Locke proscribes atheists because of their "unholiness", on the grounds (Harris declares) that atheists deny the truth of "theism" and Locke's "commonwealth" is a body that "implies the truth of theism because it required natural law" (Harris 2013: 62, 94). Contrary to Harris, for the magistrate to proscribe atheists for this theological reason would, once again, be at odds with the magistrate treating atheists as "things indifferent".

Both Harris and Stanton's error arises from their very understanding of Locke's Commonwealth itself. They wish to identify a realm of political authority ("res publica") in which the magistrate's authority is understood in secular terms as entirely separate from the realm of religion ("ecclesia") (see Harris 2013: 59-63, 73-9, 88; Stanton 2011: 18-22, 2013: 53-4). Yet, despite this, they subordinate both realms to theological imperatives, Harris declaring: "[R]es publica, as much as ecclesia, presumes the truth of theism and, of course, the validity of natural law, because both are subordinate to God's natural jurisdiction, and to no other" (Harris 2013: 63). To this end, they conceive the magistrate's authority as arising from a fundamental duty of all individuals to worship God, and magistrates themselves as entirely directed, in their actions, by divine authority (natural law) arising from that duty (see ibid.: 61-2, 63, 92, 94, 97-8, 104; Stanton 2011: 19-22). This means that, despite their best intentions, they can never truly conceive the magistrate, within the realm of "res publica", as acting in "secular" terms at all because he/she is always seeking to act in accord with God's purposes (including when they proscribe atheists). So for instance, while at times, Harris and Stanton seek to argue that Locke's magistrate acts in a purely secular manner (Harris 2013, 93, 94; Stanton 2006: 91-2; 2013: 47), treating all matters as "things indifferent", and of concern solely in terms of their civil consequences, it is not possible for them to advance this claim *and* declare (as they do) that magistrates assess the legitimacy of their actions and the limits of their authority entirely in terms of God's will (natural law) (Stanton, 2006: 90-2, 94, 95; 2011: 20-1; 2012: 230; Harris 2013: 60, 62, 63, 72-9, 81-2, 92-4). This is because for magistrates to do one is to exclude the possibility of their doing the other. The contradiction involved in Harris and Stanton's attempts to affirm both propositions, concerning the secular and divine, in relation to the magistrate's authority, is evident in contorted statements such as the following: "This was not to say that

God's requirements were irrelevant to the state.... Instead, the state's purposes could be conceived in terms of divine requirements with a purely secular bearing" (Stanton 2006: 90). For a more detailed criticism of Harris and Stanton, see Tate 2015. See also Ch. 10 (note 1).
70 See Ch. 1 ("Separation of Church and State") and Ch. 1 (notes 85 and 86).
71 Locke 1993b: 420. Locke's removal of religious "truth" from the "business of laws" is what makes possible the religious pluralism within civil society which animates his vision in the *Letter Concerning Toleration*. In the *Letter* he sees toleration applying to multiple religious groups, so that not only "Presbyterians, Independents, Anabaptists, Arminians [and] Quakers" live side by side, enjoying the same "civil rights of the commonwealth" and practising their religion with the "same liberty", but also "pagans", "Mahometans" and "Jews" (ibid.: 431). This is only possible if the Commonwealth "embraces indifferently all men that are honest, peaceable and industrious" (ibid.: 420) and such "indifference" is only possible when religious "truth" is removed from the "business of laws". It is for this reason that Locke, unlike Jonas Proast, is able to endorse the toleration of "pagans". It is not (as Ian Harris, at note 69 above, would suggest) because, like "Mahometans" and "Jews", "pagans" affirm a basic "theism", and this affirmation is a precondition of Locke's toleration. Rather, it is because the religious beliefs of "pagans" (like "Mahometans" and "Jews") are not relevant to the "indifference" with which the Commonwealth embraces all who are "honest, peaceable and industrious". For Locke on "pagans", see Locke 1963: 62 and Locke 1993b: 390, 416, 417, 420, 431. For Harris on "theism" (including "theistic" belief) as a necessary condition of toleration, see Harris 2013: 63, 94–6, 99 and note 69 above. Proast, like Harris, premises toleration on religious belief, and is opposed to Locke's toleration of "pagans" on the grounds that "they are the greatest Dishonour conceivable to God Almighty, and to Humane Nature it self" (Proast 1999: 43). No proposition could be more at odds with Locke's strategy of removing religious "truth" from the "business of laws", and therefore from the conditions that determine the scope of toleration.
72 See note 69 above where I identify my disagreement with Timothy Stanton and Ian Harris on this issue. For my disagreement with John Dunn, on similar grounds, see Tate 2013: 154–5. For my rejection of an apparent exception, within Locke's writings, to my claim that Locke proscribed atheists for the external (civil) consequences of their belief, see ibid.: 163 note 130.
73 See Ch. 1 (notes 33 and 47).
74 On Locke's declaration that liberty requires limits if it is not to degenerate into "license", see Introduction (note 22).

References

Coffey, J. (2000) *Persecution and Toleration in Protestant England, 1558–1689*. Harlow, Essex: Longman.
Harris, I. (2013) "John Locke and Natural Law: Free Worship and Toleration". In: J. Parkin and T. Stanton (eds) *Natural Law and Toleration in the Early Enlightenment*. Oxford: Oxford University Press, pp. 60–105.
Kant, I. (1949) "Foundations of the Metaphysics of Morals". In: I. Kant *Critique of Practical Reason and Other Writings in Moral Philosophy*, Chicago: University of Chicago Press, pp. 50–117.
Kant, I. (1991) "Conjectures on the Beginning of Human History". In: I. Kant *Political Writings*, 2nd ed. Trans. H. B. Nisbet. Cambridge: Cambridge University Press, pp. 221–34.
Locke, J. (1963) "A Second Letter Concerning Toleration". In: J. Locke *The Works of John Locke*. Vol. VI. Aalen: Scientia Verlag, pp. 61–137.

Locke, J. (1965) *Two Treatises of Government*. Peter Laslett (ed.). New York: New American Library.
Locke, J. (1967a) "First Tract on Government". In: J. Locke *Two Tracts on Government*. P. Abrams (ed.). Cambridge: Cambridge University Press, pp. 117–81.
Locke, J. (1967b) "Second Tract on Government: Translation". In: J. Locke *Two Tracts on Government*. P. Abrams (ed.). Cambridge: Cambridge University Press, pp. 210–41.
Locke, J. (1993a) "An Essay Concerning Toleration". In: J. Locke *Political Writings*. David Wootton (ed.). London: Penguin, pp. 186–210.
Locke, J. (1993b) "A Letter Concerning Toleration". In: J. Locke *Political Writings*. Ed. David Wootton (ed.). London: Penguin, pp. 390–436.
Locke, J. (1993c) "Letter to S.H. [Henry Stubbe]". In: J. Locke, *Political writings*. Ed. David Wootton. London: Penguin: 137–139.
Miller, J. (1983) *The Glorious Revolution*. London: Longman.
Milton, J. R. and P. Milton (2010) "General Introduction". In: J. Locke *An Essay Concerning Toleration and Other Writings on Law and Politics, 1667–1683*. J. R. Milton and P. Milton (eds). Oxford: Clarendon Press, pp. 1–161.
Proast, J. (1999) "A Third Letter Concerning Toleration: In Defense of the Argument of the Letter Concerning Toleration, Briefly Consider'd and Answer'd". In: M. Goldie (ed.) *The Reception of Locke's Politics, Vol. 5. The Church, Dissent and Religious Toleration 1689–1773*. London: Pickering and Chatto, pp. 41–116.
Rawls, J. (2005) "The Idea of Public Reason Revisited". In: J. Rawls *Political Liberalism*. Rev. ed. Columbia, OH: Columbia University Press, pp. 436–90.
Spurr, J. (1998) *English Puritanism 1603–1689*. London: Macmillan.
Stanton, T. (2006) "Locke and the Politics and Theology of Toleration", *Political Studies*, 54 (1): 84–102.
Stanton, T. (2011) "Authority and Freedom in the Interpretation of Locke's Political Theory", *Political Theory*, 39 (1): 6–30.
Stanton, T. (2012) "On (Mis)interpreting Locke: A Reply to Tate", *Political Theory*, 40 (2): 229–36.
Stanton, T. (2013) "Natural Law, Noncomformity and Toleration: Two Stages on Locke's Way". In: John Parkin and Timothy Stanton (eds) *Natural Law and Toleration in the Early Enlightenment*. Oxford: Oxford University Press, pp. 35–57.
Tate, J. W. (2010a) "Locke, Rationality and Persecution", *Political Studies*, 58 (5): 988–1008.
Tate, J. W. (2010b) "A Sententious Divide: Erasing the Two Faces of Liberalism", *Philosophy and Social Criticism*, 36 (8): 953–80.
Tate, J. W. (2013) "Dividing Locke from God: The Limits of Theology in Locke's Political Philosophy", *Philosophy and Social Criticism*, 39 (2): 133–64.
Tate, J. W. (2015) "Locke, Toleration and Natural Law: A Reassessment", *European Journal of Political Theory*, published on the journal's "early view" website in "Online First" on 8 November 2015. DOI: 10.1177/1474885115609739. Available at: http://ept.sagepub.com/content/early/2015/11/04/1474885115609739.abstract.
Vernon, R. (2013) "Lockean Toleration: Dialogical not Theological", *Political Studies*, 61 (1): 215–30.
Waldron, J. (2002) *God, Locke and Equality: Christian Foundations of John Locke's Political Thought*. Cambridge: Cambridge University Press.

4 Locke in the Dock

This chapter will begin by outlining the practical discourse of the *A Letter Concerning Toleration*, centred on civil peace and effective state governance. It will then outline its normative discourse centred on individual liberty, and the equal "rights" which, Locke believes, individuals have to this liberty. Regarding the latter, it will investigate Jeremy Waldron's claim that the *Letter* is devoid of any of these normative elements – Locke instead, Waldron insisting, identifying, in this text, with the interests of persecutors at the expense of their victims. The immense influence of Waldron's interpretation of the *Letter* makes an analysis of his claims worthwhile. The fact that they are entirely at odds with the Locke who has been presented in the chapters up to now makes it imperative.

The *Practical* Discourse of the *Letter*

The *Two Tracts*, *An Essay Concerning Toleration* and a *A Letter Concerning Toleration* are all alike in their practical concern to maintain civil peace and effective state governance within the English polity. Each recognizes that this is difficult in a context of religious difference and diversity. However, we saw that it is only the *Two Tracts* that presents this difficulty as so great that the subordination of outward religious expression entirely to the magistrate's command is perceived as the best means to achieve these ends. The *Essay*, as we have seen, revises this view, not least by revising the empirical premises upon which the argument of the *Two Tracts* is based. Indeed, the *Essay* makes clear that the strategy of the *Two Tracts*, centred on the denial of toleration, will (Catholics excepted) produce the very opposite of the civil peace and effective state governance to which it is directed.[1] Locke makes the same point in the *Letter*:

> It is not the diversity of opinions (which cannot be avoided), but the refusal of toleration to those that are of different opinions (which might have been granted), that has produced all the bustles and wars that have been in the Christian world upon account of religion.[2]

Such a position, we saw in the last chapter, could only be arrived at once Locke had thoroughly refuted premise (i) and premise (ii), as these were presented in the *Two Tracts*. It was precisely such refutation which, along with his advancement of premise (iii), allowed him to move from his negative position on toleration to his positive endorsement in *An Essay Concerning Toleration*. Locke, in the *Letter*, advances a similar proposition to the one he presented in the *Essay*, insisting that, contrary to premise (i), if those outside the established church (whom Locke in the *Essay* referred to as "fanatics" but who were conventionally called "Dissenters") are a threat to the state and its security, or to civil society in general, it is not their religious beliefs, but rather the denial of toleration, that makes them so:

> For if men enter into seditious conspiracies, 'tis not religion that inspires them to it in their meetings, but their sufferings and oppressions that make them willing to ease themselves. Just and moderate governments are everywhere quiet, everywhere safe. But oppression raises ferments, and makes men struggle to cast off an uneasy and tyrannical yoke.[3]

In this statement, Locke implies that, when it comes to "Dissenters" in England, state persecution perversely gives rise to its own purported necessity, since it produces the threats to state authority that such persecution is designed to remove.[4] Such a proposition amounts to a thorough rejection not only of premise (i) but also of premise (ii), since it implies that, left alone and subject to toleration, dissenting religions would be no threat to the state or civil society (contra premise (i)), while it also suggests that any attempt by the state to deny such toleration, and engage in "oppression", is likely to give rise to more disorder than such a policy is intended to avoid (contra premise (ii)).

As regards the practical discourse within the *Letter*, therefore, Locke affirms his previous position in the *Essay* that toleration of "Dissent" is the best means to achieve civil peace and the effective state governance that makes such peace possible. He seeks only to proscribe those religious doctrines and practices which are "opposite to the civil right of the community" or, like atheism, are likely to undermine its security.[5] Just as in the *Essay*, therefore, Locke is no longer of the view, as he was with his "leeks" and "onions" statement in the *Two Tracts*, that *any* religious diversity, in and of itself, is a possible threat to civil peace and effective state governance, nor is he of the view that conformity, rather than toleration, is the best means to achieve these ends.

The *Normative* Discourse of the *Letter*

In addition to advancing arguments for toleration directed to these practical ends, Locke, in the *Letter*, also follows the *Essay* in advancing a distinctly *normative* argument for toleration, premised on the ideal of individual liberty. Whereas Locke, in the *Essay*, refers to such liberty as applying to "speculations" and "religious worship", in the *Letter*, he ascribes such liberty to "outward form and rites of worship" and "speculative opinions ... and articles of faith". As he puts it:

> But as in every Church there are two things especially to be considered – the outward form and rites of worship, and the doctrines and articles of faith – these things must be handled each distinctly; that so the whole matter of toleration may the more clearly be understood. Concerning outward worship, I say (in the first place) that the magistrate has no power to enforce by law, either in his own Church, or much less in another, the use of any rites or ceremonies whatsoever in the worship of God. And this, not only because these Churches are free societies, but because whatsoever is practised in the worship of God is only so far justifiable as it is believed by those that practise it to be acceptable unto him.... Speculative opinions ... and articles of faith, as they are called, which are required only to be believed, cannot be imposed on any Church by the law of the land. For it is absurd that things should be enjoined by laws which are not in men's power to perform. And to believe this or that to be true, does not depend upon our will.[6]

We can see, in this passage from the *Letter*, a distinct move beyond the *Two Tracts* and its notion of "things indifferent" in matters of religion. It was precisely the magistrate's command over such "things indifferent" that Locke, in the *Two Tracts*, believed essential to civil peace, and he distinguished this realm from a purely inward realm of belief, subject to the liberty of each individual conscience and not affected by the magistrate's command.[7] But once Locke declares, in the passage above, that "whatsoever is practised in the worship of God is only so far justifiable as it is believed by those that practise it to be acceptable unto him", then the distinction between "things indifferent" and "things necessary" in matters of religion, and their relationship to individual belief, takes on a very different relationship to that in the *Two Tracts*.

This is because religious "necessity" comes to be determined by the subjective perspective of the sincere worshipper, concerning what they believe appropriate in the worship of God.[8] Locke defines "necessity" in matters of religion as "[t]hat ... part of the worship which is believed to be appointed by God, and to be well-pleasing to him, and therefore that is necessary".[9] Within the *Two Tracts*, the determination of things "necessary" in religion was not left to the liberty of the individual, as defined by their own conscience and their personal relationship with God.[10] Rather, within that text, the liberty of the individual was what was left once things "necessary" had been determined (either by natural law or divine revelation[11]) and the magistrate had determined which things "indifferent" would be subject to his or her command – Locke declaring that "the authority of the individual prevails in all matters that are not wholly prescribed by superior law ... and only when all these are silent are the commands of conscience and the vow observed".[12]

Yet Locke moves beyond this position as early as *An Essay Concerning Toleration*, telling us that:

> whatsoever the magistrate enjoined in the worship of God, men must in this necessarily follow what they themselves thought best, since no consideration could be sufficient to force a man from or to that which he was fully persuaded was the way to infinite happiness or infinite misery.[13]

Here we see an anticipation, in the *Essay*, of Locke's declaration in the *Letter*, above, that "whatsoever is practised in the worship of God is only so far justifiable as it is believed by those that practise it to be acceptable unto him". This alters the relationship, established in the *Two Tracts*, between "things indifferent" and "things necessary", because, once we accept that the subjective experience of the individual determines what is "necessary" in religion, then:

> in religious worship nothing is indifferent, for it being the using of those habits, gestures, etc. which I think acceptable to God in my worshipping of him, however they may be in their own nature perfectly indifferent, yet when I am worshipping my God in a way I think he has prescribed and will approve of, I cannot alter, omit, or add any circumstance in that which I think the true way of worship.[14]

It is true that Locke tells us in the *Letter* that "[t]hings indifferent are not otherwise lawful in the worship of God than as they are instituted by God himself; and as he, by some positive command, has ordained them to be made a part of that worship".[15] But Locke makes clear that it is ultimately individuals who must decide, in the context of their worship, what has been "instituted by God", and therefore what is "necessary" in the worship of Him, because:

> [w]hatever profession we make, to whatever outward worship we conform, if we are not fully satisfied in our own mind that the one is true, and the other well pleasing unto God, such profession and such practice, far from being any furtherance, are indeed great obstacles to our salvation.[16]

What this means is that once it is individuals who determine what is "necessary" in religious worship, Locke's distinction in the *Two Tracts*, between a purely inward liberty of conscience, and an outward realm of religious practice which, because "indifferent", can be wholly subject to the magistrate's command, with no impact on inward liberty, cannot be sustained. "Necessity", from the perspective of the sincere believer, is liable to encompass outward matters of worship (religious practice) as well as inner matters of belief, with both being fundamental to individual liberty, and therefore both placing limits on the magistrate's command.

Consequently, once Locke, in the *Essay* and the *Letter*, conceives of the liberty of the individual as extending beyond inner conscience to outward religious practice (worship), such liberty requires limits on the magistrate's command, to prevent that command intruding upon this practice.[17] Once these limits are required, an accommodation between individual liberty and the magistrate's command must be reached, if the two are not to clash, and Locke's normative imperative of individual liberty is not to be at odds with his practical imperative of civil peace and effective state governance. We have seen that the *Two Tracts* avoided this problem by conceiving of this accommodation in "vertical" terms – where there is a hierarchy of command and obedience stemming from God, to the magistrate, to the individual, and where the liberty left to the individual is what remains (in residual terms) once God and the magistrate have determined what is obligatory (in either "formal" or "material" terms[18]) and therefore what must be obeyed.[19]

By the time of the *Letter* and the *Two Treatises of Government*, however, we have seen that such an accommodation is conceived by Locke in what we might call "horizontal", as distinct from "vertical", terms, individual liberty being understood by Locke as *preceding* the magistrate's command, inaugurating that command via the contractual process of "consent", thereby placing limits upon it, but also being limited by this process in turn.[20] Liberty, therefore, no longer exists in a subordinate, and residual, relationship to the magistrate's authority (being that which remains after such authority has been exercised). Rather, via the process of "compact" and consent, it is constitutive of this authority, placing limits upon it, but also (via this same process of "compact") placing limits upon itself in relation to that authority in turn.[21]

Locke's ideal of "compact" might therefore be understood as one means by which this "horizontal" accommodation between the normative imperative of liberty, and the practical imperative of governance and civil peace, is reached. Another might be the process of "separation" discussed in Chapter 1, where Locke refers to the need to "assign what those things are which have a title to liberty", distinguishing these from "the boundaries of imposition and obedience".[22]

Of course, the ultimate corollary of this constitutive role of liberty in relation to governance is the right of resistance to the magistrate's command which Locke, by the time of the *Two Treatises* and the *Letter*, accords to each individual. We saw that the ultimate outcome of this conflict between liberty and governance is contingent and open-ended – the "appeal" being to "heaven".[23] In this respect, we see that realpolitik becomes an inescapable feature of Locke's political philosophy once he shifts to this contractual framework.[24]

Locke and Rights

We saw that Locke, in the *Essay*, referred in relation to "speculative opinions and divine worship" to an "absolute and universal right to toleration".[25] In the *Letter*, Locke is also willing to articulate such liberties in terms of "rights":

> That we may draw towards a conclusion: the sum of all we drive at is that every man may enjoy the same rights that are granted to others. Is it permitted to worship God in the Roman manner? Let it be permitted to do it in the Geneva form also. Is it permitted to speak Latin in the market-place? Let those that have a mind to it be permitted to do it also in the Church.... Let no man's life, or body, or house, or estate suffer any manner of prejudice upon these accounts.[26]

And again:

> [I]f the law of toleration were once so settled that all Churches were obliged to lay down toleration as the foundation of their own liberty; and teach that liberty of conscience is every man's natural right, equally belonging to dissenters as to themselves; and that nobody ought to be compelled in matters of religion either by law or force ... [then] [t]he establishment of this one thing would take away all ground of complaints and tumults upon account of conscience.[27]

From these passages in the *Letter* it is evident that, for Locke, a "right" is an entitlement on the part of an individual to exercise certain liberties without interference from either the state or other members of civil society. Insofar as it is toleration that, in legally prescribing such a sphere of non-interference, makes such liberty possible, toleration is also ultimately justified in terms of these same rights. In this respect we see how the *Letter*, in advancing this rights discourse, continues to build upon premise (iii), offering a distinctly normative justification of toleration quite separate from the practical arguments for toleration that, we have seen, Locke also seeks to advance. In the following chapter, where we discuss the three "considerations" that Locke offers for toleration in the *Letter*, we shall see that it is the "consent argument" that most closely encompasses the argument for toleration in terms of rights.

In justifying toleration in terms of rights, Locke is to be distinguished from those contemporary scholars who have insisted that toleration is quite distinct from "rights", on the grounds that toleration is a voluntary concession made on the part of the powerful to the less powerful, because it presumes the capacity of tolerators to reverse such toleration if they wish. Such inequality, it is argued, is inconsistent with the reciprocal equality associated with "rights", so discourses of toleration, and rights-based discourses, are entirely separate.[28]

Over two hundred years ago, George Washington, as US President, expressed a similar view of toleration, perceiving it as an unequal relationship, and contrasting it to the equality associated with a "natural right" to liberty. Writing to the Hebrew Congregation of Newport, Rhode Island, in 1790, Washington states:

> All possess alike liberty of conscience and immunities of citizenship. It is now no more that toleration is spoken of, as if it was by the indulgence of one class of people, that another enjoyed the exercise of their inherent natural rights.[29]

Indeed, even Jacques Derrida, a figure radically distant from both the liberal tradition and George Washington, has expressed a similar view, pointing to the inequality he perceives at the heart of toleration:

> Though I clearly prefer shows of tolerance to shows of intolerance, I nonetheless still have certain reservations about the word 'tolerance' and the discourse it organizes. It is a discourse with religious roots; it is most often used on the side of those with power, always as a kind of condescending concession.... Indeed, tolerance is first of all a form of charity.... Tolerance is always on the side of the "reason of the strongest", where "might is right"; it is a supplementary mark of sovereignty, the good face of sovereignty, which says to the other from its elevated position, I am letting you be, you are not insufferable, I am leaving you a place in my home, but do not forget that this is my home.[30]

The *Two Treatises* and the *Letter*

In identifying toleration with rights, Locke inscribes at the centre of toleration a reciprocal equality which distances his conception of toleration from those of Washington, Derrida and the toleration theorists referred to above. Locke, in the *Letter*, clearly associates "rights" with toleration at notes 26 and 27 above. However Locke's rights discourse is even more explicit in the *Two Treatises*. As we saw in Chapter 1, Locke, in the *Two Treatises*, places natural rights at the basis of his account of individual liberty and equality, and insists that in a state of nature "Man" is "born ... with a Title to perfect Freedom, and an uncontrouled enjoyment of all the Rights and Privileges of the Law of Nature, equally with any other Man, or Number of Men in the World".[31]

In this respect, there are normative parallels between the *Two Treatises* and the *Letter*. Just as Locke, in the *Two Treatises*, makes reference to a right of resistance to government on the part of individuals in defence of their individual liberties, so he does the same in the *Letter*, describing, in the passage below, the way in which government transgresses its lawful authority when it imposes civil penalties (including confiscation of property) upon individuals for failing to conform to state requirements in matters of religion (the very conformity Locke advocated in the *Two Tracts*). Locke insists in the passage below that resistance is likely in such circumstances. Of course this declaration, on its own, would simply make reference to a material fact – that resistance is liable to occur in a context of persecution. But Locke then goes further, in the same passage, shifting to a normative position, and justifying such resistance in terms of "natural rights" which, he says, "are not forfeitable upon account of religion":

> Now as it is very difficult for men patiently to suffer themselves to be stripped of the goods which they have got by their honest industry, and, contrary to all the laws of equity, both human and divine, to be delivered up for a prey to other men's violence and rapine, especially when they are otherwise altogether blameless, and that the occasion for which they are thus treated does not at all belong to the jurisdiction of the magistrate, but entirely to the conscience of every particular man, for the conduct of which he is accountable to God only; what else can be expected but that these men, growing weary of the evils under which they labour, should in the end think it lawful for them to resist force with force, and to defend their natural rights (which are not forfeitable upon account of religion) with arms as well as they can?[32]

In this respect, we see how the normative discourse of the *Letter*, in conceiving of religious liberty in terms of "rights", and justifying a right of resistance in defence of this liberty, is much more robust than *An Essay Concerning Toleration* when it comes to premise (iii). We saw that Locke, in that earlier text, had permitted conscientious objection to the laws of the magistrate. But the disobedience to such laws that such conscientious objection involved was always premised on a submission to the penalty the magistrate imposed for such actions.[33] The *Letter*, however, moves much more strongly in the direction of the *Two Treatises* in suggesting, in the passage above, a full-blown right of resistance to the magistrate, with no submission to the magistrate's penalty. As is pointed out at the beginning of Chapter 5, Locke's contemporaries recognized the affinity between the *Letter* and the *Two Treatises* and read these two texts in conjunction with each other.[34]

Locke as Anti-Liberal

Such, therefore, is the close connection Locke establishes between individual liberties, toleration and rights within the *A Letter Concerning Toleration*. It is in these terms that the text has been widely recognized as one of the founding documents of the liberal tradition.[35] It therefore comes as something of a surprise to encounter Jeremy Waldron's interpretation of the *Letter*, in which he argues that Locke, far from defending the rights and liberties of individuals within this text, advances no such defence, and instead identifies wholly with the interests of state persecutors, exhibiting a concern that their persecution, in threatening such liberties, be "rational", and so able to achieve its ends. As Waldron describes the *Letter*:

> [W]hat one misses above all in Locke's argument is a sense that there is anything *morally* wrong with intolerance, or a sense of any deep concern for the *victims* of persecution or the moral insult that is involved in the attempt to manipulate their faith. What gives Locke's argument its peculiar structure and narrowness is that it is, in the end, an argument about agency rather than an argument about consequences. It appeals to and is concerned with the interests of the persecutors and with the danger that, in undertaking intolerant action, they may exhibit a less than perfect rationality. Addressed as it is to the persecutors in *their* interests, the argument has nothing to do with the interests of the victims of persecution as such; rather those interests are addressed and protected only incidentally as a result of what is, in the last resort, prudential advice offered to those who are disposed to oppress them.[36]

The introduction to this book referred to the immense influence of Waldron's interpretation of the *Letter* within the wider Locke literature.[37] What makes this influence so astounding is that the interpretation Waldron offers, one of the key claims of which resides in the passage above, is so implausible. The idea that Locke, writing the *A Letter Concerning Toleration* in exile from the Stuart authorities, whom he believed were intent on persecuting him, and fearing the advances that Louis XIV was making against the Huguenots in France, could identify, in his composition of this text, with the interests of those engaged in such persecution, is counter-intuitive to say the least. Indeed, it is thoroughly at odds with all that we have discovered concerning the normative content of the *Letter*, with its emphasis on individual liberty, its defence of this liberty in terms of "rights", and Locke's claim that individuals are entitled to defend these rights by force against the depredations of those who would seek to undermine them.

Even Locke's practical discourse within the *Letter*, directed as it is to effective state governance and civil peace, cannot be aligned to any identification with the interests of state persecutors. As we have seen, although effective state governance, and the civil peace it makes possible, are practical imperatives consistent with state interests, they are also consistent with the interests of individuals within civil society, this civil peace being one of the reasons, Locke tells us, why these individuals, or their predecessors, first left the state of nature and sought the security of civil societies and government in the first place.[38] It is only when individuals perceive such practical imperatives as being pursued by the state at the expense of what they conceive to be their fundamental liberties that Locke's normative and practical imperatives are likely to come into conflict.

Waldron's Reading of the *Letter*

We shall see that Waldron's claim that Locke identified with the interests of persecutors arises from the "peculiar structure and narrowness" of his own reading of Locke's *Letter* – a reading that, we shall also see, is inherently truncated and incomplete.[39] Waldron points out that Locke opens the *Letter* with a specifically biblical argument for toleration, Locke insisting that:

> the toleration of those that differ from others in matters of religion is so agreeable to the Gospel of Jesus Christ, and to the genuine reason of mankind, that it seems monstrous for men to be so blind, as not to perceive the necessity and advantage of it in so clear a light.[40]

But other than this specifically biblical proposition, Waldron identifies only one non-biblical argument for toleration in the *Letter*. This is what Waldron refers to as the "main line of argument" in that text and which we, in this chapter and the next, shall refer to as Locke's "rationality argument".[41]

Contrary to Waldron, we shall see in the next chapter that, rather than just one, Locke in fact offered *three* non-biblical arguments (or what Locke calls "considerations") for toleration in the *Letter*, each independent of the biblical argument referred to above, only one of which is the "rationality argument". We shall also see, in subsequent chapters, that these three "considerations" were again raised by Locke in his later *Letters Concerning Toleration* which he wrote in response to Jonas Proast.

Further, far from the one non-biblical argument Waldron identifies (the "rationality argument") constituting Locke's "main line of argument" for toleration in the *Letter*, we shall see in Chapter 5 that, of Locke's three "considerations" for toleration, Locke makes clear that the "rationality argument" occupies a *subsidiary* status relative to the other two, in the sense that the other two apply, as an argument for toleration, even if the "rationality argument" does not. Further, we shall see in the same chapter that, by the time of his later debate with Proast, Locke declares that the conditions underwriting the "rationality argument", providing for its possibility, are unlikely to apply in practice. In this respect, far from the "rationality argument" being, as Waldron claims, the "main line of argument" that Locke offers for toleration in the *Letter*, Locke, in fact, ascribes to it a subsidiary status, and, by the time of his engagement with Proast, ultimately abandons it, declaring that its conditions of possibility are unlikely to be fulfilled.

Waldron's Locke

Jeremy Waldron begins his discussion of Locke's *Letter Concerning Toleration* by describing the sort of account he would like to provide of this text and the reasons he would like to provide it:

> This is a paper about John Locke's argument for toleration, or, more accurately, it is a paper about the main line of argument which appears in Locke's work *A Letter on Toleration*. It is *not* intended – as so many papers on Locke's political philosophy are these days – as a historical analysis of his position.... Rather, I want to consider the Lockian case as a political argument – that is as a practical intellectual resource that can be abstracted from the antiquity of its context and deployed in the modern debate about liberal theories of justice and political morality. To put it bluntly, I want to consider whether Locke's case is worth anything as an argument which might dissuade someone here and now from actions of intolerance and persecution.[42]

Waldron provides this account by highlighting what he believes to be the "main line of argument" that Locke provides for toleration in the *Letter*.[43] This is the argument that force is useless as a means to instil sincere and genuine belief, because such belief can only arise from an inward persuasion of the mind, which is impervious to all use of force.[44] Because force cannot achieve these ends, it is "irrational" for magistrates to use force upon those at odds with them in matters of religion, in an attempt to alter their religious belief. Instead, magistrates should adopt a policy of toleration instead, allowing religious diversity to flourish. Waldron describes this argument, as he perceives it in the *Letter*, as follows:

> The crux of the argument – the step which dominates it and on which everything else depends – is the claim that religious belief cannot be secured by the coercive means characteristic of state action. This is the essence of Locke's challenge to the rationality of religious persecution: that what the persecutors purport to be up to is something that, in the nature of the case, they cannot hope to achieve.
>
> To make this case, he needs to show that this is true *in principle*. It is not enough to show that coercion is *inefficient* as a means of religious discipline or that it is less efficient than the citizens' means of argument and persuasion. For that would leave open the possibility of using coercion as a last resort, and it would also make the case for toleration vulnerable to a reassessment of the relative values of the various effects of coercive action. Locke needs to show impossibility here. He must show that there is a gap between political means and religious ends which cannot in principle be bridged.[45]

Locke does indeed advance something akin to this "rationality argument" at a number of points in the *Essay* and *Letter*, and we shall consider his explicit articulation of this argument (one of the three "considerations" he offers for toleration in the *Letter*) in the following chapter. However, for the moment, what is clear is that the "rationality argument" assumes much more in relation to state purposes than did Locke in the *Two Tracts*. In that earlier text, Locke assumed that the magistrate would be concerned solely with the regulation of outward religious behaviour, since it was conformity at this level which (in removing the visible signs of religious difference) was perceived as necessary to ensure civil peace.[46] To this end, we saw, Locke assumed that the state, in seeking to regulate outward religious behaviour, would leave each individual's inner conscience free from coercion.[47]

The "rationality argument", on the other hand, assumes that the state is concerned to regulate not only outward behaviour, but also inner conscience, by seeking to alter religious belief. And since religious belief is only genuine if it is sincere, the "rationality argument" must assume that the state also seeks to inculcate the "sincerity" and "genuineness" with which such religious belief is held.

If the magistrate were concerned solely to regulate outward behaviour, then, as Locke assumed in the *Two Tracts*, the use of force would conceivably be capable of achieving this end. After all, outward behaviour, Locke tells us, is subject to the will, which, he says, is coercible by force.[48] The sincerity with which inner belief was held would be irrelevant to such purposes. Within the terms of the "rationality argument", however, it is the attempt to inculcate a sincere inner belief that renders force "irrational", and so presents toleration as an alternative state policy. The result is that the "rationality argument" must assume that the state is willing to use force, in matters of religion, for salvationist ends, since it is only a concern with salvation (as distinct from practical ends such as civil peace) which would make the content of an individual's inner religious belief, and the sincerity and genuineness with which it is held, a matter of concern to the magistrate, and therefore an object of his or her force. By the time of his engagement with Proast, Locke admits that the state is unlikely to use force in matters of religion for this purpose, thereby admitting that this condition of the "rationality argument" is unlikely to apply in practice.[49]

In all these respects, the "rationality argument" employs assumptions quite distinct from premise (ii). Premise (ii) assumed that the state had the material capacity to eradicate outward differences in the practice of religion, thereby ensuring conformity to the magistrate's command. It therefore assumed that the state was concerned solely with regulating outward behaviour, and Locke's refutation of premise (ii) was based on the assumption that, given the empirical circumstances of Locke's time, the use of force to this end would produce more disorder than it was intended to avoid. The "rationality argument", on the other hand, in focusing on inner belief rather than outward behaviour, is quite distinct from premise (ii). Further, we have seen that a basic assumption of the "rationality argument" is that, in contrast to outward behaviour, the use of force is *always* incapable of regulating inner belief, irrespective of empirical circumstances, because there are no conceivable circumstances in which such belief would be alterable by force. As Locke puts it in the *Letter*: "[S]uch is the nature of the understanding that it cannot be compelled to the belief of anything by outward force".[50]

The one other feature to recognise about the "rationality argument" is that it advances toleration, as the preferred policy for states to adopt, on *negative* rather than *positive* grounds – as the policy the state ought to adopt once it is shown that the magistrate is unable to instil sincere and genuine belief by force, and so unable to achieve the ends which he or she seeks. In the context of the rationality argument, therefore, toleration becomes the preferred state policy by default – not from any intrinsic worth of toleration itself, or the liberty it makes possible, but solely due to the failure of its coercive alternative.

Waldron, Locke and the State

Waldron begins his articulation of what he conceives to be Locke's "main line of argument" in the *Letter*, centred on the "rationality argument", by focusing, in the first instance, on what he believes to be Locke's conception of the state. Waldron argues that Locke defines the state not in terms of the *ends* for which it was created, and which it is therefore legitimately entitled to pursue, but rather in terms of the *means* it possesses to achieve these ends. Waldron advances this argument, initially, by appealing to a thinker very much outside of Locke's time and place – the German sociologist, Max Weber. Weber, Waldron insists, claimed "it is impossible to define the state in terms of its functions" (i.e. its ends) because in historical terms "'there is scarcely any task that some political association has not taken in hand'".[51] Waldron then insists that Weber offered an alternative definition of the state – what Waldron calls a "modal" rather than a "functional" definition of the state – i.e. a definition of the state in terms, not of its ends, but in terms of the "means" it possesses to achieve these ends. As Waldron puts it:

> Since the state cannot be defined in terms of its functions, the best way of defining it, Weber suggested, was in terms of its characteristic *means*: the means, such as the organised monopoly of legitimate force in a given territory, which are deployed to carry out whatever ends a state may happen to undertake.[52]

Waldron then insists that Locke, over two hundred years prior to Weber, defined the state very much in these "modal" terms, centred on the "means" at the state's disposal:

> Locke, like Weber, defines the state in terms of the characteristic means at its disposal. In the *Second Treatise*, he tells us: "Political power ... I take to be a right of making laws with penalties of death". Similarly, in the *Letter on Toleration* he distinguishes the means available to the magistrate from those available to the ordinary man of good will in civil society: "Every man is entitled to admonish, exhort, and convince another of error, and lead him by reasoning to accept his own opinions. But it is the magistrate's province to give orders by decree and compel with the sword".... The fact that governments and

their officials work by coercive force while other organisations do not is the fundamental premiss [sic] of Locke's argument and the basis of his distinction between church and state.[53]

I have pointed out in detail elsewhere how Waldron's ascription to Locke of a "modal" definition of the state is based on a fundamental misreading by Waldron of key passages within Locke's political philosophy – these being the passages that Waldron cites in support of this claim.[54] In one case, the textual reference that Waldron cites is flawed.[55] In the others, the series of references that Waldron refers to as evidence that Locke *defined* the state in terms of the means at its disposal only depict Locke as *describing* the state in these terms.[56] In conflating the former with the latter, Waldron has erroneously assumed that *description*, in and of itself, is tantamount to *definition*.[57]

Consequently, none of the passages Waldron cites are capable of sustaining Waldron's claim that Locke adopted a "modal" definition of the state, centred on the "means" at its disposal. Far from Locke believing that such "means" as "force" and "coercion" are definitive of the state, it is the origins of that force, in the natural right of each individual to act as executor of the law of nature and the limits other natural rights place on the authority of government once individuals contract with each other to create civil society, which are definitive of the state, since it is such a contractual process that inaugurates the state itself.[58] In other words, it is the origins of the state in a "compact", referred to in Chapter 1, and so pervasively present within the *Two Treatises* (but also, as we have seen, obliquely referred to in the *Letter*[59]), which, in making an explicit connection between the origins of government, the purposes or ends for which it was established and the limits this imposes on its authority, provides Locke with his definition of the state.[60]

In this respect, we see that Locke defines the state in what Waldron refers to as "functionalist" terms – i.e. in terms of the ends for which it was established rather than the means at its disposal – Locke insisting that these ends be confined to the "civil" purposes for which the state's authority was created (and consented to) in the first place.[61] The "consent argument" that Locke advances as one of his three "considerations" for toleration within the *Letter*, and which we shall discuss in the next chapter, encompasses this framework. Indeed, the following chapter, and later ones focusing on Locke's engagement with Proast, will show the lengths to which Locke went *not* to define the state, and the scope of its legitimate authority, in the "modal" terms to which Waldron refers – i.e. in terms of the means at its disposal.[62] Such a conception of the state is one which, we shall see, Locke explicitly rejects.

Waldron, Locke and Legitimacy

It is Waldron's (erroneous) assumption that Locke defines the state not in terms of the ends it is legitimately entitled to pursue, but rather in terms of the means at its disposal, which allows Waldron to advance the rest of his interpretation of the *Letter* and ultimately arrive at his conclusion that Locke, in this text, identified with the interests of persecutors at the expense of their victims. Waldron's first step in this direction is to present the "modal" definition of the state as a basis of the state's legitimacy. Waldron points out in the passage below that once we define the state in "modal" terms – i.e. in terms of the "means" at its disposal – it is possible to determine the legitimacy of the state's ends (i.e. the purposes for which it is entitled to exercise its authority) entirely in terms of those means. From this "modal" perspective, any particular end of the state is illegitimate, and therefore a wrongful use of the state's authority, if the state does not possess sufficient means to achieve it. This is because, in such contexts, the use of such means is rendered "irrational", being incapable of achieving the ends to which they are directed. As Waldron puts it:

> Now if we can give ... a *modal* definition of the state – if we can define it in terms of its distinctive and characteristic means – then we may have the basis for an argument about its proper ends or functions along the following lines: A state by definition is an organization which uses means of type M. But means of type M are ill-fitted for producing ends of type E. They never produce E-type effects (but perhaps at best mockeries or travesties of them). Therefore it is irrational to use M-type means in order to produce (genuine) E-type effects – and irrational in one of the most straightforward and least contestable instrumental senses. Therefore, given the type of means that it uses, it is irrational for the state to pursue E-type ends. Therefore – and in this sense – the pursuit of E-type ends cannot be one of the proper functions of government. That, it seems to me, is the form of an interesting and evidently acceptable line of argument. It is an argument from available means to possible ends – from a modal definition to a (negative) functionalist conclusion. And, in a very compressed form, it captures the structure of the main line of argument in the *Letter on Toleration* that I want to examine.[63]

It is on the basis of his belief that Locke defined the legitimate scope of state authority in these "modal" terms – i.e. in terms of the *means* at the state's disposal – that Waldron then seeks to ascribe to Locke what Waldron calls the "main line of argument" in the *Letter* and which we have called the "rationality argument". Waldron refers directly to this link between the "modal" definition of the state, and Locke's "rationality argument", as follows:

Having defined government in terms of its means, Locke then argues that those means – laws, threats, the sword – are not capable of producing genuine religious belief in the minds of the citizens who are subjected to them. Sincere and genuine (as opposed to feigned or counterfeited) belief cannot be produced by these means; so it is irrational for the authorities to use them for that purpose. Thus, from a rational point of view, the state, defined in the way Locke wants to define it, cannot have among its functions that of promoting genuine religion. And since, on Locke's definition, toleration is nothing but the absence of force deployed for religious ends, it follows that the state is rationally required to be tolerant.[64]

It is clear from this passage that Waldron conceives Locke's "main line of argument" for toleration in the *Letter* to be of the "negative" type discussed above. Waldron does not believe that Locke defends toleration in the sort of normative terms we have identified with premise (iii) – i.e. in terms of the liberty of the individual. Rather, Waldron insists that, outside of Locke's explicitly Christian endorsements, his whole case for toleration in the *Letters Concerning Toleration* is articulated in terms of the "irrationality", referred to in the passage above, in which toleration is justified on the basis of the failure of persecution to achieve its ends, and therefore the preferability of toleration as an alternative. Waldron points to Locke's "negative" case for toleration, in these terms, as follows:

Locke's position is a *negative* one: toleration, as he says in his *Second Letter* on the subject, is nothing but the absence or "removing" of force in matters of religion. The argument is about the irrationality of coercive persecution and it entails nothing more than that that sort of activity ought not to be undertaken. Nothing is entailed about the positive value of religious or moral diversity. Unlike Mill, Locke does not see anything to be gained from the existence of a plurality of views, or anything that might be lost in monolithic unanimity, in these matters. There is nothing in his argument to justify a policy of fostering religious pluralism or of providing people with a meaningful array of choices.[65]

To some extent, this comparison to Mill on the issue of "plurality" and "diversity", in the passage above, is unfair. Mill was writing in the context of a mid-nineteenth-century England in which, Mill believed, difference and diversity were under threat from an increasingly conformist, because increasingly egalitarian, society.[66] Locke, on the other hand, was writing in the context of late-seventeenth-century England – a society which, in the wake of the English Reformation and the English Civil Wars, was still deeply divided by religion. As Locke put it in one of his minor essays, written in 1676: "The great dispute in all this diversity of opinions is where the truth is".[67]

From Locke's perspective, therefore, difference and diversity were not endangered qualities in need of protection, but a political problem that, in the interests of civil peace and state security, needed to be resolved. As Locke put it in the *Letter*, "diversity of opinions" in matters of religion "cannot be avoided", and it is only toleration, he believed, that allows us to ensure that such differences can coexist peacefully with each other and the state.[68] Consequently, as a result of his historical context, Locke saw difference and diversity differently to Mill, as a political problem to be managed rather than a political virtue to be preserved. Contrary to Waldron, it is these empirical circumstances, rather than the difference of principle which Waldron identifies in the passage above, that distinguishes Locke from Mill.[69] Indeed the difference of principle between them is the converse of what Waldron supposes. The sort of normative argument that Locke advances for toleration, and which we have encapsulated in terms of premise (iii), indicates that Locke's position on toleration is not wholly "negative", and is based, in part, on individual liberty as a positive ideal. In contrast, it was Mill who subordinated individual liberty (and the "meaningful array of choices" it requires) to other ends, Mill insisting that all his commitments (including his commitment to liberty) were of value only insofar as they advanced "utility", which he defined as "utility in the largest sense, grounded on the permanent interests of a man as a progressive being".[70]

Waldron, Locke and Liberalism

We have seen above how Waldron links the "modal" definition of the state to Locke's "rationality argument" and how this "rationality argument" makes an essentially "negative" case for toleration. But how does Waldron manage to link all this to his claim that Locke identified with the interests of persecutors?

Once again, the answer lies in Waldron's insistence that Locke defined the state in "modal" terms. By focusing on the means at the state's disposal, we have seen that Waldron identifies the legitimacy of the ends the state is entitled to pursue in terms of whether the state possesses means sufficient to achieve them. Ends unable to be achieved by these means are "irrational", and therefore illegitimate. But so long as these means are capable of achieving the end in question, such legitimacy is assured. The legitimate use of state authority is therefore determined by the rationality of its activity.

For our purposes, what is significant about such a perspective is the profound shift it involves in our understanding of state legitimacy. No prior limits are placed on the legitimate scope of state activity – i.e. on the means a state might use or the ends it might conceivably pursue – so long as it possesses means sufficient to achieve these ends. As Waldron makes clear in the passage below, even "coercion", in this context, is legitimate, if "coercion" is capable of achieving the ends to which it is directed.

This "modal" framework could not be more at odds with the "contractualist" account of the state which we have ascribed to Locke in Chapter 1, where the limits on state authority, and the legitimacy of its activity, are determined by the purposes for which individuals, or their predecessors, consented to state authority in the first place.[71] It is on the basis of the "modal" account of the state, centred on the means at the state's disposal, and the specific conception of state legitimacy to which this gives rise, that Waldron is able to insist that Locke identifies with the interests of persecutors. As he puts it:

> [W]e need to see that Locke's negative argument is directed not against coercion *as such*, but only against *coercion undertaken for certain reasons* and with certain ends in mind. The argument concerns the rationality of the would-be persecutor and his purposes; it is concerned about what happens to his rationality when he selects means evidently unfitted to his ends. Coercion, as we know, is on Locke's view unfitted to religious ends. But if it is being used for other ends to which it is not so unfitted (such as Hobbesian ends of public order), then there can be no objection on the basis of this argument, even if *incidentally* some church or religious sect is harmed.[72]

In this manner, Waldron presents Locke not as a figure who, along with others, inaugurates what we have come to know as the liberal tradition, but rather as a figure very much at odds with it. After all, as Joseph Raz tells us: "The specific contribution of the liberal tradition to political morality has always been its insistence on the respect due to individual liberty."[73] Yet in the passage above, and those before it, Waldron presents Locke's case for toleration as devoid of any concern for liberty. Instead, the corollary of Waldron's position is that Locke conceives of liberty entirely in "residual" terms – as encompassing those areas of an individual or group's existence that have not yet been intruded upon by the "rational" (i.e. successful) use of the means at the state's disposal, or upon which the state has not yet decided to intrude. This is because Waldron, in his "modal" account of the state, places no limits on the legitimate scope of state activity, or upon the areas of life in which it might intervene. So long as the state possesses means capable of achieving its ends, individuals, in Waldron's account, have no "rights" upon which they might demand limits to state activity. At most, their liberty is "residual" – such individuals only possessing a "liberty" in a specific area if the state decides not to intrude upon this area or if such intrusion is shown to be "irrational" (i.e. unable to achieve its ends).[74] As Waldron states:

> The religious liberty for which Locke argues is defined *not* by the actions permitted on the part of the person whose liberty is in question, but by the motivations it prohibits on the part of the person who is in a position to threaten the liberty.... Thus it is not a right to

freedom of worship as such, but rather, and at most, a right not to have one's worship interfered with for religious ends.[75]

We can see, therefore, the extent to which Waldron's illiberal interpretation of Locke arises from the very framework of interpretation that Waldron imposes on Locke's *Letter*. Only by ascribing to Locke a "modal" account of the state, and the very specific conception of state legitimacy to which this gives rise, can Waldron conclude that Locke identified with the interests of persecutors. In this way, we see the full implications of the difference between Waldron's interpretation of Locke and that of the philosopher presented in previous chapters. For the latter, individual liberty and equality are fundamental norms.

A basic irony in Waldron's account is that, having identified within the *Letter* only one non-biblical account of toleration, Waldron accuses Locke of "simplification" and "distortion" in his reliance on this single defence. As Waldron puts it: "Locke has relied, for his indictment of the rationality of persecution, on a radical and distorted simplification of that complexity. A charge of irrationality based on that sort of simplification is likely to be returned with interest!"[76] Yet we have seen that it is precisely Waldron who has engaged in "simplification" and "distortion". This is evident in Waldron's claim that Locke advanced only one "main line of argument" for toleration in the *Letter*, when in fact we shall see in the next chapter that he offered three. But it is at its most egregious and extreme when, on the basis of this claim, and his erroneous ascription to Locke of a "modal" account of the state, Waldron can conclude that Locke identified, within the *Letter*, with the interests of persecutors at the expense of their victims.[77]

Waldron's later work on Locke seeks to situate Locke's political philosophy within Locke's theological concerns, and the conception of equality that, Waldron believes, arises from them.[78] One would imagine that such an account would be quite at odds with any suggestion that Locke identified with the interests of persecutors. Yet, to the best of my knowledge, nowhere in this later account does Waldron retract his earlier claim. Further, the later work reaffirms Waldron's assumption that the "rationality argument" is the only non-biblical argument that Locke offers for toleration in the *Letter*. This is evident when Waldron describes the content of Locke's *Letter* in his later work and mentions *only* the rationality argument. As Waldron puts it:

> The argument in the original *Letter* of 1689 had been that "true and saving religion consists in the inward persuasion of the mind.... And such is the nature of the understanding, that it cannot be compelled to the belief of anything by outward force.[79]

Notes

1. See Ch. 3 ("Premise (ii)").
2. Locke 1993a: 431. See also ibid.: 427, 428, 429.
3. Ibid.: 428. See also ibid.: 427, 429–30 and Ch. 3 (note 56). For Locke's similar claim in the *Essay*, see Ch. 3 (note 59).
4. See also Locke 2004a: 247.
5. See Ch. 1 (note 51). On "atheists", see Ch. 3 (note 69). See also Ch. 1 (notes 43–5), Ch. 2 (note 41) and Ch. 3 (notes 9 and 54). Locke engages in the same proscription of such doctrines in the *Essay* – see Locke 1993b: 188, 201.
6. Locke 1993a: 411, 420. Concerning Locke's last point in the passage that belief is not dependent on will, see also Ch. 2 (note 43), Ch. 3 (notes 24–6), Ch. 5 (notes 34 and 36) and note 50 below.
7. In this respect Locke, in the *Two Tracts*, assumed a clear and unproblematic demarcation between a realm of inner belief and an outward realm of "indifferent" religious actions subject to the magistrate's command. See Locke 1967a: 127–8, 129, 146, 164; 1967b: 214, 214–15, 216, 216–17, 218, 234–5, 238–9. See also Ch. 2 (note 23), Ch. 2 ("Locke, Liberty and the *Two Tracts*") and Ch. 3 (note 47). Concerning the magistrate's command over "things indifferent", see Ch.2 (note 20).
8. For Locke's advancement of this position in *An Essay Concerning Toleration*, see Ch. 2 (note 64). Indeed, Robert Kraynak argues that Locke comes to this new position, concerning the need for matters of worship to be acceptable to the individual conscience, quite early after the first *Tract*, in an essay entitled "Sacerdos", which Kraynak dates (following Locke's biographer, Peter King) at around 1661 (Kraynak 1980: 60).
9. Locke 1993a: 414. On "necessity" see also Ch. 2 (note 46).
10. Indeed, it could not be otherwise, since one of Locke's primary purposes in the *Two Tracts* was to limit the impact of individual consciences, and their contrary outcomes, upon civil society – see Locke 1967a: 137–40, 154, 155–6, 159–60, 161, 161–2, 167, 169, 170; 1967b: 211, 226–7, 237.
11. Ibid.: 222. See also Locke 1967a: 123, 124, 130, 135, 167–68, 175; Locke 1967b: 223, 229.
12. Ibid.: 227. See also Locke 1967a: 123, 124, 125, 156, 175; Locke 1967b: 227.
13. Locke 1993b: 189. See also Ch. 2 (note 64).
14. Locke 1993b: 190. See also Locke 1993a: 413; 2004b: 232–3 and 2004c: 276–7.
15. Locke 1993a: 412.
16. Ibid.: 394. See also ibid.: 395. We saw that Locke also affirmed the sanctity of individual conscience in the *Two Tracts* (see Ch. 2 note 43). But given that conscience, when outwardly expressed, was also perceived, in the *Two Tracts*, as a likely source of disorder (see Ch. 2 note 34), we see the importance of Locke's refutation of premise (i) (discussed in the previous chapter) which, once refuted, allowed him to perceive the outward expression of individual conscience as (largely) consistent with civil peace.
17. See Ch. 2 ("Locke's Shift") and Ch. 3 (note 11).
18. See Locke 1967b: 238. See also Ch. 2 (note 46).
19. On this hierarchy of law, see notes 11 and 12 above. See also Locke 1967b: 221–7; 1967a: 124 and 125.
20. On the contractual process of consent see Ch. 1 ("Consent, Legitimacy and Obligation" and "Consent, Legitimacy and Toleration").
21. We saw that one of the primary means by which such liberty limits itself is by individuals giving up to the magistrate, via the process of "compact", the executive authority they possessed, in the state of nature, to enforce natural law – see Ch. 1 (note 64).

22 See Introduction (note 21). On "separation" see Ch. 1 ("Separation of Church and State").
23 On the "appeal to heaven", see Ch. 1 (note 95). On Locke's right of resistance, see Ch. 1 (notes 90 and 92).
24 On realpolitik, see Ch. 1 ("Realpolitik").
25 See Ch. 2 (note 62).
26 Locke 1993a: 430. See also ibid.: 431.
27 Ibid.: 427. My additions.
28 For those who contrast toleration to "rights", see Mendus 1989: 8, 9, 15, 20, 55; Raphael 1988: 139; Heyd 2008: 175; Gray 2000: 324. For those who argue that toleration presumes a capacity, on the part of the tolerators, to reverse such toleration if they wish, see Ch. 1 (note 35).
29 Washington 2015.
30 Derrida 2003: 127–8.
31 Locke 1965: II § 87. On natural rights, see Introduction ("Theological Foundations").
32 Locke 1993a: 432. See also ibid.: 423, 424. In this respect I think Philip Abrams is in error when he declares that Locke does not endorse a right of resistance in the *Letter* (Abrams 1967: 103–4, 105–6).
33 See Ch. 1 (note 96).
34 See Ch. 5 (note 3).
35 On the influence of the *Letter*, see Gough 1948: xxxviii; Tully 1983: 11–12; Goldie 2010: xxii–xxiii.
36 Waldron 1988: 85.
37 See Introduction (notes 32–4).
38 See Ch. 1 (note 17).
39 For a more thorough demonstration of the incomplete nature of Waldron's reading of Locke's *Letter* than I am able to provide here, see Tate 2009: 762–78; 2010: 994–7, 999–1001.
40 Locke 1993a: 393. See also Waldron 1988: 62.
41 See ibid.: 61, 62, 65.
42 Ibid.: 61–2.
43 See note 41 above.
44 See Waldron 1988: 66, 67, 68, 76, 79–80, 81, 81–2. We saw Locke make the same case that belief is impervious to force as early as the *Two Tracts* – see Ch. 3 (notes 24–26). See also note 6 above.
45 Waldron 1988: 67. Waldron, in describing this "rationality argument", erroneously conflates it with a very different set of claims concerning "neutrality" – see Tate 2009: 764–6.
46 See Ch. 3 (note 20).
47 See Ch. 2 (notes 23 and 43) and Ch. 2 ("Locke, Liberty and the *Two Tracts*").
48 On the will, as distinct from "judgment", being vulnerable to coercion, see Ch. 2 ("Locke, Liberty and the *Two Tracts*"); Ch. 3 (notes 24–6).
49 See Ch. 5 (note 32). See also Ch. 5 (note 33).
50 Locke 1993a: 395. See also ibid.: 410, 411, 420; 1993b: 192–3, 204–5, 206, 207. Locke made the same point in the *Two Tracts* – see Ch. 3 (notes 24–6).
51 Max Weber "Politics as a Vocation". In H. Gerth and C. Wright Mills (eds) (1970) *From Max Weber: Essays in Sociology*. London: Routledge, p. 77, cited in Waldron 1988: 64.
52 Waldron 1988: 64. Waldron designates a "*modal* definition of the state" as one defined "in terms of its distinctive and characteristic means" (ibid.).
53 Ibid.: 65–6.
54 See Tate 2009: 775–7; 2010: 995–8.
55 Waldron claims that at "p. 91" Locke refers to the "functional definition" of the state, not as a premise of his argument but a conclusion – i.e. as "something

which in the course of his argument he has *proved*" (Waldron 1988: 66). This is in fact a misrepresentation of Locke's text. The relevant reference to "proof" that Locke makes on p. 91 of the edition of the *Letter* to which Waldron refers is: "We have already proved that the care of souls does not belong to the magistrate" (see Locke 1968: 91). Contrary to Waldron, this is not a statement suggesting Locke has "proved" the functional definition of the state "in the course of his argument" but simply a statement that the "care of souls" is not included in those functions.

56 Thus the references Waldron cites refer to Locke's description of the various "means" at the magistrate's disposal to enforce his command – all of which largely involve variations on physical and legal force – see Waldron 1988: 65. See also Tate 2009: 776.
57 See ibid; Tate 2010: 997.
58 See Ch. 1 ("Consent, Legitimacy and Obligation").
59 See Ch. 1 (note 85).
60 See Ch. 1 ("Consent, Legitimacy and Obligation" and "Consent, Legitimacy and Toleration").
61 On "civil" purposes, see Ch. 1 (notes 32, 33, 39, 40, 43–6, 82, 84, 85).
62 See Ch. 5 (notes 4, 5, 8 and 9). On how Waldron is mistaken both in his claim that only a "careless reader" would believe that Locke wanted "to define government in functional terms" (Waldron 1988: 66) and in his claim that such a "functional" account of the state "begs the question" as to why the state ought to be limited to specific ends, "at most" giving us "the *conclusion* we want to reach" but not helping us "to discharge the obligation to argue for that conclusion" (ibid.: 64), see Tate 2009: 776–7; 2010: 996–7. There were some isolated occasions when Waldron *almost* brought himself to acknowledge such "functionalist" features of Locke's political philosophy, not least the contractual processes Locke makes so much of in the *Two Treatises*, and which Locke also alludes to in the *Letter* (Waldron 1988: 74). But ultimately he does not do so (see Tate 2009: 784, note 39; 785–6, note 58). After all, any such acknowledgement would have identified Locke with a "functionalist" account of the state, and so would have undermined Waldron's ascription to Locke of a "modal account".
63 Waldron 1988: 64–5.
64 Ibid.: 66–7. See also ibid.: 67–8.
65 Ibid.: 76. See also ibid.: 70, 78.
66 See Mill 1971: 118–19, 124–9, 131.
67 Locke 2004a: 247. See also Introduction (note 20).
68 See note 2 above.
69 Susan Mendus adopts the same position as Waldron concerning the contrast between Locke and Mill, and I believe she is in error for the same reasons. See Mendus 1991: 150, 157; 1989: 27, 37. For a broader criticism of Mendus' interpretation of Locke, see Tate 2009: 778–80.
70 Mill 1971: 74.
71 On this "contractualist" account of the state, see Ch. 1 ("Consent, Legitimacy and Toleration").
72 Waldron 1988: 76. See also ibid.: 77.
73 Raz 1988: 2.
74 For others who believe Locke conceived of individual liberty, or "rights", in *residual* terms, as contingent upon what the magistrate is either unable to proscribe or chooses not to proscribe, see McCabe 1997: 252–3; Mendus 1991: 150, 159; Dunn 1991: 178; Vernon 1997: 50, 51.
75 Waldron 1988: 76–7.
76 Ibid.: 84–5.
77 Susan Mendus agrees with Waldron that Locke identified with the interests of persecutors within the *Letter* – see Mendus 1989: 27–8; 1991: 149, 150. For

my criticism of Mendus' interpretation of Locke in this respect, see Tate 2009: 778–80.
78 See Waldron 2002.
79 Ibid.: 210. For a critical evaluation of Waldron's very different account of Locke in this later work – and one which respectfully suggests that here too Waldron is in fundamental error – see Tate 2013.

References

Abrams, P. (1967) "Continuities: The 'Tracts' and Locke's Later Works". In: J. Locke *Two Tracts on Government*. P. Abrams (ed.). Cambridge: Cambridge University Press, pp. 84–107.

Derrida, J. (2003) "Autoimmunity: Real and Symbolic Suicides – A Dialogue with Jacques Derrida". In: Giovanna Borradori *Philosophy in a Time of Terror. Dialogues with Jürgen Habermas and Jacques Derrida*. Chicago: University of Chicago Press, pp. 85–136.

Dunn, J. (1991) "The Claim to Freedom of Conscience: Freedom of Speech, Freedom of Thought, Freedom of Worship?" In: O. P. Grell, J. I. Israel and N. Tyacke (eds) *From Persecution to Toleration. The Glorious Revolution and Religion in England*. Oxford: Clarendon Press, pp. 171–93.

Goldie, M. (2010) "Introduction". In: J. Locke *A Letter Concerning Toleration and Other Writings*. Indianapolis, IN: Liberty Fund, pp. ix–xxiii.

Gough, J. W. (1948) "Introduction". In: J. Locke *The Second Treatise of Civil Government and a Letter Concerning Toleration*. J. W. Gough (ed.). Oxford: Basil Blackwell, pp. vii–xxxvi.

Gray, J. (2000) "Pluralism and Toleration in Contemporary Political Philosophy", *Political Studies*, 48 (2): 323–3.

Heyd, D. (2008) "Is Toleration a Political Virtue?". In: M. S. Williams and J. Waldron (eds) *Toleration and its Limits*. New York: New York University Press, pp. 171–94.

Kraynak, R. P. (1980) "John Locke: From Absolutism to Toleration", *The American Political Science Review*, 74 (1): 53–69.

Locke, J. (1965) *Two Treatises of Government*. Peter Laslett (ed.). New York: New American Library.

Locke, J. (1967a) "First Tract on Government". In: J. Locke *Two Tracts on Government*. P. Abrams (ed.). Cambridge: Cambridge University Press, pp. 117–81.

Locke, J. (1967b) "Second Tract on Government: Translation". In: J. Locke *Two Tracts on Government*. P. Abrams (ed.). Cambridge: Cambridge University Press, pp. 210–41.

Locke, J. (1968) *Epistola de tolerantia. A Letter on Toleration*. R. Klibansky (ed.); J. W. Gough (trans.). Oxford: Clarendon Press.

Locke, J. (1993a) "A Letter Concerning Toleration". In: J. Locke *Political Writings*. David Wootton (ed.). London: Penguin, pp. 390–436.

Locke, J. (1993b) "An Essay Concerning Toleration". In: J. Locke *Political Writings*. David Wootton (ed.). London: Penguin, pp. 186–210.

Locke, J. (2004a) "Toleration B". In: J. Locke *Political Essays*. M. Goldie (ed.). Cambridge: Cambridge University Press, pp. 246–8.

Locke, J. (2004b) "Toleration A". In: J. Locke, *Political Essays*. M. Goldie (ed.). Cambridge: Cambridge University Press, pp. 230–5.

Locke, J. (2004c) "Toleration D". In: J. Locke *Political Essays*. M. Goldie (ed.). Cambridge: Cambridge University Press, pp. 276–7.

McCabe, D. (1997) "John Locke and the Argument Against Strict Separation", *The Review of Politics*, 59 (2): 233–58.

Mendus, S. (1989) *Toleration and the Limits of Liberalism*. London: Macmillan.

Mendus, S. (1991) "Locke: Toleration, Morality and Rationality". In: J. Horton and S. Mendus (eds) *John Locke: A Letter Concerning Toleration in Focus*. London: Routledge, pp. 147–62.

Mill, J. S. (1971) "On Liberty". In: J. S. Mill *Utilitarianism, Liberty, Representative Government*. London: Everyman's Library, pp. 61–170.

Raphael, D. D. (1988) "The Intolerable". In: S. Mendus (ed.) *Justifying Toleration. Conceptual and Historical Perspectives*. Cambridge: Cambridge University Press, pp. 137–53.

Raz, J. (1988) *The Morality of Freedom*. Oxford: Clarendon Press.

Tate, J. W. (2009) "Locke and Toleration: Defending Locke's Liberal Credentials", *Philosophy and Social Criticism*, 35 (7): 761–91.

Tate, J. W. (2010) "Locke, Rationality and Persecution", *Political Studies*, 58 (5): 988–1008.

Tate, J. W. (2013) "Dividing Locke from God: The Limits of Theology in Locke's Political Philosophy", *Philosophy and Social Criticism*, 39 (2): 133–64.

Tully, J. (1983) "Introduction". In: J. Locke, *A Letter Concerning Toleration*. J. Tully (ed.). Indianapolis, IN: Hackett Publishing Co.

Vernon, R. (1997) *The Career of Toleration. John Locke, Jonas Proast, and After*. Montreal: McGill-Queens University Press.

Waldron, J. (1988) "Locke: Toleration and the Rationality of Persecution". In: S. Mendus (ed.) *Justifying Toleration: Conceptual and Historical Perspectives*. Cambridge: Cambridge University Press, pp. 61–86.

Waldron, J. (2002) *God, Locke and Equality: Christian Foundations in Locke's Political Thought*. Cambridge: Cambridge University Press.

Washington. G. (2015) "GW's reply to the Hebrew congregation" (1790). In: *The Papers of George Washington*, at http://gwpapers.virginia.edu/documents/hebrew/reply.html (accessed May 2014).

5 Three "Considerations" for Toleration

Whereas the relationship between the *Two Tracts* and the *Essay* is primarily disjunctive, upholding, as they do, contrary positions on toleration, the *Essay* and the *Letter* are characterized by a significant degree of continuity. The primary point of difference, however, is that the *Letter* was written in 1685 (Richard Ashcraft extending its composition beyond this date).[1] This means that, if Peter Laslett and Richard Ashcraft's dating of the composition of the bulk of the *Two Treatises* is correct, the *Letter* was written after that text.[2] Unlike the *Essay*, therefore, the *Letter* can be read in the context of the wider framework of political philosophy that Locke advances in the *Two Treatises*. Richard Ashcraft contends that, at the time of the publication of the *Letter*, it was indeed read by Locke's contemporaries in this way – i.e. in conjunction with the *Two Treatises* – despite the fact that both texts were published anonymously: "Both [James] Tyrrell and William Molyneaux associated the *Letter on Toleration* with the *Two Treatises*, and in their view, this was a commonly held association."[3] This chapter will focus on the three primary "considerations" which Locke offers for toleration in the *A Letter Concerning Toleration* – what I have called the "truth argument", the "rationality argument" and the "consent argument". It begins by showing how Locke himself rejected the "modal" account of the state and its peculiar conception of state legitimacy, which Waldron seeks to ascribe to him and which we discussed in the preceding chapter. It then investigates each of Locke's three "considerations" for toleration, based on truth, rationality and consent, in turn.

Locke and the "Modal" Account of the State

We have seen in the previous chapter that the model of legitimacy that arises from a "modal" account of the state is one wherein the state is entitled to pursue any end for which it possesses the appropriate means. In this context, the legitimate scope of state authority is dependent entirely on the efficacy of the instruments at the state's disposal. We saw that Waldron ascribed such a model of legitimacy to Locke, at least as regards Locke's non-Christian discourse in the *Letter*. Locke in fact repudiated any such model of legitimacy, and explicitly so. As he put it in his debate with Proast, discussing the instruments at the state's disposal:

> For though it be a good argument; it is not useful, therefore not fit to be used; yet this will not be good logic; it is useful, therefore any one has a right to use it. For if the usefulness makes it lawful, it makes it lawful in any hands that can so apply it; and so private men may use it.[4]

In this passage, Locke specifically rejects the mode of reasoning that suggests that the efficacy of the means at the state's disposal – their capacity ("usefulness") to achieve their ends – determines either the legitimacy of these means ("a right to use it") or those ends themselves. Referring specifically to the "force" (or what Locke referred to in an earlier chapter as the "sword") at the state's disposal, Locke again rejects a "modal" justification of the use of such force:

> God has appointed force as useful or necessary, and therefore it is to be used; is a way of arguing, becoming the ignorance and humility of poor creatures. But I think force useful or necessary, and therefore it is to be used, has, methinks, a little too much presumption in it.[5]

In each of these passages, Locke denies any causal relationship between the usefulness of the means at the state's disposal, in terms of their capacity to achieve specific ends, and the legitimacy of those means or those ends themselves. For Locke, the relationship, giving rise to such legitimacy, is in fact the reverse. The use by the state of the means at its disposal depends, for its propriety, on the legitimacy of the ends to which those means are directed – i.e. whether these ends fall within the appropriate limits of state authority. It does not in any way depend on the capacity of those means to achieve these ends themselves (as in the "modal" account).[6] Whether a specific end falls within the appropriate limits of state authority is determined, for Locke, by the contractual process that gives rise to that authority in the first place – such a process, we have seen, ultimately arising from individual consent.[7] It is this consent which provides the "commission" for the state to pursue specific ends, and therefore bestows legitimacy on the means appropriate to achieve those ends. In the following passages, Locke explicitly contrasts such a contractual model of legitimacy to the "modal" account referred to above – an account which he again specifically rejects:

> [A]ny benefit attainable by force or natural power of a society, does not prove the society to be instituted for that end; till you also show, that those to whom the management of the force of the society is intrusted, are commissioned to use it to that end.[8]

And again:

> But suppose force, applied your way, were as useful for the promoting true religion, as I suppose I have showed it to be the contrary; it does not from hence follow that it is lawful and may be used ... because ... the magistrate has no commission or authority to do so.[9]

In these passages, Locke makes clear that, even if the state possesses means that are capable of achieving their ends, and are therefore "rational" for that purpose, this does not confer a legitimacy upon these means, or the ends to which they are directed, unless the state has been authorized to pursue such ends. Only then do such ends fall within the scope or "commission" of the magistrate's authority.[10]

The Truth Argument

In the *Letter Concerning Toleration*, Locke put forward three primary arguments for toleration – based, as we have seen, on "truth", "rationality" and "consent". At one point, all are offered consecutively, in one specific place, within the *Letter*.[11] Locke calls these his three "considerations" in favour of toleration.[12] It is these three "considerations" that then form the basis of Locke's engagement with Proast. It is to each of these three "considerations" – based on "truth", "rationality" and "consent" – that we now turn. The first that we shall consider in this section is the "truth argument".

Irrespective of the precise nature of Locke's religious beliefs, it is clear, from the content of the *Letter Concerning Toleration*, as well as Locke's more explicitly Christian texts, that he was a sincere Christian, who took religious belief seriously. As Locke declared in the *Letter*:

> Every man has an immortal soul, capable of eternal happiness or misery; whose happiness depending upon his believing and doing those things in this life which are necessary to the obtaining of God's favour, and are prescribed by God to that end, it follows from thence ... that the observance of these things is the highest obligation that lies upon mankind, and that our utmost care, application, and diligence ought to be exercised in the search and performance of them, because there is nothing in this world that is of any consideration in comparison with eternity.[13]

Locke's concern for the sanctity and integrity of religious belief informs each of his three "considerations" for toleration. Indeed, we shall see that it is clear from one of these "considerations", centred on "truth", that Locke accepted the basic Christian eschatology that the beliefs one holds in this life will determine one's eternal salvation in the next. It is open to question whether Locke believed the means of such salvation were exclusive – i.e. whether there was, as he puts it in the *Letter*, "but one truth, one way to heaven".[14] At a number of points, both in the *Letter* and in his debate with Proast, Locke indicates that this is indeed his view.[15] Yet, elsewhere in the *Letter*, he suggests that such an exclusive conception of salvation is merely an excuse for persecution, since "if there were several ways that lead thither, there would not be so much as a pretence left for compulsion".[16]

Irrespective of Locke's position on this, his "truth argument" for toleration, as presented in the *Letter*, depends on the exclusive proposition that that there is "but one truth, one way to heaven". Locke tells us that some have used such a proposition to justify "compelling men into this or the other way".[17] In the "truth argument", Locke uses this proposition to the opposite effect. He insists that, if there is but "one truth, one way to heaven", then the eternal consequences of our decisions on this matter are so dire, and opinion on it so divided, that choices regarding it should be left entirely to each individual, rather than to the magistrate whom we have no guarantee is any more in possession of this "truth" than we:

> Because there is but one way for me to escape death, will it therefore be safe for me to do whatsoever the magistrate ordains? Those things that every man ought sincerely to inquire into himself, and by meditation, study, search, and his own endeavours, attain the knowledge of, cannot be looked upon as the peculiar possession of any one sort of men. Princes indeed are born superior unto other men in power, but in nature equal. Neither the right nor the art of ruling does necessarily carry along with it the certain knowledge of other things, and least of all of the true religion.[18]

In this passage we see the role that scepticism plays in Locke's "truth argument" for toleration. Although Locke does not deny the reality of religious truth (i.e. a set of beliefs whose veracity, or otherwise, can affect our eternal salvation), he is sceptical of any individual's claim to possess knowledge of these "truths", and on this basis an entitlement to impose their opinions upon others. This is the point Locke makes against the magistrate in the passage above. He does so again as follows:

> The one only narrow way which leads to heaven is not better known to the magistrate than to private persons, and therefore I cannot safely take him for my guide, who may probably be as ignorant of the way as myself, and who certainly is less concerned for my salvation than I myself am.[19]

I have called this particular argument for toleration the "truth argument" because it rests not only on the assumption that such "truth" is necessary to our salvation, but also on Locke's scepticism concerning any individual or church's claim to have privileged access to this "truth". Indeed, in the

Letter, Locke refuses toleration to those churches or sects who, on the basis of such a claim, "arrogate to themselves, and to those of their own sect, some peculiar prerogative ... opposite to the civil right of the community", declaring, for instance, that "dominion is founded in grace" or "faith is not to be kept with heretics" or that "kings excommunicated forfeit their crowns and kingdoms".[20] In each case, Locke is not sceptical regarding religious truth itself. Rather, he is sceptical of individual claims to possess a knowledge of this truth. This is because Locke did not believe such knowledge, when it came to matters of revealed religion, to be possible, faith alone being available in such circumstances. It is this assumption that underwrites his scepticism on such matters. As he puts it to Proast:

> To you and me the Christian religion is the true, and that is built, to mention no other articles of it, on this, that Jesus Christ was put to death at Jerusalem, and rose again from the dead. Now do you or I know this? I do not ask with what assurance we believe it, for that in the highest degree not being knowledge, is not what we now inquire after. Can any magistrate demonstrate to himself, and if he can to himself, he does ill not to do it to others, not only all the articles of his church, but the fundamental ones of the Christian religion? For whatever is not capable of demonstration, as such remote matters of fact are not, is not, unless it be self-evident, capable to produce knowledge, how well grounded and great soever the assurance of faith may be wherewith it is received; but faith it is still, and not knowledge; persuasion, and not certainty. This is the highest the nature of the thing will permit us to go in matters of revealed religion, which are therefore called matters of faith: a persuasion of our own minds, short of knowledge, is the last result that determines us in such truths. It is all God requires in the Gospel for men to be saved.[21]

The "Truth Argument" Considered

We see therefore that underwriting Locke's "truth argument" is a scepticism – not concerning the reality of religious truth but rather concerning anybody's claim to possess knowledge of it. In *An Essay Concerning Human Understanding*, Locke suggests that we can have knowledge of the existence of God – based on a "natural theology".[22] But this is quite distinct from a knowledge of revealed religion and those "truths" necessary for eternal salvation ("true religion") – all of which, Locke declares, in the passage above, not to be possible, insisting instead that "faith" alone is all that is available in such matters.

Jeremy Waldron fails to perceive this scepticism at the heart of Locke's argument for toleration, instead insisting that Locke believed that knowledge of "true religion" was possible. In the passage below, Waldron begins by quoting the excerpt from the *Letter* which (at note 18 above) we have associated with Locke's "truth argument", and then declares that it reveals that Locke was not a sceptic regarding knowledge of "true religion" at all:

> "Princes are born superior in power, but in nature equal to other mortals. Neither the right nor the art of ruling carries with it the certain knowledge of other things, and least of all true religion. For if it were so, how does it come about that the lords of the earth differ so vastly in religious matters?..."
>
> But at most this is scepticism about the religious discernment of princes, not scepticism about religious matters as such. Locke maintains that 'a private man's study' is every bit as capable of revealing religious truth to him as the edicts of a magistrate.... So there are here certainly individualistic doubts about the abilities of princes; but none of these points is consistent with any more far-reaching doubts about truth or knowledge in matters of religion.[23]

Such a statement is entirely at odds with Locke's own discussion of faith and knowledge at note 21 above, where Locke denies the possibility of any knowledge of religious truth when it comes to matters of revealed religion. Waldron does concede that aspects of Locke's *Third Letter Concerning Toleration* appear to move in a sceptical direction.[24] But we have seen that Locke places scepticism at the heart of the "truth argument" from the time of the first *Letter* onwards, and it is this, along with the distinctive nature of the "truth argument" itself, that Waldron misses.[25]

In addition to scepticism concerning knowledge of "true religion" and a belief that there is "one truth, one way to heaven", Locke's "truth argument" for toleration is also underwritten by an assumption that the religious beliefs we hold in this life will determine our salvation in the next, with the result that our religious choices have eternal consequences. Without this theological assumption, the argument loses much of its force, since, in the absence of this eschatology, there would be much less at stake in any choice of religion, and so much less concern as to whether we or the magistrate chose this religion for us. Locke insists that, even if the magistrate may seem better informed on these matters, with the result that "the way to eternal life may be better known by a prince than by his subjects",[26] nevertheless given the eternal consequences of their decision, individuals should still decide their faith for themselves, as it is they who will have to bear the consequences of this choice, and the magistrate cannot compensate them if he or she is wrong:

> I would turn merchant upon the prince's command, because in case I should have ill-success in trade, he is abundantly able to make up my loss some other way.... But this is not the case, in the things that regard the life to come. If there I take a wrong course, if in that respect I am once undone, it is not in the magistrate's power to repair my loss,

to ease my suffering, or to restore me in any measure, much less entirely, to a good estate. What security can be given for the Kingdom of Heaven?[27]

Regarding the "truth argument" itself, it is questionable whether it is in fact a normative or a practical argument for toleration. After all, nothing could be more normative than the concern for individual salvation upon which the "truth argument" is based. Indeed, by upholding the liberty of the individual to make choices concerning their salvation, the "truth argument" is affirming premise (iii).

But it is our individual self-interest in salvation (and in particular our desire to avoid eternal damnation) that gives weight to the "truth argument". Does this self-interest make it a *practical* argument for toleration? I do not think so. After all, Locke makes clear that individuals have a direct interest in preserving their liberties from state intrusion and the "consent argument" (which *is* a normative argument for toleration) is premised precisely on this interest. If we assume that the desire for eternal salvation is a normative ideal, then the "truth argument" is indeed a normative argument for toleration.

Pitfalls of the "Truth Argument"

However for our purposes, what is significant about the "truth argument" is that it is *not* an effective argument for toleration at all. After all, toleration, insofar as it involves the magistrate, is a state policy. The outcome of that policy is that individuals are entitled, within limits, to freely express their religious beliefs and practices without intrusion by the state. Short of revolution, any argument for toleration, if it is to be effective, must therefore be capable of convincing state authorities that toleration is the preferred policy that the state should adopt for regulating religious differences, in preference to other policies such as enforced religious conformity. Such arguments might convince on practical grounds, insisting that toleration is the best way for the state to ensure civil peace and effective governance in a context of religious diversity. They may convince on normative grounds, persuading state authorities that they ought to adopt a policy of toleration in order to guarantee the religious liberties of the individuals subject to their jurisdiction. But in either case, it is the state authorities that must be convinced if toleration is to be adopted as state policy.

Yet it is precisely such a capacity to convince state authorities that the "truth argument" lacks. As we saw, central to the "truth argument" was the assumption that we should never trust the magistrate with our salvation because we cannot be guaranteed that the magistrate knows the "one truth, one way to heaven". Yet while such scepticism concerning the magistrate's "truth" provides a good reason why we should resist the magistrate's attempt to impose his or her religion on us, it does not in any way undermine the magistrate's own confidence or interest in doing so, Locke telling us that "the religion of every prince is orthodox to himself".[28] The "truth argument" is therefore an argument whose potency arises from the interest of those subject to the magistrate's command in ensuring their eternal life, and so resisting the magistrate's attempt to intrude upon their religion. It is *not* an argument that addresses magistrates' own assurances about their own religion or their desire to impose this religion by force.

Consequently, if magistrates wish to impose their religion on those subject to their command for the sake of salvationist ends, the "truth argument" will not be able to convince them otherwise. Equally, if they seek to impose outward religious conformity for the sake of secular ends (e.g. the "civil peace" that Locke seeks to achieve in the *Two Tracts*) then the "truth argument" will be equally impotent because the question of religious "truth" or its absence (i.e. the scepticism at the centre of the "truth argument") is likely to be irrelevant to such secular concerns. In this way, we see the inherent shortcomings of the "truth argument" as a justification of toleration.[29]

"Truth" vs. "Rationality"

What the discussion so far should have made apparent is the extent to which the "truth argument" for toleration is categorically distinct from the "rationality argument". Of course, there are some immediate affinities. Both are underwritten by theological concerns – one centred on our inability to know the "one truth, one way to heaven", the other on the fact that only sincere and genuine belief is pleasing to God and capable of achieving salvation. But along with these affinities, there are distinct differences. First, whereas the "rationality argument" is based on subjective and empirical concerns, centred on the sincerity or genuineness with which religious belief is held, and the material incapacity of the magistrate to impose this belief by force, the "truth argument" is based on veridical concerns, centred on the question of which religion is the "one truth, one way to heaven". The latter is quite distinct from any subjective concern regarding the genuineness or sincerity with which belief in such "truth" is held, since it concerns the salvationist question of whether a particular "truth" really is the truth endorsed by God. It is only if we understand "truth" in this veridical sense that Locke's injunction, at the centre of the "truth argument", not to trust the magistrate with our salvation, makes sense.

The second way in which the "truth argument" is categorically distinct from the "rationality argument" concerns their respective capacities to convince the magistrate. The "rationality argument", if effective, is capable of convincing magistrates that their own ends will be confounded if they attempt to coerce religious belief by force, because force is futile for such purposes. The argument therefore focuses on the magistrate's own interests, not least their concern with the "rationality" of their own actions, showing how these will be not be served by using force in matters of religion. In contrast, the "truth argument", we have seen, is incapable of convincing magistrates to refrain from religious coercion at all. It is, however, a persuasive argument why those subject to the magistrate's command should resist any attempt on the part of the magistrate to impose religion by force.

The final reason why the "truth argument" is categorically distinct from the "rationality argument" resides in the fact that Locke, within the *Letter*, insists that the "truth argument" applies as an argument for toleration even when the "rationality argument" does not. This is so when he declares, at the beginning of the following passage, that even if force *was* an effective means of instilling sincere and genuine religious belief (thereby overturning the conditions of the "rationality argument") this would still not justify religious coercion or persecution (at least from the perspective of those subject to such force) because there is no guarantee that the belief instilled by such force is the "one truth, one way to heaven". In other words, even when the conditions of the "rationality argument" are overturned, Locke insists that the conditions of the "truth argument" still apply as a case for toleration:

> [T]he care of the salvation of men's souls cannot belong to the magistrate, because, *though the rigour of laws and the force of penalties were capable to convince and change men's minds*, yet would not that help at all to the salvation of their souls. For their being but one truth, one way to heaven, what hopes is there that more men would be led into it, if they had no other rule to follow but the religion of the court, and were put under a necessity to quit the light of their own reason; to oppose the dictates of their own consciences; and blindly to resign up themselves to the will of their governors, and to the religion which either ignorance, ambition, or superstition had chanced to establish in the countries where they were born?[30]

In this passage, Locke renders the "rationality argument" *subsidiary* to the "truth argument", since he is declaring that the "truth argument" applies as a case for toleration even when the "rationality argument" does not. In this respect, he makes clear that the "truth argument" and the "rationality argument" are categorically distinct. Locke makes the same point in response to Proast, insisting that if force were capable of achieving its ends, so that the conditions of the "rationality argument" were undermined, what we have called the "truth" and "consent" arguments would still apply as a case for toleration

> [A]llowing that even force could work upon them, and magistrates had authority to use it in religion, then the argument you mention is not "the only one in that letter, of strength to prove the necessity of toleration".... For the argument of the unfitness of force to convince men's minds being quite taken away, either of the other would be a strong proof for toleration.[31]

The fact that Locke renders the "rationality argument" subsidiary to his other two "considerations" for toleration shows that, contrary to Waldron, Locke did not perceive the "rationality argument" as the "main line of argument" he offered for toleration in the *Letter*. The other confirmation of this occurs in Locke's debate with Proast, where Locke concedes that the two primary conditions upon which the "rationality argument" relies for its cogency are unlikely to apply in practice. The first condition concerns the propensity of magistrates to use force to instil sincere and genuine religious belief, the second concerns the efficacy of their doing so. Regarding the first condition, Locke admits (in the passage below) that the magistrate is unlikely to use force as a means to such ends. This undermines one condition of the "rationality argument" because it was the magistrate's use of force to instil sincere and genuine religious belief which provided the basis for the "irrationality" of such action (such belief being unable to be instilled by force), thereby identifying toleration as a viable alternative. Locke, in his debate with Proast, denies that magistrates are likely to use force for such purposes, instead insisting that they are likely to use it only to impose outward conformity in matters of religion:

> I think those who make laws, and use force, to bring men to church-conformity in religion, seek only the compliance, but concern themselves not for the conviction of those they punish; and so never use force to convince.... So that this exception of yours, of the "use of force, instead of arguments, to convince men", I think is needless; those who use it, not being, that ever I heard, concerned that men should be convinced.[32]

The other condition of the "rationality argument" concerned the presumed *incapacity* of force to instil sincere and genuine religious belief, thereby ensuring that all those who used force for such purposes would be engaging in irrational action. Locke denies this condition by conceding to Proast that there may be times when force, applied "indirectly" and "at a distance", might be capable of instilling sincere belief.[33] We will discuss this concession further in later chapters. However, by conceding that there may be circumstances in which force *is* capable of achieving such ends, Locke is admitting that a primary condition of the "rationality argument" may not apply in practice.

If neither of these two conditions of the "rationality argument" applies, it no longer provides a cogent case for toleration. It is in this respect that Locke, in his debate with Proast, effectively abandons the "rationality argument" and, as he points out at note 31 above, relies on his two other "considerations" for toleration in its absence.

The Rationality Argument

Yet for all its *subsidiary* and *conditional* status, Locke did advance, in the *Letter*, something akin to what we have called the "rationality argument". As he puts it:

> [T]he care of souls cannot belong to the civil magistrate, because his power consists only in outward force; but true and saving religion consists in the inward persuasion of the mind, without which nothing can be acceptable to God. And such is the nature of the understanding that it cannot be compelled to the belief of anything by outward force. Confiscation of estate, imprisonment, torments, nothing of that nature can have any such efficacy as to make men change the inward judgement that they have framed of things.[34]

Here Locke advances the fundamental proposition, central to the "rationality argument", that the use of force is incapable of instilling the sincere and genuine religious belief "acceptable to God" and therefore necessary for salvation. Locke advances this same "rationality argument" elsewhere within the *Letter* and also earlier in the *Essay*.[35] Indeed, as early as the *Two Tracts*, Locke had acknowledged that force is unable to affect inner belief, because such belief is not subject to the will but rather to the understanding.[36] Yet this was consistent with his claim in that text that outward religious behaviour could be subject to force, because such behaviour, unlike belief, was a product of individual choice (and therefore the will) and "an outward conformity", independent of belief, was "all that is here required".[37] By the time of the *Essay*, however, we have seen that Locke extends the realm of individual liberty to outward religious behaviour as well, thereby rendering such behaviour a manifestation of belief.[38]

The "rationality argument" is a distinctly *practical*, rather than *normative*, argument for toleration. This is because the "rationality" of the means at the magistrate's disposal is thoroughly dependent on the ends which the magistrate seeks to pursue, and the capacity of these means to achieve these ends. If the magistrate seeks to use means, such as force, to achieve ends (such as the inculcation of sincere and genuine belief) which force is unable to achieve, then force is "irrational" as a means to this end, and the rationality argument applies. But if, as Waldron points out, the magistrate seeks to use force for other ends – perhaps "Hobbesian ends of public order" – and seeks to impinge upon religion for this reason, then (as Locke believed in the *Two Tracts*) such a use of force might be "rational", because able to achieve its ends (sincere and genuine belief being irrelevant to such purposes).[39] The result is that, as with other practical arguments for toleration, the "rationality argument" is dependent, for its cogency, on a number of empirical circumstances, all of which are entirely contingent and subject to change.

The Consent Argument

We have already made reference to the conditions surrounding Locke's "consent argument", including the conditions underwriting it, when we discussed, in Chapter 1, Locke's conception of the origins of civil society and government, arising from the consent of individuals.[40] We also made reference to these conditions when we referred, at the beginning of this chapter, to the "authorization" or "commission" which Locke believes government receives from those who establish it and who are subject to its jurisdiction, limiting this jurisdiction to specific purposes.[41] Such "authorization" or "commission", Locke argues, arises from individual consent.[42] In all these respects, Locke perceives "consent" as a basic source of political legitimacy within civil society, limiting governments to specific ends, thereby rendering other ends open to the liberty of the individual.[43]

The editor of Locke's *Two Tracts on Government*, Philip Abrams, has argued that it is with Locke's appeal to individual consent, as a source of legitimacy for political authority, as well as a limit upon that authority, that we begin the transition from the early Locke of the *Two Tracts* to the more mature political philosopher associated with what ultimately came to be known as the liberal tradition.[44] Others, such as John Dunn, have been much more circumspect concerning the role of consent in Locke's political philosophy.[45] Timothy Stanton has gone further, arguing that "consent" plays very little role in Locke's political philosophy, indeed declaring that it is not an independent source of obligation or authority for Locke at all because "insufficient to imbue what was done with authority", unable to act as a "self-originating source of valid claims" and "not logically correlated" to the origins, ends or legitimacy of government.[46] In my journal exchange with Stanton, I have sought to refute such claims, insisting on the centrality of consent to Locke's political philosophy.[47] I also sought to demonstrate this in Chapter 1, seeking to show how consent, for Locke, by linking the origins of government, and the purposes for which it was established, with the ends it is legitimately entitled to pursue, imposed limits on its authority.[48] In this way, it was shown, Locke's consent was crucial to reconciling individual liberty with political authority, since individuals, according to Locke, were only obligated to obey political authority which, arising from consent, was perceived as legitimate.[49]

The "consent argument" for toleration is intimately connected to this wider issue of legitimacy. In Chapter 1, we saw that Locke believed government was established, and elicited the consent of the governed, solely for "civil" purposes.[50] For Locke, we have seen, civil purposes refer primarily to the material interests of individuals.[51] It was for the protection of these, Locke tells us, that individuals sought to escape the depredations of the state of nature in favour of the comparative security of civil society and government.[52] In the *Two Treatises*, Locke refers to these material interests, in broad terms, as our "Lives, Liberties and Estates".[53] In the *Letter Concerning Toleration*, he is much more specific:

> The commonwealth seems to me to be a society of men constituted only for the procuring, preserving, and advancing of their own civil interests. Civil interests I call life, liberty, health, and indolency of body; and the possession of outward things, such as money, lands, houses, furniture, and the like. It is the duty of the civil magistrate, by the impartial execution of equal laws, to secure unto all the people in general, and to every one of his subjects in particular, the just possession of these things belonging to this life.[54]

By explicitly confining the purposes of government, and the limits of its authority, to "civil" concerns centred on those "things belonging to this life", Locke reserves to individuals the religious concerns "belonging to the next". In this respect, Locke is able to insist that when it comes to the latter, "[e]very one ... must be judge for himself", so that each "must be left to their own consciences".[55] The upshot for government, Locke insists, is that religious ends are excluded from its jurisdiction, with the result that it must not intrude upon "men's souls". As Locke puts it: "We have already proved that the care of souls does not belong to the magistrate.... The care, therefore, of every man's soul belongs unto himself, and is to be left unto himself."[56] Consequently, we see how Locke's idea of consent, as a limit on the authority of government, and therefore a limit upon the ends which government might legitimately pursue, acts as a source of religious toleration for individuals. By declaring that individuals have never consented to governments intruding upon their religious lives, Locke insists that religion is excluded from the jurisdiction of government, with the result that governments must leave individuals alone in matters of religion.[57] Toleration consists in this "leaving alone". Locke makes explicit reference to this process in the *Letter* as follows:

> [T]he care of souls is not committed to the civil magistrate, any more than to other men. It is not committed unto him, I say, by God; because it appears not that God has ever given any such authority to one man over another as to compel anyone to his religion. Nor can any such power be vested in the magistrate by the consent of the people, because no man can so far abandon the care of his own salvation as blindly to leave it to the choice of any other, whether prince or subject, to prescribe to him what faith or worship he shall embrace. For no man can, if he would, conform his faith to the dictates of another. All the life and power of true religion consists in the inward and full persuasion of the mind; and faith is not faith without believing.[58]

It is in this passage that Locke provides, within the *Letter*, his most explicit articulation of the "consent argument". Within this passage, Locke refers, just as in the "rationality argument", to the necessity of "sincere" and "genuine" belief ("inward and full persuasion of the mind") and also to the assumption of the "truth argument" that we cannot leave our "own salvation ... to the choice of any other". But it is the elements of the passage that concern the authority of the magistrate, and the "consent" from whence such authority derives, which is fundamental to the "consent argument", since it is this process which, we have seen, limits the jurisdiction of government to the purposes for which it was established, thereby leaving other matters to the liberty of the individual. To this end, Locke declares:

> Nothing can "in reason be reckoned amongst the ends of any society", but what may in reason be supposed to be designed by those who enter into it.[59]

We have seen that Locke makes the same link in the *Letter* between the origins of government, the purposes for which it was established, and the ends it is legitimately entitled to pursue.[60] He does so again in the *Essay* when he states that "what was the end of erecting of government ought alone to be the measure of its proceeding".[61] It is upon this link that the "consent argument" is based, since it is premised on the assumption that, since no individuals would "consent" to governments having an authority over their own religious beliefs and practices, these matters are excluded from the jurisdiction of governments, because they could not be among the purposes for which governments are established.[62]

The "Three Considerations"

Like the "truth argument", Locke's "consent argument" for toleration is categorically distinct from the "rationality argument". This is because, in confining the magistrate's jurisdiction to "civil" matters, the "consent argument" excludes from that jurisdiction any concern, on the part of the magistrate, with the inculcation of "sincere" and "genuine" religious belief – a concern which, we have seen, lies at the heart of the "rationality argument". In this respect, by excluding the very condition which the "rationality argument" presupposes for its existence, we can see that the "consent argument" is not only categorically distinct from the "rationality argument", but also inconsistent with it.

Further, we can see how different, in other respects, is the "consent argument" from both the "truth" and "rationality" arguments. Far from being premised on the need for individuals to ensure their eternal salvation ("truth argument") or the fact that governments possess "means" insufficient to achieve their ends ("rationality argument"), the "consent argument" is premised on the normative right of individuals to obey only that government authority to which they or their predecessors have given their consent.[63] Individual liberty therefore lies at the foundations of the "consent argument", as does the equal right of individuals to this liberty, as expressed in their equal entitlement to withhold or bestow consent.[64] In this respect, the "consent argument" upholds premise (iii), and is a *normative* as distinct from a *practical* argument for toleration.

Notes

1. On Ashcraft, see Ch. 2 (note 1).
2. Laslett and Ashcraft date the bulk of the composition of the *Two Treatises* to either the period of the Exclusion Crisis (1679–80) (Laslett) or the years 1681–82 in the wake of Charles II's Oxford Parliament and the lead up to the Rye House Plot (Ashcraft). See Laslett 1965: 74–75; Ashcraft 1980: 431, 436, 438–47.
3. Ashcraft 1986: 476n.
4. Locke 1963a: 80.
5. Ibid.: 85. This is a specific response to Proast's attempt, in his first response to Locke, to premise the "lawfulness" (i.e. legitimacy) of "means" on their usefulness in achieving ends (Proast 1999a: 31–2). For other places in his debate with Proast where Locke insists that the "usefulness" of means in achieving a specific end does not give rise to any "lawfulness" in their use, see Locke 1963a: 69, 80, 82, 85, 112–13, 113–14, 119–22, 134; Locke 1963b: 162. In his second response to Locke, Proast insists that he premised the "lawfulness" of "means" not only on their "usefulness" but also on their "necessity" in achieving specific ends (such as salvation) (Proast 1999b: 56). Locke responds by insisting that only God knows what is "necessary" for ends such as salvation (Locke 1963b: 162); that Proast is unable to categorically prove any specific means as "necessary" to such ends (ibid.: 165, 166, 169, 300, 331, 495–6); and even if "necessary", means are not "lawful" unless those that wield them have a "commission" to do so (see ibid.: 164 and note 9 below).
6. See note 5 above.
7. See Ch. 1 ("Consent, Legitimacy and Obligation" and "Consent, Legitimacy and Toleration").
8. Locke 1963b: 218. See also ibid.: 214.
9. Locke 1963a: 80. For Locke's other references to the necessity of "commission" as a source of legitimacy, see ibid.: 80, 112, 113, 119, 120, 120–1, 121–2, 126, 134; Locke 1963b: 164, 166–7, 169.
10. Yet one must not assume that just because an end is legitimate, *any* means are justified if they are capable of achieving it. This would suppose a Machiavellian process of ends justifying means. Locke rejects such an implication by use of a medical analogy: "Running a man through may save his life, as it has done by chance, opening a lurking imposthume. But will you say, therefore, that this is lawful, justifiable chirurgery?" (Locke 1963a: 69). In other words, just as Locke rejects a "modal" account which ascribes a legitimacy to ends on the basis of (efficacious) means, so he rejects a Machiavellian account which ascribes a legitimacy to (efficacious) means on the basis of their (legitimate) ends.
11. See Locke 1993a: 394–6.
12. Ibid.: 394, 396.
13. Ibid.: 421. At times, even Leo Strauss seems to have accepted that Locke was a sincere Christian – see Strauss 1959: 202, 207, 208.
14. Locke 1993a: 396.
15. See ibid.: 407, 408. See also Locke 1963a: 133; 1963b: 320, 326, 327, 328, 332–3, 356, 422; and also Ch. 9 (notes 9 and 68).
16. Locke 1993a: 406. Locke, at one point, provides a definition of "true religion", but one that capaciously, and circularly, defines "true religion" and "salvation" in terms of each other:

> For that, and that alone, is the one only true religion, without which nobody can be saved, and which is enough for the salvation of every one who embraces it. And therefore whatever is less or more than this, is not the only true religion.
>
> (Locke 1963b: 422)

17 Locke 1993a: 406. Certainly such an allegation applies to Jonas Proast. See Proast 1999b: 42, 46–7, 48–51, 59, 60.
18 Locke 1993a: 407. See also ibid.: 396. Locke makes the same point in *An Essay Concerning Toleration* – Locke 1993b: 188.
19 Locke 1993a: 408.
20 See Ch. 1 (notes 44 and 51).
21 Locke 1963b: 144. See also ibid.: 402, 422, 424 and Ch. 9 (note 38). I would tentatively suggest that Locke's scepticism in this passage is of an Academic rather than Pyrrhonist kind. Richard Popkin, referring to these two types of scepticism, defines Academic scepticism (deriving from Plato's Athenian Academy) as a belief that no knowledge is possible, and Pyrrhonist scepticism (deriving from the ancient Greek philosopher, Pyrrho of Elis) as a belief that we lack sufficient evidence to determine if any knowledge is possible, and so we should suspend all judgment concerning questions of knowledge (Popkin 1960: ix–x). The passage in the main text clearly shows that Locke believes that *no* knowledge of revealed religion is possible (at least as regards Christianity), thereby aligning him, on this question, with Academic scepticism.
22 As Locke puts it: "the knowledge of a GOD, be the most natural discovery of humane Reason" (Locke 1975: Bk. I, ch. iv, § 17, p. 95). See also Locke 2004: 278–9. For a broader discussion, including why Locke believes competing and contrasting conceptions of God arise, despite this natural propensity towards knowledge of Him, see Tate 2013: 152–3.
23 Waldron 1988: 70–1.
24 Ibid.: 72.
25 Indeed, Waldron fails to make any distinction between what we have called Locke's "truth" and "rationality" arguments at all, simply coupling "truth" with "sincere" and "genuine" belief as one more thing that the magistrate cannot coerce by force – thereby subsuming Locke's references to "truth" within the *Letter* to the "rationality argument", and failing to see how the "truth argument" is a categorically distinct argument for toleration on its own (see ibid.: 80–1). For a more comprehensive development of this point, see Tate 2009: 767–8.
26 Locke 1993a: 407.
27 Ibid.: 407–8.
28 Ibid.: 416.
29 I have discussed these shortcomings of the "truth argument" at Tate 2009: 768, 2010: 992.
30 Locke 1993a: 395–6. Emphasis added.
31 Locke 1963a: 67. See ibid.: 80, 111–12. See also Ch. 8 (note 45).
32 Locke 1963a: 73. See ibid.: 99.
33 See ibid.: 67–8, 69, 69–70, 77, 78. However, Locke insists that, although force may at times, "indirectly" and "at a distance", be useful in instilling sincere belief, the preponderant weight of evidence is that in most cases it will be harmful to this end (ibid.: 78–9). Hence Locke, in addressing Proast, refers to "your indirect and at a distance usefulness, which amounts but to the shadow and possibility of usefulness, but with an overwhelming balancing weight of mischief and harm annexed to it" (ibid.: 79–80).
34 Locke 1993a: 395. Locke advances a similar argument in *An Essay Concerning Toleration* – Locke 1993b: 189, 204–5.
35 See Ch. 4 (note 50).
36 See Ch. 3 (notes 24–6). See also Ch. 4 (note 50).
37 See Ch. 3 (notes 20 and 26).
38 See Ch. 2 ("Locke's Shift"). See also Ch. 4 ("The *Normative* Discourse of the *Letter*") where outward religious behaviour is also presented as a manifestation of inner belief.

39 For Waldron, see Ch. 4 (note 72).
40 See Ch. 1 ("Consent, Legitimacy and Obligation").
41 See notes 8 and 9 above.
42 See Ch. 1 ("Consent, Legitimacy and Obligation").
43 See Ch. 1 (notes 52, 67 and 72–6).
44 Abrams 1967: 91.
45 See Dunn 1980: 30–2.
46 Stanton 2011: 20, 21.
47 See Tate 2012: 227 (note 8); 2015: 7–8, 12 (note 8).
48 See Ch. 1 ("Consent, Legitimacy and Obligation" and "Consent, Legitimacy and Toleration").
49 See Ch. 1 (notes 72–4).
50 See Ch. 1 (notes 32, 33, 39, 40, 82, 84, 85) and note 54 below.
51 See Ch. 1 (note 40) and note 54 below.
52 See Ch 1 (notes 17 and 54).
53 Locke 1965: II § 123. See also ibid.: II, § 87, 171, 222.
54 Locke 1993a: 393–4. See also Ch. 1 (note 40).
55 Locke 1963a: 89; 1993a: 410. See also Ch. 1 (notes 25, 29 and 40).
56 Locke 1993a: 405–6.
57 See Ch. 1 (notes 75 and 76).
58 Locke 1993a: 394.
59 Locke 1963a: 119. See also ibid.: 121. Similarly, Locke declared in an earlier chapter: "[I]n all societies instituted by man, the ends of them can be no other than what the institutors appointed" (Ch. 1 note 76. See also Ch. 1 note 72 and Ch. 8 note 52).
60 See Ch. 1 (note 85).
61 Locke 1993b: 186.
62 See Ch. 1 (notes 75 and 76).
63 See Ch. 1 (notes 52 and 67). Locke is able to move beyond the problem that only the original contractarians might have given their "express" consent to government by referring to "tacit consent" – the consent individuals can be presumed to have given to government if they derive benefits from the effective governance and civil peace it ensures (see Locke 1965: II § 119. See also Ch.1 (note 70).
64 See Ch. 1 (note 67). See also Ch. 1 ("Consent, Legitimacy and Obligation").

References

Abrams, P. (1967) "Continuities: The 'Tracts' and Locke's Later Works". In: J. Locke *Two Tracts on Government*. Cambridge: Cambridge University Press, pp. 84–111.
Ashcraft, R. (1980) "Revolutionary Politics and Locke's *Two Treatises of Government*: Radicalism and Lockean Political Theory", *Political Theory*, 8 (4): 429–86.
Ashcraft, R. (1986) *Revolutionary Politics and Locke's Two Treatises of Government*. Princeton, NJ: Princeton University Press.
Dunn, J. (1980) "Consent in the Political Theory of John Locke". In: J. Dunn *Political Obligation in its Historical Context. Essays in Political Theory*. Cambridge: Cambridge University Press: pp. 29–52.
Laslett, P. (1965) "Introduction". In: J. Locke *Two Treatises of Government*. Peter Laslett (ed.). New York: New American Library, pp. 15–148.
Locke, J. (1963a) "A Second Letter Concerning Toleration". In: J. Locke *The Works of John Locke*. Vol. VI. Aalen: Scientia Verlag, pp. 61–137.

Locke, J. (1963b) "A Third Letter for Toleration". In: J. Locke *The Works of John Locke*. Vol. VI. Aalen: Scientia Verlag, pp. 141–546.

Locke, J. (1965) *Two Treatises of Government*. Peter Laslett (ed.). New York: New American Library.

Locke, J. (1975) *An Essay Concerning Human Understanding*. P. H. Nidditch (ed.). Oxford: Oxford University Press.

Locke, J. (1993a) "A Letter Concerning Toleration". In: J. Locke *Political Writings*. David Wootton (ed.). London: Penguin, pp. 390–436.

Locke, J. (1993b) "An Essay Concerning Toleration". In: J. Locke *Political Writings*. David Wootton (ed.). London: Penguin: pp. 186–210.

Locke, J. (2004) "Religion". In: J. Locke *Political Essays*. M. Goldie (ed.). Cambridge: Cambridge University Press, pp. 278–80.

Popkin, R. (1960) *The History of Scepticism from Erasmus to Descartes*. Rev. ed. Assen: Van Gorcum & Comp.

Proast, J. (1999a) "The Argument of the Letter Concerning Toleration, Briefly Consider'd and Answer'd". In: M. Goldie (ed.) *The Reception of Locke's Politics, Vol. 5. The Church, Dissent and Religious Toleration 1689–1773*. London: Pickering and Chatto, pp. 25–37.

Proast, J. (1999b) "A Third Letter Concerning Toleration: In Defense of the Argument of the Letter Concerning Toleration, Briefly Consider'd and Answer'd". In: M. Goldie (ed.) *The Reception of Locke's Politics. Vol. 5. The Church, Dissent and Religious Toleration, 1689–1773*. London: Pickering & Chatto, pp. 41–116.

Stanton, T. (2011) "Authority and Freedom in the Interpretation of Locke's Political Theory", *Political Theory*, 39 (1): 6–30.

Strauss, L. (1959) "Locke's Doctrine of Natural Law". In: L. Strauss *What is Political Philosophy and Other Studies*. Glencoe, IL: The Free Press, pp. 197–220.

Tate, J. W. (2009) "Locke and Toleration: Defending Locke's Liberal Credentials", *Philosophy and Social Criticism*, 35 (7): 761–91.

Tate, J. W. (2010) "Locke, Rationality and Persecution", *Political Studies*, 58 (5): 988–1008.

Tate, J. W. (2012) "Locke, God and Civil Society: Response to Stanton", *Political Theory*, 40 (2): 222–8.

Tate, J. W. (2013) "Dividing Locke from God: The Limits of Theology in Locke's Political Philosophy", *Philosophy and Social Criticism*, 39 (2): 133–64.

Tate, J. W. (2015) "Locke, Toleration and Natural Law: A Reassessment", *European Journal of Political Theory*, published on the journal's "early view" website in "Online First" on 8 November 2015. DOI: 10.1177/1474885115609739. Available at: http://ept.sagepub.com/content/early/2015/11/04/1474885115609739.abstract.

Waldron, J. (1988) "Locke: Toleration and the Rationality of Persecution". In: S. Mendus (ed.) *Justifying Toleration: Conceptual and Historical Perspectives*. Cambridge: Cambridge University Press, pp. 61–86.

6 Locke vs. Proast

A Letter Concerning Toleration, when published anonymously in 1689, caused an immense stir. The reason why there was such speculation concerning the identity of the author was precisely because of the impact of the text and the rigorous way in which it engaged with the most salient issues of religious toleration prevalent at that time. The English translation, published by William Popple in 1689, elicited two responses in quick succession from individuals holding official positions within the Anglican Church. The first response was delivered in 1689 by Thomas Long, Archdeacon of Exeter, and the second in 1690 by Jonas Proast, a former Chaplain of All Souls College, Oxford.[1] Only Proast's response elicited a reply from Locke, and they exchanged two letters each between 1690 and 1692. This was followed by a long hiatus, after which Proast published a third, much shorter, letter in 1704, to which Locke responded with a reply that was unfinished at the time of his death in 1704. Locke maintained the fiction, throughout their engagement, that he was unaware of the identity of the author of the *A Letter Concerning Toleration*. Regarding the long hiatus in the Locke/Proast debate, and their final encounter in 1704, Mark Goldie states:

> Proast had been struck silent by Locke's massive *Third Letter for Toleration* of 1692 (it is 405 pages long in the 1801 edition of the *Works*). His brief and belated response came in 1704, after he was publicly goaded into a further reply. The anonymous author of *A Just and Impartial Character of the Clergy*, a latitudinarian tract which emphasised the moderation of modern Anglican churchmen, claimed that he knew of no work which "calmly and deliberately maintained, that 'twas lawful and proper, to punish men meerly for not conforming to the laws and customs of our church" – "unless it be a small discourse, in answer to a letter concerning toleration", the author of which, he had heard, had now "upon further reflexion, given up, and quitted" his view. Proast had not quitted his view, though his final reply to Locke only tackles remarks made in the opening pages of the *Third Letter for Toleration*.[2]

Indeed, regarding Locke and Proast's final exchange, Mark Goldie sees very little in it. He declares that although the political circumstances surrounding toleration had changed much by the time of the ascension of Queen Anne in 1702, with Tories seeking to limit toleration for Dissenters by passing legislation outlawing "occasional conformity", neither Locke or Proast "had anything new to say".[3]

This is by no means true. New ground was broken in Locke and Proast's final exchange. For instance, whereas in his first response to Locke, Proast claimed that what we have called the "rationality argument" constituted the "whole Strength" of Locke's argument for toleration,[4] in his third and final response, Proast shifts position. He insists that Locke now places the "greatest Strength" of his argument on a very different proposition – this being that if one magistrate is entitled to advance his or her religion by force, simply on the grounds that he or she is persuaded it is the "true religion", then all magistrates are so entitled, because indubitable knowledge of "true religion" being unobtainable, each magistrate's "faith" is equal in this regard.[5] Such a proposition places the question of knowledge of "true religion" at the centre of Locke and Proast's exchange, and it is in his final response to Locke that Proast offers a criterion by which, he insists, such knowledge can be obtained – what he calls a "third sort or degree of Perswasion" which, he says, only arises in the case of "true religion".[6] Locke responds to this claim in his *Fourth Letter For Toleration*. We shall discuss this "third sort or degree of Perswasion" further below, but for the moment, what the above suffices to show is that, contrary to Mark Goldie, Locke and Proast did break new ground in their final exchange of letters on toleration.

The Revolution of 1688

In order to understand the Locke/Proast debate, it is important to situate Proast's response to Locke's *A Letter Concerning Toleration* in terms of the circumstances prevalent within England at this time. The year before the publication of Locke's *Letter* had been the year of England's "Glorious Revolution" (1688), a time when both Whigs and Tories had temporarily united to oust James II from the English throne and invite William of Orange, and his wife Mary, to replace him as Protestant monarchs. In 1689, Parliament enshrined this revolutionary settlement in legislation, among which was a *Toleration Act* and a *Bill of Rights*. The first of these statutes sought to devise a religious settlement giving greater toleration to Dissenters worshipping outside the confines of the Church of England; the second sought to give greater authority to Parliament in its dealings with the Crown.[7] While James, during his reign, had offered toleration to Dissenters in the hope of dividing them from the Anglicans who opposed him, it was his Catholicism which alienated both Anglicans and Dissenters alike.[8] Religion was therefore at the centre of the Revolution of 1688 and its settlement afterward, as was the relative authority of Crown and Parliament.

Yet, while the Revolution of 1688 had involved a certain measure of unity between Whigs and Tories in order to achieve its ends, the same unity did not characterize the revolutionary settlement which followed. From the perspective of High Church Tories, traditionally committed to the ideal of royal as distinct from parliamentary supremacy, their relationship to the Revolution itself was exceptional, because at odds with their deepest commitments to the Crown. Many justified their revolutionary actions within their own minds only by the very specific and exigent circumstances of James's reign.[9] Indeed, in the wake of the Revolution, six bishops and "over four hundred of the lower clergy" found that, in conscience, they could not swear an oath of allegiance to William and Mary as ruling monarchs (as distinct from "regents"), it being at odds with the previous oath that they had sworn to James. They therefore became "nonjurors" and were deprived of their positions within the Church.[10]

Yet it was the religious settlement, arising once James had been ousted, that many High Church Tories saw as moving away from the principles for which they had stood in 1688. John Miller describes their outlook, even before the passage of the key statutes of the revolutionary settlement, as follows:

> It was one thing to build a common Protestant front against James. It was quite another to find oneself saddled with a foreign Calvinist king who favoured Dissenters, [and] distrusted High Churchmen.... Anxious Anglicans blamed William for the destruction of the episcopal church in Scotland, although it is doubtful whether he could have prevented it, and feared that the same would happen to the Church of England.[11]

This belief that the Revolution, having been won, was now moving in an excessively Whig direction – not least towards the toleration of Dissenters – aroused the ire of some High Church Tories. After all, in many cases, these individuals had fought the Revolution of 1688 in order to preserve the Restoration settlement of the 1660s, in which the persecution of Dissent was central, not do away with that settlement in favour of a new one embracing toleration of such Dissent.[12] Certainly one can surmise that Thomas Long, the archdeacon of Exeter who penned the first public response to Locke's *Letter*, was of such a view, seeing the Restoration settlement as under threat from the new revolutionary settlement after 1688, with its statutory toleration of dissenters in the *Toleration Act*. Mark Goldie has described Long's motives in responding to Locke's *Letter* in these terms as follows:

> Long (1621–1707), prebendary of Exeter, was a savage polemicist against the Protestant Dissenters, a type of the High Tory ideologists who dominated public debate in the 1670s and 1680s.... Long assumes that the anonymous author of *A Letter Concerning Toleration* is a spokesman for the Dissenters and a fanatical extremist within

that camp. His riposte is a tirade against sectarianism and schism, licentiousness and heresy. He includes the familiar Anglican charge that toleration of Protestant sects is a Trojan horse for Catholicism. The bulk of his tract is taken up with showing that the Presbyterians, who now begged for toleration, themselves had preached intolerance in their heyday during the revolutionary 1640s, when they tried to withstand the spread of the more radical Puritan sects. Long goes on to cite the most venerable Christian authority on behalf of coercive religious discipline, St. Augustine, who grounded his strictures against the Donatist schism upon an explication of Christ's words, "compel them to come in". Long's tract appeared a few months after the passage of the Toleration Act, which he plainly found distasteful. He alludes to it, speaking of the recent "condescensions" to the Dissenters. For a generation afterwards High Churchmen fought a rearguard action against the advent of Protestant pluralism.[13]

Jonas Proast was also among these "High Churchmen" to whom Goldie refers in the passage above. Referring to Proast, Goldie describes the politics of this sort of Anglican churchman, particularly those holding positions, as Proast once did, within the universities, as follows:

In politics they inclined to absolutism, though protective of the Church. In ecclesiology, they remained imbued with a militant desire to destroy the Dissenters. Their time of triumph was the period 1681–5, when they set about achieving a purified Anglican and Tory polity, and when an unprecedentedly savage onslaught upon the Dissenters was undertaken.[14]

Indeed, one indication of Proast's outlook is evident in his exchange with Locke, where Proast quite openly expresses his horror regarding the period, prior to Charles II's Restoration, in which Puritanism was in the ascendant and the Anglican Church under siege:

The *Toleration* the *Fruits* whereof I say *give no encouragement to hope for any advantage from* our Author's *Toleration, to true Religion,* is that (as I thought you would easily have guess'd) which almost all, but those of the Church of *England,* enjoyed in the times of the *Blessed Reformation,* as it was call'd. And for the *Fruits* of it, *viz.* the *Sects* and *Heresies* which it produced (*some of which* I say *still remain with us*) how numerous, and of what quality they were, some yet living remember, and the Writers of those times do sufficiently discover.[15]

Given his opposition to toleration during the Interregnum, Proast was equally opposed to its resurgence in 1689, however limited was the toleration accorded to Dissenters in the *Toleration Act*.[16] As Goldie tells us, "Proast was a defender of the regime of religious uniformity that ended decisively with the passage of the Toleration Act in 1689, and a spokesman for those Tories who deplored the Act."[17]

In their respective responses to Locke's *Letter*, both Long and Proast can therefore be understood as part of that "rearguard action against the advent of Protestant pluralism" in which, Goldie tells us at note 13 above, "High Churchmen" engaged in the wake of the *Toleration Act*. Indeed Locke, at one point in his debate with Proast, makes oblique reference to this recent religious settlement in England, and Proast's apparent attitude to it, when he states in his *Third Letter*: "For you seem not well satisfied with what the magistrates have lately done, without your leave, concerning religion in England."[18]

Locke and Proast

Locke did not respond to Long's criticism of the *Letter*. Instead he responded to Proast. The explanation for this, according to Mark Goldie, resides in the small world of Oxford University and Anglican Church politics in the immediate pre- and post-revolutionary years. In the wake of the Revolution of 1688 and its settlement, the Anglican authorities, having excluded Dissenters from the established church by resisting comprehension within the Church of England, found themselves immersed in an internal struggle between the High Church faction of the Anglican Church, which had orchestrated this exclusion, and an emergent wing of increasingly rationalist Latitudinarians, more willing to adopt a broad, moderate and more inclusive view of the Church and its principles.[19] Thus, "[t]he opposition to High churchmen within the Church of England thus consisted partly of old-style Puritans and partly of new-style Latitudinarians".[20] Goldie argues that Locke, in his engagement with Proast, represented the Latitudinarian interest in this divide, while Proast represented the High Church faction. Their clash, according to Goldie, therefore reflected a wider struggle between competing factions within the Church of England in the immediate aftermath of 1688. As Goldie puts it:

> Jonas Proast was not an isolated target. In assaulting him, Locke placed himself firmly amid the developing quarrel between High and Low Church factions within the established Church. He publicly associated himself with the Latitudinarian wing, and more particularly with the circle of John Tillotson, archbishop of Canterbury from 1691 to 1694.... In Locke's contest with Proast, the crucial polarity was not between Anglicanism and Dissent, but between the High Church ideals of the deposed Archbishop William Sancroft, and a new type of churchmanship which sought to seize the pastoral initiative in the aftermath of the Act of Toleration. If Tillotson was to make headway, then the squadron of Oxford theologians who provided the doctrinal backbone to Sancroft's church and to whom Proast was adjutant, had to be defeated. In this task Locke was Tillotson's servant.[21]

Goldie adds to this specific contextualization of the Locke/Proast debate by pointing to particular grievances which, he says, Proast had against the new Anglican Church regime established by John Tillotson and supported by Locke. This concerned Proast's desire for reinstatement as chaplain of All Souls College, Oxford. He had been expelled in 1688 by the warden of the college for his role in a university election in which he had opposed the candidacy of the warden, a man, it was widely recognised, who was a client of James II.[22] Goldie presents Proast as one of those High Churchmen, referred to above, who saw themselves as having valiantly opposed the depredations of James, in the name of the Restoration settlement and its ideals, but yet found the post-revolutionary regime moving away from these ideals in whose name they had been willing to sacrifice so much.[23] As Goldie describes the conception such men had of their own position: "they had heroically withstood King James, but were cast aside when James was vanquished".[24] The result, Goldie says, is that "Proast's defiant stand is symptomatic of the reluctance of High-Churchmen to accept the Toleration Act of 1689, and of the persistence of Restoration orthodoxies".[25]

Pitfalls

Mark Goldie provides a very useful service to Locke scholarship in offering this contextual background to the Locke/Proast debate. In particular, Goldie points out that, in stressing Locke's association with Latitudinarian bishops who wielded immense power within the Church of England in the aftermath of 1688, he is countering the idea that "Locke's natural home was amongst Dissenters and sectaries, amid Puritan rebels" rather than amidst the post-revolutionary Anglican elite.[26]

But I think in seeking to contextualize the Locke/Proast debate in terms of the immediate church politics of the post-Revolution years, and the recent history of All Souls, Goldie misses the broader set of interests, and the wider agenda, in terms of which Locke and Proast confronted each other in the 1690s. To insist, as Goldie does, that the exchange between Locke and Proast can be explained in terms of the respective political agendas of different factions among the Anglican elite in the post-1688 environment is to reduce the compass of the debate to very narrow terms, and above all to fail to recognize how the issues within the debate arose primarily from the content of Locke's original *Letter*, which, in being penned by Locke in 1685–86, was written before the Revolution of 1688 and so before the appointment of Archbishop Tillotson to the Canterbury Diocese and the internal Anglican politics to which, Goldie says, this gave rise. For this reason, neither the origins of Locke and Proast's exchange, nor its implications and consequences, can be reduced to the limited circumstances to which Goldie refers, nor can Locke's role in the debate be confined to the narrow purview implied by Goldie's declaration that Locke, in his confrontation with Proast, acted as Archbishop Tillotson's "servant".[27]

Indeed, this is not the only shortcoming in Goldie's account of the Locke/Proast debate. One other key claim he makes in that account is even more problematic. Goldie quotes a letter from Locke to Philip van Limborch who, as we saw in Chapter 1, was the addressee of the first *Letter Concerning Toleration*. In this letter, dated 2 June 1692, Locke says he is "impatient to see" a forthcoming work of Limborch's, which he does not mention by name but which Goldie tells us is Limborch's *Historia Inquisitionis*, which, Goldie says, Limborch wrote on the basis of his discovery of the records of the thirteenth-century Inquisition in Toulouse.[28] Goldie then quotes Locke, in the letter to Limborch, as stating that "those who do not love and promote Christian liberty as is right" nevertheless seek to distance themselves from the "monstrous cruelty of the Holy Office".[29] In reference to this statement, and without offering any additional evidence, Goldie immediately declares: "Locke plainly had Proast in mind here" – the reason being, Goldie says, that Locke, in his engagement with Proast, "wanted to show that Anglican persecution was but a branch and remnant of popery".[30] It is on the basis of this highly circumstantial claim that Goldie then arrives at his definitive conclusion, which again follows immediately – that Locke's "*Third Letter* was intended to be thought of as an addendum to Limborch's great indictment of Romish persecution".[31]

The *Third Letter For Toleration*, as reprinted in Locke's ten volume *Works*, is 406 pages long – very long for an "addendum" in anyone's estimation. But my point is that Goldie arrives at this conclusion concerning this very substantial and complex text on the basis of very little substantiation of his own. As we have seen above, he simply provides a single quotation from Locke's letter to Limborch (at note 29 above) in which Locke refers to those who are not in favour of Christian liberty (i.e. who practice persecution), but who at the same time wish to distance themselves from the Holy Office, and on the basis of this excerpt, declares that Locke "plainly had Proast in mind". However nowhere in Locke's letter to Limborch does Locke mention Proast or his debate with him – the presence of either of which might have given some substance to Goldie's claim.[32] The bulk of the letter concerns Locke's tardiness in writing to Limborch, the dearth of learning in Locke's locale given the presence of war, the health of the Limborch family and references to their mutual friends.[33] The quote at note 29 above, upon which Goldie bases his conclusions, arises solely from what Locke says is his "impatience" to read Limborch's forthcoming work, given its "profitability" to the "Christian world".[34] There is no basis, given the content of the quote at note 29, or the letter from which it arises, for Goldie's conclusion that Locke, in his references to "Christian liberty" and the "Holy Office", "plainly had Proast in mind", nor Goldie's wider claim that Locke wrote the letter to Limborch "in terms which show that he linked the publication of the *Historia* with his own impending *Third Letter*".[35] Further, nowhere in the third *Letter For Toleration* itself does Locke mention Limborch or the *Historia*

Inquisitionis, which would be quite extraordinary if the *Letter* really was an "addendum" to Limborch's text, as Goldie claims. In all these respects, therefore, Goldie's declaration that the third *Letter* was intended by Locke to be "an addendum to Limborch's great indictment of Romish persecution" is entirely lacking in confirmation, there being no evidence advanced by Goldie capable of supporting this conclusion.

The only other link Goldie seeks to make between Limborch's work and the third *Letter* is equally tenuous. This is the coincidental fact that Limborch's work discusses "popish cruelties", while "a central theme in Locke's *Letters* was the moral, and almost the physical, equivalence between the English repression of Dissent and the contemporary archetype of popish persecution, Louis XIV's attack on the Huguenots".[36] This parallel is intended by Goldie not simply to reveal an affinity between the two texts in terms of subject matter, but, again, is used to support Goldie's much more robust proposition that the relation between these two texts is a causal one – the third *Letter* being written by Locke as an "addendum" to Limborch's *Historia Inquisitionis*. Once again, the evidence advanced by Goldie – the coincidental fact that each text refers to Catholic persecution – establishes no such thing.

We saw in the introduction to this book that Quentin Skinner insisted on the need to situate texts within the specific circumstances of their own time and place if we are to understand their content aright, and this is certainly what Goldie seeks to do in his account of Locke's third *Letter* above. But surely the conclusions reached via such a process, concerning lines of influence and intent, must be based on at least some semblance of evidence arising from the texts or the circumstances themselves. The evidence that Goldie presents above falls short in this regard. Far from being an "addendum" to a work by Limborch, Locke's third *Letter* is a refutation, almost line by line, of Proast's second *Letter*, which in turn is a reply to Locke's second *Letter*, which in turn responds to Proast's first *Letter*, which itself sought to respond to Locke's original *Letter Concerning Toleration*. Most of this correspondence preceded Locke's letter to Limborch in which, Goldie tells us, Locke makes indirect reference to the *Historia Inquisitionis*. It is this wider sequence of engagements, stretching back some years to an original text written in 1685–86, rather than an entirely unstated concern with Limborch's *Historia Inquisitionis*, which informs the content of Locke's third *Letter*.

"*Indirectly* and *At a Distance*"

The range of Locke and Proast's disagreement is wide. But one of the fundamental points at issue between them is whether "force" ought to be used by the magistrate as a means to advance religion among those subject to the magistrate's command. Such force is, of course, absolutely inconsistent with toleration, which requires that the magistrate leave individuals alone to make their own decisions on such matters. We have seen that Locke, in the *Letter*, provides three "considerations" (along with a range of biblical arguments) why the magistrate ought to eschew such force and embrace a policy of toleration in its place. Proast, by contrast, claimed to have found means of force which, when applied "indirectly" and "at a distance" by the magistrate, could lead individuals toward "sincere" and "genuine" religious belief and so aid in their salvation.[37]

Proast concedes to Locke that "*Belief is to be wrought in men by Reason and Argument, not by outward Force and Compulsion*".[38] He therefore concedes Locke's claim that "Penalties, or Force is *absolutely impertinent in this case, because it is not proper to convince the Mind*".[39] However he then distinguishes his own position, stating:

> though Force be not proper to *convince the Mind*, yet it is not *absolutely impertinent in this case*, because it may ... do some service towards the bringing men to embrace the Truth which must save them, by bringing them to *consider those Reasons and Arguments which are proper to convince the Mind, and which without being forced, they would not consider*.[40]

To this end, Proast insists, in the passage below, that the use of force, applied by the magistrate, not directly, but "*indirectly* and *at a distance*", may have these beneficial effects, with the result that the use of force is able to assist in the advancement of "true religion" and individual salvation:

> *But notwithstanding this, if Force be used, not in stead of Reason and Arguments, i.e.* not to convince by its own proper Efficacy (which it cannot do), but onely to bring men to consider those Reasons and Arguments which are proper and sufficient to convince them, but which, without being forced, they would not consider: who can deny, but that *indirectly* and *at a distance*, it does some service toward the bringing men to embrace that Truth, which otherwise, either through Carelessness and Negligence they would never acquaint themselves with, or through Prejudice they would reject and condemn unheard, under the notion of Errour?[41]

On this basis, Proast concludes:

> And by this we see how little of Truth there is in the ... *Proposition* ... That *all outward Force is utterly useless for the promoting True Religion and the Salvation of Souls*. For if Force so applied as is above mentioned, may, in such sort as has been said, be serviceable to the bringing men to receive and embrace Truth; there can be no reason assigned, why this should not hold with respect to the Truths of Religion, as well as with respect to any other Truths whatsoever.[42]

Proast's advocacy of the magistrate's use of force for religious ends is quite distinct from the sort of advocacy that Locke himself engaged in within the

Two Tracts on Government. In that early text, Locke advocated the use of force only to ensure outward conformity to the magistrate's religion.[43] Locke made quite clear that such conformity was not meant to impinge on the inner liberty of belief – the magistrate's command, in this respect, only imposing itself upon the will, not the judgment, of individuals.[44] Locke was not concerned, therefore, in the *Two Tracts*, with the "sincerity" or "genuineness" with which individuals adhered to their religious beliefs, only that their outward behaviour conformed to the magistrate's command, and so was consistent with civil peace.

Proast, on the other hand, eschews all such practical political concerns. He does not seek to advance a particular religion because it is consistent with civil peace, but rather because it is "true", and so a means to salvation. As he puts it: "All therefore that is here requisite to be considered for the clearing this matter, is, Whether there be any *need* of outward Force, for the bringing men to the True Religion, and so to Salvation."[45] Consequently, unlike Locke in the *Two Tracts*, Proast is concerned with the "sincerity" and "genuineness" with which religious belief is held, because this (along with the "truth" of religion) is what is necessary for salvation. As he writes:

> [T]he Authority of the Magistrate is not an Authority to compel any one to his Religion, but onely an Authority to procure all his Subjects the means of Discovering the Way of Salvation.[46]

It is this salvation which, in Proast's mind, justifies the magistrate's use of indirect force. "True religion", therefore, performs a crucial role of legitimation for Proast, since from Proast's perspective, force is only justified, on the magistrate's part, if it leads to the "promoting True Religion and the Salvation of Souls".[47]

Proast and Restoration England

Mark Goldie has pointed out how Proast's propositions above, concerning the use of force in matters of religion, fall within one of three distinct arguments for religious persecution which were present within Restoration England. Of these three, one is an insistence that Dissenters ought to be repressed because (given recent English political history) they are a potential source of sedition; the other is an argument (advanced by Locke in the *Two Tracts*) that the magistrate, for the sake of "order and decency in divine worship", ought to have authority over "things indifferent" in matters of religion.[48] The third, advanced by Proast above, is based on the distinction, already discussed by Locke in the *Two Tracts*, between the will and the understanding.[49] The will, it was assumed, was coercible by force whereas the understanding was not.[50] Proast's argument (anticipated, Goldie tells us, by many Anglican divines throughout the Restoration period) is that if the will is directed (via the use of force) to attend to the

"Reasons and Arguments" for religious "truth", then the "understanding" may eventually come to embrace such "truth" voluntarily and of its own accord.[51] In this respect, Goldie calls Proast's discourse "the sharpest formulation of a ubiquitous Restoration argument".[52]

The important point to note, for our purposes, is that, of the three Restoration arguments for religious coercion identified by Goldie, only the argument advanced by Proast has, as a basis for its justification, the idea that force ought to be applied for the sake of "true religion", and therefore individual salvation. The argument based on sedition justifies force not on the grounds of "true religion", but on the grounds that sedition is thereby avoided; while the "things indifferent" referred to in the second argument are "indifferent" precisely because they are not linked to any religious "truths", and so are not necessary for salvation at all.

Consequently, the argument wielded by Proast must assume that force, applied by the magistrate "indirectly and at a distance", to "bring men to consider those Reasons and Arguments which are proper and sufficient to convince them", is justified only if those "Reasons and Arguments" lead individuals to "true religion". It is for this reason that "true religion" performs such a crucial role of legitimation for Proast and why the question of whether knowledge of such "true religion" is possible occupies such a central position in the Locke/Proast debate. Indeed, throughout his debate with Locke, Proast continually insists that he justifies the use of force only in those instances where force is used to serve the advancement of the "one true Religion".[53]

Indeed, so central is the proposition that there is "one true Religion" to the position Proast seeks to advance, and that it is possible to *know* which religion this is, that he declares that an inability to affirm either of these propositions results in his entire "Cause" being conceded to Locke, and his case for the use of force in matters of religion being abandoned:

> Indeed if either of the two Principles but now mention'd, be true, *i.e.*, if all Religions be equally *true*, and so *indifferent*; or all be equally *certain* (or *uncertain*): then without more adoe, the Cause is yours. For then, 'tis plain, there can be no reason why any man, in respect to his Salvation, should change his Religion: and so there can be no room for using any manner of Force, to bring men to consider what may reasonably move them to change.[54]

Waldron, Goldie and Dunn

Jeremy Waldron, in his account of Locke's *Letters Concerning Toleration*, argued that Locke failed to provide a case for toleration able to "dissuade someone here and now from actions of intolerance and persecution".[55] One of the primary bases upon which Waldron arrived at this conclusion was his belief that Locke had failed to offer an adequate response to Proast's claim to have found means of force which, when applied "indirectly" and "at a distance", were capable of leading individuals toward "sincere" and "genuine" religious belief.[56] In failing to provide an adequate response to this claim, Waldron insists, Locke had failed to defend his "rationality argument" in favour of toleration. The "rationality argument" had insisted that the magistrate should adopt a policy of toleration in the context of religious diversity because force was "useless" as a means to instil sincere belief. Because Proast claimed to have found a type of force which was "useful" in such a context, and Locke, according to Waldron, had provided no refutation of this claim, Waldron insisted that Proast's claims were conclusive against Locke:

> Proast had conceded Locke's point that beliefs could not be imposed or modified directly by coercive means, but he insisted that force applied "indirectly and at a distance" might be of some service in concentrating the minds of recalcitrants and getting religious deviants to reflect on the content of the orthodox faith. Force may be unable to inculcate truth directly, but it may remove the main obstacles to the reception of the truth, namely "negligence" and "prejudice". Despite the enormous amount of ink that he devoted to his response, Locke failed to provide any adequate answer to this point.[57]

Locke's failure to defend his "rationality argument", Waldron insists, leaves him with only a "pragmatic" argument in defence of toleration, based on the material circumstances in which force, when applied, might fail to achieve its ends.[58] By contrast, Waldron says, Locke's "case in principle" against the use of force in matters of religion – a case which, Waldron says, depended on "the claim that religious belief cannot be secured by the coercive means characteristic of state action"[59] – has "collapsed".[60] Waldron therefore concludes:

> It is impossible ... to agree with J. D. Mabbott that Locke provides a "complete and effective" response to Proast's critique. On the contrary, the response he provides completely and effectively demolishes the substance of his position. I do not see any other way of reconstructing Locke's argument to meet the criticisms that I have outlined.[61]

Waldron comes to the same conclusions concerning the Locke/Proast debate in his subsequent book on Locke.[62]

Once again, Waldron can only arrive at such conclusions as a result of his erroneous belief that the "rationality argument" is the only non-biblical argument that Locke offers for toleration in the *Letter*. Because this is the only argument he believes Locke offers, Waldron assumes that once Proast refutes this argument, by showing that force can have an efficacious impact on belief, Locke has only the pragmatic argument, referred to above, or the *Letter's* biblical arguments, to fall back on in defence of toleration. But we have seen that Locke offers "three considerations" for toleration in the

Letter, and effectively abandons the "rationality argument" (the argument to which Waldron refers) in the face of Proast's critique, on the grounds that the conditions underwriting this argument are unlikely to apply in practice.[63] Locke then insists that his other arguments for toleration will apply in its place.[64] Once again, it is only Waldron's incomplete reading of the *Letter*, and his inadequate understanding of Locke's subsequent engagement with Proast, that allows him to assume that, in refuting the "rationality argument", Proast's case is conclusive against Locke.

Waldron is joined, in his account of the Locke/Proast debate, by Mark Goldie and John Dunn. Like Waldron, John Dunn insists that Locke's "case" for toleration "rests on the empirical claim that it is impossible to change men's beliefs by coercion", so that "sincere" and "genuine" religious belief can never arise by these means.[65] In other words, like Waldron, Dunn appears to be of the view, outlined in the passage below, that Locke's entire non-biblical case for toleration, which he advances against Proast, "rests" on what we have called Locke's "rationality argument". Thus, referring to the claim that "[i]ndividual religious behaviour ... is necessarily defined by subjective conviction [and] [s]uch conviction cannot in principle be generated by governmental action", Dunn declares:

> This claim was at the heart of Locke's controversy with Jonas Proast.... Proast argues throughout that religious establishments do over a period of time exert a causal influence on the religious beliefs of those subject to them. As Locke repeatedly complains, [Proast] is often slightly disingenuous in his discussion of the means which they may employ to further this end. But the argument, if crudely positivist, is not a weak one and Locke handles it pretty feebly. *His case rests on the empirical claim that it is impossible to change men's beliefs by coercion. But he also wishes to argue as a sort of logical truth that it is a defining characteristic of a religious belief that it be not the product of human coercion.* The falsity of the first of these claims becomes increasingly obvious and the force of the second has diminished with the lower status accorded to religious beliefs in the contemporary world. Hence it has become difficult to see why Locke found his own argument so convincing. But in the historical context the first was a plausible extrapolation from the religious and political history of England over the preceding thirty years and the second is almost the central axis of Locke's own distinctive development of Puritan religious individualism.[66]

This passage makes clear that Dunn, like Waldron, believes that Locke's entire (non-biblical) case for toleration "rests" on the incapacity of force to affect individual belief (the "rationality argument"), Dunn insisting, in the passage above, that this proposition constitutes the "heart" of Locke's "controversy" with Proast. In offering this assessment of Locke's case for toleration, and his debate with Proast, Dunn is just as remiss as Waldron in failing to perceive how so much of each depend, for Locke, not on the alleged incapacity of force to generate sincere religious belief (a point which, we have seen, Locke concedes to Proast early in their engagement[67]) but on the categorically distinct questions of the entitlement ("commission") of the magistrate to use force for such purposes ("consent argument") and the inability of the magistrate to guarantee that such force is used for the sake of "true religion" ("truth argument").[68] In other words, Dunn, like Waldron, misses what, for Locke, are the central points at issue in his engagement with Proast and which, we shall see, he advances at length in that debate.

Mark Goldie arrives at the same truncated conception of the Locke/Proast debate as Waldron and Dunn, insisting that the debate is conducted on a "narrow front", centred, once again, on the issue central to the "rationality argument" – the capacity of force to instil "sincere" and "genuine" belief, or what Goldie calls the "efficacy of coercion on behalf of 'true religion' ".[69] As Goldie puts it:

> The debate between the two men was conducted on an apparently narrow front. No general theory of toleration was at issue. The topic was the efficacy of coercion on behalf of "true religion". Reliable knowledge of the "true religion" was taken as the starting point: what was contested was whether the civil magistrate could or should use physical pressure to bring people to that religion.[70]

With all due respect to Professor Goldie, it would be difficult to find a more mistaken account of the Locke/Proast debate expressed in such succinct terms. In the first place, as mentioned, Goldie repeats in this passage the error of Waldron and Dunn, concerning their Procrustean attempt to reduce the Locke/Proast debate to the efficacy of force in matters of religion. In the second place, "[r]eliable knowledge of the 'true religion' " was *not* "taken as the starting point" of this debate. Indeed, quite the contrary was the case. We saw that one of the three "considerations" Locke advanced for toleration in the *Letter* – what we have called the "truth argument" – was based on the assumption that no such "reliable knowledge" was available at all, leading Locke to the conclusion that we should not trust another with the means to our own salvation.[71] Further, we saw in the previous chapter that Locke made clear to Proast his belief that, in matters of revealed religion, "faith", but not "knowledge", is all that is available to individuals, with the result that, although he acknowledges that there may be "one true religion", he insists we have no means of determining which religion is "true".[72]

Indeed, far from "[r]eliable knowledge of the 'true religion' " being "taken as the starting point", it is on this question that Locke and Proast are most profoundly at odds. For instance, we have seen, repeatedly, that Proast justified the use of force, by the magistrate, solely on the grounds that such force would be used to advance the "true religion".[73] Such "truth" implied knowledge. Proast is quite explicit that it is because knowledge of "true religion" *is* possible, that the use of force that seeks its advancement is capable of being justified. As Proast puts it:

> [I]f ... there be one true Religion, and no more; and that may be known to be the onely true religion by those who are of it; and may by them to be manifested to others, in such sort as has been said: then 'tis altogether as plain, that it may be very reasonable and necessary for some men to change their Religion; and that it may be made to them to be so. And then if such men will not consider what is offer'd, to convince them of the Reasonableness and Necessity of doing it; it may be very fit and reasonable, for any thing you have said to the contrary, in order to the bringing them to Consideration, to require them under convenient Penalties, to forsake their false Religions, and to embrace the true. Now as these things are all that I need to *suppose*; so I shall take leave to suppose them, till you shew good reason why I should not.[74]

The cogency of Proast's entire position, therefore, rests on the assumption that knowledge of "true religion" is possible. Indeed, so much is this the case that, as we saw above, Proast declared to Locke that the "Cause is yours" if such knowledge is not possible.[75]

"Third Sort or Degree of Perswasion"

In his third response to Locke, Proast sought to provide some account of how such knowledge of "true religion" is possible. He denied Locke's strict distinction between faith and knowledge in matters of revealed religion, advanced in the previous chapter, in which Locke insisted that only faith was possible in such circumstances.[76] Instead, he insisted that there is a "third sort or degree of Perswasion", which arises in the case of "true religion" and "true religion" only, which amounts to "Full Assurance" or "Knowledge" of its truth, thereby distinguishing "true religion" from all other religions on this basis. As Proast states:

> [T]here is a third sort or degree of Perswasion, which though not grounded upon strict Demonstration, yet, in Firmness and Stability, does far exceed that which is built upon slight appearances of Probability; being grounded upon such clear and solid Proof, as leaves no reasonable Doubt in an attentive and unbyas'd mind: So that it approaches very near to that which is produced by Demonstration, and is therefore, as it respects Religion, very frequently and familiarly call'd in Scripture, not *Faith*, or *Belief* only, but *Knowledge*.... Now this kind of Perswasion, this *Knowledge*, this *Full Assurance* men may and ought to have of the True Religion: but they can never have it of a False one. And this it is, that must point out that Religion to the Magistrate, which he is to promote by the Method I contend for.[77]

On the basis of this "third sort or degree of Perswasion", Proast assumed that magistrates had the capacity to *know* that their religion was the "true religion". Or, more to the point, since there were many magistrates, and not all of their religions could be true, Proast had to assume that he – Proast – had the capacity, on the basis of this "third sort or degree of Perswasion", to distinguish between those magistrates who were in possession of the "true religion", and those who were not, since, as we saw, only the former were, in Proast's opinion, justified in using force to advance their religion.

Locke, in his final response to Proast, rejects, on a number of grounds, the possibility that the "third sort or degree of Perswasion" to which Proast refers amounts to knowledge of "true religion". In the first instance, he suggests that Proast's claims for this "third sort or degree of Perswasion" are made in an inherently "question-begging" manner, since Proast declares, in the passage above, that this "Perswasion" only arises in cases of "true religion", and yet we have no criterion of determining whether it has indeed arisen in the case of "true religion" other than the fact that such "Perswasion" is said to have occurred:

> I say the magistrates are not in a capacity to perform their duty, if they be obliged to use force to promote the true religion, since they have nothing to determine them but their own persuasion of the truth of any religion; which, in the variety of religions which the magistrates of the world have embraced, cannot direct them to the true. Yes, say you, their persuasion, who have embraced the true religion, will direct them to the true religion. Which amounts at last to no more but this, That the magistrate that is in the right, is in the right: a very true proposition without doubt; but whether it removes the difficulty I proposed, any better than begging the question, you were best consider.[78]

Further, Locke rejects Proast's claim, which Proast advances in the earlier passage above, that the reason we can be certain that the "third sort or degree of Perswasion" amounts to knowledge of "true religion" is because of the degree of "Assurance" it provides to believers, based on its "Firmness" and "Stability". In response, Locke insists, as he did when he first distinguished between "faith" and "knowledge" in matters of religion at note 21 in the previous chapter, that there is a categorical distinction between belief on the one hand and knowledge on the other, which cannot be bridged by the degree of "Assurance" of either – "for knowledge upon strict demonstration is not belief or persuasion, but wholly above it".[79] In this respect, he says, the "boundaries" between "knowledge and belief" "must be kept, and their names not confounded".[80] Further, Locke insists that the strength or intensity of "Perswasion", such as Proast refers to with his reference to "Firmness" and "Stability", is again no indication of "truth" or "knowledge", since such "Firmness" and "Stability" is equally possible in regard to "false" religions. As Locke puts it:

> Another false supposition you build upon is this, that the true religion is always embraced with the firmest assent. There is scarce any one so little acquainted with the world, that hath not met with instances of men most unmoveably confident, and fully assured in a religion which was not the true.[81]

The result, Locke says, is that

> believing in the highest degree of assurance is not knowledge ... [and] ... whatever is not capable of demonstration is not, unless it be self-evident, capable to produce knowledge, how well grounded and great soever the assurance of faith may be wherewith it is received.[82]

Goldie Revisited

When all this is taken into account, we see that nothing could be further from an accurate depiction of the Locke/Proast debate than Professor Goldie's claim, at note 70 above, that "[r]eliable knowledge of the 'true religion' was taken as the starting point". Far from being in agreement on this matter, we have seen that it is precisely on this issue that Locke and Proast are most profoundly at odds.[83]

There are other pitfalls in Professor Goldie's account of the Locke/Proast debate. Because Goldie does not perceive the full range of issues at stake in the debate, he fails to perceive its full significance. For instance, Goldie seeks to dismiss the debate as lacking in productive momentum:

> Proast was concerned almost exclusively with restating Augustine's claim that the conscience can, in a sense, be coerced.... He forced Locke to address the point more closely, though somewhat fruitlessly, as both writers rapidly descended into mutually incomprehending counter-assertion.[84]

Contrary to Goldie, we shall see that the debate did have productive momentum. Each protagonist was forced by the other to develop, and at times abandon, positions, with Locke ultimately cornering Proast on the basis of a theological proposition concerning the "grace of God".

Again, because Goldie does not perceive the full range of issues at stake in the Locke/Proast debate, he fails to perceive the distance that divides Locke from Proast, presenting their respective positions as far closer to each other than they actually were. This is most apparent in his claim that not only are Locke and Proast in agreement concerning "[r]eliable knowledge of the 'true religion'", but they share a common purpose of seeking to "bring people to the true religion", simply being divided (Goldie tells us in the last line of the passage below) on the "best means" of achieving this end:

> Noting that Locke concedes that there *is* a "true religion", the ensuing debate almost wholly concerns the efficacy of compulsion on its behalf. Hence their battle was fought on a narrow front, with limited attention paid to the larger question of the inroads of scepticism upon the idea of "true religion". This has the effect (quite properly) of portraying Locke not as a defender of a secular, sceptical pluralism, but as a Low Church Anglican who differs about the best means to bring people to true religion.[85]

Once again, it would be difficult to arrive at a more mistaken understanding of the Locke/Proast debate, or the position that Locke attempts to advance within it. Far from seeking to "bring people to the true religion", we have seen, again repeatedly, that Locke believes that on all such matters, individuals should be left to make these choices for themselves. As Locke puts it, when it comes to such concerns, "[e]veryone ... must be judge for himself", with the result that each "must be left to their own consciences".[86] His "truth", "rationality" and "consent" arguments all seek to affirm this proposition, upholding the liberty of individuals to decide their religious fate for themselves, with the inevitable religious pluralism that results. Equally, Locke's scepticism concerning anyone's claim to possess authoritative knowledge of "true religion", widely discussed in the preceding chapter, would also preclude a strategy of "bringing people to the true religion".

Of course, Locke upheld a right for individuals to exhort, encourage and admonish each other on matters of religion, which he strictly distinguished from any attempt at coercion.[87] But Locke did not perceive this exhortation and encouragement as likely to result in any convergence on a single "true religion", as would be implied by the "Low Church" strategy that Goldie seeks to ascribe to him in the passage above. And the reason, once again, is Locke's belief that knowledge of "true religion" is not possible. The absence of such knowledge means there is no indubitable criterion to decide between rival truth claims in matters of religion. The result, Locke says, is that, in such matters, "every man in what he believes has so far this persuasion that he is in the right", with the result that "everyone is orthodox to himself".[88] Indeed, Locke made this point as early as *An Essay Concerning Toleration*.[89] For this reason, Locke is able to declare to Proast that "true and false ... when we suppose them for ourselves, or our party, in effect, signify just nothing, or nothing to the purpose".[90] This again undermines any possibility that consensus on "true religion", of the type implied by Goldie's "Low Church Anglican" strategy above, is possible. Consequently, far from Locke seeking the "best means" to "bring people to the true religion", with all the convergence and agreement that this would involve, Locke tells us, in the *A Letter Concerning Toleration*, that, in matters of religion, "diversity of opinions ... cannot be avoided".[91]

Indeed, so far was Locke from insisting that individuals should be "brought to the true religion" that he insisted, in the first *Letter*, that individuals should be left alone even when we know they are "neglecting" the "care" of their "own soul".⁹² Further, Locke, in the third *Letter*, directly denies that the Church of England has any exclusive claim to being the "only true religion", thereby again casting doubt on Goldie's claim that he, like Proast, is concerned with the "best means" to "bring people" to it.⁹³

Yet all this evidence notwithstanding, Goldie has elsewhere repeated this extraordinary claim that Locke's purpose is one of seeking to "bring people to the true religion", or what he describes in the passage below as bringing the "wayward to truth":

> It is not just that Locke excludes Roman Catholics and atheists from tolerance, but also that his very premises [in the *Letter*] are rooted in Christian evangelism.... [I]ts argument is grounded in the question: What are the legitimate means at the disposal of Christians to bring the wayward to the truth?⁹⁴

Once again, Locke's scepticism concerning all claims to "truth" in matters of religion precludes any possibility of attributing to him such an evangelical strategy. The only reason Goldie can repeatedly arrive at such erroneous conclusions is that he continually misses this scepticism in Locke's theory of toleration. This is evident when Goldie tells us at note 70 above that Locke and Proast are in agreement concerning "[r]eliable knowledge of the 'true religion'", with the result that, within their debate, "limited attention" was paid "to the larger question of the inroads of scepticism upon the idea of 'true religion'" (note 85).

Contrary to Goldie, we have seen that none of this is true. We saw in Chapter 5 that Locke's "truth argument", from the time of the first *Letter* onwards, relied on precisely such scepticism concerning knowledge of "true religion" for its cogency. Locke reiterates such scepticism at note 21 in the previous chapter, and in Chapter 9 we go into detail concerning the extensive attention that Locke and Proast did pay, within their debate, "to the larger question of the inroads of scepticism upon the idea of 'true religion'". It is because Goldie fails to perceive this scepticism at the heart of Locke's case for toleration that he also fails to perceive it in his debate with Proast, thereby failing to understand the distance that divides these two antagonists. The result, as we have seen above, is that, not only does Goldie misunderstand basic aspects of the debate itself, but he presents Locke and Proast's respective positions as far closer to each other than they actually were.

Notes

1 Goldie 1999a: 2.
2 Goldie 1999b: 118. Maurice Cranston suggests that perhaps Proast's delay in replying to Locke's "Third Letter on Toleration" was a result of the latter's length:

> The first edition ran to no fewer than 350 pages. It would probably have been better if it had been a quarter of its length.... It took Proast twelve years to publish a rejoinder; one might well believe that it took him twelve years to read it.
>
> (Cranston 1957: 368)

3 Goldie 2002: 170–1.
4 Proast 1999a: 26.
5 Proast 1999b: 119, 120–4. On Locke's advancement of this particular argument, see Ch. 7 (note 44).
6 Proast 1999b: 121.
7 See Schochet 1992: 147; Hoak 1996: 2–11; Miller 1983: 34–8, 47–9.
8 See ibid.: 46–7.
9 As Mark Goldie states:

> [I]t is important to stress how total was the political and moral desertion of James by most Tories and Churchmen. They hated popery as much as Puritanism and Whiggery; and James, a Catholic who decreed toleration, managed to embody all these evils. Tories challenged James's schemes at every opportunity.
>
> (2002: 148)

10 Miller 1983: 49.
11 Ibid.: 47.
12 On how both Thomas Long and Jonas Proast fit this category of Tory, see notes 13, 14, 17 and 23–5 below.
13 Goldie 1999a: 2.
14 Goldie 2002: 147.
15 Proast 1999c: 52.
16 Indeed it was these limits that ensured sufficient support for the passage of the Act. As Thomas Babington Macaulay famously put it, the *Toleration Act* "removed a vast mass of evil without shocking a vast mass of prejudice" (Macaulay 1958: 446). On these limits to the Act, see Miller 1983: 48–9; Coffey 2000: 199; Marshall 1996: 369–70.
17 Goldie 1999c: 24.
18 Locke 1963a: 425.
19 Miller 1983: 64–5.
20 Ibid.: 65.
21 Goldie 2002: 144–5.
22 As Goldie states: "In his expulsion from the chaplaincy of All Souls [Proast] became a minor martyr in the Anglican counter-revolution against James" (Goldie 2002: 148. See also ibid.: 145, 146, 149–50).
23 Ibid.: 151, 152.
24 Ibid.: 152.
25 Goldie 1991: 362–3.
26 Goldie 2002: 144.
27 See note 21 above.
28 Goldie 2002: 168, 169.
29 Ibid.: 169.
30 Ibid.
31 Ibid.
32 See Locke 1979: 457–9.
33 Ibid.
34 Ibid.: 458.
35 Goldie 2002: 169.
36 Ibid.: 168.

37 Proast states his basic position at a number of points in the debate – Proast 1999a: 27, 28, 30, 31; 1999c: 55–6, 65, 68, 72, 73–4, 76, 81, 83, 85–6, 101, 113, 114; 1999b: 123–4.
38 Proast 1999a: 26, 27.
39 Proast 1999c: 65. See Proast 1999a: 27, 31. For Locke's original claim on these lines, see Locke 1993a: 395. See also Ch. 3 (notes 24–6).
40 Proast 1999c: 65.
41 Proast 1999a: 27.
42 Ibid. See also Proast 1999c: 65.
43 See Ch. 3 (note 20).
44 See Ch. 2 ("Locke, Liberty and the *Two Tracts*"). See also Ch. 3 (notes 24–6).
45 Proast 1999a: 28.
46 Ibid.: 34. See also Ch. 7 (note 14).
47 Ibid.: 31–2. See also note 53 below.
48 Goldie 1991: 332–3.
49 See Ch. 2 ("Locke, Liberty and the *Two Tracts*"). See also Ch. 3 (note 24).
50 Goldie 1991: 333–5, 354. For Locke's confirmation of this point, see Ch. 3 (notes 24–6). For Locke and Proast's agreement on this point, see notes 38 and 39 above.
51 See notes 40–2 above. For the widespread use of this argument in Anglican circles during the Restoration period, see Goldie 1991: 346–50.
52 Ibid.: 363.
53 See Proast 1999c: 59, 63, 65, 66, 67, 68, 82, 85, 85–6, 86, 104, 104–5, 108, 109, 111. See also notes 45–7 above. Goldie points to how such justification was widespread upon the part of Anglican authorities, wherein the use of force upon Dissenters "was premised on an assumption of an objectively known true religion" (Goldie 1991: 361).
54 Proast 1999c: 85–6.
55 See Ch. 4 (note 42).
56 Waldron 1988: 83–4.
57 Ibid.
58 See ibid.: 84. In Waldron's view, Locke, of course, also retained the Christian arguments for toleration to which Waldron refers in the opening pages of Waldron 1988. See also Ch. 4 (note 40).
59 See Ch. 4 (note 45).
60 Waldron 1988: 84.
61 Ibid.
62 Waldron 2002: 209–11.
63 For Locke's statement that the conditions of the "rationality argument" are unlikely to apply in practice, see Ch. 5 (notes 32 and 33).
64 See Ch. 5 (note 31) and Ch. 8 (note 45).
65 Dunn 1969: 33n.
66 Ibid. Emphasis added.
67 See Ch. 5 (note 33).
68 On Locke's references to "commission", see Ch. 5 (notes 8 and 9). On the question of religious "truth", and our capacity to "know" it, being central to the Locke/Proast debate, see Ch. 5 (note 21), and notes 5, 6, 45–7, 53 and 54 above.
69 Indeed, Goldie refers directly to Waldron's account, declaring it "similar" to his own (Goldie 1991: 364n). See also note 85 below.
70 Goldie 1999c: 24.
71 See Ch. 5 ("The Truth Argument" and "The 'Truth Argument' Considered").
72 Concerning Locke's claim in the previous chapter that faith, but not knowledge, is all that is available to individuals in matters of religion, see Ch. 5 (note 21). On his claim that there may be "one true religion", and his associated hesitations in this regard, see Ch. 5 (notes 14–16).

73 See notes 6, 45–7, 53 and 54 above.
74 Proast 1999c: 86.
75 See note 54 above.
76 See Ch. 5 (note 21).
77 Proast 1999b: 121.
78 Locke 1963b: 567.
79 Ibid.: 559.
80 Ibid.: 558.
81 Ibid.: 563. See also Ch. 9 (note 17). Here we see once again the distinction Locke makes between scepticism concerning claims to knowledge of "true religion", and his belief in the existence of a "true religion" itself. Locke's declaration, in the passage, that some religions are "not the true" clearly implies the existence of a "true religion", even if the existence of such false religions are not sufficient proof of this.
82 Locke 1963b: 558.
83 As Locke declares to Proast in the third *Letter Concerning Toleration*:

> I shall desire you but to set down what you mean here by true religion, that we may know what in your sense is, and what is not contained in it. Would you but do this fairly, and define your words, or use them in one constant settled sense, I think the controversy between you and me would be at an end, without any farther trouble.
>
> (Locke 1963a: 423)

84 Goldie 1991: 363.
85 Ibid.: 363–4. Indeed, Goldie cites Waldron as one important influence on his conclusions in this regard. As he states: "For a similar discussion to that provided in the following paragraphs see J. Waldron, "Locke: Toleration and the Rationality of Persecution", in S. Mendus (ed.) *Justifying Toleration: Conceptual and Historical Perspectives* (Cambridge, 1988), 61–86" (Goldie 1991: 364n.).
86 See Ch. 5 (note 55). See also Ch. 1 (notes 25, 29 and 40) and Ch. 5 (note 56).
87 See Ch. 1 (notes 28–30, 34) and Ch. 2 (note 38).
88 Locke 1993a: 390; 1993b: 205.
89 Locke refers to those who resisted state persecution for their religion and asks how they managed to resist. He then states: "Let them not say it was because they knew they were in the right, for every man in what he believes has so far this persuasion that he is in the right" (Locke 1993b: 205).
90 Locke 1963c: 90.
91 See Locke 1993a: 431. See also Ch. 4 (note 2).
92 Locke 1993a: 406. See also Ch. 7 (note 87).
93 On Locke's insistence that Proast should not assume the Church of England to be the "only true religion", see Locke 1963a: 320, 326, 327, 328, 332–3, 334, 422, 423.
94 Goldie 2010: xi-xii. My addition.

References

Coffey, J. (2000) *Persecution and Toleration in Protestant England, 1558–1689*. Harlow: Longman.

Cranston, M. (1957) *John Locke. A Biography*. London: Longmans, Green and Co.

Dunn, J. (1969) *The Political Thought of John Locke*. Cambridge: Cambridge University Press.

Goldie, M. (1991) "The Theory of Religious Intolerance in Restoration England". In: O. P. Grell, J. I. Israel and N. Tyacke (eds) *From Persecution to Toleration*.

The Glorious Revolution and Religion in England. Oxford: Clarendon Press, pp. 331–68.
Goldie, M. (1999a) "Introduction to Thomas Long, 'The Letter for Toleration Decipher'd and the Absurdity and Impiety of an Absolute Toleration Demonstrated, by the Judgement of Presbyterians, Independents, and by Mr. Calvin, Mr. Baxter, and the Parliament, 1662'". In: M. Goldie (ed.) *The Reception of Locke's Politics, Vol. 5. The Church, Dissent and Religious Toleration 1689–1773*. London: Pickering and Chatto, p. 2.
Goldie, M. (1999b) "Introduction to Jonas Proast 'A Second Letter to the Author of the Three Letters for Toleration'". In: M. Goldie (ed.) *The Reception of Locke's Politics, Vol. 5. The Church, Dissent and Religious Toleration 1689–1773*. London: Pickering and Chatto, p. 118.
Goldie, M. (1999c) "Introduction to Jonas Proast, 'The Argument of the Letter Concerning Toleration Briefly Consider'd and Answer'd'". In: M. Goldie (ed.) *The Reception of Locke's Politics, Vol. 5. The Church, Dissent and Religious Toleration 1689–1773*. London: Pickering and Chatto, p. 24.
Goldie, M. (2002) "John Locke, Jonas Proast and Religious Toleration 1688–1692". In: J. Walsh, C. Haydon and S. Taylor (eds) *The Church of England c.1689–c.1833: From Toleration to Tractarianism*. Cambridge: Cambridge University Press, pp. 143–71.
Goldie, M. (2010) "Introduction". In: J. Locke *A Letter Concerning Toleration and Other Writings*. Indianapolis, IN: Liberty Fund, pp. ix–xxiii.
Hoak, D. (1996) "The Anglo-Dutch Revolution of 1688–89". In: D. Hoak and M. Feingold (eds) *The World of William and Mary: Anglo-Dutch Perspectives on the Revolution of 1688–89*. Stanford, CA: Stanford University Press, pp. 1–26.
Locke, J. (1963a) "A Third Letter for Toleration". In: J. Locke *The Works of John Locke*. Vol. VI. Aalen: Scientia Verlag, pp. 141–546.
Locke, J. (1963b) "A Fourth Letter for Toleration". In: J. Locke *The Works of John Locke*. Vol. VI. Aalen: Scientia Verlag, pp. 549–74.
Locke, J. (1963c) "A Second Letter Concerning Toleration". In: J. Locke *The Works of John Locke*. Vol. VI. Aalen: Scientia Verlag, pp. 61–137.
Locke, J. (1979) "Locke to Philippus van Limborch", 2 June 1692. In: J. Locke *The Correspondence of John Locke*, Vol. 4. E. S. De Beer (ed.). Oxford: Clarendon Press, pp. 457–59.
Locke, J. (1993a) "A Letter Concerning Toleration". In: J. Locke *Political Writings*. David Wootton (ed.). London: Penguin, pp. 390–436.
Locke, J. (1993b) "An Essay Concerning Toleration". In: J. Locke *Political Writings*. David Wootton (ed.). London: Penguin, pp. 186–210.
Macaulay, T. B. (1958) *Macaulay's History of England. From the Accession of James II*, Vol. 2. London: Dent.
Marshall, J. (1996) *John Locke. Resistance, Religion and Responsibility*. Cambridge: Cambridge University Press.
Miller, J. (1983) *The Glorious Revolution*. London: Longman.
Proast, J. (1999a) "The Argument of the Letter Concerning Toleration, Briefly Consider'd and Answer'd". In: M. Goldie (ed.) *The Reception of Locke's Politics, Vol. 5. The Church, Dissent and Religious Toleration 1689–1773*. London: Pickering and Chatto, pp. 25–37.
Proast, J. (1999b) "A Second Letter to the Author of the Three Letters for Toleration, from the Author of the Argument of the Letter Concerning Toleration, Briefly Consider'd and Answer'd, and of the Defense of It". In: M. Goldie (ed.)

The Reception of Locke's Politics, Vol. 5. *The Church, Dissent and Religious Toleration 1689–1773*. London: Pickering and Chatto, pp. 119–28.

Proast, J. (1999c) "A Third Letter Concerning Toleration: In Defense of the Argument of the Letter Concerning Toleration, Briefly Consider'd and Answer'd". In: M. Goldie (ed.) *The Reception of Locke's Politics*, Vol. 5. *The Church, Dissent and Religious Toleration 1689–1773*. London: Pickering and Chatto, pp. 41–116.

Schochet, G. J. (1992) "John Locke and Religious Toleration". In: L. G. Schwoerer, *The Revolution of 1688–1689. Changing Perspectives*. Cambridge: Cambridge University Press, pp. 147–64.

Waldron, J. (1988) "Locke: Toleration and the Rationality of Persecution". In: S. Mendus (ed.) *Justifying Toleration: Conceptual and Historical Perspectives*. Cambridge: Cambridge University Press, pp. 61–86.

Waldron, J. (2002) *God, Locke and Equality: Christian Foundations of John Locke's Political Thought*. Cambridge: Cambridge University Press.

7 Proast's Response: "True Religion and the Salvation of Souls"

This chapter begins the account of the Locke/Proast debate. It will consider Jonas Proast's response to each of Locke's three "considerations" for toleration, which Locke first presented in *A Letter Concerning Toleration*, along with some of Locke's rejoinders to Proast. The following chapter will then consider, in more detail, Locke's response to Proast, which Locke advances in his second, third and fourth *Letters Concerning Toleration*.

This chapter begins with Proast's account of the content of Locke's *Letter*, in particular the arguments for toleration Proast perceives within it, before moving on to consider Proast's response to Locke's "truth argument". The chapter then covers a number of related themes, including Proast's response to the religious diversity of his own time, before considering Proast's response to Locke's "consent argument" and "rationality argument".

Proast and the *Letter*

At first glance, Jonas Proast seems to advance an analysis of Locke's *Letter* similar to that which, centuries later, Jeremy Waldron would provide. Just as Waldron identified only one (secular) argument for toleration within Locke's text, which he dubbed the "main line of argument", so Proast identifies this same argument as the "single Argument" that, he believes, Locke advances in the *Letter*:

> For, if I understand this *Letter*, the whole Strength of what it urgeth for the Purpose of it, lies in this Argument:
>
> *There is but one Way of Salvation, or but one True Religion.*
> *No man can be saved by this Religion, who does not believe it to be the True Religion.*
> *This Belief is to be wrought in men by Reason and Argument, not by outward Force and Compulsion.*
> *Therefore all such Force is utterly of no use for the promoting True Religion, and the Salvation of Souls.*

> *And therefore no body can have any Right to use any Force or Compulsion, for the bringing men to the True Religion; neither any Private Person; nor any Ecclesiastical Officer (Bishop, Priest, or other;) nor any Church, or Religious Society; nor the Civil Magistrate.*
>
> This, upon a careful perusal of this *Letter*, I take to be the single Argument by which the Author endeavours in it to establish his Position. And if every Point of this were sufficiently proved, I must confess I think he would need no more for the accomplishing his Design. But whether he has sufficiently made out this Argument in all the Parts of it, is that which I am now to examine.[1]

What Proast makes reference to in the passage above is, of course, what we have dubbed the "rationality argument" – centred on the capacity (or rather, incapacity) of force to instil, within individuals, sincere and genuine religious belief. It is this, Proast claims in the passage above, which is "the single Argument by which the Author endeavours … to establish his Position".

Yet, despite this apparent anticipation of Waldron's "main line of argument", Proast is in fact far more sensitive than Waldron to the full content of Locke's *Letter* and the range of arguments Locke deploys in defence of toleration within it. Although at times suggesting that the "rationality argument" is the "single Argument" that Locke employs to "establish his Position",[2] Proast acknowledges the other two arguments that Locke advances to this end, based on "truth" and "consent".[3] It is these three arguments, centred on "truth", "rationality" and "consent", which, we have seen, constitute Locke's "three considerations" for toleration in the *Letter*. Proast, in his engagement with Locke, ultimately acknowledges all three of these, stating *"the Author offers three Considerations to prove that the Civil Power neither can nor ought in any manner to be extended to the Salvation of Souls"*.[4] In offering this assessment, Proast demonstrates a more comprehensive understanding of the content of the *Letter* than does Waldron almost three centuries later.

The Truth Argument

As explained in Chapter 5, the one assumption central to the "truth argument", as Locke presented it within the *Letter*, was Locke's claim that, although there may be "but one truth, one way to heaven", we can never be entirely sure who possesses access to this "truth", and therefore we can never be sure who we should entrust with our salvation. Because we each have to bear the eternal consequences of this decision – such choices determining the fate of our immortal souls – Locke insists that we would be best to make these decisions for ourselves, rather than trust the magistrate, or indeed any other authority, to make them for us, since we have no guarantee that these authorities are in possession of "true religion" and, further, they cannot compensate us if they are wrong.⁵ Indeed, Locke insists that we ought to make these decisions for ourselves even if it is "probable the way to eternal life may be better known by a prince than by his subjects".⁶ Proast quotes Locke's articulation of the "truth argument" along these lines in the *Letter* as follows:

> *For there being but one Truth, one way to Heaven; what hope is there that more men would be led into it, if they had no Rule but the Religion of the Court, and were put under a necessity to quit the Light of their own reason, and oppose the Dictates of their own Consciences, and blindly to resign up themselves to the Will of their Governours, and to the Religion, which either Ignorance, Ambition, or Superstition has chanced to establish in the Countries where they were born?*⁷

Proast agrees that there is "but one Truth, one way to Heaven".⁸ However he insists that the "truth argument", as outlined by Locke, does not apply to Proast's own justification of the use of force in matters of religion – a justification which we considered in the previous chapter.⁹ The reason for this, Proast insists, is that his justification does not seek to endorse the magistrate's use of force in order to advance *any* religion to which the magistrate may happen to subscribe, irrespective of its truth. Rather, Proast declares, he seeks to justify the magistrate's use of force only when that force is used to advance the "true religion".¹⁰ Proast identifies the use of force with "true religion" as follows:

> For if Force so applied … may, in such sort as has been said, be serviceable to the bringing men to receive and embrace Truth; there can be no reason assigned, why this should not hold with respect to the Truths of Religion, as well as with respect to any other Truths whatsoever. For as the True Religion, embrac'd upon such Consideration as Force drives a man to, is not the less *True*, for being so embraced; so neither does it upon that account lose its *Acceptableness with God*, any more then that Obedience does, which God himself drives men to by chastening and afflicting them.¹¹

In his first response to Locke, Proast does not identify this "true religion" with the religion of the magistrate.¹² This is despite the fact that it is certainly those who are at odds with the magistrate on matters of religion to whom the "force" that Proast refers to in the passage above (and in the previous chapter) is applied.¹³ For example, responding directly to the passage from the *Letter* quoted at note 7 above, in which Locke refers to individuals "*blindly … resign[ing] up themselves to the Will of their Governours*", Proast declares:

> Now all this I acknowledge to be very true. But to what purpose it is here alleged, I do not understand. For who requires that *men should*

> *have no Rule but the Religion of the Court? Or that they should be put under a necessity to quit the Light of their own reason, and oppose the Dictates of their own Consciences, and blindly resign up themselves to the Will of their governors, &c.?* No man certainly, who thinks Religion worthy of his serious Thoughts. The Power I ascribe to the Magistrate, is given him, to bring men, not to his *own*, but to the *true* Religion; And though (as our Author puts us in mind) *the Religion of every Prince is Orthodox to himself*; yet if this Power keep within its bounds, it *can* serve the Interest of no other Religion but the true, among such as have any concern for their Eternal Salvation; (and those that have none, deserve not to be consider'd).[14]

Here we see the fundamental distinction that Proast makes in his first response to Locke. He makes clear, in the passage above, that the "true religion" he refers to is not necessarily the religion of the magistrate ("The Power I ascribe to the Magistrate, is given him, to bring men, not to his *own*, but to the *true* Religion"). But he nevertheless affirms that the magistrate possesses the necessary "Power" by which to lead individuals to this "true religion" – this "Power" being that which, if kept "within its bounds ... *can* serve the Interest of no other Religion but the true." This "Power" is therefore, in Proast's view, an instrumental means by which "true religion" can be achieved. The "Power" referred to is, of course, those means of force ("Penalties") which, Proast declares, magistrates impose on those individuals, at odds with them on religion, in order bring these individuals to a "thorough" and "impartial" examination of these matters:

> When Men fly from the means of a right Information, and will not so much as consider how reasonable it is, throughly [sic] and impartially to examine a Religion, which they embraced upon such Inducements as ought to have no sway at all in the matter, and therefore with little or no examination of the proper Grounds of it: what humane method can be used, to bring them to act like Men, in an affair of such consequence, and to make a wiser and more rational Choice, but that of laying such Penalties upon them, as may balance the weight of those Prejudices which enclined them to prefer a false Way before the True, and recover them to so much Sobriety and Reflexion, as seriously to put the question to themselves, Whether it be really worth the while to undergo such Inconveniences, for adhering to a Religion, which, for any thing they know, may be false, or for rejecting another (if that be the case) which, for any thing they know, may be true, till they have brought it to the Bar of Reason, and given it a fair Tryal there. Where Instruction is stiffly refused, and all Admonitions and Perswasions prove vain and ineffectual, there is no room for any other Method but this.[15]

Given the distinction that Proast makes, at note 14 above, between the magistrate possessing the means to the "true religion", but not necessarily possessing knowledge of the "true religion" itself, why can Proast assume, in the same passage, that such means, if kept "within its bounds", "*can serve the Interest of no other Religion but the true*"? The answer lies, Proast insists, in the sort of force ("Penalties") that the magistrate imposes, "indirectly and at a distance". If properly applied, such "Penalties", he declares, have the effect (as per the passage at note 15 above) of making those at odds with the magistrate on religion "seriously" and "impartially" reflect upon their religious commitments (not least whether these commitments are of sufficient worth to endure the penalties which the magistrate imposes). They do not, however, have the effect (Proast claims) of making individuals give up a "true religion" in favour of a false one, and so to this extent serve the interest of "true religion":

> [T]he Penalties it enables him that has it to inflict, are not such as may tempt such Persons either to renounce a Religion which they believe to be true, or to profess one which they do not believe to be so; but only such as are apt to put them upon a serious and impartial examination of the Controversy between the Magistrate and them: which is the way for them to come to the knowledge of the Truth.[16]

Proast provides one other significant reason why he believes the magistrate's "Power", if kept "within its bounds", can "serve the Interest of no other Religion but the true". This concerns Proast's conception of God. Proast believes that the qualities of God are such that He would never deny true knowledge of Himself, and therefore the knowledge of the "true religion" necessary for salvation, to those among His creatures who genuinely and diligently seek it. As Proast puts it: "(if we believe the Scriptures) no Man can fail of finding the way of Salvation, who seeks it as he ought; and in this case all Men are supposed so to seek it".[17] As Proast believes it is the purpose of the magistrate's use of force to encourage individuals to diligently seek "true religion" in this way ("such as are apt to put them upon a serious and impartial examination of the Controversy between the Magistrate and them"[18]) this use of force, if "kept within its bounds", once again "serves the Interest of no other Religion but the true".

Indeed Proast, in his first response to Locke, goes so far as to argue that, even if the magistrate is mistaken about the "true religion", and therefore imposes penalties on individuals for the sake of a false religion, the cause of "true religion" is still served. This is because those individuals subject to the magistrate's "penalties", in realizing the magistrate's error, now know "better than they did before, where the Truth does lie".[19]

In all these ways, therefore, Proast responds to Locke's "truth argument", insisting that Locke's concern that "true religion" and salvation will not be served if individuals "*resign up themselves to the Will of their Governours*", is unfounded. This is because, for all the reasons above, Proast insists that the exercise of the magistrate's "Power" in matters of religion, if kept "within its bounds ... *can* serve the Interest of no other

Religion but the true", even in those cases where the magistrate is not in possession of the "true religion".

Proast and "True Religion"

In the last chapter, we saw that central to Proast's position was the claim that force, if used by the magistrate "indirectly and at a distance", may do "some service toward the bringing men to embrace that Truth, which otherwise, either through Carelessness and Negligence they would never acquaint themselves with, or through Prejudice they would reject and condemn unheard, under the notion of Errour".[20] Throughout the *Second Letter Concerning Toleration*, Locke continually insists that Proast be open and explicit as to what "Truth" he is referring to here, and therefore which religion, being the "true religion", has the exclusive entitlement to be backed by the magistrate's use of force.

Locke suggests that perhaps Proast is referring to his *own* religion as the "true".[21] At the very least, Locke insists that Proast is assuming the "magistrate's" religion to be "true" and is therefore supposing that all those at odds with the magistrate on matters of religion are in error:

> But why, I pray, all this boggling, all this loose talking, as if you knew not what you meant, or durst not speak it out? Would you be for punishing somebody, you know not whom? I do not think so ill of you. Let me then speak out for you.... To show you that I do not speak wholly without book, give me leave to mind you of one passage of yours. The words are, "Penalties to put them upon a serious and impartial examination of the controversy between the magistrates and them". Though these words be not intended to tell us who you would have punished, yet it may be plainly inferred from them. And they more clearly point out whom you aim at than all the foregoing places where you seem to (and should) describe them. For they are such as between whom and the magistrate there is a controversy; that is, in short, who differ from the magistrate in religion. And now indeed you have given us a note by which these you would have punished may be made known.... Therefore, say you, let all dissenters be punished. Why? Have no dissenters considered of religion? Or have all conformists considered? That you yourself will not say.[22]

We saw that in his first response to Locke, Proast denied that he was assuming the magistrate to be in possession of the "true religion".[23] Initially, he advances the same line of argument in his second response, declaring that, for the success of his "Method", he does not have to assume either his own or the magistrate's religion to be "true", but only that there be "one true religion".[24]

Yet Locke continues to insist that Proast be open and up-front about which religion he believes to be "true" and therefore entitled to be backed by force. Again, he suggests that Proast is really assuming either his own or the magistrate's religion to be "true" and that conversion to this religion is the purpose of his "Method":

> For though you do all you can to cover it under the name of rejecting the true religion duly proposed; yet it is in truth no more but being of a religion different from yours, that you would have them punished for: for all that the author pleads for, and you can oppose in writing against him, is toleration of religion. Your scheme therefore being thus mended, your hypothesis enlarged, being of a different religion from the national found criminal, and punishments found justly to belong to it.[25]

Eventually, in response to Locke's entreaties, Proast ultimately pushes all prevarication aside and, rather than affirming the general necessity of "one true Religion", goes further and declares that the "one true Religion" to which he refers encompasses the Church of England:

> But as to my *supposing* that the National Religion now in England, back'd by the Publick Authority of the Law, is the onely true Religion; if you own, with our Author, that there is but one true Religion, I cannot see how you your self can avoid *supposing* the same. For you own your self of the Church of *England*; and consequently you own the National Religion now in England, to be the true Religion; for that is her Religion. And therefore if you believe there is but one true Religion; there is no help for it, but you must suppose, with me, that the National Religion now in England, back'd with the Publick Authority of the Law, is the onely true Religion.[26]

In this passage, Proast has moved beyond his claim that the means the magistrate possesses "*can* serve the Interest of no other Religion but the true". He has gone further and declared that English magistrates, in particular, are in *possession* of the "one true Religion". In other words, Proast is claiming to possess that very knowledge of "true religion" which, we saw, Locke declares to be unavailable. Once more, therefore, we see how (contrary to Mark Goldie) far from "[r]eliable knowledge of the 'true religion'" being the "starting point" of agreement between Locke and Proast, it was upon this question that they were most profoundly divided.[27] Despite the fact that both shared a sincere Christianity, both fundamentally disagreed on whether it is possible to *know* if this Christianity, or any particular variant of it, is the "true religion".

"Begging the Question"

Indeed, at those points in Proast's second response to Locke that Proast assumes knowledge of, as distinct from "faith" in, the "one true Religion",

Locke accuses Proast of "begging the question". He declares that Proast has no indubitable criterion by which to affirm his own religion, or that of any other, to be the "onely true Religion" – the sole authority for such claims, Locke insisting, being Proast's own arbitrary declarations to this effect.[28] So for instance, in response to Proast's proposition that those who ought to be punished in matters of religion are those "that are got into a wrong Way" and are "deaf to all Perswasions",[29] Locke responds:

> And your church, doubtless, as well as all others, is orthodox to itself in all its tenets. If you mean by all persuasion, all your persuasion, or all persuasion of those of your communion; you do but beg the question, and suppose you have a right to punish those who differ from, and will not comply with you.[30]

From Locke's perspective, "begging the question" arises when an individual declares that a particular religion is the "true religion" without conclusive proof or substantiation. After all, as Locke states: "certainly no one of our church, nor any other, which claims not infallibility, can require any one to take the testimony of any church, as a sufficient proof of the truth of her own doctrine".[31] Consequently, to justify force in matters of religion on the grounds that one does so in the name of "true religion" is, in Locke's view, unjustified on epistemic grounds, because knowledge of "true religion" being unavailable, all "beg the question" when they make such claims.[32]

Locke's injunction against "begging the question" is related to the "truth argument" in that both are premised on Locke's assumption that no knowledge of "true religion" is possible. Further, we shall see in Chapter 10 that Locke applies this same injunction to circumstances of civil debate, directed towards public agreement (what we shall call Locke's "civil perspective"). In such circumstances, Locke declares that nobody ought to advance, as justification for their views, propositions based on "true religion", since, there being no authoritative criterion for the truth of such claims, they are not propositions capable of impartial or authoritative adjudication, and so cannot form a basis of public agreement with others.[33] On these same grounds, and for these same reasons, Locke insists that Proast ought to advance his case

> without supposing all along your church in the right, and your religion the true; which can no more be allowed to you in this case, whatever your church or religion be, than it can be to a papist or a Lutheran, a presbyterian or anana baptist; nay, no more to you, than it can be allowed to a Jew or a Mahometan.[34]

"Non-Neutral Principles"

Locke, in his references to "begging the question", is making the point that, due to the absence of an indubitable criterion of "true religion", claims to "true religion", or accusations that others lack possession of it, are something that either side in a dispute can advance, since at no point can they be shown to be in error, with the result that agreement or resolution on such issues is unlikely and, at times, impossible. Locke makes this point to Proast as follows:

> [A]nd you build all you say, upon this lurking supposition, that the national religion now in England, backed by the public authority of the law, is the only true religion, and therefore no other is to be tolerated; which being a supposition equally unavoidable, and equally just in other countries, unless we can imagine that every where but in England men believe what at the same time they think to be a lie.[35]

The point Locke makes in this passage, concerning "true religion", was conveyed some centuries later by the American moral philosopher, Gerald Dworkin, in his discussion of "non-neutral principles".[36] Dworkin writes that it is "characteristic" of "non-neutral principles" that "their application to particular cases is a matter of controversy for the parties whose conduct is supposed to be regulated by the principle in question".[37] This is because individuals, although possibly agreeing on the "principle" at a general level, will differ as to whether it has been correctly applied in specific circumstances, which means that such application will always be open to dispute. Dworkin describes this difficulty as follows:

> It is important to realize that the controversy in question here is not one concerning the correctness or incorrectness, rightness or wrongness, of the principle, but one concerning whether or not the controversial predicate in question applies to the particular case. Thus a principle which states that killing of redheaded people is justified is neutral in my sense – since one can tell which people are redheaded and which are not – while one which states that killing in self-defense is legitimate is non-neutral since parties will often differ as to when a case is one of self-defense.[38]

In this respect, it is clear that "true religion" would qualify as a "non-neutral principle". While Anglicans, Catholics and Dissenters in seventeenth-century England might all affirm the existence of a "true religion" and all agree that specific aspects of their society ought to be governed by the principles of "true religion" – thereby securing agreement that "true religion" exists and ought to be a regulative principle within society – they will all differ concerning what constitutes "true religion" and so over when "true religion" has been correctly applied in practice, there being no "neutral" criteria by which such application can be determined. This makes public agreement between these different faiths on the basis of "true religion" impossible.

We therefore understand why Locke tells us, in the passages above, that because "true religion" lacks an authoritative criterion, it lacks validity and cogency when used to support positions on which individuals seek public agreement – each side being equally capable of advancing these propositions against the other, with no possibility of resolution. In making this point Locke is advancing the same position as Gerald Dworkin all these years later. It is for this reason that Locke can tell us that "true and false, as it commonly happens, when we suppose them for ourselves, or our party, in effect, signify just nothing, or nothing to the purpose", with the result that each individual should be "judge for himself" in such matters.[39] The alternative, Locke makes clear, is interminable conflict, since the principle of "true religion" can be equally advanced by each side in a dispute, but with no possibility of mutual resolution.[40]

"Geneva" and the "Indies"

As pointed out above, it is on the question of whether knowledge of "true religion" is possible that Locke and Proast most fundamentally divide, thereby making Locke's "truth argument", which denies all such knowledge, a basic source of dispute between them. As we shall see at note 55 below, it would appear that Jeremy Waldron, for one, has no problems with Proast's proposition that knowledge of "true religion" is possible, nor with Proast's resort to this proposition to advance his case against toleration. In his own engagement with Locke, Waldron points to a variant of the "truth argument" that Locke employs in the *Letter* (or at least one which, Waldron tells us, has "a slightly stronger sceptical content"[41]). This is Locke's declaration that because "the civil power is the same everywhere", if "a power be granted to the civil magistrate in religious matters" – for instance, to advance his or her own religion by force on the grounds that it is the "true religion" – then this power must be granted to all magistrates, with the result that "at Geneva he may extirpate by force and blood the religion which there is regarded as false or idolatrous", and in another country, "by the same right", another magistrate may "oppress the orthodox religion, and in the Indies the Christian".[42]

The relation of this argument to what we have called the "truth argument" resides in Locke's declaration that there is no distinction between these different magistrates on the grounds of "true religion", because there is no indubitable criterion to determine which of them is in possession of this. Each magistrate has "no other guide but his own persuasion of what is the true religion, and must be led by that in his use of force, or else not use it at all in matters of religion", and, because there is no criterion of religious "truth" capable of authoritatively deciding between magistrates on this question, we can have no means of determining which magistrates use force for the sake of "true religion" and which use it for contrary ends.[43] Locke's scepticism therefore leads him to the universalist conclusion above – a conclusion he repeats throughout his third and fourth *Letter* – that if one magistrate is entitled to use force to advance their religion, on the grounds that they believe this religion to be "true", then all magistrates are so entitled.[44]

Locke's hypothetical generalization in his reference to "Geneva" and the "Indies" – from one magistrate's presumed entitlement to use force in matters of religion, to that of all magistrates being entitled to do so – is an example of what I have called Locke's "criterion of reciprocity".[45] This is where a right or entitlement accorded to one party is presumed, by Locke, to be ascribable to all similar parties in all similar circumstances. Locke refers to such an ideal of reciprocity at various points within the first *Letter*.[46] He also does so in his later engagement with Proast, such as in the context of Locke's articulation of what I call his "civil perspective", discussed in Chapter 10. The normative force of this ideal of reciprocity is seen in the fact that, in those instances where a right or entitlement cannot be accorded to all, and so fails to fulfil this "criterion of reciprocity", the "right" appears arbitrary. Gerald Dworkin has given expression to the sort of normative commitments underwriting the criterion of reciprocity, and the generalization (or what Dworkin calls "universalization") of entitlement it implies, as follows:

> It is by now widely accepted that those who act claiming moral justification for their conduct must be prepared to accept as legitimate certain universalizations of their action. There must be a consistency in conduct, a refusal to make special pleas on one's own behalf or to consider oneself an exception to general principles.[47]

Locke affirms the criterion of reciprocity, and its idea that equal rights or entitlements be generalized to all relevant parties, when he declares, in the first *Letter Concerning Toleration*, that "the sum of all we drive at is that every man may enjoy the same rights that are granted to others".[48] The criterion of reciprocity can also work as a negative injunction, seeking to limit our behaviour towards others. This is evident when Locke declares that no matter how

> clearly we may think this or the other doctrine to be deduced from Scripture, we ought not therefore to impose it upon others as a necessary article of faith because we believe it to be agreeable to the rule of faith; unless we would be content also that other doctrines should be imposed upon us in the same manner.[49]

The relation of this criterion of reciprocity (as it is applied here) to the "truth argument" is that it too relies on a scepticism concerning all claims to knowledge of "true religion". It is only because nobody's claims to such knowledge can be affirmed as authoritative that we reach the reciprocal outcome, discussed in the "Geneva" and "Indies" example above, that if one magistrate is entitled to advance their religion by force, on the grounds that it is the "true religion", then all are. And since, Locke tells us, "the national religions of the world are, beyond comparison, more of them false or erroneous, than such as have God for their author, and truth for their standard",[50] a right of all magistrates to use force to advance their religions will have ill consequences in regard to the advancement of "true religion" in general and therefore the salvation of souls (with the result, Locke implies, that toleration is the preferable alternative):

> And now I desire it may be considered, what advantage this supposition of force, which is supposed put into the magistrate's hands ... to be used in religion, brings to the true religion, when it arms five hundred magistrates against the true religion, who must unavoidably in the state of things in the world act against it, for one that uses force for it.[51]

Proast rejects this line of reasoning and the conclusions Locke reaches. He does so by declaring that the only people who would think all magistrates equally entitled to use force in matters of religion are those who do not "think Religion worthy of [their] serious Thoughts" or have no concern for their "Eternal Salvation".[52] In his second response to Locke, Proast similarly declares that "no man that has any Religion will assert" that "every Magistrate has a Right to use Force to promote his own Religion, whatever it be" – a position, he says, that only an "Atheist, will assert".[53] In his third response, he again directly addresses Locke's proposition that if one magistrate is entitled to advance their religion by force, then all are. Proast declares, in the passage below, that no such conclusion is justifiable if we are able to distinguish those magistrates who are in possession of the "true religion" from those who are not. In other words, Proast's response to the scepticism that drives Locke's conclusions concerning "Geneva" and the "Indies" is to deny such scepticism by declaring, once again, that knowledge of "true religion" (and therefore knowledge of who is in possession of "true religion") is possible:

> Now that every Magistrate, who upon just and sufficient grounds believes his Religion to be true, is obliged to use some moderate Penalties (which is all the *Force* I ever contended for) to bring men to his Religion, I freely grant; because that must needs be the True Religion; since no other can upon such grounds be believed to be true. But that any Magistrate, who upon weak and deceitful grounds believes a False Religion to be true (and he can never do it upon better grounds) is obliged to use the same (or any other) means, to bring men to his Religion, this I flatly deny; nor can it by any Rules of reasoning, be inferr'd from what I assert.[54]

Equally, Jeremy Waldron rejects Locke's line of reasoning above – and he does so on the same grounds as Proast, insisting that knowledge of "true religion" (and therefore knowledge of who is in possession of "true religion") is (at least in principle) possible. Waldron advances this position in response to Locke's same "Geneva" and "Indies" passage, where an entitlement of a magistrate to use force in "Geneva", on the basis of "true religion", yields the same entitlement to a magistrate in the "Indies". Like Proast, Waldron seeks to undercut such reciprocal conclusions by denying the scepticism that allows Locke to reach them. Just as Proast argues that Locke's argument does not apply in those instances where we can distinguish between those magistrates who are in possession of the "true religion" and those who are not, Waldron, in the passage below, insists that Locke's argument does not apply in those instances where a magistrate seeks to advance by force a religion which "is *in fact* objectively correct":

> Notice that this is a good argument only against the following rather silly principle:... that the magistrate may enforce *his own* religion or whatever religion *he thinks* is correct. It is not a good argument against the somewhat more sensible position ... that a magistrate may enforce the religion, whatever it may be, which is *in fact* objectively correct. It may, of course, be difficult to tell, and perhaps impossible to secure social agreement about, whether the view that the magistrate believes is correct is in fact the correct view.... But opposition to intolerance based on awareness of these difficulties is not opposition to intolerance as such, but only opposition to particular cases of it.[55]

From the perspective of Proast's and Waldron's assumption that knowledge of "true religion" is possible, Locke's "truth argument" (which denies such knowledge) is far from being an unconditional argument for toleration valid in all instances where a magistrate seeks to use force in matters of religion. On the contrary, if "truth" can be known in such circumstances, then Locke's "truth argument" is rendered a *contingent* argument for toleration, valid only in relation to "particular cases" of intolerance, where magistrates use force to advance *false* religions, but not in those instances where such force is used to advance "true religion" – i.e. the religion which, in Waldron's words, "is *in fact* objectively correct".

Locke, we have seen, affirms (with some reservations) the existence of a "true religion" and therefore the existence of "one truth, one way to heaven".[56] He just denies any individual's capacity to have knowledge of which religion this is. To this extent, Locke makes clear that, when it comes to actions by the magistrate, we are always in the realm of what Waldron calls, in the passage above, the "silly principle", because even if there is a religion which "is *in fact* objectively correct" – and so the "one truth, one way to heaven" – we can never have indubitable certainty which religion this is and so can never know which magistrate exercises force for the sake of this truth.

Contrary to Waldron's dismissal, as a "silly principle", the idea "that the magistrate may enforce *his own* religion or whatever religion *he thinks* is correct", Locke's point is that, if we allow the magistrate to use force in matters of religion, this is the *only* option available. This is because "the religion of every prince" being "orthodox to himself", and there being no indubitable criterion of religious "truth" to distinguish between the religious claims of rival "princes" (i.e. magistrates), all advance the religion which they only *think* is correct, so all fall within the purview of Waldron's "silly principle". As Locke puts it: "[I]f the magistrates of the world cannot know, certainly know, the true religion to be the true religion … then that which gives them the last determination herein must be their own belief, their own persuasion".[57]

We have seen above the crucial role that scepticism performs within Locke's theory of toleration, not least in the fact that scepticism concerning knowledge of "true religion" (if not scepticism concerning the existence of a "true religion" itself) underwrites Locke's "truth argument", which he advances in his first *Letter Concerning Toleration*.[58] We have seen that such scepticism also underwrites a further argument for toleration, centred on the proposition that if one magistrate is entitled to exercise force for the sake of "true religion", simply because he or she believes their religion to be "true", then all are, with deleterious consequences for "true religion". Locke's scepticism also allows him to declare that Proast's attempt, at note 54 above, to demarcate between those magistrates who use force for the sake of "true religion" and those who use force for all other religions (the very demarcation that underwrites Waldron's "silly principle") is a "useless distinction".[59] Once scepticism concerning knowledge of "true religion" is applied, then all magistrates, we have seen, who seek to advance their religion by force, are in the realm of Waldron's "silly principle" – these being the religions that they only *believe* to be true. In Chapter 9, we shall return to this issue of scepticism, engaging with the arguments of those Locke scholars who claim that scepticism is not present in Locke's justification of toleration at all.

Proast and Religious Diversity

As Locke tells us, "diversity of opinions" in matters of religion "cannot be avoided".[60] The result is that "in this great variety of ways that men follow, it is still doubted which is this right one".[61] Confronted with this reality of religious diversity, Locke is a firm advocate of toleration. Proast, however, when confronted with this same reality, comes to the directly opposite conclusion. This is due to what we have seen is his faith in God and his belief that God would not deceive those who sincerely seek His "truth".[62] As Proast puts it:

> Now here I grant, that if all men were but so faithful to their own Souls, as to seek the way of Saving them, with such Care and Diligence

as the Importance of the matter deserves, and with Minds free from Prejudice and Passion; there could be no need of Force to compel any man to do, what in that case every man would be sure to voluntarily, and of his own accord.... Because (if we believe the Scriptures) no Man can fail of finding the way of Salvation, who seeks it as he ought; and in this case all Men are supposed so to seek it.[63]

Of course, the necessary corollary of this proposition – that all who genuinely seek the "true religion" necessary for "Salvation" cannot "fail of finding" it – is that those who, in Proast's opinion, have not found "true religion", must have been in some way negligent in their search for it. Indeed, this is the very conclusion that Proast draws. His proof of this is the existence of religious diversity itself – the fact that many individuals in Proast's time were divided on matters of faith. He declares that, if all individuals sought their salvation in the diligent manner he describes above, then "as there is indeed but one true Religion, so there could be no other Religion but that in the world".[64] And yet as there are "many Religions in the World" and "only one of them can be true", the very fact of this diversity is clear evidence that "Men have not sought the Truth ... with that application of mind, and that freedom of Judgement, which was requisite to assure their finding it".[65] This, he believes, justifies the magistrate's use of force to ensure this.[66] What we see, therefore, is that whereas Locke, by the time he has moved beyond the *Two Tracts*, uses the existence of religious diversity as reason for toleration, Proast, on the basis of this very same reality, arrives at the directly opposite conclusion.

It is within this context, and within the framework of this set of assumptions, that we can understand Proast's claim, at note 14 above, that if the magistrate's "Power" is kept "within its bounds", it is able to "serve the Interest of no other Religion but the true". This statement depends for its coherence on Proast's assumptions, evident above, that (a) there is but "one true religion"; (b) it is possible to know which religion this is; (c) all those who have not found this religion "have not sought the Truth ... with that application of mind, and that freedom of Judgement, which was requisite to assure their finding it"; because, (d) God would not deceive those who genuinely seek His truth, with the result that "no Man can fail of finding the way of Salvation, who seeks it as he ought". If all of these assumptions are affirmed, Proast is able to conclude that, if individuals, by the appropriate use of force, are brought "to consider those Reasons and Arguments which are proper and sufficient to convince them", they will "come to the knowledge of the Truth", and those that do not "deserve not to be consider'd".[67]

Proast and the Consent Argument I

We saw that Locke's "consent argument" refers, not to the "means" at a magistrate's disposal, but to the "ends" which he or she is legitimately entitled to pursue. Such ends, being the purposes for which the magistrate's authority was originally established, make up the legitimate scope of the magistrate's authority and therefore incorporate those matters over which he or she has a rightful jurisdiction. As explained in Chapter 1, Locke insists that political power (or what Locke calls the "sword") belongs exclusively to the magistrate, and it is to "civil" ends alone that such power may be legitimately directed.[68]

Jeremy Waldron, we saw, denied that these aspects of Locke's political philosophy were present in the *Letter Concerning Toleration*.[69] He therefore denied the existence of a "consent" argument, within the *Letter*, qualitatively different from the "rationality argument". By contrast, Proast is more sensitive to the content of Locke's *Letter*. In his first response to Locke, he directly acknowledges the existence of the "consent argument" and the limits it seeks to place on government, as follows:

> But in reference to the *Civil magistrate*, our Author tells us, That *the Commonwealth seems to him to be a Society of men constituted onely for the procuring, preserving, and advancing of their own Civil Interests*. By which *Interests* he tells us he means *Life, Liberty, Health and Indolency of Body; and the Possession of outward things, such as Money, Lands, Houses, Furniture, and the like*. And agreeably to this *Hypothesis*, he would perswade us, That *the whole Jurisdiction of the Magistrate reaches onely to these Civil Concernments: and that all Civil Power, Right, and Dominion, is bounded and confined to the onely care of promoting these things: and that it neither can nor ought in any manner to be extended to the Salvation of Souls*.[70]

Proast then surprises us by not only acknowledging the existence of this consent argument in the *Letter* but also apparently endorsing it – insisting that he too believes the magistrate's authority ought to be limited to the ends for which it was established:

> I acknowledge (as this Author here seems to do) that the extent of the Magistrate's Jurisdiction is to be measured by the End for which the Commonwealth is instituted. For in vain are men combined in such Societies as we call Commonwealths, if the Governours of them are not invested with sufficient Power to procure the End for which such Societies are intended.[71]

But Proast then takes this argument further and, rather than limiting the ends of the magistrate's authority to that specific class of interests ("Civil Interests") to which he refers at note 70 above, expands these ends to include whatever "Benefits" magistrates are capable of procuring, with the "means" at their disposal, for those under their jurisdiction:

> I must say, that our Authour does but beg the Question, when he affirms that the Commonwealth is constituted *onely* for the procuring,

preserving, and advancing of the Civil Interests of the Members of it. That Commonwealths are instituted for these Ends, no man will deny. But if there be any other Ends besides these, attainable by Civil Society and Government; there is no reason to affirm that these are the *onely* Ends for which they are designed. Doubtless Commonwealths are instituted for the attaining of the Benefits which Political Government can yield. And therefore if the *Spiritual* and *Eternal* Interests of men may any way be procured or advanced by Political Government; the procuring and advancing those Interests must in all reason be reckon'd among the Ends of Civil Societies, and so, consequently, fall within the compass of the Magistrate's Jurisdiction.[72]

By defining the "compass of the Magistrate's Jurisdiction" in terms of the "Benefits which Political Government can yield", and then insisting that "*Spiritual* and *Eternal* Interests" fall within this "compass" because they are "Benefits" government is capable of "procuring", Proast seems to be anticipating Waldron's "modal" account of the state. This is the account which, we saw, underwrote Waldron's depiction of Locke's "rationality argument" and declares that the ends a magistrate seeks to pursue are legitimate so long as he or she possesses the requisite means to achieve them. In insisting, in the passage above, that the scope of the magistrate's legitimate authority extends to all those "Benefits" he or she is capable of "procuring", "advancing" or "attaining" for those under their command, Proast seems to be endorsing such a "modal" account of the state, and in so doing, displacing the terms of the "consent argument", which he endorsed at note 71 above, with those of the "rationality argument", in which it is the efficacy of the means at the magistrate's disposal which underwrites the legitimate scope of the magistrate's command.

Proast is even more direct in his appeal to the "modal" account elsewhere in his first response to Locke. As he puts it:

> And certainly, if there be so great *Use* and *Necessity* of outward Force (duly temper'd and applied) for the promoting True Religion and the Salvation of Souls, as I have endeavoured to shew there is; this is as good an Argument, to prove there is somewhere a Right to use such Force for that purpose, as the utter *Uselessness* of Force (if that could be made out) would be, to prove that no body has any such Right.[73]

By appealing to this "modal account", Proast is able to side-step the connection between the origins of government, the purposes for which it was established, and the ends it is legitimately entitled to pursue, which, we saw, was so central to Locke's "consent argument". Whereas Locke, in this argument, sought to reconcile individual liberty with government authority by prescribing the limits of that authority in terms of the consent of the governed, Proast's "modal" approach to such authority – where government has a "Right" to employ authority to "attain" those "Benefits" which, given the means at its disposal, it is able to "yield" – allows him to avoid the issue of individual consent altogether.

As we shall see in the following chapter, Locke responds to Proast's attempt to circumvent the "consent argument" by re-emphasising this argument, declaring (as in previous chapters) that the magistrate is only entitled to pursue those ends for which he or she has a "commission", arising from the "consent" of the individuals (or their predecessors) subject to the magistrate's jurisdiction, and insisting that religion is not a matter upon which individuals would grant such "commission". But we shall see that Locke and Proast's engagement also moves beyond the consent argument to a theological level, centred on God's purposes for government, quite distinct from the consent of the governed.

Proast and the Consent Argument II

Yet, before moving to this theological level, we must discuss one other way in which Proast seeks, in his first letter to Locke, to respond to the consent argument. This concerns Proast's appeal to the "true Interests" of those subject to the magistrate's command. Proast directly quotes Locke's claim in the *Letter* that no "Power" over religion can

> be vested in the Magistrate by the consent of the People; because no man can so far abandon his own Salvation as blindly to leave it to the choice of any other, whether Prince or Subject, to prescribe to him what Faith or Worship he shall embrace.[74]

It is in direct response to this passage that Proast appeals to "true Interests":

> For if men, in choosing their Religion, are so generally subject, as has been shewed, when left wholly to themselves, to be so much swayed by Prejudice and Passion, as either not at all, or not sufficiently to regard the Reasons and Motives which ought alone to determine their Choice: then it is every man's true Interest, not to be left wholly to himself in this matter, but that care should be taken, that in an affair of so vast Concernment to him, he may be brought even against his own inclination, if it cannot be done otherwise (which is ordinarily the case) to act according to Reason and sound Judgement. And then what better course can men take to provide for this, then by vesting the Power I have described, in him who bears the Sword?[75]

With this appeal to "true Interest", Proast challenges Locke's "consent argument" at its core. This is because Locke, in the "consent argument", conceives of individuals exercising consent on behalf of such interests. It is precisely their own true interests which, Locke tells us in the *Two Treatises*, motivates individuals to leave the state of nature and consent to the establishment of civil society and government.[76] By appealing to the "true Interests" of individuals – albeit interests centred on their eternal salvation – Proast, far from seeking to circumvent the "consent argument", as he does with his "modal" account in the previous section, aligns his claims with the terms of the "consent argument" itself. This then allows Proast to conclude, in the passage above and below, that, far from individuals having an interest in excluding religion from the magistrate's jurisdiction (as Locke claims), individuals would consent to the magistrate having authority over their religion, because it is in their "true Interests" to do so:

> And so I proceed to shew that it is every man's *interest*, in respect of his Salvation, that the Magistrate should have such a Power committed to him.... For if the Power I speak of, be of such a nature as I have represented it; it will follow unavoidably, not onely that the People may vest it in the Magistrate without *abandoning the care of their Salvation*, or *leaving it blindly to the choice of another to prescribe to them what Faith and Worship they shall embrace*; but likewise, that it is every one's *Interest* (supposing it in his power) to vest it in him.[77]

How does Proast justify such a proposition, identifying the "true Interest" of individuals with an authority, on the part of the magistrate, over their religion? The key phrase resides in the passage above, which begins "if the Power I speak of, be of such a nature as I have represented it". It is his description of this "Power" that enables Proast to link it to the "true Interests" of individuals. This "Power", of course, is the magistrate's authority to use force in matters of religion and we have seen that Proast describes this "Power" as one which, if kept "within its bounds", is able to "serve the Interest of no other Religion but the true".[78] If this proposition is maintained, then Proast's description of this "Power" is such that it is indeed in the "true Interest" of each individual that the magistrate should possess such "Power" and exercise it over religion. This is because such "Power", in serving "no other Religion but the true", is a "Benefit" conducive to each individual's salvation. In such circumstances, the ascription of such a "Power" to the magistrate is not a case (as per Locke's "truth argument") of an individual abandoning his own salvation so as to "blindly ... leave it to the choice of any other, whether Prince or Subject, to prescribe to him what Faith or Worship he shall embrace".[79] Rather, in serving "no other Religion but the true", such "Power" is a "Benefit" which, in assisting the path to salvation, accords with individuals' "true Interests".[80]

Consequently, in addition to seeking to circumvent the "consent argument" by affirming a "modal" account of the state, in which the legitimacy of the magistrate's authority is determined, not by the "consent" of the governed, but by the efficacy of the means the magistrate has at his or her disposal, Proast, in his reference to "true Interests", also seeks to abide by the terms of the "consent argument", but uses this to arrive at the very opposite conclusion to Locke concerning the magistrate's authority over religion. Of course, the two types of argument, advanced by Proast, are linked. Proast begins, in the "modal" account, with the "Benefits" that governments can "yield", with the means at its disposal, and then shows how these "Benefits" are consistent with the "true Interests" of individuals. It is this appeal to "true Interests" which turns what would otherwise be a purely "modal" account of the state, of the type we perceive in the "rationality argument", into a version of the "consent argument", since it seeks to justify government authority in terms of the interests of individuals rather than the means at the magistrate's disposal. Even though Proast does not attempt to show that individuals have ever *actually* bestowed their consent on government in these terms (indeed at note 75 above he argues that such authority can be employed "even against [their] own inclination") nevertheless Proast's implicit position is that such consent can be assumed if individuals are aware of their "true Interests".

Proast's Appeal to God

Proast does not leave the justification of the magistrate's authority over religion solely to the terms he articulates above. Instead, he ultimately appeals to God as the final confirmation of the magistrate's jurisdiction in this regard. In so doing, Proast moves beyond the terms of Locke's "truth", "rationality" and "consent" arguments altogether.

Proast makes this appeal to God in the passage that follows. In the first instance, he repeats the "modal" account of the state, justifying the ends of the magistrate's authority in terms of the means he or she possesses to achieve them. But in the final line, he provides a *theological* justification for why the means at the magistrate's disposal, if capable of achieving their ends, ultimately justify those ends themselves:

> If all Force and Compulsion be utterly useless and unserviceable to the promoting these Ends; then to use it for that purpose, will be only to abuse it; which no man can have a Right to do: But if, on the contrary, such a degree of outward Force as has been mentioned, be really of great and even necessary use for the advancing these Ends (as, taking the World as we find it, I think it appears to be;) then it must be acknowledged, that there is a Right somewhere to use it for the advancing those Ends; *unless we will say (what without Impiety cannot be said) that the Wise and Benign Disposer and Governour of all things has not furnish'd Mankind with competent Means for the promoting his own Honour in the World, and the Good of Souls.*[81]

Consequently, it is clear that, for Proast, the ultimate justification of the magistrate's authority, and the ends he or she is entitled to pursue, is not the "usefulness" and "necessity" of the means he or she has at their disposal (as in the "modal" account) or indeed the "true Interests" of individuals (as in Proast's version of the "consent argument"). Rather, it is the will of God

Himself. This is because Proast is insisting, in the last line of the passage above, that if the magistrate possesses means capable of achieving specific ends, then it must be the will of God that these ends be achieved, and it is this which incorporates these ends within the legitimate scope of the magistrate's authority. In other words, Proast is ultimately justifying the authority of government in terms of God's purposes – what he refers to in the passage above as God's "*own Honour in the World, and the Good of Souls*".

Proast makes a similar point in his second response to Locke, insisting that the means at the magistrate's disposal must entitle the magistrate to pursue the ends these means are capable of achieving, since otherwise such "means" would have been given to the magistrate in "vain":

> For if what has hitherto been universally acknowledged, be true, *viz.* That *no Power is given in vain*, but to be *used* upon occasion; I think a very little *Logick* may serve a man to draw this Conclusion from it, That all Societies are instituted for the attaining *all the good*, or *all the benefits* they are *enabled* to attain: Because if you except any of those benefits, you will be obliged to admit, that *the Power* of attaining them was given in vain.[82]

Once again, such a justification of the magistrate's authority only makes sense if the idea that the magistrate might have been given possession of "Power" in "vain" is an unthinkable possibility. And this is only unthinkable if we consider the magistrate's authority as ultimately arising from divine purposes, as Proast appears to in the passage at note 81 above – since only then can we follow Proast, in his assumption in this same passage, that it would be "Impiety" to presume that the magistrate's means do not accord with the ends he or she is supposed to pursue.

In ultimately resorting to God to justify the authority of government, it is clear that Proast, like Locke, advances a "functional" rather than a "modal" account of the state. As we have seen, a "functional" account is an account in which the legitimacy of the magistrate's authority is justified in terms of the ends which the magistrate is entitled to pursue, rather than the means the magistrate possesses to achieve these. Whereas, for Locke, these ends are determined by the purposes for which individuals establish government, and consent to its authority, for Proast, in the passages above, they are ultimately determined by God's purposes, and His intention as to what the ends of government should be.[83] In this way, Proast's various gestures towards a "modal" account of the state, such as those quoted earlier, are ultimately overridden by an authoritative appeal to God, as the consummate source of the magistrate's authority and the basis of his or her legitimacy (though Proast is insistent throughout his letters that the only magistrates whose authority he seeks to justify in this way are those who seek to advance the "true religion"[84]).

Needless to say, the fact that Locke's "functional" account of the state is based on consent, and Proast's on God's purposes, gives rise to profound differences between them. Locke's appeal to consent means that individual liberty (expressed as a capacity to withhold or bestow consent) plays a central role in his justification of government authority, the limits he places upon it and therefore his defence of toleration. Proast's appeal to God and His purposes means that he does not have to appeal to individual liberty in relation to such matters at all, since he can assume that God, as "*the Wise and Benign Disposer and Governour of all things*", would not engage in any purposes which were not ultimately to the "Benefit", and in the "true Interests", of individuals. Whereas I suggested earlier that it is Proast's "modal" account of the state that allows him to "side-step" the emphasis on individual liberty and consent so central to Locke, we see here that it is also Proast's appeal to God that allows him to do so.

The upshot is that whereas Locke's framework allows him to exclude matters of religion from the legitimate ends of the magistrate's authority, on the grounds that these are not purposes for which individuals are likely to have conceded consent to government, Proast, with his appeal to God and His purposes, is able to insist that the "promoting True Religion and the Salvation of Souls", as well as the means necessary to achieve this, fall well within the purview of the magistrate's authority, and the "true Interests" of the individuals subject to it, and it would be "Impiety" to suggest otherwise.

Proast, Berlin and Mill

Once Proast appeals to God and His purposes as the primary source of government authority, as well as the legitimacy of that authority, we saw, at note 75 above, that he is able to justify the exercise of that authority even against the "inclinations" of those subject to it. This is because his appeal to God ensures that this exercise can still be conceived as being in the "true Interests" of these individuals, irrespective of their "inclinations" (God, presumably, being a better judge of their "true Interests" than these individuals themselves).

Of course, such a proposition is a definite instance of the more extreme manifestations of what Isaiah Berlin has called "positive liberty", where what counts as the "liberty" of the individual is determined independently of the choices of individuals themselves, in terms of a "higher" reason or some other normative ideal.[85] The significant difference, however, is that the argument as advanced by Proast refers to "Interests", not liberty, and has God, not temporal ideals of rationality, as its "higher ideal".

Needless to say, from Locke's perspective, just as from John Stuart Mill's some one hundred and seventy years later, the "true Interests" of individuals were not a legitimate reason for the magistrate to impinge upon individual liberty. Mill made this point very clear in his essay *On Liberty*.[86] Locke makes it clear in the *Letter Concerning Toleration*, when he specifically precludes the magistrate from interfering with the religious affairs of an individual even if the latter "neglects the care of his soul".[87] The fate of an individual's soul is, for Locke, a purely "private" matter, and, in *An Essay Concerning Toleration*, he clearly distinguishes "private" concerns from those of the magistrate:

> [I]n things of this world over which the magistrate has an authority he never does, and it would be injustice if he should any further than it concerns the good of the public, enjoin men the care of their private civil concernments, or force them to a prosecution of their own private interests.[88]

For Locke, therefore, even if an individual is neglecting their private interests, including the salvation of their own soul, this provides no justification for others, including the magistrate, to forcibly interfere beyond the personal exhortations and admonitions that Locke endorses in Chapter 1, because they have no authority to do so:

> No man has power to prescribe to another what he should believe or do in order to the saving of his own soul, because it is only his own private interest, and concerns not another man. God has nowhere given such power to any man or society, nor can man possibly be supposed to give it [to] another over him absolutely.[89]

Consequently, the fact that Locke was unwilling to countenance the coercion of individuals in their "private" affairs, even when this was in the "true Interests" of the individuals concerned, shows the central role that "negative" liberty (to use Berlin's term) – and the equal entitlement to this liberty – plays within Locke's conception of toleration, placing limits on the authority of others to intrude into individual lives.[90] Indeed, we shall see in Chapter 9 that Locke makes this same point, insisting that even if the magistrate had knowledge of "true religion" and therefore possessed the means by which individuals could ensure their eternal salvation (a purely hypothetical proposition given that Locke denies the possibility of all such knowledge) this would still not justify the imposition of the magistrate's religion, and the coercion of individual liberty that would accompany this, because the magistrate would still have no "commission", arising from individual consent, to intrude upon "men's souls".[91] In this respect, we shall see in Chapter 9 the crucial role which the "consent argument" continues to play in Locke's defence of toleration – and how it applies even in the hypothetical circumstances above, in which a knowledge of "true religion", on the part of the magistrate, undermines the conditions of the "truth argument" (which, of course, rests on the assumption that no such knowledge is possible).

The Rationality Argument

As the previous chapter made clear, it is Proast's claim to have found a means by which the use of force, exercised "*indirectly* and *at a distance*", is able to create the conditions for the inculcation of sincere and genuine religious belief, which is the primary basis upon which Locke scholars such as Jeremy Waldron, Mark Goldie and John Dunn have concluded that Locke's *Letters Concerning Toleration* fail to provide a cogent defence of toleration in the face of Proast's critique. As Waldron put it, "[d]espite the enormous amount of ink that he devoted to his response, Locke failed to provide any adequate answer to this point".[92]

We saw that Waldron's account foundered on the fact that, unlike Proast, he failed to perceive the full range of arguments that Locke did advance for toleration within the *Letter*, only one of which is affected by the capacity of force to inculcate sincere religious belief. However, the preceding discussion shows a further way in which Waldron has misread the Locke/Proast debate. In the sections above, we have seen that the ultimate basis of Proast's response to Locke resides not in his discovery of means of force capable of instilling sincere and genuine religious belief, but rather in Proast's appeal to God and His purposes. The latter, as a "functional" account of state authority, is qualitatively distinct from the "modal" account which Waldron seeks to ascribe to Proast, and provides a completely different reason why, from Proast's perspective, the magistrate is entitled to use force in matters of religion.

Proast's appeal to God and his purposes, as the ultimate basis of the magistrate's authority, and the scope of his or her legitimate jurisdiction, therefore "trumps" his "modal" account of the state, which had sought to perform the same service. Contrary to Waldron, Goldie and Dunn, therefore, it is not Proast's discovery of "means" capable of instilling sincere and genuine religious belief which is the ultimate basis of Proast's purported refutation of Locke's theory of toleration, and Proast's defence of the magistrate's use of force in matters of religion, but rather his insistence that such toleration, in allowing individuals to be left alone in such concerns, is not in accord with their "true Interests", nor in accord with God and His purposes.

Notes

1 Proast 1999a: 26–7. See also Proast 1999b: 53.
2 See Proast 1999a: 27; Proast 1999b: 53–4, 59, 90.
3 Ibid.: 94. Indeed, at one point in his second response to Locke, Proast even declares that the issue central to Locke's "consent argument" – whether the magistrate has been given authority to impose penalties on those who do not embrace "true religion" – "is the very thing in question between us" (ibid.: 102).
4 Ibid.: 94.
5 See Ch. 5 ("The Truth Argument" and "The 'Truth Argument' Considered").
6 See Ch. 5 (note 26).

7 Proast 1999a: 36. For Locke's original statement, see Ch. 5 (note 30).
8 Proast makes this point clear when he states "there are so many Religions in the World, and ... only one of them can be true" (Proast 1999a: 28).
9 For Proast's justification of the use of force, see Ch. 6 ("*Indirectly* and *At A Distance*'").
10 See Ch. 6 (notes 45–7, 53 and 73–5).
11 Proast 1999a: 27.
12 See, for instance, Ch. 6 (note 46) and note 14 below.
13 So for instance, Proast says at note 16 below that the purpose of penalties, imposed by the magistrate, is to ensure that individuals at odds with the magistrate on religion engage in "a serious and impartial examination of the Controversy between the Magistrate and them".
14 Proast 1999a: 36.
15 Ibid.: 30. See also Ch. 6 (note 74).
16 Proast 1999a: 36.
17 Ibid.: 28. See also Proast 1999b: 67–8, 69, 72, 83, 96, 107. For the full quote see note 63 below.
18 See note 16 above.
19 Proast 1999a: 36–7. For Locke's criticism of this argument, see Locke 1963a: 132–3.
20 See Ch. 6 (note 41).
21 See Locke 1963a: 111.
22 Ibid.: 92–4. See also ibid.: 71, 74.
23 See Ch. 6 (note 46) and note 14 above.
24 Proast 1999b: 85–6.
25 Locke 1963b: 301.
26 Proast 1999b: 50. Although Proast insists that the "one true Religion" encompasses the Church of England, he also declares that "I am far enough from thinking that the true Religion is confined to this *Kingdom*, or this *Island*" (ibid.). This, it would seem, conflicts with his subsequent, and somewhat exclusive, statement, in the last line of the passage in the main text, that "the *National Religion now in* England, *back'd with the Publick Authority of the Law, is the onely true Religion*" (ibid.).
27 See Goldie at Ch. 6 (note 70).
28 See Locke 1963a: 88–9.
29 Proast 1999a: 29.
30 Locke 1963a: 89. See also Locke 1963b: 296–7.
31 Locke 1963a: 90.
32 See ibid.: 65, 89, 90, 111; 1963b: 296–7, 332–4, 419.
33 See Locke 1963a: 90; 1963b: 296–7, 419.
34 Locke 1963a: 111.
35 Ibid.: 65. See also ibid.: 89, 90, 111; 1963b: 296–7, 332–34, 419.
36 For others who have applied Dworkin to Locke, see Waldron 1988: 72: Vernon 2013: 222.
37 Dworkin 1975: 126.
38 Ibid.: 127.
39 See Ch. 6 (note 90); Locke 1963c: 561. On each individual being "judge for himself", see also Ch. 1 (notes 25, 29 and 40); Ch. 5 (notes 55 and 56).
40 See Locke 1963a: 89; 1963b: 419; 1963c: 561; Locke 1993a: 403.
41 Waldron 1988: 71.
42 Ibid.: 72. The original quote from Locke that Waldron cites is at Locke 1993a: 416, though in my text Locke refers to "India" rather than the "Indies".
43 Locke 1963b: 145. See also notes 44 and 57 below.
44 See ibid.: 143–6, 163, 184, 205, 213, 262, 365, 370, 374, 378, 382, 398, 399, 402, 408–9; 1963c: 505–6, 514, 535–6, 541, 555–6; 1993a: 416. I have

already made reference to Locke's use of a version of this argument at Ch. 6 (note 5).
45 For Locke's "criterion of reciprocity", see Ch. 3 (note 32). For Richard Vernon's identification of the role of "reciprocity" in Locke, see Ch. 3 (note 33).
46 See Locke 1993a: 416, 417, 430, 435.
47 Dworkin 1975: 125. Locke has also articulated such a commitment to universalization. Speaking of his authorship of the *Letter Concerning Toleration* in the third person, he says to Proast: "The author's letter pleased me, because it is equal to all mankind, is direct, and will, I think, hold every where; which I take to be a good mark of truth" (Locke 1963a: 95).
48 Locke 1993a: 430.
49 Ibid.: 435.
50 Locke 1963a: 78.
51 Locke 1963c: 566. See also Locke 1963b: 146, 147–8, 163, 184, 205, 213, 374, 378; 535–6. Locke makes a similar point in his second *Letter* at Locke 1963a: 76–7, 78, 114.
52 Proast 1999a: 36.
53 Proast 1999b: 54, 66.
54 Proast 1999c: 121.
55 Waldron 1988: 72. Indeed, Waldron also denied that Locke exhibited scepticism about "religious matters" – see Ch. 5 (note 23). On how Waldron can only advance the "somewhat more sensible position", that he refers to in his passage in the main text, because of his failure to recognize, not only the full scope of Locke's "truth argument", but also the full scope of Locke's "consent argument", see Ch. 9 (note 75).
56 On Locke's belief in "one true religion", and associated reservations, see Ch. 5 (note 14–16).
57 Locke 1963b: 143. See also notes 43 and 44 above.
58 Concerning the role of scepticism in Locke's "truth argument", see Ch. 5 ("The Truth Argument" and "The 'Truth Argument' Considered").
59 Thus Locke, in addressing Proast, refers to "your useless distinction of force to be used, not for any, but for the true religion" (Locke 1963b: 146).
60 See Ch. 4 (note 2). Equally, in the *Two Treatises*, Locke also mentions the inevitability of diversity, referring to "the variety of Opinions, and contrariety of Interests, which unavoidably happen in all collections of Men" (Locke 1965: II § 98). I am indebted to the late Richard Ashcraft for the *Two Treatises* reference (see Ashcraft 2009: 57), but although Ashcraft also mentions the *Letter Concerning Toleration* reference, I had already discovered that on my own.
61 See Introduction (note 20).
62 See note 17 above.
63 Proast 1999a: 28.
64 Ibid.
65 Ibid.
66 Ibid.
67 See Ch. 6 (note 41), and note 14 and 16 above.
68 On the "sword" being the exclusive possession of the magistrate, see Ch. 1 (notes 31 and 50). On its limitation to civil ends alone, see Ch. 1 (notes 32, 33, 39, 40, 82–5) and Ch. 5 (note 54).
69 See Ch. 4 (notes 62, 65 and 72).
70 Proast 1999a: 32–3.
71 Ibid.: 33. See also Proast 1999b: 97.
72 Proast 1999a: 33. See also Proast 1999b: 95.
73 Proast 1999a: 31–2.
74 Ibid.: 34. For Locke's original statement on these lines, see Ch. 5 (note 58). See also ibid. (note 30).

75 Proast 1999a: 35.
76 See Ch. 1 (notes 17 and 54).
77 Proast 1999b: 103. See also ibid.: 114, 114–15.
78 See Ch. 7 (note 14).
79 See note 74 above.
80 At one point, in his second response, Proast seeks to respond to Locke's consent argument by insisting that, although the magistrate cannot be a "Judge of Truth" for others, nevertheless if he or she has "knowledge" of the "Truth", then he or she "may easily judge whether other men be *alienated*" from the "Truth" and can therefore apply "Penalties" to bring individuals "to judge more sincerely for themselves" (Proast 1999b: 102). This appears to be a spurious distinction, since it is not apparent how, in laying "Penalties" upon others, on the grounds that they are "alienated from the Truth", a magistrate has avoided being a "Judge of Truth" for these others. Locke makes this point as follows: "That which I say ... is, that, whoever punishes others for not being of the religion he judges to be true, judges of truth for others" (Locke 1963b: 174. See also ibid.: 173–4, 175–6, 185, 186, 187).
81 Proast 1999a: 32. Emphasis added.
82 Proast 1999b: 95.
83 In his second response to Locke, Proast also sought to argue that there is nothing inconsistent in his account with such authority of the magistrate (over religion) also coming from the consent of the people (ibid.: 103–4).
84 See Ch. 6 (notes 45–7, 53 and 74–5) and notes 14 and 54 above.
85 See Berlin 2008: 178–212.
86 See Mill 1971: 72–3.
87 See Ch. 6 (note 92).
88 Locke 1993b: 188. For other explicit references to the "private", see ibid.: 195; Locke 1993a: 404. See also Locke 1993b: 188–9 and 1993a: 404–5.
89 Locke 2004: 276. On "personal exhortation and admonition", see Ch. 1 (note 28). On why Proast was unlikely to see religious belief as a purely "private" interest, see Conclusion (note 1) where he argues that such belief can affect the fate of an entire polity.
90 It is in this respect that Isaiah Berlin is thoroughly mistaken to identify Locke with his "positive" conception of liberty – see Berlin 2008: 193–4. Locke's conception of liberty is, within the framework of limits provided by law, adulthood and sanity, largely "negative", premised on freedom from restraint (see Locke 1965: II § 22, 57, 190. See also Ch. 1 note 61). I have made this point elsewhere in the journal literature, and identified where Berlin, in aligning Locke with "positive" liberty, misinterprets his political philosophy (Tate 2013: 823–7).
91 See Ch. 9 ("Ultimate Conditions of Possibility I"). On "men's souls", see Ch. 5 (notes 56 and 58). See also Ch. 1 (notes 25, 29 and 40).
92 See Ch. 6 (note 57).

References

Ashcraft, R. (2009) "Locke and the Problem of Toleration". In: H. E. Bödeker, C. Donato and P. H. Reill (eds) *Discourses of Tolerance and Intolerance in the European Enlightenment*. Toronto: University of Toronto Press, pp. 53–72.

Berlin, I. (2008) "Two Concepts of Liberty". In: I. Berlin *Liberty*. Henry Hardy (ed.). Oxford: Oxford University Press, pp. 166–217.

Dworkin, G. (1975) "Non-Neutral Principles". In: N. Daniels (ed.) *Reading Rawls. Critical Studies on Rawls' A Theory of Justice*. Oxford: Basil Blackwell, pp. 124–140.

Locke, J. (1963a) "A Second Letter Concerning Toleration". In: J. Locke *The Works of John Locke*. Vol. VI. Aalen: Scientia Verlag, pp. 61–137.

Locke, J. (1963b) "A Third Letter for Toleration". In: J. Locke *The Works of John Locke*. Vol. VI. Aalen: Scientia Verlag, pp. 141–546.

Locke, J. (1963c) "A Fourth Letter for Toleration". In: J. Locke *The Works of John Locke*. Vol. VI. Aalen: Scientia Verlag, pp. 549–74.

Locke, J. (1965) *Two Treatises of Government*. P. Laslett (ed.). New York: New American Library.

Locke, J. (1993a) "A Letter Concerning Toleration". In: J. Locke *Political Writings*. David Wootton (ed.). London: Penguin, pp. 390–436.

Locke, J. (1993b) "An Essay Concerning Toleration". In: J. Locke *Political Writings*. David Wootton (ed.). London: Penguin, pp. 186–210.

Locke, J. (2004) "Toleration D". In: J. Locke *Political Essays*. M. Goldie (ed.). Cambridge: Cambridge University Press, pp. 276–7.

Mill, J. S. (1971) "On Liberty". In: J. S. Mill *Utilitarianism, Liberty, Representative Government*. London: Everyman, pp. 61–170.

Proast, J. (1999a) "The Argument of the Letter Concerning Toleration, Briefly Consider'd and Answer'd". In: M. Goldie (ed.) *The Reception of Locke's Politics, Vol. 5. The Church, Dissent and Religious Toleration 1689–1773*. London: Pickering and Chatto, pp. 25–37.

Proast, J. (1999b) "A Third Letter Concerning Toleration: In Defense of the Argument of the Letter Concerning Toleration, Briefly Consider'd and Answer'd". In: M. Goldie (ed.) *The Reception of Locke's Politics, Vol. 5. The Church, Dissent and Religious Toleration 1689–1773*. London: Pickering and Chatto, pp. 41–116.

Proast, J. (1999c) "A Second Letter to the Author of the Three Letters for Toleration, from the Author of the Argument of the Letter Concerning Toleration, Briefly Consider'd and Answer'd, and of the Defense of It". In: M. Goldie (ed.) *The Reception of Locke's Politics, Vol. 5. The Church, Dissent and Religious Toleration 1689–1773*. London: Pickering and Chatto, pp. 119–28.

Tate, J. W. (2013) "'We Cannot Give One Millimetre'? Liberalism, Enlightenment and Diversity", *Political Studies*, 61 (4): 816–33.

Vernon, R. (2013) "Lockean Toleration: Dialogical not Theological?", *Political Studies*, 61 (1): 215–30.

Waldron, J. (1988) "Locke: Toleration and the Rationality of Persecution". In: S. Mendus (ed.) *Justifying Toleration: Conceptual and Historical Perspectives*. Cambridge: Cambridge University Press, pp. 61–86.

8 Locke's Reply: "That Which Without Impiety Cannot be Said"

This chapter focuses on Locke's reply to Proast, which he provides in his second, third and fourth *Letters Concerning Toleration*. This reply extends to hundreds of pages, and as Locke's strategy, within these pages, is to respond to each of Proast's letters, almost line by line, the result is often repetitive, prolix and verbose. Nevertheless, within this reply there is a kernel of hard, robust political philosophy in which Locke continues to maintain most of the key positions he advanced within the first *Letter Concerning Toleration*, building upon these in various ways, but also moving beyond them, not least in the fourth *Letter*, where, as discussed in an earlier chapter, new ground is broken in the debate. Far from Mark Goldie's view that Locke's debate with Proast took place on an "apparently narrow front", with "[n]o general theory of toleration ... at issue", and Goldie, Waldron and Dunn's view that the key issue in the debate, upon which Locke's case for toleration either succeeded or failed, was the capacity of force to instil sincere and genuine religious belief, we shall see that the debate involved much more than this, taking place across a very broad front, with Locke continuing to advance, in a number of ways, two of his three "considerations" for toleration, based on "truth" and "consent", first put forward in the *Letter Concerning Toleration*.

The chapter begins with Locke's criticism of the content and structure of what he calls Proast's "Method" – i.e. Proast's advocacy of force, applied "*indirectly*" and "*at a distance*", for "promoting True Religion and the Salvation of Souls". I have divided this criticism into two categories, each referring to the content and structure of the "Method". These categories are "proportion" and "Design" – categories which arise from Proast's own description of his "Method".

Locke's criticism of Proast's "Method", in terms of its "proportion" and "Design", is primarily instrumental in focus, centred on whether Proast's "Method" is capable of achieving the ends that Proast assigns to it. But Locke also advances a normative critique of this "Method", arising from his "consent argument", which focuses on the legitimacy of the "Method", when force, employed "*indirectly* and *at a distance*", is applied to realize its ends. We consider Locke's instrumental critique, centred on the "proportion" and "Design" of Proast's "Method", first, before considering his normative critique, arising from his "consent argument". Finally, as with the previous chapter, we shall see that Locke's engagement with Proast eventually moves to a theological level, with Locke and Proast each appealing to God in a quite different way to advance their case either for or against toleration. Ultimately it is Locke's appeal which is the more successful in this respect, Proast ultimately finding himself mired in contradiction on the issue of the "Grace of God".

"Penalties"

As the previous chapter made clear, central to Proast's position is his claim that the magistrate's "Power", if kept "within its bounds", is able to "serve the Interest of no other Religion but the true".[1] This proposition implies the possession of a "Method" that is instrumentally capable of achieving such ends. Proast makes reference to such a "Method" when he refers to the "great *Use* and *Necessity* of outward Force (duly temper'd and applied) for the promoting True Religion and the Salvation of Souls".[2] Proast conceives of such a "Method", involving the use of such "outward Force", in terms of "Penalties", where these "Penalties" are applied, by the magistrate, upon those who have "got into a wrong Way" and so refuse to affirm the "true religion", in order to bring them "to consider those Reasons and Arguments which are proper and sufficient to convince them".[3] As Proast puts it:

> Where to shew the Necessity of Penalties to bring men to *hearken to Instruction*, and to *consider* and *examine* matters of Religion as they ought to do, I allege that such as are out of the right Way, are usually so prejudiced against it, that no intreaties or Perswasions will prevail with them so much as to give an ear to those who call them to it; so that there seems to be no other means left (besides the Grace of God) but Penalties onely, to bring them to *hear* and *consider*; and so to embrace the Truth.[4]

Regarding the use of such force (in the form of "Penalties") we have seen that Proast insists that if these are applied "*indirectly* and *at a distance*", they can do "some service toward the bringing men to embrace that Truth, which otherwise, either through Carelessness and Negligence they would never acquaint themselves with, or through Prejudice they would reject and condemn unheard, under the notion of Errour?"[5] It is this which constitutes Proast's "Method".

"Proportion" and "Design"

But it is one thing for Proast to make reference to such a "Method". It is quite another to give a clear idea of how "Penalties", "duly temper'd and applied", are able to bring individuals "to embrace that Truth, which otherwise, either through Carelessness and Negligence they would never acquaint themselves with", thereby promoting "True Religion and the Salvation of Souls". In other words, in making reference to such a "Method", Proast also needs to give a clear idea of the terms of its application and how these will allow it to achieve its ends. Only then will Proast have affirmed the instrumental effectiveness (or what Jeremy Waldron would call the "rationality") of his "Method".

Proast himself conceded this point. Just like Locke in the *Two Tracts*, he declared that "*if it be rightly used … the Force applied [must] be duly proportioned* to the Design of it".[6] And yet, as Locke himself declares over numerous pages, it is at the level of both "proportion" and "Design" that he finds Proast's "Method" most wanting. We shall consider each of these elements of Proast's "Method" – "proportion" and "Design" – in turn.

"Proportion" can be broken down into two halves. First, it can refer to the *content* of Proast's "Method", meaning the identity of those specific instruments of "force", applied "*indirectly*" and *at a distance*", of which Proast seeks to make use. Second, it can refer to the *application* of this force, or more particularly, the conditions of its *successful* application, where this force, so applied, is capable of achieving its ends. The latter is what Proast refers to above when he describes such instruments of force as having been "duly temper'd and applied".[7]

"Design" refers not only to the content of Proast's "Method" but also to the ends it seeks to achieve. As we saw in relation to Locke's *practical* arguments for either religious conformity (*Two Tracts on Government*) or toleration, "means" are only effective (or what Waldron would call "rational") when they are capable of achieving their ends. So, irrespective of the content or application of Proast's "Method" ("Proportion"), its "Design" is only successful if it encompasses ends which it is capable of achieving.

Now it is at the level of "ends" that Proast's "Method" undergoes a profound shift between his first and second response to Locke. We saw in the previous chapter that Proast, in his first response to Locke, insisted that his "Method", as applied by the magistrate, was a "Power" for the magistrate "to bring men, not to his *own*, but to the *true* Religion".[8] Now it may be, as a matter of contingent fact, that these two religions are one and the same – although Locke insists that, as knowledge of "true religion" is denied us, this is not something we can ever *know*, such matters being left to "the supreme judge of all men, to whom also alone belongs the punishment of the erroneous".[9]

But Proast, in his first response to Locke, does not declare these religions to be one and the same. Rather, we saw, Proast acknowledged that the magistrate may be mistaken about the "truth" of the religion to which he or she seeks to direct individuals, in which case, Proast insists, little harm is done, even though "Penalties" have been applied, because the individuals concerned will "know better than they did before, where the Truth does lie".[10]

Yet, as we also saw in the previous chapter, by the time of his second response to Locke, Proast had moved beyond this position. Although acknowledging that the magistrate may be mistaken about "true religion", Proast denies that this can be the case in regard to the English magistrate, because the "true religion", he insists, encompasses the Church of England.[11]

Once Proast makes this admission, the "Design" of his "Method" shifts. Of all magistrates, the English magistrate, at least, can no longer be *wrong* about the "truth" of religion. Rather, the only thing he or she can be wrong about is whether the "Method" they possess is capable of bringing individuals "to embrace that Truth, which otherwise, either through Carelessness and Negligence they would never acquaint themselves with".

The question, therefore, of whether the "Penalties" applied by the magistrate are "duly *proportioned* to the Design of it" will have a very different answer depending on whether that "Design" is directed to (i) "True Religion and the Salvation of Souls" in general (in which the "truth" of religion is not identified with the magistrate) or (ii) "True Religion and the Salvation of Souls" when "true religion" is identified with the English magistrate. In each case, the "Design" encompasses a very different end, with the result that the use of force that is "duly *proportioned*" to achieve that end will differ.

In the case of (i), Proast insists that the force which is sufficient to achieve the end in question is that amount necessary to put those individuals, at odds with the magistrate on religion "upon a serious and impartial examination of the Controversy between the Magistrate and them: which is the way for them to come to the knowledge of the Truth".[12] Because "truth", in the case of (i), is not identified with the magistrate's religion, Proast is able to declare that, in such instances, "*the Authority of the Magistrate is not an Authority to compel any one to his Religion*, but onely an Authority to procure all his Subjects the means of Discovering the Way of Salvation".[13]

In the case of (ii), on the other hand, where "true religion" is identified with the English magistrate, the only possible criterion of success for Proast's "Method" – given that the "Method" is designed for the "promoting True Religion and the Salvation of Souls" – is conversion to the English magistrate's religion.[14] Proast makes himself very clear on this point as follows:

> For (to come to the Point;) the *National Religion* is either true, or not true. If it be not true, no man is bound to *believe* it: And it is no *fault* in him that is not bound to believe it, not to *profess* it. If it be true; then either there is sufficient provision made for instructing men in the truth of it, or there is not. If there be not; then all men are not bound to *believe* it; And (as was said before) in those who are not bound to believe it, it will be no *fault* not to profess it. But if there be sufficient means of Instruction provided for all; then it must be a *fault* in all not

to *profess it*: because, in that case, it is a *fault* in all not to *believe* it. And the like is to be said concerning *Communion with the Magistrate in Divine Worship*.

This I take to be very plain. And from hence these two things will unavoidably follow. 1. That no man ought to be punish'd for not being of any false Religion, though it be the *National Religion*; Because it is no *fault* not to be of any false Religion. 2. That all who have sufficient means of Instruction provided for them, may be justly punish'd for not being of the *National Religion*, where the true, is the National Religion: Because it is a *fault* in all such, not to be of that Religion. And so *all Punishment* for the sake of Religion, will not be *unjustifiable Severity*. For though, *where there is no Fault, there can be no moderate Punishment*; yet all Punishment is not *immoderate, where there is* a Fault to be punish'd.[15]

Consequently, if the "true religion" is the Church of England, then given that the purpose of Proast's "Method" is the "promoting True Religion and Salvation of Souls", anything short of conversion to that "national religion" would be a failure of the "Method" to achieve its ends. But it would also be, in Proast's view, a failure on the part of the individuals to whom the "Method" is applied. After all, as Proast tells us, "no man ever *studied* the true Religion with such care and diligence as he might and ought to use, and with an honest mind, but he was *convinced of the truth of it*".[16] Therefore, assuming such "care" and "diligence", "the *Light of their own Reason*, and the *Dictates of their own Consciences* (if their *Reason and Consciences* were not perverted and abused) would undoubtedly lead them to the same thing, to which the Method we speak of, is designed to bring them".[17] Consequently, for individuals to have been subjected to Proast's "Method" and yet fail to be "convinced of the truth" of the "true religion", would be an instance of that "Carelessness and Negligence" which Proast identified earlier as the justification for the application of his "Method" in the first place.[18] As he put it:

> [M]y Method punishes men with Punishments ... for rejecting the true Religion, proposed to them with sufficient Evidence, (which certainly is a Fault), to bring them to consider and examine the Evidence with which it is proposed, that so they may embrace it (which is both lawful for them, and their duty to do).[19]

Proast could not reach these conclusions without assuming that knowledge of "true religion" is not only possible for all who seek it, but also conclusive, thereby giving individuals no excuse for not having embraced the "true religion" "proposed to them with sufficient Evidence". He is able to make such assumptions because of his belief, discussed in the preceding chapter, that God would not deceive those who sincerely and diligently seek Him, with the result that "no Man can fail of finding the way of

Salvation, who seeks it as he ought".[20] Consequently, given Proast's assumption that knowledge of "true religion" is both possible and conclusive, and failure to recognize that "truth" is evidence of "carelessness" and "negligence", it would seem that in relation to (ii) above, the "Design" of his "Method" – not least its criterion of success – would require that "Penalties" not cease until conversion to the English magistrate's religion has taken place, and indeed *ought* to increase until such conversion takes place.

Certainly Locke makes this point to Proast.[21] Proast himself, in his first response to Locke, admits that, when it comes to this crucial question of "proportion" – i.e. the level of force "duly temper'd and applied" necessary to promote "True Religion and the Salvation of Souls" – his "Method" lacks certainty and precision.[22] Indeed such difficulties does this issue of "proportion" (the "Degrees" and "just Measures" of force) pose for Proast, that, in his first response to Locke, he says he will postpone any consideration of it, stating that it is not an issue that he would "take upon me to determine", admitting it was the "onely Point", in his debate with Locke, in which there was "any ground for Controversy, in this whole matter".[23]

However by the time of his second response to Locke, in which he has conceded that the "true religion" encompasses the Church of England, Proast is much more certain concerning the question of "proportion" and agrees with Locke's assessment of his "Method" that "Penalties" will not cease until conversion to the "true religion" has taken place:

> But because my Designe does rather oblige me to consider *how long* men may *need* Punishment, than *how long* it may be *just* to punish them; therefore I shall add, That as long as men refuse to embrace the true Religion, *so long* Penalties are necessary for them, to dispose them to consider and embrace it: And that therefore, as Justice allows, so Charity requires that they be kept subject to Penalties, *till* they embrace the true Religion.[24]

This confirmation on Proast's part concerning the "proportion" of the "Penalties" he seeks to apply resolves an important ambiguity for Locke. Locke had insisted, in his first response to Proast, that if the purpose of Proast's "Method", in its application of "Penalties", was (as Proast declared) to force those at odds with the magistrate's religion to engage "upon a serious and impartial examination of the Controversy between the Magistrate and them", the "Method" had no means of determining when such "serious and impartial examination" had taken place, and so no means of determining when the "Method" had achieved its goal and "Penalties" should cease.[25] In other words, Proast had no means of determining when force had been "duly temper'd and applied". As Locke puts it, when it comes to such "serious and impartial examination", "it is impossible for you ever to know whether [an individual] has done his duty, or whether he be desperately perverse and obstinate".²⁶ This is because "the fault is undefined, and the guilt not to be proved", with the result, Locke says, that Proast does "but regulate one uncertainty by another".²⁷ Locke points to how this uncertainty undermines the overall purpose of Proast's "Method", this being the "promoting True Religion and the Salvation of Souls":

> [T]o punish men for that, which it is visible cannot be known whether they have performed or no, is so palpable an injustice, that it is likelier to give them an aversion to the persons and religion that uses it than to bring them to it.²⁸

However, once Proast makes clear that the fault to be punished is not the absence of "serious and impartial examination" but rather a failure to affirm the "true Religion" (as per (ii) above) and that "Penalties" must continue to be applied until such affirmation (conversion) takes place, the level of force which, "*if it be rightly used* ... [must] be duly *proportioned* to the Design of it", becomes more apparent, because the point at which the "Method" has achieved its end, and "Penalties" should cease, becomes more evident. However, such clarification having taken place, Locke then points to the spurious nature of Proast's earlier claim, that "*the Authority of the Magistrate is not an Authority to compel any one to his Religion, but onely an Authority* to procure all his Subjects the means of Discovering the Way of Salvation".²⁹ As Locke puts it:

> To deny the magistrate to have a power to compel men to his religion; but yet to say the magistrate has a power, and is bound to punish men to make them consider, till they cease to reject the true religion; of which true religion he must be judge, or else nothing can be done in discharge of this his duty; is so like going round about to come to the same place, that it will always be a circle in mine and other people's imagination, and not only there, but in your hypothesis.³⁰

Punishment and Conversion

When Locke was under the impression that the purpose of Proast's "Method" was to force upon Dissenters (i.e. those at odds with the magistrate on religion) "a serious and impartial examination of the Controversy between the Magistrate and them", Locke had pointed out that this was unfair, since, he declared, those who were members of the magistrate's religion were, on the whole, much less likely to have "seriously" and "impartially" examined their religious beliefs, and much more likely to hold to these beliefs on unexamined grounds, than Dissenters, who had chosen the more arduous prospect of non-conformism and residence outside the established church for the sake of their religion.³¹ As Locke puts it, pointing to the restrictions imposed by English law on dissenting places of worship:

For what sense is it, to punish a man "to dispose him to submit to instruction, and give a fair hearing to reasons offered for enlightening his mind, and discovering truth to him", who goes two or three times a week several miles on purpose to do it, and that with the hazard of his liberty or purse?[32]

Yet once Proast admits that the "Design" of his "Method" has, as its end, not merely "serious and impartial" examination of religion, but conversion to the Church of England, Proast is able to give a clear rationale as to why his "Method" applies only to Dissenters, rather than members of the Church of England who have not "seriously" and "impartially" "examined":

Now here I acknowledge, that though want or neglect of Examination be a general Fault, yet the Method I propose for curing it, does not reach to all that are guilty of it, but is limited to those who reject the true Religion, proposed to them with sufficient Evidence.... So that how much soever any of those who own the true Religion, may be guilty of neglect of Examination; 'tis evident, I was onely concern'd to shew how it may be *cured* in those, who, by reason of it, reject the true Religion, duly proposed or tender'd to them.[33]

Indeed, Proast perceives the "guilt" on the part of Dissenters, in failing to affirm the "true Religion", to be so palpable, that the application of his "Method" entails no more than their just deserts:

For there is nothing more evident, than that those who do so reject the true Religion, are *culpable*, and *deserve* to be punish'd. And it is easy enough to *know* when men do so reject the true Religion. For that requires no more than that we know that that Religion was tender'd to them with sufficient Evidence of the truth of it.... Now if the persons I describe, do really *deserve* to be punish'd; and may be *known* to be such as I describe them; than as they *deserve* to be punished; so they *may* be punish'd. Which is all that needs to be said upon this Head, to shew the *Consistency* and *Practicableness* of this *Method*.[34]

Once Proast admits that the end of his "Design" is conversion to the English magistrate's religion, Locke points to two reasons why he believes Proast's "Method" is not "practicable". The first concerns the process of conversion itself. Since Proast tells us, at note 24 above, that Dissenters will "be kept subject to Penalties, *till* they embrace the true Religion", Locke insists that these "Penalties" are likely to be most effective on those Dissenters willing to adopt mere outward conformity to the Church of England, so as to escape "Penalties", and so is unlikely to produce the "serious and impartial examination" of religion which, Proast declares, "is the way for [Dissenters] to come to the knowledge of the Truth".[35] As Locke puts it:

[I]t is manifest that embracing the true religion in your sense is only embracing the outward profession of it, which is nothing but outward conformity. And that being the farthest you would have your penalties pursue men, and there leave them with as much of their ignorance of the truth, and carelessness of their souls, as they please: who can deny but that it would be impertinent in you to consider how want of impartial examination, or aversion to the true religion, should in them be cured?[36]

Yet what of those Dissenters who refuse to convert to the magistrate's religion, even for opportunistic reasons? This gives rise to the second reason why Locke believes Proast's "Method", and its end of seeking conversion to the English magistrate's religion, is not "practicable". Proast admits, at note 24 above, that "Penalties" must be applied until conversion to the "true religion" takes place. In *An Essay Concerning Toleration*, Locke declared that the sort of force needed to convince the most recalcitrant Dissenters "cannot stop short of the total destruction and extirpation of all dissenters at once".[37] He makes the same point twenty-five years later, declaring that Proast cannot "limit the punishment to any degree short of the highest, if you will use punishments at all in matters of religion".[38] Locke gives his reasons for this conclusion as follows:

> Non-conformity to the national, when it is the true religion, as in England, is a fault, a vice, say you, to be corrected by the coactive power of the magistrate. If so, and force be the stronger remedy, he must increase it, till it be strong enough to work the cure, and must not neglect his duty; for so you make it, when he has force enough in his hand to make this remedy more powerful. For wherever force is proper to work on men, and bring them to a compliance, its not producing that effect can only be imputed to its being too little.... For to continue inefficacious penalties, insufficient upon trial to master the fault they are applied to, is unjustifiable cruelty; and that which nobody can have a right to use, it serving only to disease and harm people, without amending them.[39]

Consequently, in relation to Proast's reference to "outward Force (duly temper'd and applied)", which he says ought to be directed to "the promoting True Religion and the Salvation of Souls", Locke's conclusion is that Proast can impose no justifiable limit on such force if the end of his "Method" has not yet been achieved:

> For, as I have said, and you deny not, "Where there is no fault, there no punishment is moderate"; so I add, Where there is a fault to be corrected by the magistrate's force, there no degree of force, which is ineffectual, and not sufficient to amend it, can be immoderate; especially if it be a fault of great moment in its consequences, as certainly that must be, which draws after it the loss of men's eternal happiness.[40]

As such, Locke says, Proast must, in terms of the "Design" of his "Method", either "condemn all" "Penalties", imposed for the sake of religion, or, for the reasons above, "retain all" – "you must either take or leave all together".[41] Yet if Proast "retains all", then Locke concludes that his "Method" will be unable to achieve its end of converting Dissenters to the English magistrate's religion without applying, on some, the upmost force, and therefore destroying those whom it seeks to convert – an outcome which, Locke insists, is "absurd".[42] In confounding its own ends in this way, Proast's "Method", from Locke's perspective, is not only "impracticable", but also (to use Waldron's term) "irrational".

Locke, Proast and Consent

In the preceding sections of this chapter, Locke offers a variety of reasons why, at the level of "proportion" and "Design", Proast's "Method" is unlikely to achieve the ends which Proast assigns to it. Yet we have seen that, in his response to Proast, Locke did admit that "indirectly" and "at a distance", Proast's "Method" might, on occasion, actually succeed in achieving these assigned ends, centred on the inculcation of sincere and genuine religious belief.[43]

Such an admission that force, applied "indirectly" and "at a distance", may at times achieve the ends which Proast assigns to it, certainly (we saw) undermines one of the key conditions of the "rationality argument". The other condition of that argument was undermined once Locke conceded that the magistrate was unlikely to use force to achieve such ends in any case.[44]

Yet, in abandoning the "rationality argument", Locke in no way assumed that this left him devoid of other arguments to advance in favour of toleration. When Proast sought to make such a claim, Locke responded as follows:

> And you tell us, "the whole strength of what that letter urged for the purpose of it, lies in this argument", which I think you have no more reason to say, than if you should tell us, that only one beam of a house had any strength in it, when there are several others that would support the building, were that gone.[45]

Locke's "truth" and "consent" arguments, we saw, are categorically distinct from the "rationality argument", and even in the absence of the "rationality argument", remain intact as normative arguments for toleration (though we saw in Chapter 5 that the "truth argument" was more an argument why we should resist the magistrate's command in matters of religion than an argument capable of convincing the magistrate not to exercise this command). Unlike the "rationality argument", we have seen that the "truth" and "consent" arguments are in no way dependent, for their cogency, on the empirical question of whether force is capable of achieving the ends which the magistrate assigns to it. Indeed, in the case of the "consent argument", we saw that it sought to exclude from the magistrate's jurisdiction these very ends, based on the inculcation of sincere and genuine religious belief, which underwrote the "rationality argument".[46]

One reason for this exclusion is that, at the level of "compact", the "consent argument" assumes that religion is not something concerning which individuals either wish, or can, "stipulate about ... one with another", nor "submit ... to the power of the society, or any sovereign they should set over it".[47] One primary reason Locke offered for this was the material fact that "nobody else is concerned" in these matters, nor can "receive any prejudice" from the conduct of individuals "therein".[48] It is therefore a matter in which "[n]obody is obliged ... to yield obedience unto the admonitions or injunctions of another", with the result that Locke insists that "[e]very man ... has the supreme and absolute authority of judging for himself".[49] Indeed, as Locke makes clear in the first *Letter Concerning Toleration*, the only issues upon which individuals are obliged to "stipulate about ... one with another", at the level of compact, are those that "by mutual assistance, and joint force, they may secure unto each other".[50] Because religion does not fall within this category, Locke did not believe it was something that individuals, at the level of compact, would submit to the judgment of others, and so it was not something over which they would cede any authority to the magistrate.[51] From the perspective of the "consent argument", therefore, religion was not a matter that would be included among the ends of the magistrate, to be pursued by force or other means.

This is the essence of Locke's "consent argument", centred on what, in Locke's opinion, it was possible for individuals to contract about with each other when establishing civil society and government. The "consent argument" provides a normative argument against Proast's "Method", and the force it assigns to the magistrate in matters of religion, by insisting that, irrespective of whether the "Method" is or is not capable of achieving its ends, centred on religion, these are ends that ought to be excluded from the magistrate's jurisdiction altogether, the magistrate having no "commission" to pursue them. The result is an argument for toleration in those areas where the magistrate is not entitled to interfere. We saw that this argument was a central part of Locke's first *Letter Concerning Toleration*, but Locke, in response to Proast, is still articulating it in detail in the third *Letter*:

> The end of a commonwealth constituted can be supposed no other than what men in the constitution of, and entering into it, proposed; and that could be nothing but protection from such injuries from other men, which they desiring to avoid, nothing but force could prevent or remedy; all things but this being as well attainable by men living in a neighbourhood without the bounds of a commonwealth, they could propose to themselves no other thing but this in quitting their natural liberty, and putting themselves under the umpirage of a civil sovereign,

who therefore had the force of all the members of the commonwealth put into his hands to make his decrees to this end be obeyed. Now since no man or society of men can, by their opinions in religion or ways of worship, do any man who differed from them any injury, which he could not avoid or redress if he desired it, without the help of force; the punishing any opinion in religion or ways of worship by the force given the magistrate, could not be intended by those who constituted or entered into the commonwealth; and so could be no end of it, but quite the contrary. For force from a stronger hand, to bring a man to a religion which another thinks the true, being an injury which in the state of nature every one would avoid; protection from such injury is one of the ends of a commonwealth, and so every man has a right to toleration.[52]

Locke, Proast and God

Proast, we saw, recognized the presence of the "consent argument" among those "considerations" Locke advanced in the original *Letter Concerning Toleration*. Indeed, as the previous chapter made clear, Proast's ultimate strategy for overcoming the "consent argument" and substantiating his case for the magistrate's use of force in matters of religion, is by an appeal to God. The following sections investigate this appeal further and also consider Locke's response to it. We shall see that Proast's appeal to God, centred on God's "Grace", ultimately mires his argument in contradiction.

We saw, in the preceding chapter, that the ultimate foundation for Proast's justification of the magistrate's use of force in matters of religion was not, as Waldron, Dunn and Goldie claim, the effectiveness of that force as a *means* to instil sincere religious belief and thereby advance "true religion". Rather, it was that such force, when used for these purposes, was in accord with the will of God. In this respect, Proast insists, Commonwealths are instituted by God, with the result that their purposes must include God's purposes.[53]

Locke's response to such claims is not to deny that Commonwealths are instituted by God. As a sincere Christian, with a belief in God's omnipotence and omnipresence, Locke must have seen all aspects of the world as, in some respect, a product of God's creation, or at least His acquiescence.[54] And yet, as we shall see below, Locke is clearly reluctant to endorse such divine origins for Commonwealths, insisting at note 57 below that it is "man", not God, who inaugurates Commonwealths, and the political authority they exercise, and that he does so via "consent", on the basis of material, as distinct from spiritual, interests. But then, after confrontation with Proast on this point, Locke reluctantly seeks a compromise, admitting at note 66 below that profane and divine origins of Commonwealths can coincide, given that it is through the medium of natural law (which arises from God's will) that individuals acquire the authority to create governments on the basis of their own consent. But, as these passages below make clear, Locke remains reluctant to affirm such divine origins for Commonwealths, such concessions notwithstanding.

The result is that when it comes to the origins of political authority, it seems there is a tension, within Locke's political philosophy, between his recognition of the omnipotence and omnipresence of God and his commitment to the idea that it is the liberty of individuals and the consent to which this gives rise, not divine authority, which inaugurates Commonwealths and places limits on government authority. After all, as Locke puts it in the *Two Treatises*, "*the Consent of Free-men, born under Government* [is that] which only *makes them Members of it*".[55] Locke's reluctance to endorse divine origins for Commonwealths, evident in his engagement with Proast below, may be considered as one more example of Locke seeking to "bracket" his political conclusions from any theological foundations.[56]

God, Man and Commonwealths

Locke's attempt to reconcile these two sources, God and man, in relation to the origin of Commonwealths, arises as a late response to Proast – in particular, to Proast's objection to the following passage in Locke's *Second Letter Concerning Toleration*. In this passage, Locke, in the interests of excluding religion from the magistrate's jurisdiction, excludes God from the origins of Commonwealths, insisting that Commonwealths arise from the mutual consent of individuals alone:

> Commonwealths, or civil societies and governments, if you will believe the judicious Mr. Hooker, are, as St. Peter calls them ... the contrivance and institution of man.... You must show them such a commission, if you say it is from God. And in all societies instituted by man, the ends of them can be no other than what the institutors appointed; which I am sure could not be their spiritual and eternal interest.[57]

Immediately after the passage above, Locke justifies his proposition that the ends of "civil societies and governments" cannot include the "spiritual and eternal interests" of individuals by making the point, central to the "consent argument", that religion is not something that these individuals, in the process of inaugurating civil society and government, would have "stipulated about ... one with another", these being interests which they were either unwilling or unable to "submit ... to the power of the society, or any sovereign they should set over it".[58]

Proast responds by rejecting each one of the propositions that Locke advances above. These are that (a) civil societies and governments arise from the consent of individuals rather than from God; (b) that the ends of government are therefore not determined by God; with the result that (c) "spiritual and eternal interests" do not fall within the jurisdiction of governments because (d) these are not among the matters which individuals, in the creation of civil society and government, were willing to "stipulate about ... one with another, nor submit ... to the power of the society, or any sovereign they should set over it".

Regarding (a), Proast states:

> St. *Paul* teaches us that the Supreme Powers are ... *order'd, disposed,* or *set in their places by God. That they are accordingly ... the Disposition,* or *Ordinance of God: And that they bear the Sword and punish them that do evil,* as the *Ministers of God, i.e.* as *appointed* and *comission'd* by him so to do: For how they can be his *Ministers,* for that, or any other purpose, without his appointment and Commission, is not to be understood. So that, if you will believe the *Scriptures,* the *Civil Powers,* or, if you please, *Civil Society* and *Government* are so the *Contrivance and Institution of Man,* as to be withall the *Ordinance and Institution of God.*[59]

In this way, Proast seeks to counter Locke's claim that the "commission" of government – i.e. the basis of its authority – arises from individual consent, insisting instead that it arises directly from God. Regarding (b) Proast states:

> Now if according to the *Scriptures,* and even to the *judicious Mr.* Hooker, *God* is the Author and *Institutor* of Civil Society in general; then the *Ends* of it, as your self must grant, can be no other than what *He* has appointed: and all that is left to the Choice and Contrivance of Man, is onely the framing and modelling Commonwealths, and the Government of them, as Prudence shall direct, for the better attaining the Ends which he has fix'd and prescribed.[60]

In this passage, Proast has subverted Locke's "consent argument", rewiring it in a divine direction. He agrees with Locke's statement at note 57 above that the "ends" of civil society and government can be "no other than what the institutors appointed". But the "institutor" is, in Proast's opinion, God, and so it is His "ends" which are authoritative, leaving individuals within civil society only a "framing and modelling" role, within these divine limits, "as Prudence shall direct", so that God's "ends" may be "better" achieved. In these respects, divine authority has replaced individual consent as the source of political legitimacy and authority.

Regarding (c) and (d) Proast states:

> But you say you are *sure the Ends of Commonwealths, appointed by the Institutors of them, could not be their Spiritual and Eternal Interests.* But why not, if their Spiritual and Eternal Interests may be promoted by Political Government, as I think I have shewn they may? Why, say you, *they cannot stipulate about these one with another,* (which I suppose you explain by the following words) *nor submit this*

> *Interest to the Power of the Society, or any Sovereign they should set over it.* Very true, Sir: But they can submit to be punish'd in their Temporal Interests, if they despise or neglect those greater Interests. Which is all they need to do.[61]

We saw in Chapter 7 that it was on the basis of Proast's appeal to the authority of God that he was able to sidestep the issue of individual liberty and consent so central to Locke's "consent argument". In the last two lines of the passage above, we see how Proast overrides these concerns altogether. In response to Locke's claim, at note 58 above, that religious interests are not among those matters which individuals are willing to put to common agreement – "stipulating about … one with another" – Proast replies that these individuals are nevertheless able to "submit to be punish'd in their Temporal Interests, if they despise or neglect those greater Interests". Such a conclusion can only arise if these "greater Interests" override these "Temporal Interests". For Proast they do, because these "greater Interests" refer to the "spiritual and eternal interests" which Locke, at note 57 above, seeks to exclude from the jurisdiction of governments, but to which Proast, by contrast, believes individuals can be "brought", by government, "even against [their] own inclination, if it cannot be done otherwise", because this is in their "true Interest", of which they are not the best judge.[62] It is these sort of assumptions, advanced by Proast, that underwrite the last line of Proast's passage above, justifying the "punishment" to which he refers, and the overriding of individual liberty and consent which is the inevitable corollary of this. In this way, Proast seeks to confirm that "spiritual and eternal interests" fall firmly within the jurisdiction of governments, and are an end for which governments are entitled to exercise authority over individuals.

Locke's Response to Proast's Appeal to God

What is clear, from the discussion above, is that Locke and Proast perceive the Commonwealth as inaugurated not only for different purposes, but as serving entirely different ends, each of which have very different implications for individual liberty. This can be seen in the following declaration where Proast implies that, because the Commonwealth is instituted for God's purposes, individuals can (again) be punished by the magistrate if they subvert these purposes, thereby revealing that, in such matters, issues of individual liberty and consent have no status within Proast's conception of the Commonwealth at all:

> You say St. *Peter* shews, in the place you referr to, *for what End Commonwealths are instituted,* viz. *for the punishment of evil-doers, and the praise of them that do well.* But you say you do not find any where, *that it is for the punishment of those who are not in Church Communion with the Magistrate.* Nor do I any where say it is. But if

rejecting the true Religion, or declining the Communion of the Church of God, be *doing evil*; then they that do so, are *Evil-doers*: and then you see what you get by St. *Peter's* words.[63]

Locke, in his third *Letter Concerning Toleration*, responds to Proast's explicit appeal to God in the passages above. To Proast's insistence, at note 61 above, that individuals, in civil society, can be punished by government if they neglect their "Spiritual and Eternal Interests", Locke responds by reasserting the terms of the "consent argument", insisting that individuals cannot be punished for that which they have not submitted to the authority of government (or anybody else) in the first place:

> To my saying, "the ends of commonwealths appointed by the institutors of them, could not be their spiritual and eternal interest, because they could not stipulate about those one with another, nor submit this interest to the power of the society, or any sovereign they should set over them". You reply, "very true, sir; but they can submit to be punished in their temporal interest, if they despise or neglect those greater interests". How they can submit to be punished by any men in their temporal interest, for that which they cannot submit to be judged by any man, when you can show, I shall admire your politics.[64]

Concerning the origins of Commonwealths, however, which was the subject of Locke's original appeal to St Peter at note 57 above, Locke's response to Proast is to reluctantly adopt the compromise referred to earlier, where he concedes that Commonwealths can have both divine and profane origins, given that it is God-given natural law that provides individuals with the authority to create governments (and the natural rights governments are inaugurated to protect).[65] It is this authority, and these rights, which form the basis of the contractual negotiations (and ultimately consent) to which Locke refers at notes 55 and 58 above, and which (he tells us at note 57) are part of the "contrivance and institution of man":

> And now, sir, if you can but imagine that men in the corrupt state of nature might be authorized and required by reason, the law of nature, to avoid the inconveniences of that state, and to that purpose to put the power of governing them into some one or more men's hands, in such forms, and under such agreements as they should think fit; (which governors so set over them for a good end by their own choice, though they received all their power from those, who by the law of nature had a power to confer it on them, may very fitly be called powers ordained by God, being chosen and appointed by those who had authority from God so to do: for he that receives commission, limited according to the discretion of him that gives it, from another who had authority from his prince so to do, may truly be said, so far as his commission reaches,

> to be appointed or ordained by the prince himself;) it may serve ... to show that there is no opposition or difficulty in all that St. Peter, St. Paul, or the judicious Mr. Hooker says; nor any thing, in what either of them says, to your purpose. And though it be true, those powers that are, are ordained of God; yet it may nevertheless be true, that the power any one has, and the ends for which he has it, may be by the contrivance and appointment of men.[66]

Thus we see that, at least from Locke's perspective, although God might be an ultimate source of political authority, Locke makes clear in the last line of the passage above that it is the free consent of individuals ("the contrivance and appointment of men") that determines the limits and ends of government, and therefore those purposes for which the magistrate might legitimately exercise authority. Locke's attempt to retain his original emphasis, at note 57 above, on the "contrivance and institution of man", so evident in the last line of the passage above, shows his eagerness to resist Proast's attempt to reduce the origins and ends of government entirely to God's purposes. His reluctance to concede ground to Proast, in this respect, evident in his unwillingness to shift from his original position at note 57, makes no sense unless he wished to preserve a separate role, in the creation of government, for individual consent, as a source of political legitimacy and as an expression of individual liberty, quite independent from God.

Christian History

Jonas Proast's reading of Locke's *Letter Concerning Toleration* is informed, we have seen, by one overriding concern – "the promoting True Religion and the Salvation of Souls". In his first response to Locke, Proast makes clear that his primary objection to the toleration Locke proposes in the *Letter* is that Proast does not see how "true religion" would be "any way a gainer by it". As he declares:

> I do not believe this Author intends any prejudice, either to Religion in general, or to the Christian Religion. But yet it seems hard to conceive how he should think to do any Service to either, by recommending and perswading such a Toleration as he here proposeth. For how much soever it may tend to the Advancement of Trade and Commerce (which some seem to place above all other Considerations;) I see no reason, from any Experiment that has been made, to expect that True Religion would be any way a gainer by it; that it would be either the better preserved, or the more widely propagated, or rendered any whit the more fruitful in the Lives of its Professours by it. I am sure the Fruits of a Toleration not quite so large as our Author's (some of which still remain with us) give no encouragement to hope for any such Advantage from it.[67]

As Proast was a devout Anglican clergyman, one should not be surprised that his primary concern should be the advancement of "true religion", rather than the normative concerns of individual liberty, or the practical concerns of effective state governance or civil peace, which inform Locke's commitment to toleration. Indeed, in the last line of the passage above he shows he has a jaundiced view of the history of toleration, as applied within England. Locke, in the *Two Tracts*, shared such a jaundiced view, though for different reasons – Proast insisting that such toleration did not advance "true Religion" while Locke, with his focus on civil order, declaring that toleration was "the first inlet to all those confusions and unheard of and destructive opinions that overspread this nation".[68] We saw in Chapter 3 that it was only Locke's reassessment of what we have called premise (i) and premise (ii), as well as his advancement of premise (iii), which moved him beyond this position.

In his second response to Locke, Proast appeals to the history of Christianity as further evidence to underwrite his proposition that "true Religion" would not be "any way a gainer" by toleration. It was Locke who first raised this history, seeking to refute this proposition, when Proast first advanced it in the passage above. Locke argued that the historical proof that "true Religion" *would* be a "gainer" by toleration can be found in the experience of Christianity in the first "several hundreds of years" after its inauguration:

> "You see no reason, you say, from any experiment that has been made, to expect that true religion would be a gainer by it." True religion and Christian religion are, I suppose, to you and me, the same thing. But of this you have an experiment in its first appearance in the world, and several hundreds of years after. It was then "better preserved, more widely propagated, in proportion, and rendered more fruitful in the lives of its professors", than ever since; though then Jews and pagans were tolerated, and more than tolerated, by the governments of those places where it grew up.... This, as I take it, has been made use of by Christians generally, and by some of our church in particular, as an argument for the truth of the Christian religion; that it grew, and spread, and prevailed, without any aid from force, or the assistance of the powers in being; and if it be a mark of the true religion, that it will prevail by its own light and strength, but that false religions will not, but have need of force and foreign helps to support them, nothing certainly can be more for the advantage of true religion, than to take away compulsion every where.... The inventions of men in religion need the force and helps of men to support them. A religion that is of God wants not the assistance of human authority to make it prevail.[69]

It is on the basis of this reading of Christian history, as well as his other arguments discussed above, that Locke concludes that "force, to make men examine matters of religion, is not necessary at all".[70] Instead, he insists that, in relation to such objectives, the "grace of God" is "a proper and sufficient means; and, which is more, the only means; such means as can work by itself, and without which all the force in the world can do nothing".[71] Thus Locke insists that we should confine ourselves to only those means which God has authorized for the propagation of religion (preaching, exhortation and the use of Scripture),

> unless we will say, that which without impiety cannot be said, that the wise and benign Disposer and Governor of all things does not now use all useful means for promoting his own honour in the world, and the good of souls.[72]

This last statement is a gloss on Proast's use of very similar words in his first response to Locke, quoted in the previous chapter.[73] Yet, in using such words, both Locke and Proast appeal to God as a source of authority and veracity underwriting their respective positions.

Proast, in his second response to Locke, takes issue with Locke's reading of the history of Christianity, and the support, Locke claims, it provides for toleration as the appropriate policy for magistrates to adopt within civil society. In the first instance, Proast denies Locke's proposition that "the Christian Religion prevail'd at first meerly by its own *Beauty, Force, or Reasonableness, without the help of Authority or Force*".[74] On the contrary, Proast argues, the early period of Christianity was accompanied by miracles, which buttressed the authority of Christian claims with visible demonstrations of God's power, of which the later period of Christianity is devoid.[75] Then, in response to Locke's claim, at note 69 above, that Christianity's expansion in this period, without the aid of force, is evidence of its status as the "true religion" and therefore of the fact that "true religion" needs no use of force in order to prevail, Proast, in the passage below, makes a distinction between matters of fact and matters of principle. He points out that the *fact* that Christianity did prevail *is* evidence of its truth. But as a matter of principle, it is by no means the case that "true religion" will always prevail or that it therefore has no need of the use of force in order to prevail:

> For neither does the true Religion always *prevail, without the Assistance of the Powers in being*; nor is that always the *true religion*, which does so *spread and prevail*: As I doubt not but you will acknowledge with me, when you have but consider'd within how few Generations after the Flood, the Worship of False Gods prevail'd against the Religion which *Noah* profess'd, and taught his Children (which was undoubtedly the true Religion) almost to the utter exclusion of it (though that at first was the onely Religion in the World) *without any Aid from Force*, or the *Assistance of the Powers in being*.... Of which (besides the Corruption of Humane Nature) I suppose there can no other Cause be assigned, or none more probable than this, that the

> *Powers* then *in being*, did not do what they might and ought to have done, towards the preventing, or checking that horrible Apostasy.⁷⁶

It is at this point that we gain a deeper insight into why Proast does not believe that "True Religion would be any way a gainer" by toleration. Although he agrees, with Locke, that "true religion" does contain its own persuasive force, yet he also believes that the "Corruption of Humane Nature", referred to in the passage above, is likely to prevail at the expense of "true religion", if both are left to their own devices – as they would be within a regime of toleration, where neither would suffer the punitive sanction of state force. In this he sees the biblical example of Noah as conclusive:

> That the true Religion has always *Light and Strength* of its *own*, sufficient to prevail with all that consider it seriously, and without Prejudice, I readily grant. But if, when you make *it a mark of the true Religion*, that it will *prevail by its own Light and Strength*, you mean (as it is plain you must) that it will always prevail in the World against other Religions, *meerly* by its own Light and Strength, without the Assistance either of *Miracles*, or of *Authority*; then I must tell you, that *prevailing by its own Light and Strength*, is so far from being a *mark of the true religion*, that it is not *true*, that the *true Religion* will *so prevail* by its own *Light and Strength*. The Instance [of Noah] but now given, is too great a proof of this.... [i]dolatry prevailing against it, not by its own *Light* and *Strength*, you may be sure, (for it could have nothing of either;) nor yet by the *help of Force* ... but meerly by the advantage which it had in the Corruption and Pravity of Humane Nature, left (as it is most reasonable to suppose) to it self, unbridled by *Authority*.⁷⁷

It is in order to "bridle" "Humane Nature" and avoid its "Corruption and Pravity", or what he elsewhere calls the "Folly, Perverseness, and Wickedness of Men", so detrimental to the advancement of "true religion", that Proast insists, in this and the preceding chapter, that "true religion" be supported by the use of the magistrate's force, "indirectly" and "at a distance".⁷⁸ "True Religion" may have, he says above, "always *Light and Strength* of its *own*, sufficient to prevail with all that consider it seriously, and without Prejudice", but Proast's point is that few do so consider it, independent of the encouragement (or constraint) of the magistrate's authority. It is to this encouragement and constraint that, we have seen, Proast claims his "Method" is directed.⁷⁹

Toleration, on the other hand, as either a policy or an ideal, is seen by Proast as giving a free hand to "Corruption and Pravity", by leaving it to its own devices in matters of religion. The result, Proast declares, is that "in England, or wherever else the true Religion is Nationally received", "true Religion" would not "reap any advantage by having its present Establishment taken away, and our *Author's, i.e.* an *universal Toleration* of Religions *set up* instead of it".⁸⁰ Proast's conclusion, therefore, is that individuals should not be left to "their own Consciences" in matters of religion.⁸¹

Once again, we see an interesting parallel here between Proast and Locke in the *Two Tracts on Government*. Proast's concerns about the "Corruption and Pravity" of "Humane Nature", which underwrite his case against toleration, strike a chord with Locke's similarly pessimistic view of humanity, in the *Two Tracts*, upon which he also advanced his case against toleration.⁸² But once again, there are important differences. Proast's concerns about this "Corruption and Pravity" are primarily pastoral, he believing it will lead, as in the days of Noah, to the advance of a "false religion" at the expense of the "true". Locke's concerns, in the *Two Tracts*, by contrast, are entirely practical in nature, centred on the threat which an unruly humanity poses to civil peace.⁸³ In each case, Locke and Proast assume that individuals cannot be trusted with their own liberty, and so toleration ought to be denied, but one for theological and the other entirely for civil reasons.

Proast and the Will of God

Proast appeals not only to Christian history, but to the will of God, in his justification of the magistrate's use of force in matters of religion. Indeed, to this end, Proast imputes motive and strategy to God Himself. In response to Locke's proposition above that force was absent in the early years of Christianity, and yet the Christian religion proliferated (thereby confirming that force is not necessary for this purpose), Proast insists that God, nevertheless, wishes such force to be applied in the years afterwards, once the persuasion wrought by miracles has been removed:

> Indeed when God takes the matter wholly into his own hands; as he does at his first revealing and planting a Religion; there can then be no need of the Assistance of Humane Authority: because then, to make such a Religion appear to be his, God himself does all that is requisite to *make it prevail*. But when once God has sufficiently settled his Religion in the World, so that if Men will but thenceforth do what they may and ought, in their several Capacities, to preserve and propagate it, it may subsist and prevail without that extraordinary Assistance from him which was necessary for its first establishment: then he leaves it to their care, under his ordinary Providence, to try whether they will do their Duties, or not: leaving them answerable for all that may follow from their neglect. And then, if that religion will not prevail without the Assistance of *Humane Authority*, it cannot be said not to *need that Assistance to make it prevail*.⁸⁴

Proast admits that, in supposing such motives on the part of the divine, he is presuming to "guess at the Counsils of infinite Wisdom".⁸⁵ However he argues that, insofar as miracles "were not withdrawn, till by their help

Christianity had prevail'd to be received for the Religion of the Empire, and to be supported and encouraged by the Laws of it", then

> I cannot but think it highly probable ... that God was pleas'd to continue [miracles] till then, not so much for any necessity there was of them ... for the evincing the Truth of the Christian Religion, as to supply the want of the Magistrate's Assistance.[86]

Proast's Contradiction

Such is Proast's response to Locke's appeal to the early history of Christianity as proof that Christianity had no need of force in order to prevail and could coexist even with the toleration of "Jews and pagans".[87] Proast next seeks to answer Locke's charge that, not only had Christianity no need of such force, but there is no biblical authority, in the words of Christ or elsewhere, for the use of force by magistrates or anyone else for such purposes. Locke makes this point as early as the opening page of his first *Letter Concerning Toleration*.[88]

Proast's response is that there was no need for Christ to invest magistrates with the authority to use force for such purposes because, in Christ's time, they possessed this authority already.[89] Proast arrives at this conclusion by insisting that the Christian duty, which Jesus imposes on each Christian to look after the spiritual welfare of others, applies even more to magistrates given their greater capacity to fulfil this duty.[90]

Locke, we saw, had argued that one reason why force is inappropriate as a means to advance Christianity and inculcate religious belief in individuals (and therefore why the magistrate does not possess authority to use force for these purposes) is because the "grace of God" Himself is "a proper and sufficient means; and, which is more, the only means; such means as can work by itself, and without which all the force in the world can do nothing".[91]

It is in Proast's response to this claim that he encounters the *greatest* difficulty in his engagement with Locke and ultimately finds himself mired in contradiction. Like Locke in the paragraph above, Proast acknowledges God's omnipotence and His concern to provide individuals with all that is necessary for their salvation. We saw this in the previous chapter where Proast declared it would be an "Impiety" to suggest that "the Wise and Benign Disposer and Governour of all things has not furnish'd Mankind with competent Means for the promoting his own Honour in the World, and the Good of Souls".[92] Yet, in order to justify the magistrate's use of force in matters of religion, Proast must declare, contrary to Locke's view in the paragraph above, that *more* than simply God's "grace" is necessary for salvation, since, as we have seen at note 71 above, such "grace" does not, in and of itself, include the use of the magistrate's force. Yet how is Proast to do this without casting doubt on God's omnipotence and so moving in the direction of the "Impiety" that he refers to above?

Proast's strategy, in confronting this conundrum, is to concede Locke's proposition that the "grace of God" is a "proper and sufficient" means of salvation and yet implicitly deny this by insisting that "human" (or what Proast calls "Humane") means may also be necessary to ensure such salvation:

> And therefore though the *Grace of God* be *both a proper and sufficient Means*, and *such as can work by it self*, and without which neither Penalties, nor any other Means can do any thing; yet it may be true however, that when Admonitions and Intreaties fail, there is no *Humane Means* left, but Penalties, to bring prejudiced Persons to hear and consider what may convince them of their Errors, and discover the Truth to them. And then *Penalties* will be *necessary* in respect to that end, as an *Humane Means*.[93]

From any conventional Christian perspective, such a statement moves in the direction of the "Impiety" to which Proast refers above. This is because it appears to deny that the "Grace of God" is a "proper and sufficient Means" of salvation, since such "Grace" requires, in some circumstances, the assistance of "Humane Means" ("Penalties") to ensure salvation.

As if aware of this, Proast seeks to clarify his position. In the passage below, he once again appears to endorse Locke's proposition, at note 91 above, that the "grace of God" is a "proper and sufficient" means of salvation. He does so by referring to the "Grace of God" as "the *onely necessary* Means" of salvation, "as being able to do its work without any help of other Means", and insisting that all other means are "vain and ineffectual" in the absence of it. Yet, in the same passage, he insists that this "Grace" does not "ordinarily exclude all other means" of salvation:

> What you intend by saying that the *Grace of God* is the *onely Means*, I do not well understand. If you mean onely that it is the *principal* and *most necessary* Means, and that without which all other Means are vain and ineffectual; I grant it is so. Or if you mean that it is the *onely necessary* Means, as being able to do its work without any help of other Means: This I have already granted. But if by calling it the *onely Means*, you intend to say that it does either always, or ordinarily exclude all other means; I see no ground you have to say it.[94]

Such a statement, on Proast's part, confronts him with an invidious either/or. Either the "Grace of God" is "a proper and sufficient" means of salvation – being "the *onely necessary* Means ... able to do its work without any help of other Means" – thereby making "all other means" of salvation not only "vain and ineffectual", but unnecessary and superfluous. Or these "other Means" of salvation are also, at times, necessary, in which case the "Grace of God", in these instances, is not "sufficient". Proast can affirm one or the other of these propositions. However it is his attempt to affirm *both*, as he appears to in the passages above, that leads him to contradiction, since the propositions are mutually exclusive. Further, it is the second proposition – that the "Grace of God" is not a sufficient means of salvation because other means are, at times, "necessary" – that contains the seeds of the "Impiety" that Proast identifies at note 92 above, something that, given his Christian commitments, he would wish to avoid.

Proast Agonistes

We saw both in this chapter and the previous one that Proast's ultimate appeal, to justify the magistrate's use of force in matters of religion, is to the will of God. His appeal to the "modal" account of the state, in which the legitimacy of the magistrate's authority is based on the "usefulness" and "necessity" of the means at the magistrate's disposal, is, we saw, ultimately subordinate to this appeal to God.[95] By appealing to God, we saw that Proast ultimately resorted to what Waldron calls a "functional" conception of the state to justify the ends that the magistrate seeks to achieve.[96]

However, in his appeal to God in the section immediately above, we have seen that Proast encounters a contradiction. Locke's insistence that the "grace of God" is a "proper and sufficient" means of salvation, excluding all other means, implies that any other means of salvation are not only "insufficient" but also "improper" to this end and therefore ought not to be used. This proposition has effectively outflanked Proast, because Proast needs to deny the proposition if he is to justify the magistrate's use of force in matters of religion, but he cannot deny it without the implications of "Impiety" that he refers to above.

Proast's ultimate response to this conundrum is a circular one. He justifies the means the magistrate uses in seeking to ensure what the magistrate (and Proast) perceives as individuals' salvation (including "Humane" means involving the use of force) on the grounds that whatever means are made use of by the magistrate to this end, must nevertheless be means "made use of" by God, and so must be consistent with the "Grace of God", since it is God alone that ultimately ensures salvation:

> Yes, say you: *God alone can open the Ear that it may hear, and open the Heart that it may understand.* But, by your favour, this does not prove that he makes use of no *Means* in doing it. For whatever Means we may suppose him to make use of, it is *he alone* still that does it, though he does it by the Means he makes use of.[97]

Proast advances the same sort of argument in the following passage, insisting that if the magistrate's use of force is capable of achieving its ends, and ensuring that individuals embrace the magistrate's ("true") religion, then this again can only be in accord with the "Grace of God", since it is ultimately only the "Grace of God" that can produce such outcomes:

> I suppose you mean, that the Magistrate has no ground to hope that God will *bless* any Penalties that he may use, to bring men to *hear* and *consider* the Doctrine of Salvation: or (which is the same thing) that God does not (at least not ordinarily) afford his Grace and Assistance to them who are brought by such Penalties to hear and consider that Doctrine, to enable them to hear and consider it as they ought, *i.e.* so as to be moved heartily to embrace it. If this be your meaning; then to let you see that it is not true, I shall onely desire you to tell me, whether they that are so brought to hear and *consider*, are bound to *believe* the Gospel, or not? If you say they are; (and I suppose you dare not say otherwise) then it evidently follows that God does afford them that Grace which is requisite to enable them to believe the Gospel: Because without that Grace, it is impossible for them to believe it; and they cannot be bound to believe what it is impossible for them to believe.[98]

In each of the two passages above, Proast seeks to avoid the "either/or" referred to earlier (between the magistrate's force, on the one hand, and the "Grace of God" on the other) by identifying the successful use of one wholly with the other. Aside from the inherent circularity in this process (based, as it is, on a tautological identification of the successful use of the magistrate's force with the "Grace of God") it places no limits on the means a magistrate might use to achieve religious ends, since, by Proast's reasoning in these passages, the achievement of these ends (by whatever means the magistrate might use) is considered consistent with the "Grace of God", because such ends are presumed to be unachievable without this "Grace".

Once this reasoning is in place, Proast is able to justify the magistrate's use of force and, at least to his own satisfaction, escape any implications of "Impiety", throwing the onus of proof back onto Locke with a demand that *he* prove that the "penal" means in use by the magistrate, and shown to achieve their ends, do *not* arise from "God's Grace", and therefore do *not* have God's approval:

> Though the *Work of our Salvation* be, as you justly call it, *stupendous and supernatural*; yet I suppose no sober man doubts but it both admits, and ordinarily requires the use of *natural* and *humane* means, in subordination to that *Grace* which works it. And therefore till you have shewn (as you have not yet) that no Penal Laws that can be made, can do any service towards the salvation of men's Souls, in subordination to God's Grace; or that God has forbidden the Magistrate to serve him in that great *Work*, with the Authority which he has given him; there will be no occasion for the Caution you give us, *not to be wiser than our Maker in that stupendous and supernatural Work*.[99]

Proast encounters what appears to be an insurmountable conundrum once he is confronted by the "either/or", to which we have referred, centred on the magistrate's use of force and the "Grace of God". His resort to a circular and question-begging process of argumentation, in the passages above, is evidence of his difficulty in this respect, and shows that Proast, in confronting Locke's propositions concerning the "Grace of God", ultimately encounters the limits of his own intellectual and theological outlook. This is because he is unable, in any plausible fashion, to reconcile the magistrate's use of force, in matters of religion, with Locke's proposition concerning the "Grace of God", without either recognizing such force as "insufficient" and "improper", and therefore an illegitimate means for the magistrate to use, or else engaging in "Impiety", should he assume the opposite, and insist that such force is a necessary means for salvation, thereby denying the sufficiency of the "Grace of God". To paraphrase Jeremy Waldron: I do not see any other way of reconstructing Proast's argument to meet the criticisms that I have outlined.[100]

Notes

1. See Ch. 7 (note 14).
2. Proast 1999a: 31–2.
3. See Ch. 6 (note 41). For Proast's reference to those who have "got into a wrong Way", see Proast 1999a: 29.
4. Proast 1999b: 76. See also Proast 1999a: 36.
5. See Ch. 6 (note 41).
6. Proast 1999a: 30. For Locke's similar claim in the *Two Tracts*, see Ch. 3 (note 21). Mark Goldie points out that it was this emphasis, on the part of the Anglican authorities, on the "due proportion" of force which, in their minds, was one of the features distinguishing their persecution of non-conformists from the more excessive Catholic persecution of Protestants on the Continent (Goldie 1991: 365). The other feature, of course, was their assumption that, unlike Catholics, they employed such force for the sake of "true religion" (ibid.: 359–60).
7. See note 2 above.
8. See Ch. 7 (note 14).
9. Locke 1993a: 402.
10. See Ch. 7 (note 19).
11. See Ch. 7 (note 26).
12. See Ch. 7 (note 16).
13. See Ch. 6 (note 46).
14. See Proast 1999b: 50–2.
15. Ibid.: 59. See also ibid.: 63.
16. Ibid.: 96.
17. Ibid.: 83.
18. See Ch. 6 (note 41). Indeed, we saw that Proast perceived the very existence of religious diversity as evidence of such "Carelessness" and "Negligence" (see Ch. 7 "Proast and Religious Diversity").
19. Proast 1999b: 83. See also ibid.: 63, 67, 86, 88–9, 96.
20. See Ch. 7 (notes 17 and 63). See also notes 16 and 17 above.
21. See Locke 1963a: 193, 197, 263, 264, 275, 279–86, 288, 290, 301, 302, 311, 412, 481–2, 507; 1963b: 72, 77, 108–9, 109.
22. Proast 1999a: 30.
23. Ibid.: 30, 31.

24 Proast 1999b: 89. See also ibid.: 86, 87, 88, 88–9. At times, in his second response to Locke, Proast prevaricates between asserting that conversion to the "true religion" is the end-point and goal of his "method", so that "Penalties" should continue until such conversion takes place, and his earlier position that the goal is to ensure that dissidents "weigh matters of Religion carefully and impartially" (as he claims at Proast 1999a: 31 and which Locke declares at notes 25 to 28 below to be an illusory goal because it is impossible to determine when such impartial consideration has taken place). On Proast's prevarication, compare Proast 1999b: 101, 106 and 111 to ibid.: 112.

25 See Locke 1963b: 78, 87–8, 92, 93–4, 97, 102, 103, 104, 105–7, 124. Indeed, Locke declared that only God knew when someone had "seriously" and "impartially" examined (ibid.: 103). For Proast's reference to "serious and impartial examination", see Ch. 7 (note 16).

26 Locke 1963b: 106. My addition. See also ibid.: 103. Proast responds by insisting that Locke's demand for such precision, concerning the "rule" by which "penalties" will be applied, is "unreasonable", since "rules" do not include the "particulars" of their application (Proast 1999b: 88).

27 Locke 1963b: 105. Locke makes a similar point in the third *Letter*, declaring: "[Y]ou ordinarily shift off the doubtfulness of one place, by appealing to as doubtful an expression in another" (Locke 1963a: 273).

28 Locke 1963b: 78. Indeed, Locke argued in *An Essay Concerning Toleration* that it is precisely such aversion that makes toleration a more practical means for the magistrate to respond to religious diversity within his or her jurisdiction (Locke 1993b: 192–3, 207).

29 See Ch. 6 note 46. See also Ch. 7 (note 14).

30 Locke 1963a: 185.

31 On Locke's belief that Dissenters are more likely to have "seriously and impartially examined", and adherents of the magistrate's church less likely to have "seriously and impartially examined", see: Locke 1963b: 78, 94, 94–5, 97, 131. Locke continues to make the same point in the third *Letter* at Locke 1963a: 306, 372–3, 390. Hence Locke declares that it is the "highest injustice" to "punish the innocent considering dissenter with the guilty; and, on the other side, let the inconsiderate guilty conformist escape with the innocent" (Locke 1963b: 94).

32 Locke 1963b: 97.

33 Proast 1999b: 106. See also ibid.: 101, 111.

34 Ibid.: 86. See also ibid.: 60, 63, 67, 67–8, 83, 88–9, 96, 101, 111.

35 For Proast's declaration, see Ch. 7 (note 16).

36 Locke 1963a: 351. Locke makes the same point elsewhere that opportunistic conformity to the English magistrate's religion is the most that Proast's "method" can guarantee (ibid.: 168–9, 198, 199, 245, 314–15, 317–19, 323–4, 324, 332, 334–5, 337–40, 343, 350–3, 374, 379, 384, 385, 391, 393–4, 397, 427, 480, 542, 543). As Locke declares: "For your use of authority and force, being only to bring men to an outward conformity to the national religion, it leaves the corruption and pravity of human nature as unbridled as before" (ibid.: 480). Further, Locke insists that "if all your magnified and necessary means of force, in the way you contend for, reaches no farther than to bring men to a bare outward conformity to the church of England", then it would appear that it is less "true religion" than a specific church "party" that "you write for" (ibid.: 542).

37 See Ch. 3 (note 47).

38 Locke 1963a: 262.

39 Ibid.: 285. See also note 21 above.

40 Ibid.: 282.

41 Ibid.

42 Thus Locke refers to "the extreme absurdity they are guilty of, who, under pretence of zeal for the salvation of souls, proceed to the taking away their lives" (Locke 1963b: 72. See also Locke 1993a: 392). For Locke's insistence that the logical conclusion of the application of "penalties" upon Dissenters are precisely these deadly outcomes, see Locke 1963a: 264–5, 285, 286, 288, 380; 1963b: 77, 107–9; 1993b: 204, 208. See also Chapter 3 (note 47) and note 21 above. Indeed, Locke declares that, under the auspices of Proast's "Method", it is likely that the upmost force will have to be employed against some Dissenters:

> For such men being awed by the fear of hell-fire, if that fear will not make them consider better than they have done, moderate penalties will be too weak to work upon them. It is well if dragooning and martyring can do it.
> (Locke 1963a: 380. See also ibid.: 275)

43 See Ch. 5 (note 33).
44 See Ch. 5 (note 32).
45 Locke 1963b: 67. See also Ch. 5 (note 31).
46 See Ch. 5 ("The 'Three Considerations'").
47 See Ch. 1 (note 76).
48 Locke 1993a: 422. Of course, as we shall discuss in Chapter 9, one primary argument against toleration, advanced by figures like Proast, is premised on the assumption that individuals can receive "prejudice" from the religious beliefs of others, particularly if those beliefs are erroneous and so liable to lead these individuals into error. From this perspective, religion can never be merely the "private" concern of an individual.
49 Locke 1993a: 421–2.
50 Ibid.: 422.
51 Indeed, Locke makes this point as early as the *Two Tracts* – see Ch. 1 (note 75).
52 Locke 1963a: 212. See also Locke 1993a: 422–3; 1963b: 117, 119, 120–1, 121, 121–2, 126, 135. See also Ch. 1 (notes 72 and 76) and Ch. 5 (note 59).
53 Proast 1999a: 32, 34; Proast 1999b: 98–9, 99. See also Ch. 7 ("Proast's Appeal to God").
54 It is in this respect that I interpret Locke's claim, in a passage of the *Two Treatises*, that "God hath certainly appointed Government to restrain the partiality and violence of Men" (Locke 1965: II § 13). I do not perceive this "appointment" as in any way a substitute for individual consent, as the immediate source of the origin and legitimacy of government, that Locke elsewhere emphasises in the *Two Treatises* (see Chapter 1 notes 52 and 57) but rather as a reflection of Locke's belief in God's omnipotence and omnipresence (on consent, see Ch. 1 notes 52 and 67).
55 Locke 1965: II § 117.
56 On this "bracketing" process, see Introduction ("The Limits of Theology"). On why I believe Waldron is mistaken in his assumption that Locke does *not* engage in this "bracketing" process, see Tate 2013.
57 Locke 1963b: 121. On Locke's claim that the "ends" of civil society and government can be "no other than what the institutors appointed", see Ch. 1 (notes 72 and 76), Ch. 5 (note 59) and note 52 above.
58 See Ch. 1 (note 76) and note 47 above.
59 Proast 1999b: 98–9.
60 Ibid.: 99.
61 Ibid.: 100.
62 See Ch. 7 (note 75).
63 Proast 1999b: 99–100.
64 Locke 1963a: 224–5.
65 On natural law and natural rights, see Introduction (notes 13–15).

66 Locke 1963a: 224.
67 Proast 1999a: 26. He makes the same point about toleration undermining the advance of "true religion" at Proast 1999b: 48, 49, 50, 52, 73, 89, 101. See also Ch. 6 (note 15).
68 See Ch. 2 (note 59).
69 Locke 1963b: 63–4.
70 Ibid.: 85.
71 Ibid.: 84. By the "grace of God", Locke means the idea of God acting directly in individuals' lives to bring them to salvation. As Locke states: "God alone can open the ear that it may hear, and open the heart that it may understand: and this he does in his own good time, and to whom he is graciously pleased" (ibid). See also ibid.: 78, 81, 83, 85. Locke also identifies Scripture as an appropriate "means", declaring that it contains "all the means and methods of salvation" (ibid.: 85. See also ibid.: 82, 130). Concerning "all the means and methods of salvation", Locke declares in the third *Letter*: "And I hope you acknowledge, that preaching, admonitions, and instructions, and that grace which God denies to none who seriously ask it, are sufficient for salvation" (Locke 1963a: 487).
72 Locke 1963b: 82. Concerning the confining ourselves to "only those means which God has authorized for the propagation of religion", Locke declares:

> It is not for the magistrate, or any body else, upon an imagination of its usefulness, to make use of any other means for the salvation of men's souls than what the author and finisher of our faith hath directed.
> (Ibid.: 81)

73 See Ch. 7 (note 81).
74 Proast 1999b: 45. For Locke's statement to this effect, see Locke 1963b: 63.
75 Proast 1999b: 45. For Locke's discussion of miracles, see Locke 1963b: 82.
76 Proast 1999b: 46.
77 Ibid.: 46–7. My addition.
78 For Proast's reference to the "Folly, Perverseness, and Wickedness of Men", see ibid.: 47.
79 See Ch. 6 (notes 37, 40–2). However we have seen that, ultimately, Proast goes further and claims that "conversion" to the Church of England is the end to which his "method" is directed (see Ch. 7 note 26 and note 15 above).
80 Proast 1999b: 48.
81 Ibid.: 52.
82 On Locke's pessimistic views, see, for instance, Ch. 2 (notes 31 and 32).
83 See Ch. 2 (notes 34, 37, and 40).
84 Proast 1999b: 47–8. See also ibid.: 81.
85 Ibid.: 75.
86 Ibid. My addition.
87 On "Jews" and "pagans", see note 69 above.
88 Locke 1993a: 390–1.
89 Proast 1999b: 70. See also ibid.: 74. For those other places where Proast insists the magistrate has the authority to use force in matters of "true religion", see ibid.: 74, 75, 76, 78, 81, 90, 95, 99, 100, 101, 102. Locke, in the *Two Tracts*, adopts a similar position to Proast, insisting that Scripture does not limit an authority which the magistrate already possessed (though in Locke's case, only in relation to "things indifferent" in religion) – Locke 1967: 130, 172.
90 Proast 1999b: 70–1.
91 See note 71 above.
92 See Ch. 7 (note 81).
93 Proast 1999b: 78.

94 Ibid.
95 See Ch. 7 ("Proast's Appeal to God").
96 See Ch. 7 ("Proast's Appeal to God").
97 Proast 1999b: 78. The citation from Locke that Proast provides at the beginning of this passage is located at note 71 above.
98 Ibid.: 79.
99 Ibid.: 73–4. See also ibid.: 76, 81, 102.
100 See Ch. 6 (note 61).

References

Goldie, M. (1991) "The Theory of Religious Intolerance in Restoration England". In: O. P. Grell, J. I. Israel, and N. Tyacke (eds) *From Persecution to Toleration. The Glorious Revolution and Religion in England.* Oxford: Clarendon Press, pp. 331–68.

Locke, J. (1963a) "A Third Letter for Toleration". In: J. Locke *The Works of John Locke.* Vol. VI. Aalen: Scientia Verlag, pp. 141–546.

Locke, J. (1963b) "A Second Letter Concerning Toleration". In: J. Locke *The Works of John Locke.* Vol. VI. Aalen: Scientia Verlag, pp. 61–137.

Locke, J. (1965) *Two Treatises of Government.* Peter Laslett (ed.). New York: New American Library.

Locke, J. (1967) "First Tract on Government". In: J. Locke *Two Tracts on Government.* P. Abrams (ed.). Cambridge: Cambridge University Press, pp. 117–81.

Locke, J. (1993a) "A Letter Concerning Toleration". In: J. Locke *Political Writings.* David Wootton (ed.). London: Penguin, pp. 390–436.

Locke, J. (1993b) "An Essay Concerning Toleration". In: J. Locke *Political Writings.* D. Wootton (ed.). London: Penguin, pp. 186–210.

Proast, J. (1999a) "The Argument of the Letter Concerning Toleration, Briefly Consider'd and Answer'd". In: M. Goldie (ed.) *The Reception of Locke's Politics, Vol. 5. The Church, Dissent and Religious Toleration 1689–1773.* London: Pickering and Chatto, pp. 25–37.

Proast, J. (1999b) "A Third Letter Concerning Toleration: In Defense of the Argument of the Letter Concerning Toleration, Briefly Consider'd and Answer'd". In: M. Goldie (ed.) *The Reception of Locke's Politics, Vol. 5. The Church, Dissent and Religious Toleration 1689–1773.* London: Pickering and Chatto, pp. 41–116.

Tate, J. W. (2013) "Dividing Locke from God: The Limits of Theology in Locke's Political Philosophy", *Philosophy and Social Criticism*, 39 (2): 133–64.

9 Locke, Scepticism and Consent

Far from Locke's "rationality argument" being the "main line of argument" that Locke advances for toleration in the *Letter*, we have seen that it is in fact one of three "considerations" that Locke advances to this end. Further, we have seen that although each of these "considerations" are categorically distinct, offering different arguments for toleration, their relative status is not equal. The "rationality argument" occupies a subordinate and subsidiary position relative to the other two, based on "truth" and "consent", with Locke telling us that these other two arguments for toleration apply even when the "rationality argument" does not.[1] Indeed, this subordinate status is evident in the fact that Locke ultimately abandoned the "rationality argument", conceding to Proast that there may be times when, "indirectly and at a distance", force is able to instil sincere and genuine religious belief, and insisting that the magistrate is unlikely to use force for this purpose in any case.[2]

But of the remaining two "considerations" for toleration, based on "truth" and "consent", what is the relationship between these? Each of these "considerations" is, of course, founded on an entirely distinct set of propositions. The "truth argument" depends on Locke's scepticism concerning anyone's claim to possess knowledge of "true religion". The "consent argument" is dependent on Locke's account of the origins of civil society and government and the limits placed on government by the consent of those subject to its jurisdiction. Does one of these "considerations" for toleration apply in the absence of the other, as is the case with the "rationality argument", with the result that it provides the ultimate conditions of possibility for Locke's commitment to toleration? Or are the two "considerations" entirely equal, and independent, in this respect?

This chapter will address these and a range of other issues. First it will consider Locke's response to Proast's charge that, in advancing his case for toleration, Locke also advances a scepticism and a relativism concerning matters of religion. These were charges which, highly stigmatic in late seventeenth-century England, Locke sought to deny, though ultimately, I seek to show, without the success he would have wished. The chapter will then address the competing views of those within the secondary literature concerning whether Locke does advance scepticism as a basis for toleration and evaluate these against my own account which insists that this is so.

The chapter then considers the "moral challenge" which toleration poses for both Locke and Proast, in terms of their respective commitments to Christianity. This "moral challenge" is fundamentally important, because Locke and Proast's respective responses to this challenge go far to explaining how these individuals could share a sincere Christianity and yet arrive at completely contrary positions concerning toleration. We shall see that Locke needed to overcome this moral challenge in order to affirm toleration, otherwise (as with Proast) his Christian commitments might have precluded a commitment to toleration altogether.

We shall see that it is Locke's "truth argument" which allows him to overcome this moral challenge, but that it is in fact Locke's "consent argument" which provides the ultimate conditions of possibility for Locke's commitment to toleration. This is because, as Locke makes clear in the discussion below, his "consent argument" applies as an argument for toleration even if the "truth argument" does not. In this respect, the "truth argument", in Locke's account of toleration, goes the same way as the "rationality argument", each occupying a subsidiary and subordinate position relative to the "consent argument".

Locke and Scepticism I

There has been some dispute among contemporary Locke scholars concerning the role which scepticism plays in Locke's account of toleration and in his engagement with Proast. Certainly the matter was an explicit point of discussion between Locke and Proast themselves. Proast, in his second response to Locke, makes the distinction we have often encountered in these pages between two types of scepticism. He distinguishes between a scepticism concerning the existence of "true religion" (where one doubts or denies that a "true religion" exists) and a scepticism concerning anyone's claim to have knowledge of this "true religion" (where one does not deny that a "true religion" exists, but rather denies the capacity of anyone to *know* which religion this is). Proast declares, in the passage below, that Locke must affirm either one or the other of these two types of scepticism – which Proast designates as (1) and (2) respectively. The impetus behind Proast's declaration is Locke's insistence, in the second *Letter* (quoted in Chapter 7) that Proast should not suppose

> all along your church in the right, and your religion the true; which can no more be allowed to you in this case, whatever your church or religion be, than it can be to a papist or a Lutheran, a presbyterian or anana baptist; nay, no more to you, than it can be allowed to a Jew or a Mahometan.[3]

It is this statement which, Proast insists, reveals that Locke endorses a scepticism of either type (1) or (2). Proast makes this point as follows:

> You say this can be no more allow'd to me in this case, whatever my Church or Religion be, than it can be to a papist or a Lutheran, a *Presbyterian or an Anabaptist; nay no more to me, than it can be allow'd to a Jew or a Mahometan. No Sir? Not whatever my Church, or Religion be?* That seems somewhat hard. And methinks you might have given us some Reason for what you say: For certainly it is not so self-evident as to need no proof. But I think it is no hard matter to guess at your Reason, though you did not think fit expressly to own it. For 'tis obvious enough that there can be no other Reason for this Assertion of yours, but either the equal *Truth*, or at least the equal *Certainty* (or *Uncertainty*) of all Religions. For whoever considers your Assertion, must see, that to make it good, you will be obliged to maintain one of these two things: Either 1. That no Religion is *the true Religion*, in opposition to other Religions: Which makes all Religions *true*, or all *false*, as so either way *indifferent*. Or, 2. That though some one Religion be *the true Religion*; yet no man can have any more reason, than another man of another Religion may have, to believe his to be *the true Religion*. Which makes all Religions equally *certain* (or *uncertain*; whether you please) and so renders it vain and idle to enquire after *the true Religion*, and onely a piece of good luck if any man be of it, and such good luck as he can never know that he has, till he come into the other World. Whether of these two Principles you will own, I know not. But certainly one or the other of them *lies at the bottom* with you, and is the *lurking Supposition upon which you build all that you say.*[4]

A charge of either scepticism or relativism in matters of religion was a highly stigmatic one in Locke's time and place. As mentioned in a previous chapter, Proast asserts that only "Atheists" or those who do not "think Religion worthy of [their] serious Thoughts", and have no concern for their "Eternal Salvation", would advance such scepticism or relativism.[5] Certainly Thomas Hobbes was, among Locke and Proast's contemporaries, highly suspected of "Atheism", and Locke was purportedly eager, at all times, to avoid any association with Hobbes.[6] As Maurice Cranston writes:

> Locke's borrowings from Hobbes were not confined to the treatise he wrote in answer to Bagshawe, but at no time in his life would Locke admit his debt to Hobbes. He even came to pretend he had never read Hobbes properly. Partly, perhaps, this pretence was the repudiation of a former master; it may also have been due to the fact that the word "Hobbist" came to be a pejorative one in all but a very few quarters, and Locke was forever anxious to avoid a bad name.[7]

Not surprisingly, therefore, Locke responds to Proast's accusations of scepticism in the negative. As he puts it: "Certainly no, sir, neither of these reasons you have so ingeniously and friendly found out for me, lies at the bottom."[8] He therefore denies the scepticism, of either type (1) or (2), that Proast seeks to impute to him, as well as the relativism that Proast insists is their necessary consequence – that all religions are either equally "true" or "false", and therefore "indifferent", or "equally *certain* (or *uncertain*; whether you please)".

Locke proclaims this denial in both the third and fourth *Letters Concerning Toleration*. Concerning scepticism (1), which involves a denial of the existence of "true religion" itself, Locke declares (without the reservation that we saw in the first *Letter Concerning Toleration*) that there is "one true religion", and on this, he insists, he is in agreement with Proast:

> You suppose "there is one true religion, and but one". In this we are both agreed: and from hence, I think, it will follow ... whoever is of this true religion shall be saved, and without being of it no man shall be saved.[9]

In other words, Locke responds to Proast's accusation that he is guilty of scepticism of type (1) by directly denying this, and insisting that he and Proast are at one in their belief that there is but "one true religion". Concerning Locke's response to Proast's accusation that he affirms scepticism of type (2), this involves a somewhat more convoluted denial, and is dependent on a crucial distinction that Locke makes in the third *Letter* – a distinction whose components I shall designate as (a) and (b).

(a) and (b)

Locke's denial that he is guilty of scepticism of type (2) is based on a distinction he makes, in response to Proast, at note 13 below. Locke distinguishes between two propositions: (a) that "men of all religions cannot be equally allowed to suppose their religions true"; and (b) their equal entitlement to suppose their religion true, on the grounds that

> the assurance wherewith one man supposes his religion to be true, being no more an argument of its truth to another than *vice versa*, neither of them can claim by the assurance, wherewith he supposes his religion the true, any prerogative or power over the other, which the other has not by the same title an equal claim to over him.[10]

As we shall see at note 13 below, Locke affirms (a), but for the purposes of (b), declares that (a)'s contrary assumption ("men of all religions *are* equally allowed to suppose their religions true") "may and ought to be allowed or denied equally to all men". He then insists that his position concerning (a) and (b) allows him to reject Proast's claim that he is guilty of scepticism of type (2). We shall consider (a) and (b) in turn, before considering whether Locke is entitled to arrive at his position concerning each of them. We shall then determine if the position Locke adopts concerning (a) and (b) allows him to conclude, as he does, that he has successfully rejected Proast's claim that he is guilty of scepticism of type (2).

Scepticism of type (2) involves allegations of relativism as well as scepticism. As Proast puts it in the passage at note 4 above, if "no man can have any more reason, than another man of another Religion may have, to believe his to be *the true Religion*", then this "makes all Religions equally *certain* (or *uncertain*; whether you please) and so renders it vain and idle to enquire after *the true Religion*". As we have seen, Proast, at a number of points in his response to Locke, suggests that only an "Atheist", or those that did not think "Religion worthy of [their] serious Thoughts" or had no concern for their "Eternal Salvation", would affirm such propositions, and further, affirm what, we have seen, Locke takes to be their corollary – that if there is no means to determine who is in possession of the "true religion", then if such "truth" is sufficient justification for the use of force, *any* magistrate is entitled to advance their own religion by force, on the basis of their assumption that their religion is "true".[11]

It is this last proposition – that each magistrate is equally entitled to advance their religion by force should they suppose their religion "true" – that arises from (b), since, as we have seen, (b) refers to the inability of any person to have authoritative knowledge of "true religion", with the result that, in epistemic terms, all such competing claims are "equal" (because equally uncertain). Indeed, we saw in Chapter 7 that Locke's proposition concerning each magistrate's equal entitlement to advance their religion by force was central to one of his arguments for toleration, Locke insisting that such an outcome would have such detrimental consequences for the advancement of "true religion" that toleration of rival religions would be the preferable alternative.[12]

In the passage below, therefore, Locke seeks to affirm (a) – that "men of all religions cannot be equally allowed to suppose their religions true". But he says that for the purposes of (b), we ought to be able to assume the contrary because this places individuals (and magistrates) in that position of "equality", concerning their respective claims to "true religion", referred to above, and so places them in a position (necessary for mutual toleration) in which neither has any "prerogative or power over the other, which the other has not by the same title an equal claim to over him":

> But, sir, if you will add but one more to your plentiful stock of distinctions, and observe the difference there is between the ground of any one's supposing his religion is true, and the privilege he may pretend to by supposing it true, you will never stumble at this again; but you will find, that though, upon the former of these accounts, men of all religions cannot be equally allowed to suppose their religions true, yet in reference to the latter, the supposition may and ought to be allowed

or denied equally to all men. And the reason of it is plain, viz. because the assurance wherewith one man supposes his religion to be true, being no more an argument of its truth to another than *vice versa*, neither of them can claim by the assurance, wherewith he supposes his religion the true, any prerogative or power over the other, which the other has not by the same title an equal claim to over him.[13]

In the passage above, Locke directly affirms proposition (a), insisting that "men of all religions cannot be equally allowed to suppose their religions true". In this respect, he clearly assumes that there are some grounds upon which some individuals are more entitled to claim "truth" for their religion than others, thereby denying scepticism of type (2) and the relativism between religions that Proast believes is the inevitable consequence of this. He does the same again in the fourth *Letter*:

[T]he question between us is not what religion has the most clear and solid grounds for the belief of it; much less whether "there are as clear and solid grounds for the belief of false religions as there are for the belief of the true", *i.e.* whether falsehood has as much truth in it as truth itself? a question which, I guess, no man, but one of your great pertinency, could ever have proposed.[14]

Elsewhere in the fourth *Letter*, Locke again rejects any suggestion that he denies proposition (a) or endorses a scepticism of type (2), declaring any such suggestion to be "absurd":

It is with the same pertinency, that to this proposition, "that there are as clear and solid grounds for the belief of a false religion as there are for the belief of the true", you join this following as an equivalent, "Or that men may both as firmly and as rationally believe and embrace false religions as they can the true"; and you would fain have it thought that your cause is gained, unless I will maintain these two absurd propositions, which my argument has nothing to do with.[15]

Yet, such statements notwithstanding, the arguments which Locke advances for toleration within the *Letters* do not allow him to sustain the claim, in the three passages above, that he affirms proposition (a) or denies scepticism of type (2). After all, any such claim would require him to assert that we can categorically distinguish between "true" and "false" religions, clearly identifying the one from the other. As Locke puts it in the passages above, "men of all religions cannot be equally allowed to suppose their religions true" and may not "as firmly and as rationally believe and embrace false religions as they can the true". Such statements are only meaningful on the basis of a prior assumption that there is an indubitable criterion by which we can distinguish between "true" and "false" religions, thereby justifying belief in the one but not in the other. In other words, to affirm proposition (a) and deny scepticism (2), Locke must affirm that we have a capacity to *know* the "true religion".

Yet we have seen that it is precisely such a capacity that Locke repeatedly denies. He denies it in the context of the "truth argument", which is premised on the assumption that knowledge of the "true religion" is not possible. He also denies it in the context of his argument, discussed in Chapter 7 and referred to at note 12 above, concerning the entitlement of *all* magistrates to advance their religion by force. He denies it when insisting to Proast, in Chapter 5, that "faith", but not "knowledge", is all that is available when it comes to revealed religion.[16] Indeed, the whole thrust of Locke's criticism of Proast's "third sort or degree of Perswasion", as a criterion of "true religion", which we discussed in Chapter 6, was his insistence that there was no degree of "Perswasion", concerning religion, sufficient to attain the status of knowledge, and therefore none by which any individual would be entitled to claim knowledge of "true religion", or justify the use of force on this basis – with the result that everyone's "assurances" in such matters are sufficient only unto themselves.[17]

The ultimate consequence, therefore, is that, if there is no knowledge of "true religion", and therefore no indubitable criterion to distinguish between the claims to "truth" arising from competing religions, then there is no criterion to distinguish between "true" and "false" religion, and Locke's implicit assumption to the contrary, in the passages at notes 13 to 15 above (where he seeks to endorse proposition (a) and deny scepticism of type (2)) is in error. Locke, in other words, is not entitled to affirm proposition (a) – that "men of all religions cannot be equally allowed to suppose their religions true". On the contrary, to sustain his case for toleration, he must reject proposition (a) and uphold a scepticism of type (2) – in which (to use Proast's words) he must assume that "though some one Religion be *the true Religion*, yet no man can have any more reason, than another man of another religion may have, to believe his to be *the true Religion*".[18] Indeed, we have seen in the paragraph above that this is *precisely* the position that Locke does affirm at a number of points in his *Letters*.

In all these ways, therefore, we see a basic conflict in Locke's discourse between his eagerness to deny Proast's charge of scepticism (and the relativism in matters of religion that Proast says is a necessary consequence of this) and the very same scepticism and relativism which Locke must suppose at those points where, in order to advance his case for toleration, he declares that knowledge of "true religion" is not possible. Locke's eagerness, in later *Letters*, to rebut Proast's charges of scepticism – perhaps, as Cranston might suggest, to "avoid a bad name" – has led him to contradict the very positions upon which some of his arguments for toleration depend.[19]

Locke and Scepticism II

Scepticism therefore plays an important role in Locke's engagement with Proast. Not all Locke scholars have recognized this. One who has is Peter Nicholson. Indeed, Nicholson believes that Locke's scepticism, concerning knowledge of "true religion", is conclusive against Proast. He points out that Proast's "own account" presumes the possibility of such knowledge if his argument against Locke is to be "effective and legitimate" – Proast's position being continually dependent (as we have seen) on the assumption that knowledge of "true religion" is possible.[20] Yet it is Locke's sceptical denial of such knowledge, Nicholson declares, which undermines Proast's position:

> Since it is impossible for the magistrate to have the kind of knowledge which Proast's scheme requires, the magistrate will never be in a condition to exercise the power Proast gives him. Here is the final blow, an impracticability grounded in an epistemological argument, which finishes off Proast's case conclusively.[21]

In contrast to Nicholson, Richard Vernon (like Mark Goldie in Chapter 6) is insistent that Locke's case against Proast does *not* rely on scepticism, and that Locke does not affirm such scepticism at any point in his arguments for toleration. Vernon writes that although "[i]t is true that Locke distinguishes matters of faith from matters of knowledge, declaring that items of faith cannot be demonstrated in the way that items of knowledge can be ... this is not the basis of his case".[22] Instead, Vernon declares that Locke premises toleration on the political and moral relations between individuals, "arising from the recognition of [their] background equality", not upon a foundation arising from sceptical judgments concerning "epistemology".[23]

Vernon insists that the equality that Locke perceives between individuals in their political and moral relations leads him to affirm requirements of reciprocity in public dialogue, where each interlocutor seeks, as a basis of public justification, "to appeal to what can secure agreement in a reasoned way, rather than deploying arguments that others, we can safely predict, will disclaim".[24] Vernon identifies Locke's lineage with Rawls in this respect, not least Rawls' proposition that individuals, "as reasonable and rational", ought to "be ready to explain the basis of their actions to one another in terms each could reasonably expect that others might endorse".[25]

Vernon perceives this ideal of reciprocity, within Locke's framework, as premised not only on Locke's background assumption that individuals are equal in their relations with each other. He also perceives it as premised upon the public requirements and constraints of the communicative process itself and the propositions that can "expect to win assent" within it.[26] Vernon does not perceive this ideal of reciprocity as arising from the epistemological status of those propositions themselves and therefore any scepticism in relation to them. On the contrary, Vernon declares: "Locke rests his argument on the constraints of exchange, not on what it is open to humans to know".[27]

The result, Vernon insists in the passage below, is that what, in the Locke/Proast debate, appears to be Locke's sceptical claims concerning knowledge of "true religion", is not a denial of such knowledge but, rather, simply the communicative posture that Locke requires individuals to adopt in a process of mutual exchange, to comply with the reciprocal requirements and constraints of public dialogue – constraints which are necessary if such individuals are to reach public agreement with each other and engage in mutually acceptable processes of public justification. Outside of this public context, however, Vernon does not believe that Locke demands that individuals abandon a conviction concerning the truth of their religious beliefs, or engage in any sceptical distinction between faith and knowledge at all:

> Locke surely cannot be taken to be saying, to an audience whose Christian credentials (of one kind or another) he has taken to be secure from the outset, that they can accept his argument only if they suppose Judaism or Islam to be just as good as Christianity.... So what he must mean, in denying Proast the option of "supposing" his view to be true, is that it is not a valid dialogical move: you cannot begin a discussion with the "supposition" – that is, a premise that your interlocutor is obliged to accept – that you are right and your interlocutor wrong. In short, dialogue is possible only if neither interlocutor is guaranteed a win in advance. It is not that no-one is allowed to suppose their own belief to be true (for surely to believe something is to believe that it is true).[28]

What Vernon falls short of recognizing here is what, I believe, was at the forefront of Locke's consciousness in his debate with Proast – what I have called the "moral challenge of toleration". This moral challenge arises from the fact that religious faith, when sincerely held, claims a status, within individuals' lives, of ultimate significance, with the result, as Locke puts it, that "the observance of these things is the highest obligation that lies upon mankind".[29] It is from such obligations that arise Proast's concern with "promoting True Religion and the Salvation of Souls".[30]

Toleration, on the other hand, requires such individuals to permit beliefs and practices to which they are opposed, and perhaps believe to be in grave error – error perhaps fatal to individual souls, and the eternal salvation open to them. A moral challenge arises, therefore, because to tolerate such error is to allow for its propagation, with the result that others may fall into similar error. In this respect, from the perspective of the religiously devout, toleration may involve complicity in the damnation of souls. John Coffey articulates such a perspective as follows:

> To fail to employ all the means at one's disposal to re-educate erroneous consciences was to allow one's neighbours to persist in soul-destroying heresy. In seeking to be kind, tolerationists were simply being cruel. To grant "the publique freedome of heresies", suggested Bilson, was to countenance the "murder of souls". [St] Augustine, Thomas Crane noted, had declared that those who called for liberty of conscience only gained "Libertatem perditionis", liberty to destroy themselves. Instead of shepherding their subjects along the path to heaven, towards true freedom, irresponsible magistrates allowed them the liberty to choose hell.[31]

John Rawls makes the same point, indicating how toleration was seen by many, at the time of the Reformation and after, as the acquiescence in heresy:

> The problem was ... How is society even possible between those of different faiths? What can conceivably be the basis of religious toleration? For many there was none, for it meant the acquiescence in heresy about first things and the calamity of religious disunity.[32]

In this way, toleration gives rise, among the devout, to a moral challenge. Locke therefore had to find some means of blunting or removing this moral challenge if he was to convince those of devout religious belief to tolerate that to which their faith was at odds, or else convince them to limit their faith in ways that made public agreement with those of differing faith possible. One of the ways he chose to do so was the sceptical distinction between faith and knowledge discussed in Chapters 5 and 6. Locke knew that, if individuals presumed that they possessed an absolute knowledge of their religion as "true", they may not limit the claims they make upon others in the name of that religion, either for the sake of toleration, or public agreement or any other consideration, not least because (in line with the moral challenge above) they would perceive their own or others' eternal salvation to be at stake. In other words, they would not limit religious faith to the personal terms referred to in a previous chapter, where religion is recognized to be a matter for individual conscience, involving preaching and exhortation, and voluntary church attendance, and does not extend to coercive imposition upon others.[33]

Locke recognised the unlimited nature of religious claims, and the upheaval they could cause, as early as his *Two Tracts on Government*, insisting that "men find no cause that can so rationally draw them to hazard this life ... as that which promises them a better", with the result that they "adopt themselves children of God, and from thence assume a title to inheritance here and proclaim themselves heirs of the world".[34] Of course, by the time of his later writings, Locke had a much more benign view of Christianity, and its propensity to produce disorder, than he had in the *Two Tracts*.[35] But he still recognized that religion could be a source of disorder whenever individuals refused to limit the claims arising from it, such as when they "arrogate to themselves, and to those of their own sect, some peculiar prerogative ... opposite to the civil right of the community".[36]

From Locke's perspective, therefore, those who perceive their faith to be "true", with no doubt conceded either to themselves or others, may find it difficult to limit their religious claims or adopt an attitude of toleration towards those at odds with their faith. This is because they will not be able to overcome the "moral challenge" of toleration, seeing any toleration of that which is at odds with this "truth" as a negligent action likely to endanger the salvation of souls.

Scepticism, with its categorical distinction between "faith" and "knowledge", is one means for individuals to overcome this "moral challenge" and find ways of limiting their religious claims in relation to others, adopting an attitude of toleration towards those at odds with their faith. Scepticism makes this possible because it undermines the assumptions of "truth" upon which their intransigence towards others arises. Contrary to Vernon, therefore, it is scepticism, not communicative reciprocity, which is one of the bases upon which Locke seeks to underwrite his case for toleration (and reciprocal dialogue) in his debate with Proast. Locke does, therefore, require individuals to abandon claims to knowledge concerning the truth of their religious beliefs, and to do so by engaging in a sceptical distinction between faith and knowledge.

Vernon's position, articulated above, is that surely Locke cannot be suggesting that "no-one is allowed to suppose their own belief to be true", because, he says, "to believe something is to believe that it is true". But when it comes to revealed religions like Christianity and Islam, this is precisely what Locke is suggesting (if we mean by "truth" that which is an object of knowledge rather than faith). His grounds for doing so are (as Locke explains in Chapter 5) that the central truth claims of these religions are not open to empirical confirmation, and therefore are not capable of becoming an object of knowledge, only an object of faith.[37] Locke makes the same point to Proast elsewhere in the third *Letter* as follows:

> [Y]ou say ... that "that one true religion may be known by those who profess it".... At first, it will be necessary to inquire what you mean by known; whether you mean by it knowledge properly so called, as contradistinguished to belief – or only the assurance of a firm belief? ... If you mean, that the true religion may be known with the certainty of knowledge properly so called; I ask you farther, whether that true religion be to be known by the light of nature, or needed a divine revelation to discover it? If you say, as I suppose you will, the latter; then I ask whether the making out of that to be a divine revelation depends not upon particular matters of fact, whereof you were no eye-witness, but were done many ages before you were born? and if so, by what principles of science they can be known to any man now living?

> The articles of my religion, and of a great many such other short-sighted people as I am, are articles of faith, which we think there are so good grounds to believe, that we are persuaded to venture our eternal happiness on that belief.... But we neither think that God requires, nor has given us faculties capable of knowing in this world several of those truths which are to be believed to salvation.[38]

Such scepticism, as Locke advocates in the passage above, does not mean that individuals will "suppose Judaism or Islam to be just as good as Christianity", as Vernon suggests. Locke, after all, declared the beliefs attaching to Catholicism, Judaism, and "heathenism" to be "false and absurd", and did so on the basis of his faith in his *own* religion.[39] But such scepticism *will* mean that, although the devout will continue to make these disparaging comparisons, on the basis of their faith, between their own religion and that of others, they will have no epistemological basis for knowing these comparisons to be "true", in any veridical sense, and therefore (according to Locke) no indubitable basis for acting upon them to the detriment of others.

Unlike Richard Vernon, Adam Wolfson insists that Locke's case for toleration does rely on scepticism. Yet it is a scepticism upon which, Wolfson declares, Locke seeks to initiate a secularization of religious belief, involving a fundamental reorientation between believers and their beliefs themselves. It is upon this reorientation that Wolfson pins not only Locke's conception of toleration, but Wolfson's conception of Locke's "modernity" – Locke's status as an inaugurator of a modern liberal secular outlook.

Wolfson argues that Locke's case for toleration depends not only upon institutional features of civil society, such as the separation of church and state discussed in an earlier chapter, but also on a fundamental reorientation of the relationship between individuals and their religious beliefs, arising from scepticism. Drawing on Locke's distinction between faith and knowledge, discussed in Chapters 5 and 6, Wolfson declares:

> We might formulate Locke's point in this way: Toleration's institutional expression is manifested in the separation of church and state. Yet the full scope of Locke's argument for toleration, as it was developed in his quarrel with Proast, suggests that what would make this separation seem plausible (or, more importantly, necessary) was scepticism of a certain kind. That is to say, the separation of church and state is supported by a more fundamental separation, that between faith and knowledge. If toleration is to be anything more than a temporary modus vivendi among warring religious faiths, religion itself must, to paraphrase Locke, be made reasonable.[40]

Consequently, Wolfson believes that Locke ultimately rests his case for toleration, and the institutional mechanisms such as the separation of church and state which underpin it, on "a fundamental inner adjustment in the religious believer himself".[41] Belief, for Locke, becomes more "reasonable", Wolfson argues, to the extent that it becomes less fervent, and this requires an "overcoming" of the "traditional Christian view".[42] What enables this "overcoming", Wolfson insists in the paragraph below, is the strong dose of scepticism that arises once we internalize Locke's distinction between "faith" and "knowledge", and recognize that our religious beliefs lack the certainty of the latter.

Wolfson argues that Locke's case for toleration is based on "a new moral outlook rooted in broadly liberal notions of consent, human dependency and the limits of human knowledge".[43] What this required, Wolfson says, was for Locke to

> overcome the traditional Christian view up to that point or, more broadly, the view of religion as such. Thus rather than emerging out of certain Christian or theological assumptions, as many scholars argue, toleration requires, according to Locke, an overcoming of the religious worldview.[44]

Wolfson declares that Locke engages in this "overcoming" by his "sceptical exploration of the distinction between faith and knowledge" which, he hopes, will give rise to "more moderate religious attachments".[45]

According to the terms of Wolfson's perspective, Locke becomes a key point along the path of European "secularization", somewhat akin to the Locke we find in parts of Alasdair MacIntyre's *After Virtue*.[46] Indeed, Wolfson makes this clear when he states that "as Proast and Locke understood their quarrel, one of them represented the cause of Christianity, and the other a new, liberal humanism".[47]

In this way, Wolfson takes Locke's scepticism, present in his engagement with Proast, and ascribes to it what, from our perspective, appears to be a distinctly "modern" outlook – a "liberal humanist" perspective, based on an "overcoming" of the "traditional Christian view", and resulting in "more moderate religious attachments". Wolfson argues that this process of diluting the religious commitments of individuals, making these more "rational" and "moderate", also underpins the institutional basis of toleration, centred, as Wolfson points out above, on the separation of church and state.

I think that, in advancing these arguments, Wolfson misunderstands the role which scepticism plays in Locke's case for toleration. We have seen that Locke does make a strong distinction between "faith" and "knowledge", denying the proposition upon which Proast most relies to legitimate the use of force in matters of religion – that knowledge of "true religion" is possible. Equally, in *An Essay Concerning Human Understanding*, Locke makes a strong distinction between "faith" and "reason", and insists on the primacy of the latter, declaring that reason "can never require or enable me to believe that which", arising from "faith" or "revelation", "is contrary to it self: It being impossible for Reason, ever to procure any Assent to that, which to it self appears unreasonable".[48] It is on these grounds that Locke warns against "enthusiasm" in religion, which he defines as an arbitrary assertion of "faith" or "revelation", independent of both reason and Scripture, based on an individual's self-assurance or persuasion that he or she has direct access to God's truths – what Locke calls an "inner light".[49] Indeed, it is precisely this assertion of "faith" or "revelation", independent of "reason", that Locke perceives as a source of conflict and excess in religion.[50] Consequently, Locke insists that any instance of "faith" or "revelation", in order to be valid, must be in accord with either the tenets of reason or Scripture, and that it is reason alone that determines if a particular instance of "faith" or "revelation" is in accordance with these sources.[51]

But while Locke insists that our religious "faith" be constrained by reason and Scripture, I do not think Wolfson is correct in concluding that, at the level of personal religious belief, Locke advocates some sort of "secularization" of religious belief, on "liberal humanist" grounds, involving a dilution of faith, or a diminution in the fervency with which it is held – or that this then underwrites the institutional separation of church and state which Locke advocates in the *Letter Concerning Toleration*. In the first place, Locke's account of scepticism in matters of religion does not require this diminution or dilution of belief. We saw that Locke distinguished between a scepticism concerning the existence of "true religion" and a scepticism concerning anyone's claim to have knowledge of this "truth". As made clear in previous chapters, Locke affirmed only the second type of scepticism, which he used as a basis for denying anybody a right to use force in matters of religion on the assumption that their religion, as distinct from all others, is "true".[52] So long as individuals stop short of the use of such force, and such claims to knowledge, Locke's scepticism does not preclude individuals from believing, with all the intensity of their faith and all the fervency at their disposal, that their own religion is "true".[53] After all, as Locke tells us at the beginning of the *Letter Concerning Toleration*, "everyone is orthodox to himself".[54] They just must recognize that they cannot have any *knowledge* of this "truth", only a faith in it. The result is that Locke's scepticism denies knowledge of "true religion", not a faith in one's religious belief.

Second, Locke himself advocated such fervency, insisting that religion ought to be placed at the centre of our lives. As he put it in the first *Letter Concerning Toleration*, the "believing and doing those things in this life which are necessary to the obtaining of God's favour" are

> the highest obligation that lies upon mankind, and ... our utmost care, application, and diligence ought to be exercised in the search and performance of them, because there is nothing in this world that is of any consideration in comparison with eternity.[55]

This expression of religion as an ultimate commitment governing our personal lives is consistent with Locke's insistence that it ought to remain within the bounds of reason and Scripture (and so not degenerate into the "enthusiasm" described above), but it is not consistent with Wolfson's view that Locke advocated a "liberal humanist" "overcoming" of the "traditional Christian view", involving a decline in the fervency of belief as a result of a sceptical detachment between individuals and their religious commitments.

As to Wolfson's other claims, far from Locke assuming that his institutional foundations of toleration, such as the separation of church and state, would be underwritten by a decline in the fervency of individual religious belief, and a greater detachment of individuals from those beliefs, I would suggest that Locke assumed the very opposite. As Locke makes clear in his "eternity" passage, in the paragraph above, and in his account in the *Letter* of those religious beliefs which threaten civil peace, mechanisms such as the separation of church and state are necessary precisely because, Locke assumed, individuals would continue to hold their religious beliefs with an intense commitment.[56] What I believe Locke was attempting to do with mechanisms such as separation was not reduce the fervency of religious beliefs, or the intensity of religious attachments (along "liberal humanist" lines). Rather his intention was (for want of a better term) to "privatize" these beliefs and attachments, removing them from the public sphere, and ensuring that those matters of faith upon which individuals were most devoted (and divided), and therefore least able to agree, would not become matters of civil and political deliberation (or conflict) but instead would be issues of private debate and admonishment (absent the use of force).[57] We saw the extent to which Locke went in order to ensure this, insisting that, if a matter of religion did become an object of state regulation, thereby placing it outside of the private sphere, it had to be treated by the magistrate as a thing "indifferent", completely separate from its religious concerns, and subject to state regulation solely insofar as it impacted on civil concerns, for which the magistrate has authority.[58]

In this way, although such a strategy of "privatization" did not reduce the fervency with which individual religious belief was held, or make individuals any more likely to agree on such matters, it did (if successful) ensure that such issues were no longer a matter of political contestation, upon which individuals were divided in the public sphere. When religion did remain a source of political contestation, Locke (as is evident in the passage below) saw this as a source of "discord and war". To avoid this, what Locke required was that individuals recognize and abide by the civil limits placed on their religious beliefs (resulting in the privatization strategy above), not that they hold them with any less attachment or fervency. As he put it:

> Nobody therefore, in fine, neither single persons, nor Churches, nay, nor even commonwealths, have any just title to invade the civil rights and worldly goods of each other, upon pretence of religion. Those that are of another opinion would do well to consider with themselves how pernicious a seed of discord and war, how powerful a provocation to

endless hatreds, rapines, and slaughters they thereby furnish unto mankind. No peace and security, no, not so much as common friendship, can ever be established or preserved amongst men, so long as this opinion prevails, that dominion is founded in grace, and that religion is to be propagated by force of arms.[59]

Toleration and Moral Choice

We saw that, in any comparison of the "truth" and "consent" arguments, the "consent argument" is by far the strongest "consideration" that Locke offers for toleration. This is because the "truth argument" – based as it is on a scepticism concerning all claims to "true religion" – was less an argument capable of convincing magistrates that, in seeking to impose their religions by force, they were exceeding the limits of their authority, and more an argument capable of convincing individuals, subject to the magistrate's authority, that they should resist the magistrate's intrusion in this regard.[60]

Having said this, however, we have seen that the scepticism at the heart of the "truth argument", concerning competing claims to "true religion", plays a much larger role in Locke's defence of toleration than the specific confines of the "truth argument" would suggest. Not least, it is a defining difference between Locke and Proast. We have seen that central to the legitimacy of Proast's position is a belief that knowledge of "true religion" is possible. Locke, on the other hand, denies the possibility of all such knowledge.

This distinction between Locke and Proast means that they respond very differently to the moral challenge, discussed above, which a policy of toleration presents to any sincere Christian. This challenge arises, we have seen, from the fact that toleration allows for the existence, and indeed proliferation, of religious diversity. If we assume, with Proast, that "there are so many Religions in the World, and ... only one of them can be true"[61] – a proposition that Locke, with only some hesitation, also seems to endorse[62] – then the religious diversity allowed by toleration will, from the perspective of a sincere Christian, increase the likelihood of the propagation of religious error, and therefore the damnation of individual souls.[63] Locke made reference to this diversity when he stated that "in this great variety of ways that men follow, it is still doubted which is this right one", while in reference to the religion of magistrates, he refers to "the variety and contradiction of opinions in religion, wherein the princes of the world are as much divided as in their secular interests".[64]

From Proast's perspective, the primary concern, in this context of diversity, is to engage in "promoting True Religion and the Salvation of Souls". His primary reference point, in evaluating toleration, is therefore whether it serves this end and his response to the "moral challenge of toleration" is informed by this position. He makes clear in his first response to Locke that he believes toleration does not serve this end, insisting that "true religion" will not "be any way a gainer" by it.⁶⁵ In his second response to Locke, Proast repeats this view, insisting that, when it comes to "true religion", "an universal Toleration would ruine it both there and every where else in the end".⁶⁶ Indeed, we saw that, from Proast's perspective, the propagation of religious "error" was even more likely in a context of toleration, given his assumptions concerning the "Corruption and Pravity of Humane Nature", wherein "false Religions are ever more agreeable than the true".⁶⁷ When it comes to the "moral challenge of toleration", therefore, Proast's response is to repudiate toleration altogether.

We have seen that Locke, in order to endorse toleration, and yet still retain his Christian commitments, must in some way overcome this moral challenge. The "consent argument" does not provide Locke with the means of doing so, because although it might seek to circumvent this challenge, by insisting that religion is no concern of the magistrate, this does not exclude Locke himself, as a sincere Christian, from such concerns, or the damage to individual souls that might arise from his advocacy of a policy of toleration.

Does the scepticism, at the heart of the "truth argument", fare better as a means of overcoming this moral challenge? We saw earlier in the chapter that scepticism did provide means for individuals to overcome this challenge. But, while such scepticism casts doubt on anyone's claim to possess knowledge of "true religion", such scepticism is still consistent with a belief that there is only "one truth, one way to heaven" – a position, as explained above, that Locke, at times, endorsed. It is also consistent with the much wider assumption that, even if there is not one single way to heaven, there may be many "false" ways that might exclude one from it. Once Locke assumes either of these, he is confronted with the moral challenge of toleration, because each gives rise to the possibility that the religious diversity facilitated by toleration allows for the propagation of religious error and therefore the damnation of souls.

Yet it is the scepticism at the basis of the "truth argument" which, once again, provides a means to overcome this moral challenge. This is because it denies our capacity to make the epistemological distinction, between "true" and "false" religion, upon which this challenge is based. It is true that a sceptical incapacity to distinguish between "true" and "false" religion is consistent with the possibility that there is "one truth, one way to heaven". But if we are unable to categorically distinguish between "true" and "false" religions, in terms of this ultimate end, and so identify, on a basis of knowledge rather than faith, the *one* religion by which "heaven" might be achieved, or the "false" ones by which it will not, the moral challenge to which toleration gives rise is undermined.

Although Locke can declare to Proast that the Christian Scriptures have "for at least these sixteen hundred years contained the only true religion in the world", we have seen that, upon his own admission, he has no indubitable basis upon which to assert that such a proposition is "true".⁶⁸ For this reason, the "truth argument" allows Locke to overcome the moral challenge, presented by toleration, far more readily than the "consent argument", because the scepticism at the heart of it allows Locke to avoid complicity, and therefore responsibility, for the propagation of religious error and the damnation of souls – such responsibility only being meaningful if the religion/s capable of ensuring salvation, or those responsible for denying it, are identifiable.

Ultimate Conditions of Possibility I

Yet, while the "truth argument" provides Locke with the means to overcome the moral challenge to his Christianity posed by toleration, it is the "consent argument" that provides him with the ultimate conditions of possibility for his commitment to toleration itself. This is apparent when Locke makes clear, in the passages below, that the "consent argument" applies as an argument for toleration, even if the "truth argument" does not.[69] The necessary condition upon which the "truth argument" relies is the sceptical proposition referred to above – that knowledge of "true religion" is not possible. However, in the passages below, Locke insists that, even if (in hypothetical circumstances) we *did* possess knowledge of "true religion", so that we knew which of the diverse religious faiths in existence was the "one truth, one way to heaven" (thereby undermining the conditions of the "truth argument" and preventing it from overcoming the moral challenge of toleration) this would still not justify a policy of coercion towards those at odds with "true religion", in order to guide them towards salvation, because the conditions of the "consent argument" for toleration would still apply.

The first instance where Locke moves in this direction is in the first *Letter Concerning Toleration*. Locke offers the hypothetical example of two rival churches in the city of Constantinople, "the one of Arminians, the other of Calvinists".[70] He states:

> [I]f it could be manifest which of these two dissenting Churches were in the right way, there would not accrue thereby to the orthodox any right of destroying the other. For Churches have neither any jurisdiction in worldly matters, nor are fire and sword any proper instruments wherewith to convince men's minds of error, and inform them of the truth.[71]

In this passage, Locke is quite clear that, even if it could be confirmed that one of these churches possessed knowledge of "true religion", thereby undermining the conditions of the "truth argument", this would not justify it coercing or denying toleration to the other, since (a) it has no "jurisdiction" to do so, and (b) force cannot instil genuine belief. In other words, Locke here makes clear that even in the absence of the "truth argument", and the scepticism upon which it relies, the conditions of the "consent argument" and the "rationality argument" would still apply. Locke is even more explicit on this point elsewhere in the first *Letter*, insisting that toleration applies, for reason of the "consent argument", irrespective of whether the religion in question "be true or false":

> The care of each man's soul, and of the things of heaven, which neither does belong to the commonwealth nor can be subjected to it, is left entirely to every man's self.... And, therefore, the magistrate cannot take away these worldly things from this man, or party, and give them to that; nor change property amongst fellow-subjects (no, not even by a law) for a cause that has no relation to the end of civil government – I mean, for their religion, which, *whether it be true or false*, does no prejudice to the worldly concerns of their fellow-subjects, which are the things that only belong unto the care of the commonwealth.[72]

Locke is insisting here that toleration applies, irrespective of whether a religion be "true" or "false" – and the reason is because religion does not fall within those civil matters ("worldly" concerns) which are the sole concern of the magistrate, and the reason for which the magistrate's authority exists, with the result, Locke tells us, that "peace and goodwill", and therefore toleration, are owed to the "erroneous" as well as to the "orthodox".[73] So long as the adherents of the various religions within the Commonwealth do "no prejudice to the worldly concerns of their fellow-subjects", Locke insists that the magistrate has no grounds upon which to interfere with them, irrespective of the "truth" or "falsity" of their religion.[74]

In this way, Locke insists in the first *Letter* that the "consent argument" applies, as a justification for toleration, even if, as a result of some ideal circumstance, we possessed knowledge of "true religion", with the result that the "truth argument" is undermined. In the second *Letter Concerning Toleration*, Locke advances the same position, insisting that the "consent argument" applies as a justification of toleration even when both the "truth" and "rationality" arguments do not. He makes this point by insisting that even if Proast's "Method" could achieve its end of instilling sincere religious belief (thereby undermining the conditions of the "rationality argument") and "true religion" was thereby promoted (undermining the conditions of the "truth argument"), the "Method" itself, and the force it imposes on "false" religious beliefs, would still not be justified, because the magistrate has no "commission" to engage in such activity:

> But suppose force, applied your way, were as useful for the promoting true religion, as I suppose I have showed it to be the contrary; it does not from hence follow that it is lawful and may be used ... because ... the magistrate has no commission or authority to do so.[75]

Finally, in his *Third Letter For Toleration*, Locke once again insists that possession of "true religion", and therefore knowledge of the "one way" to heaven, does not in any way preclude the case for toleration:

> But supposing all the truths of the Christian religion necessary to salvation could be so known to the magistrate, that, in his use of force for the bringing men to embrace these, he could be guided by infallible certainty; yet I fear this would not serve your turn, nor authorize the magistrate to use force to bring men in England, or anywhere else, into the communion of the national church.[76]

Of course, all such reference to possession of religious "truth" is hypothetical because, as Locke makes clear in Chapters 5 and 6, "faith", not knowledge, is all that is available to individuals in matters of revealed religion. But, as the passages above show, even with this hypothetical assumption in place, with the result that the conditions of the "truth argument" are overturned, Lock believes the "consent argument" still applies as a case for toleration, and therefore as a reason why the magistrate should not impose force upon what he or she knows to be "false" religions. The "truth argument" is therefore able to go the same way as the "rationality argument", with neither applying as a case for toleration, and yet the "consent argument" still remains in place. It is for this reason that the "consent argument" provides Locke with the ultimate conditions of possibility for his commitment to toleration.

Ultimate Conditions of Possibility II

Locke, in the passages above, gives clear reasons why toleration ought to apply even in those circumstances where the magistrate is (hypothetically speaking) in possession of religious "truth". But elsewhere in his first *Letter Concerning Toleration*, Locke provides another reason why toleration should apply in such circumstances. This is because, even if the magistrate was in possession of religious "truth", and sought to impose it upon those subject to his or her jurisdiction, this would be of no use to the salvation of souls unless individuals freely assented to that religion, independent of all force and coercion. In other words, Locke is declaring that, in such circumstances, the basic conditions of the "rationality argument" would continue to apply as a case for toleration even if those of the "truth argument" did not, thereby providing one more reason why the magistrate would not be justified in advancing "true religion" by force. Locke makes this point as follows:

> But after all, the principal consideration, and which absolutely determines this controversy, is this: although the magistrate's opinion in religion be sound, and the way that he appoints be truly evangelical, yet if I be not thoroughly persuaded thereof in my own mind, there will be no safety for me in following it. No way whatsoever that I shall walk in, against the dictates of my own conscience, will ever bring me to the mansions of the blessed.[77]

Of course, we saw that Locke, by the time of his engagement with Proast, admitted that, "indirectly" and "at a distance", force may ultimately be capable of inculcating in individuals a "genuine" and "sincere" belief in matters of religion, thereby undermining the conditions of the "rationality argument" as a case for toleration. But short of such circumstances, the "rationality argument" provides one more reason why, even in (hypothetical) circumstances, where religious "truth" is known by the magistrate, toleration ought still to be the required policy of government.

Locke, Truth and Diversity

We have seen that, although Locke was a sceptic regarding individual claims to "true religion", he did not seem to be a sceptic regarding the existence of "true religion" itself.[78] Indeed, the moral challenge of toleration notwithstanding, Locke has a more optimistic prognosis concerning the fate of religious "truth" in a context of toleration and diversity than does Proast. Proast, we saw, believed that if individuals were provided with liberty in religion, "false religion" would outstrip the "true", because "false religion" is "more agreeable" to individuals, given the "Corruption and Pravity of Humane Nature".[79] It was for this reason, we saw, above all others, that Proast concluded that "true religion" would not be "any way a gainer" by toleration, and why individuals should not be left to "their own Consciences" in matters of religion.[80] In the passage below, Locke arrives at the directly opposite conclusion, insisting (contrary not only to Proast but also to John Stuart Mill in the introduction to this book) that "truth", left to its own devices, is sufficiently robust to win out against error:

> For truth certainly would do well enough, if she were once left to shift for herself. She seldom has received, and I fear never will receive, much assistance from the power of great men, to whom she is but rarely known, and more rarely welcome. She is not taught by laws, nor has she any need of force to procure her entrance into the minds of men. Errors indeed prevail by the assistance of foreign and borrowed succours, but if truth makes not her way into the understanding by her own light, she will be but the weaker for any borrowed force violence can add to her.[81]

Consequently, whereas Proast was of the view that it is religious "truth" that requires the aid of external force to prevail, Locke insists, in the passage above, that it is "error" that requires the assistance of such "foreign and borrowed succours". On what grounds can Locke assume, in this way, that it is religious "truth", rather than "error", which will ultimately prevail without assistance? We have already seen that he believes there is no authoritative criterion by which, within our temporal lives, we can "know" a religion to be the "true religion", so on what basis can he combine this scepticism with an assumption that, in a context of toleration, it is "truth", rather than "error", which "certainly would do well enough, if she were once left to shift for herself"?

The source of Locke's optimism in this regard would seem to be theological. In Chapter 8, in response to Proast's insistence that force is necessary for the propagation of "true religion", Locke declared that Scripture, and the "grace of God" are "a proper and sufficient means; and, which is more, the only means; such means as can work by itself, and without which all the force in the world can do nothing".[82] He declared that we must affirm this proposition

> unless we will say, that which without impiety cannot be said, that the wise and benign Disposer and Governor of all things does not now use all useful means for promoting his own honour in the world, and the good of souls.[83]

We saw in Chapter 8 that it was precisely such a theological claim, used in defence of toleration, to which Proast was ultimately unable to find a convincing answer. But it would also seem to be the basis for Locke's proposition above that it is religious "truth", rather than "error", which will ultimately prevail if "left to shift for herself", since, given the circumstances of his scepticism, there would seem to be no other foundation, other than this faith in God, upon which Locke could advance such an optimistic prognosis.

Notes

1 See Ch. 5 (notes 30 and 31).
2 See Ch. 5 (notes 32 and 33).
3 See Ch. 7 (note 34).
4 Proast 1999: 85.
5 See Ch. 7 (notes 52 and 53).
6 On Hobbes' association with atheism in the minds of the seventeenth-century English, see Tuck 1990: 29, 33, 89, 93.
7 Cranston 1957: 62–3. Part of Peter Laslett's purpose, in his editorship of the *Two Treatises*, was to distance Locke from Hobbes, challenging the conventional wisdom that Locke wrote the *Two Treatises* in response to Hobbes' *Leviathan* (Laslett 1965: x).
8 Locke 1963a: 419. Locke denies the presence of scepticism in the first and second *Letters Concerning Toleration* and declares that Proast's accusations to this effect are self-serving:

> [W]hatever agrees not with your system must presently, by interpretation, be concluded to tend to the promoting of atheism or scepticism in religion. For I challenge you to show, in either of those two letters you mention, one word tending to Epicureanism, atheism, or scepticism in religion.
> (Ibid.: 415)

9 Ibid.: 422. See also Ch. 5 (notes 14–15) and note 68 below. Concerning the reservation that Locke expressed regarding the idea of "one true religion" in the first *Letter*, see Ch. 5 (note 16).

10 See note 13 below.
11 See Ch. 7 (notes 44, 52 and 53).
12 See Ch. 7 (notes 50 and 51).
13 Locke 1963a: 420. See also ibid.: 419.
14 Locke 1963b: 562.
15 Ibid.: 563.
16 See Ch. 5 (note 21). See also Ch. 6 (notes 79–82).
17 See Ch. 6 ("Third Sort or Degree of Perswasion"). As Locke puts it elsewhere: "The strength of our Perswasions are no Evidence at all of their own rectitude … and Men may be as positive and peremptory in Error as in Truth" (Locke 1975: Bk. IV, ch. XIX § 11, 703).
18 See note 4 above.
19 In this respect, propositions (a) and (b) are at odds with each other. In order to affirm proposition (a), and deny scepticism of type (2), Locke had to deny the scepticism and relativism upon which proposition (b) depends. He is, however, unable to affirm proposition (a), and deny scepticism of type (2), because, as we have seen, some of his key arguments for toleration depend on the scepticism (and consequent relativism) presumed by proposition (b).
20 Nicholson 1991: 182. Concerning Proast's need to assume that knowledge of "true religion" is possible, see Ch. 6 (notes 45–7, 53 and 74–5) and Ch. 7 (notes 10, 11, 14 and 54).
21 Nicholson 1991: 177–8.
22 Vernon 1997: 62. Equally, Vernon has argued that it does not "make sense to say that a sceptic exercises tolerance" (ibid.: 53). For my attempt to refute Vernon's view, see Tate 2016.
23 Vernon 1997: 61, 65; 2013: 223. Concerning Locke's assumptions regarding equality, see Locke 1965: II § 4, 6, 54. See also Introduction (note 11).
24 Vernon 2013: 229.
25 Rawls 2005: 218. See also Vernon 2013: 223.
26 Ibid.: 219, 220.
27 Ibid.: 219.
28 Ibid.
29 Locke 1993a: 421.
30 See Ch. 6 (note 47).
31 Coffey 2000: 35. See also Goldie 1991: 348.
32 Rawls 2005: xxiv.
33 On "preaching" and "exhortation", see Ch. 1 (notes 28–30, 34) and Ch. 2 (note 38). On the exclusion of coercion in matters of religion, see Ch 1. (notes 30, 31, 34, 36, 49, 50).
34 Locke 1967: 121, 160.
35 See Locke 1993b: 189; 1993a: 390–3. See also Ch. 3 (note 55).
36 See Ch. 1 (note 51). See also Ch. 1 (note 44), Ch. 2 (note 41) and Ch. 4 (note 5).
37 See Ch. 5 (note 21).
38 Locke 1963a: 424. Concerning Locke's distinction, in the passage, between the "light of nature" as a basis for religious knowledge and "divine revelation", see Ch. 5 (note 22).
39 Locke 1993a: 420.
40 Wolfson 2010: 76. See also ibid.: xv–xvi.
41 Ibid.: xvi.
42 Ibid.: xv.
43 Ibid.
44 Ibid. My addition.
45 Ibid.: 10, 76.
46 See MacIntyre 1997: 217, 250–1.

47 Wolfson 2010: 10.
48 Locke 1975: Bk. IV, ch. XVIII § 6, p. 693.
49 Ibid.: Bk. IV, ch. XIX, § 3, p. 698; Bk. IV, ch. XIX § 5–9, pp. 699–700. See also Locke 2004a: 289.
50 Locke 1975: Bk. IV, ch. XVIII § 11, p. 696. See also ibid.: Bk. IV, ch. XIX § 11, p. 703.
51 See ibid.: Bk. IV, ch. XVIII § 10, p. 695; Bk. IV, ch. XIX § 15, pp. 704–5. See also 2004b: 249; 2004c: 279; 2004a: 290.
52 Concerning Locke's affirmation of the second type of scepticism, see the section "Locke and Scepticism I" above. Concerning the first type of scepticism, we saw that Locke (although at times equivocating on this) often affirmed his belief in the existence of "one true religion" and so denied scepticism of type 1 (see Ch. 5 notes 14–15. See also note 9 above and 68 below).
53 Indeed, Richard Vernon makes this point when he states that, just because Locke "insists that religious belief is not a matter of knowledge, it is wrong to imply, anachronistically, that it must therefore be tentative" (Vernon 1997: 62). Of course, the contrary argument is that, unless individuals believe they possess *knowledge* that their religion is "true", they cannot have a "faith" that it is true, with the result that, once knowledge is removed, so is faith. Locke's distinction between "faith" and "knowledge", most clearly enunciated in Ch. 5 note 21, does not presume this is so.
54 Locke 1993a: 390.
55 See Ch. 5 (note 13).
56 For beliefs that threaten civil peace, see Locke 1993a: 424–26. See also Ch. 1 (notes 44, 45, and 51), Ch. 3 (notes 54 and 69) and Ch. 4 (note 5).
57 For private debate and admonishment, see Ch. 1 (notes 28–30, 34) and Ch. 2 (note 38). On "absent the use of force", see Ch 1. (notes 30, 31, 34, 36, 49, 50). Ian Harris has rejected the idea that, for Locke, religion was a "private" matter, instead insisting on the duty which he believed Locke established, on the basis of natural law, for all individuals to worship God (see Harris 2013: 89–90. See also ibid.: 61, 90–1). Contrary to Harris, we have seen Locke directly refers to the "private" as a means to describe the realm of individual liberty when it comes to religious worship (see Ch. 7 notes 88 and 89). My use of "private" (for want of a better term) is meant to refer to Locke's desire to remove religion entirely from the public sphere, and instead situate it within the realm of individual conscience, and voluntary church attendance, wherein "the care of each man's salvation belongs only to himself" (see Ch. 1 notes 25, 29, 40; Ch. 5 notes 55 and 56; Ch. 6 note 86; Ch. 7 note 39 and Ch. 8 note 49).
58 See Ch. 1 (notes 33 and 47).
59 Locke 1993a: 403.
60 See Ch. 5 ("Pitfalls of the 'Truth Argument'").
61 See Ch. 7 (note 8).
62 See Ch. 5 (notes 14–16) and note 9 above and 68 below.
63 On Proast's response to religious diversity, see Ch. 7 ("Proast and Religious Diversity").
64 Locke 1993a: 396, 407. See also Introduction (note 20).
65 See Ch. 8 (note 67).
66 Proast 1999: 49. See also ibid.: 48, 50, 52, 73, 89, 101.
67 Ibid.: 47. See also Ch. 8 (note 77).
68 For Locke's statement concerning the "truth" of the Christian Scriptures, "for at least these sixteen hundred years", see Locke 1963a: 356.
69 Richard Vernon also makes this same point. See Vernon 1997: 30–1, 65; 2013: 219, 221.
70 Locke 1993a: 401.
71 Ibid.: 402.

72 Ibid.: 423–4. Emphasis added.
73 Locke 1993a: 404.
74 See note 72 above. We saw Locke apply the same principles in the case of "animal sacrifice" in Chapter 1, with Locke insisting (in his first *Letter Concerning Toleration*) that the only reason animal sacrifice should be proscribed by the magistrate is if it interferes with "civil" concerns (such as public food supplies), not because the magistrate perceives it to be at odds with the will of God (see Ch. 1 note 43). Equally, Locke insists, again in the first *Letter*, that the magistrate ought to tolerate those religious practices which he or she believes to be "sinful" (such as "idolatry") when these are "not prejudicial to other men's rights, nor … break the public peace of societies" (Locke 1993a: 417. See also Ch. 1 note 46). In each case, Locke is clearly demonstrating that, in his view, the "business of laws" has no concern with the "truth of opinions" (see Ch. 3 note 71), with the result that such laws are only exercised by the magistrate for "civil" purposes. On the magistrate's authority being justified only if exercised for "civil" purposes, see Ch. 1 (notes 32, 33, 39, 40, 82, 84, 85) and Ch 5 (note 54).
75 See Ch. 5 (note 9). See also Locke 1963c: 120–1. Of course, such statements entirely undermine Waldron's purported distinction, at Ch. 7 (note 55), between his "silly principle" and "sensible position". This distinction trades on Waldron's assumption that Locke's arguments for toleration do not preclude a magistrate from using force to advance a religion "which is *in fact* objectively correct". Earlier I pointed out that this failed to take account of Locke's "truth argument" which denied our capacity to know when a religion is "objectively correct" – see Ch. 7 ("'Geneva' and the 'Indies'"). We now see it also fails to take account of his "consent argument" which Locke, in this chapter, insists applies even if we know which religion is "objectively correct".
76 Locke 1963a: 145. See also Locke 1963a: 326–7. At one point in the third *Letter*, Locke, in a direct address to Proast, appears to imply the contrary – that knowledge of "true religion" would justify coercion: "For whatever may be known, besides matter of fact, is capable of demonstration; and when you have demonstrated to any one any point in religion, you shall have my consent to punish him if he do not assent to it" (ibid.: 424–5). However this might be disregarded as a moment of rhetorical excess, perhaps arising from exasperation, since Locke is elsewhere convinced that, in matters of religion, no such "demonstration" is possible.
77 Locke 1993a: 410. See also Locke 2004d: 276.
78 See Ch. 5 (notes 14–16) and note 9 and 68 above.
79 See Ch. 8 (note 77) and note 67 above.
80 See Ch. 8 (notes 67 and 81).
81 Locke 1993a: 420–1. See also Ch. 8 (note 69).
82 See Ch. 8 (note 71).
83 See Ch. 8 (note 72).

References

Coffey, J. (2000) *Persecution and Toleration in Protestant England, 1558–1689*. Harlow: Longman.

Cranston, M. (1957) *John Locke. A Biography*. London: Longmans, Green and Co.

Goldie, M. (1991) "The Theory of Religious Intolerance in Restoration England". In: O. P. Grell, J. I. Israel and N. Tyacke (eds) *From Persecution to Toleration. The Glorious Revolution and Religion in England*. Oxford: Clarendon Press, pp. 331–68.

Harris, I. (2013) "John Locke and Natural Law: Free Worship and Toleration". In: John Parkin and Timothy Stanton (eds) *Natural Law and Toleration in the Early Enlightenment*. Oxford: Oxford University Press, pp. 60–105.

Laslett, P. (1965) "Foreword". In: J. Locke *Two Treatises of Government*. P. Laslett (ed.). New York: New American Library, pp. ix–xiv.

Locke, J. (1963a) "A Third Letter for Toleration". In: J. Locke *The Works of John Locke*. Vol. VI. Aalen: Scientia Verlag, pp. 141–546.

Locke, J. (1963b) "A Fourth Letter for Toleration". In: J. Locke *The Works of John Locke*. Vol. VI. Aalen: Scientia Verlag, pp. 549–74.

Locke, J. (1963c) "A Second Letter Concerning Toleration". In: J. Locke *The Works of John Locke*. Vol. VI. Aalen: Scientia Verlag, pp. 61–137.

Locke, J. (1965) *Two Treatises of Government*. P. Laslett (ed.). New York: New American Library.

Locke, J. (1967) "First Tract on Government". In: J. Locke *Two Tracts on Government*. P. Abrams (ed.). Cambridge: Cambridge University Press, pp. 117–81.

Locke, J. (1975) *An Essay Concerning Human Understanding*. P. H. Nidditch (ed.). Oxford: Clarendon Press.

Locke, J. (1993a) "A Letter Concerning Toleration". In: J. Locke *Political Writings*. David Wootton (ed.). London: Penguin, pp. 390–436.

Locke, J. (1993b) "An Essay Concerning Toleration". In: J. Locke *Political Writings*. David Wootton (ed.). London: Penguin, pp. 186–210.

Locke, J. (2004a) "Enthusiasm". In: J. Locke *Political Essays*. M. Goldie (ed.). Cambridge: Cambridge University Press, pp. 289–91.

Locke, J. (2004b) "Faith and Reason". In: J. Locke *Political Essays*. M. Goldie (ed.). Cambridge: Cambridge University Press, pp. 248–50.

Locke, J. (2004c) "Religion". In: J. Locke *Political Essays*. M. Goldie (ed.). Cambridge: Cambridge University Press, pp. 278–80.

Locke, J. (2004d) "Toleration D". In: J. Locke *Political Essays*. M. Goldie (ed.). Cambridge: Cambridge University Press, pp. 276–7.

MacIntyre, A. (1997) *After Virtue. A Study in Moral Theory*. London: Duckworth.

Nicholson, P. (1991) "John Locke's Later Letters on Toleration". In: John Horton and Susan Mendus (eds) *John Locke. A Letter Concerning Toleration in Focus*. London: Routledge, pp. 163–87.

Proast, J. (1999) "A Third Letter Concerning Toleration: In Defense of the Argument of the Letter Concerning Toleration, Briefly Consider'd and Answer'd". In: M. Goldie (ed.) *The Reception of Locke's Politics, Vol. 5. The Church, Dissent and Religious Toleration 1689–1773*. London: Pickering and Chatto, pp. 41–116.

Rawls, J. (2005) *Political Liberalism*. Rev. ed. New York: Columbia University Press.

Tate, J. W. (2016) "Toleration, Skepticism and Blasphemy: John Locke, Jonas Proast, and Charlie Hebdo", *American Journal of Political Science*, forthcoming in 2016. DOI: 10.1111/ajps.12245.

Tuck, R. (1990) *Hobbes*. Oxford: Oxford University Press.

Vernon, R. (1997) *The Career of Toleration. John Locke, Jonas Proast and After*. Montreal: McGill-Queens University Press.

Vernon, R. (2013) "Lockean Toleration: Dialogical not Theological?", *Political Studies*, 61 (1): 215–30.

Wolfson, A. (2010) *Persecution or Toleration. An Explication of the Locke–Proast Quarrel, 1689–1704*. Lanham, MD: Lexington Books.

10 Locke's "Civil Perspective"

This chapter will consider what we shall call Locke's "civil perspective". This perspective provides another way by which we can highlight the differences between Locke and Proast, because Proast's outlook is devoid of any such perspective altogether. From the time of the *Two Tracts on Government*, Locke was confronted, in England, with the reality of a civil society in which individuals were fundamentally divided by religious belief, but in which these individuals also needed to secure public agreement on the terms of their coexistence if civil society itself was to be possible. Locke's "civil perspective" was the means by which Locke sought to secure such public agreement in the midst of such difference. In this respect, Locke's "civil perspective" arises from Locke's practical concern, evident from the time of the *Two Tracts*, to find means of ensuring civil peace between individuals deeply divided by religious faith. But, as we shall see, it also reflects a normative concern with individual liberty as well.

It is the "civil perspective" that connects Locke to more recent developments within the liberal tradition, not least to John Rawls's account of political liberalism. By connecting Locke to recent developments in this way, and showing how his ideas have been highly influential on specific aspects of the liberal tradition, this chapter will show how Locke's political philosophy sustains its cogency over time, and is relevant to contemporary liberal democratic societies. Given that these societies are just as divided today as in Locke's own time, but on a number of dimensions in addition to religion, the problem of peaceful coexistence that so occupied Locke from the *Two Tracts* onwards, and in terms of which he came to see toleration playing such an important role, has lost none of its salience over time.[1]

The Civil Perspective

Several aspects of Locke's political philosophy give rise to what we might call his "civil perspective". The "civil perspective" refers to the position which, Locke insists, protagonists in public debate ought to adopt in their engagement with each other if they wish to reach mutual agreement and understanding on public matters, despite their personal differences.

We shall see that Locke articulates the "civil perspective" at a number of points in his engagement with Proast but also, in the first passage below, in the original *Letter Concerning Toleration*. The "civil perspective" is one more feature of Locke's political philosophy in which his differences from Proast are most pronounced.

As we shall see, the "civil perspective" arises from Locke's practical commitment to civil peace, oriented as it is to reaching mutual public agreement between individuals deeply divided by religious belief. But we shall see further below that this civil perspective also advances Locke's normative commitment to individual liberty, insofar as it ensures that the key issues it excludes from public debate are left to the personal liberty of the individual. Proast, we have seen, is animated by none of these concerns – instead being solely committed to the "promoting True Religion and the Salvation of Souls".[2] A fundamental difference between Locke and Proast's position, therefore, can be seen in the fact that Proast's position, in being oriented solely to the advancement of "true religion", is devoid of a "civil perspective", while Locke's "civil perspective", in being oriented to reaching public agreement in civil society, seeks to exclude propositions concerning "true religion".

The "civil perspective" is defined not so much by the content of public debate as by the limits it seeks to impose upon it. There are certain matters Locke believes ought to be excluded from public debate because unable to elicit mutual agreement between individuals. Among these are propositions concerning "true religion", or propositions justified in terms of "true religion". The reason for this is not only because individuals are thoroughly divided on this question, but also, as we saw in our discussion of "non-neutral principles" in Chapter 7, because such claims lack a neutral, impartial or authoritative criterion of adjudication, capable of resolving disagreement, with the result that they cannot form a consensual basis for the exercise of public authority. On the contrary, because of the absence of an impartial and authoritative criterion, each side in a dispute is equally capable of advancing such claims in relation to the other, with no possibility of resolution between them.[3] Locke makes this point in the first *Letter Concerning Toleration*, using as his example the two hypothetical churches in Constantinople, referred to in Chapter 9, with their competing claims to religious "truth":

> But if one of these Churches hath this power of treating the other ill, I ask which of them it is to whom that power belongs, and by what right? It will be answered undoubtedly, that it is the orthodox Church which has the right of authority over the erroneous or heretical. This is, in great and specious words, to say just nothing at all. For every Church is orthodox to itself; to other, erroneous or heretical. Whatsoever any Church believes, it believes to be true; and the contrary thereunto it pronounces to be error. So that the controversy between these Churches about the truth of their doctrines, and the purity of their

worship, is on both sides equal; nor is there any judge, either at Constantinople or elsewhere upon earth, by whose sentence it can be determined. The decision of that question belongs only to the supreme judge of all men, to whom also alone belongs the punishment of the erroneous.[4]

Once again, Locke is declaring that, without an indubitable criterion of "true religion", "true and false ... when we suppose them for ourselves, or our party, in effect, signify just nothing, or nothing to the purpose".[5] This is because either side is capable of advancing such claims, based on their own faith, with no authoritative means of deciding between them. Locke makes precisely the same point in his third *Letter For Toleration*:

> [W]hatever privilege or power you claim, upon your supposing yours to be the true religion, is equally due to another, who supposes his to be the true religion, upon the same claim: and therefore that is no more to be allowed to you than to him.... You believe yours to be the true religion, so does he believe his: you say you are certain of it; so says he, he is: you think you have "arguments proper and sufficient" to convince him, if he would consider them; the same thinks he of his. If this claim, which is equally on both sides, be allowed to either, without any proof; it is plain he, in whose favour it is allowed, is allowed to be judge in his own cause, which nobody can have a right to be, who is not at least infallible. If you come to arguments and proofs, which you must do, before it can be determined whose is the true religion, it is plain your supposition is not allowed.[6]

It is because there is no authoritative criterion of "true religion", capable of resolving such competing claims, that Locke declares, in the passage from his first *Letter* above, that to advance, in public debate, justifications based on "true religion" (or "orthodoxy") is "in great and specious words, to say just nothing at all". What allows Locke to reach these conclusions is, of course, his scepticism. It is because Locke endorses (despite his own denials) the scepticism Proast identified as type (2) – "That though some one Religion be *the true Religion*; yet no man can have any more reason, than another man of another Religion may have, to believe his to be *the true Religion*" – that he is able to insist that we cannot decide between competing claims to "true religion", and so propositions advanced in these terms cannot form a basis of mutual public agreement or understanding.[7] In this respect, we see that, in addition to a concern for individual liberty and civil peace, Locke's "civil perspective" is underwritten by scepticism.

Public Agreement

Public agreement will only be likely to arise on those matters upon which there is sufficient mutual interest for such agreement to be meaningful.

However, as is evident from the preceding discussion, it will also only arise on those matters upon which such agreement is possible. "True religion" is a matter on which, in Locke's time, there was widespread mutual interest, but for the reasons explained above, it was not a matter on which public agreement was possible, there being no indubitable criterion upon which "truth" in such matters could be determined, and so generally affirmed by all. The result is that Locke seeks to exclude such matters from public debate because, in being unable to elicit mutual agreement, they cannot form a consensual basis for the exercise of public authority. It is for this reason that Locke, in his second *Letter Concerning Toleration*, admonishes Proast not to advance his position, seeking to justify the magistrate's public use of force in matters of religion, by

> supposing all along your church in the right, and your religion the true; which can no more be allowed to you in this case, whatever your church or religion be, than it can be to a papist or a Lutheran, a presbyterian or anana baptist; nay, no more to you, than it can be allowed to a Jew or a Mahometan.[8]

Locke makes the same point to Proast in the third *Letter For Toleration*:

> [I]n using punishments in religion, your supposing yours to be the true religion, gives you or your magistrate no more advantage over a papist, presbyterian, or Mahometan, or more reason to punish either of them for his religion, than the same supposition in a papist, presbyterian or Mahometan, gives any of them, or a magistrate of their religion, advantage over you, or reason to punish you for your religion: and therefore this supposition, to any purpose or privilege of using force, is no more to be allowed to you than to any one of any other religion.[9]

In these statements, by seeking to exclude propositions concerning "true religion" from public debate, and declaring that they are "no more to be allowed to you than to any one of any other religion", Locke advances not only his "civil perspective" but also what we have called his "criterion of reciprocity", discussed in Chapters 3 and 7. Indeed, the limits Locke imposes on public debate, by removing religion from its purview, are comparable to the limits which he places on the judgment of the magistrate, when he insists that the magistrate treat all matters of religion as "things indifferent".[10] In each case, the capacity of religion to become an object of public deliberation, and therefore a source of public disagreement, is excluded. Both processes are therefore part of that broader strategy of "privatization" of religious differences, referred to in the previous chapter, in which Locke sought to shift all matters of religion to the sphere of individual conscience and voluntary church attendance. Although Locke did not believe that such a strategy would make individuals any more likely to agree on religious matters, he did believe it would defuse the capacity of religion to become a source of division within civil society – Locke seeking to ensure that "the care of each man's salvation" is left "only to himself", and disagreement on such matters be limited to individual debate, exhortation and admonishment (in which the use of force is absent).[11]

We have seen that Locke refers to the "private" quite explicitly in this context and justifies the removal of religion to the sphere of individual conscience and voluntary church attendance on the practical grounds that this is conducive to civil peace.[12] But this removal is also justified on normative grounds, because, in not being an object of public deliberation or a basis for public agreement, religion is not enforceable by the magistrate's command, and so, in being left to the conscience and free choice of the individual, is subject to individual liberty.[13] The "civil perspective", in being one means whereby Locke seeks to remove religion from the public sphere, is therefore justified in terms of its capacity to realize a normative objective of individual liberty as well as a practical objective of civil peace.

Proast, on the other hand, in being possessed of no such normative or practical concerns, imposes no such limits on public debate. This is evident in Proast's response to Locke's suggestion, in the passage above, that Proast should not seek to advance his position, concerning the use of force in matters of religion, by "supposing all along your church in the right, and your religion the true". Proast replies:

> For if my *Church* be *in the right*; and my Religion be the true; why may I not all along suppose it to be so?[14]

The assumption of "truth" that Proast adopts in this passage is precisely what Locke, with his scepticism in such matters, places in question, and which his "civil perspective" seeks to exclude. It was such responses, on Proast's part, that, in earlier chapters, Locke criticized as "begging the question", since they made assumptions, concerning the accessibility of "truth" in matters of religion, the possibility of which Locke sought to deny.[15] Yet, for our purposes, what is important to note is that, in advancing his position in the passage above, Proast shares none of the assumptions that inform Locke's "civil perspective". Rather, Proast's is an explicitly "theological perspective", underwritten by an epistemic assumption that knowledge of religious "truth" is possible, with the result that if one is in possession of this "truth", one ought to promote, by political force if necessary, "True Religion and the Salvation of Souls".[16]

Locke and the "Legislative Point of View"

The "civil perspective" differs in significant ways from what Alex Tuckness, in investigating Locke's political philosophy, has referred to as the "legislative point of view". The "civil perspective" is a dialogic process between interlocutors, where one individual consciously seeks to limit his or her public propositions to the terms which others are likely to find meaningful, and upon which mutual agreement is therefore likely to be possible. The process is a "dialogical" one because the practical requirements for reaching public agreement, and consensus, are worked out by the protagonists themselves, in terms of those propositions and assumptions upon which each can agree.

Tuckness's "legislative point of view", by contrast, appears to be a monological procedure in which each individual evaluates public principles, in particular the principles upon which the exercise of public authority is to be justified, by considering the outcome if all other individuals affirmed and acted on those same principles as well. As Tuckness puts it: "If we adopt a legislative point of view, we have a reason to take into consideration the way others would interpret and apply a principle when deciding whether or not to act on that principle."[17] Tuckness's procedure appears designed to ensure, from each individual's monological perspective, a certain unanimity, concerning appropriate public rules and principles, among individuals with otherwise disparate outlooks. But I think any reading of Locke's *Letters Concerning Toleration* make clear that Locke's commitment to civil peace made him much more concerned with dialogic processes, since it is public dialogue, oriented to mutual agreement, between individuals deeply divided in their personal commitments, which he saw as a necessary means of securing civil peace. It is therefore to these dialogic processes that the "civil perspective" refers.

Locke's Legacy: John Rawls and *Political Liberalism*

We have seen in previous chapters that Locke is clearly distinguishable from those theorists of toleration who conceive of toleration in unequal terms, as a concession on the part of the powerful to the subservient, and indeed a concession the powerful have the capacity to reverse.[18] Such theorists contrast a policy of toleration to a framework of equal rights precisely because, they believe, toleration is characterized by such inequality, and so lacks the reciprocal equality associated with rights doctrines.[19] Yet we saw that Locke's conception of toleration is framed in terms of equality – not least, the equal entitlement of all individuals to their natural rights of liberty – and is therefore understood by Locke in terms of a theory of rights. As Locke put it in *A Letter Concerning Toleration*, "the sum of all we drive at is that every man may enjoy the same rights that are granted to others".[20] It is this which constitutes the normative (as distinct from practical) basis of Locke's conception of toleration. Locke therefore provides a strong alternative to those theorists who claim that toleration is outmoded in contemporary multicultural liberal democracies because it is at odds with the entitlements to equal rights which theories of multiculturalism presume.[21]

Yet Locke's legacy is not only one of strong contrasts to contemporary political theorists. It is also one of continuity. We can perceive definite elements of Locke's position in the later political philosophy of John Rawls. Rawls reoriented much of the contemporary liberal tradition when, with the publication of *A Theory of Justice* in 1971, he resurrected social contract theory, and an ideal of individual rights, against a dominant utilitarian tradition.[22] However, in so doing, Rawls identified his philosophical ambitions primarily with Immanuel Kant rather than John Locke.[23] Indeed, the universalist elements of Kant's position have their parallel in a passage Rawls advances at the end of *A Theory of Justice*, in which he claims for the "original position", at the centre of his theory, the same apodictic and universal ambitions as Kant's categorical imperative when it comes to establishing principles of right.[24] As Rawls states:

> Thus to see our place in society from the perspective of this position is to see it *sub specie aeternitatis*: it is to regard the human situation not only from all social but also from all temporal points of view. The perspective of eternity is not a perspective from a certain place beyond the world, nor the point of view of a transcendent being; rather it is a certain form of thought and feeling that rational persons can adopt within the world. And having done so, they can, whatever their generation, bring together into one scheme all individual perspectives and arrive together at regulative principles that can be affirmed by everyone as he lives by them, each from his own standpoint. Purity of heart, if one could attain it, would be to see clearly and to act with grace and self-command from this point of view.[25]

Yet by 1980, Rawls was clearly seeking to depart from this comprehensive, universalist perspective. In an article he published that year in the *Journal of Philosophy*, he eschews universalist ambitions such as those advanced in the passage above:

> I should emphasize that what I have called the "real task" of justifying a conception of justice is not primarily an epistemological problem. The search for reasonable grounds for reaching agreement rooted in our conception of ourselves and in our relation to society replaces the search for moral truth interpreted as fixed by a prior and independent order of objects and relations, whether natural or divine, an order apart and distinct from how we conceive of ourselves.... What justifies a conception of justice is not its being true to an order antecedent to and given to us, but its congruence with our deeper understanding of ourselves and our aspirations, and our realization that, given our history and the traditions embedded in our public life, it is the most reasonable doctrine for us.[26]

Indeed, in *Political Liberalism*, published in 1993, Rawls expands on this position, which he now defines as "political", and which he explicitly contrasts to the more "comprehensive" position he sought to advance in *A Theory of Justice*. He does so by insisting that the "political" perspective of *Political Liberalism* seeks a more limited, and contingent, basis of justification and agreement than *A Theory of Justice*:

> In *Theory [of Justice]* a moral doctrine of justice general in scope is not distinguished from a strictly political conception of justice. Nothing is made of the contrast between comprehensive philosophical and moral doctrines and conceptions limited to the domain of the political. In the lectures in this volume, however, these distinctions and related ideas are fundamental.... In this respect a political conception of justice differs from many moral doctrines, for these are widely regarded as general and comprehensive views.... By contrast, a political conception tries to elaborate a reasonable conception for the basic structure [of society] alone and involves, so far as possible, no wider commitment to any other doctrine.[27]

Indeed, Rawls explains his shift to a "political", as distinct from "comprehensive", conception of justice in terms of his recognition of the pervasive pluralism and disagreement present within contemporary liberal democratic societies. In the context of such pluralism, individuals adhere to rival moral, religious and philosophical doctrines, and yet need, amidst these differences, to secure political agreement, concerning the terms of their coexistence, if civil society is to be possible.[28] Political agreement between individuals (or what Locke would call mutual "consent") is fundamental for Rawls, because, like Locke, his theory is based on contractarian ideals, where such agreement (consent) forms the basis of the political legitimacy, and stability, of government.[29] However Rawls insists that, in a context of pervasive pluralism, a limited consensus, centred on the "political", is all that is possible, and this requires agreement on political principles of justice, capable of regulating and ordering society, and ensuring political stability over time.[30] The reason for such limits, centred on the "political", Rawls says, is because, in the midst of such pluralism within liberal democratic societies, there is not sufficient unanimity among individuals to justify these principles of justice on the sort of broad, "comprehensive" basis assumed in *A Theory of Justice*.[31] Rawls therefore explains his transition from *A Theory of Justice* to his later position, culminating in *Political Liberalism*, in terms of the "unrealistic" expectations of comprehensive agreement inherent in his earlier position, arising from his failure to recognize the pervasive pluralism present in contemporary liberal democracies:

> Now the serious problem is this. A modern democratic society is characterized not simply by a pluralism of comprehensive religious, philosophical, and moral doctrines but by a pluralism of incompatible yet reasonable comprehensive doctrines. No one of these doctrines is affirmed by citizens generally. Nor should one expect that in the foreseeable future one of them, or some other reasonable doctrine, will ever be affirmed by all, or nearly all, citizens. Political liberalism

assumes that, for political purposes, a plurality of reasonable yet incompatible comprehensive doctrines is the normal result of the exercise of human reason within the framework of the free institutions of a constitutional democratic regime...

The fact of a plurality of reasonable but incompatible comprehensive doctrines – the fact of reasonable pluralism – shows that, as used in *Theory*, the idea of a well-ordered society of justice as fairness is unrealistic. This is because it is inconsistent with realizing its own principles under the best foreseeable conditions.... This problem sets the stage for the later essays beginning in 1980.[32]

Rawls and Locke

What the discussion above makes clear is that the later Rawls was preoccupied with a problem very close to that which Locke had to confront over three centuries earlier from the time of the *Two Tracts on Government* onwards. This was the problem of how to secure political agreement and stability (or what Locke would call civil peace) between individuals in a context of "deep doctrinal conflict with no prospect of resolution".[33] Rawls gives expression to this problem as follows:

> [T]he problem of political liberalism is: how is it possible that there may exist over time a stable and just society of free and equal citizens profoundly divided by reasonable though incompatible religious, philosophical, and moral doctrines? Put another way: how is it possible that deeply opposed though reasonable comprehensive doctrines may live together and all affirm the political conception of a constitutional regime? What is the structure and content of a political conception that can gain the support of such an overlapping consensus? These are among the questions that political liberalism tries to answer.[34]

Both Locke and Rawls, therefore, confront a society in which individuals are divided in their deepest personal commitments, and each faces the basic political problem of finding, in the midst of this difference, terms of civil and political coexistence, based on mutual consent, capable of ensuring civil peace and political stability over time. Just as Locke referred to the persistence of diversity, in his own time, as something which "cannot be avoided", so Rawls presents the diversity and disagreement that he confronts as "the normal result of the exercise of human reason within the framework of the free institutions of a constitutional democratic regime".[35]

Some of the strategies that Rawls deployed to achieve political agreement, and therefore peaceful coexistence, in such circumstances, have their broad parallel in Locke. Rawls insists, for instance, that, in seeking agreement between individuals, limited to the "political", political liberalism should not attempt to elicit judgment from individuals on substantive issues (such as questions of "truth" or "morality" central to individuals' comprehensive doctrines) because it is upon these that individuals are most profoundly divided, and such issues can be avoided because they fall outside the realm of the "political", not being essential to the "basic structure" of society.[36] As Rawls tells us, to demand such substantive judgments, as a condition of political agreement, would be to go "beyond the bounds of a political conception of justice framed so far as possible to be acceptable to all reasonable comprehensive doctrines".[37] Instead, political liberalism deliberately reserves judgment on all matters falling outside the realm of the "political", perceiving these as not essential to political agreement:

> Political liberalism sees its form of political philosophy as having its own subject matter: how is a just and free society possible under conditions of deep doctrinal conflict with no prospect of resolution? To maintain impartiality between comprehensive doctrines, it does not specifically address the moral topics on which those doctrines divide.[38]

Indeed, by reserving judgment on such contentious issues, political liberalism seeks to remove them from the realm of political deliberation and therefore from the scope of political agreement altogether:

> Faced with the fact of reasonable pluralism, a liberal view removes from the political agenda the most divisive issues, serious contention about which must undermine the bases of social cooperation.[39]

This concern to abstract from all comprehensive questions upon which individuals differ, and instead focus purely on "political" issues, upon which public agreement is possible, has its rough analogy in Locke's "civil perspective", not least its attempt to remove matters of "true religion" from public deliberation. It also has its rough analogy in Locke's insistence that magistrates not make judgments concerning the intrinsic qualities of the matters that fall within their purview, but instead treat all such issues as "things indifferent", and so of concern only if they impact on the "civil" matters for which the magistrate has authority. In each case, there is an attempt by Locke to remove from the sphere of political deliberation, and its justification of political authority, controversial matters upon which individuals are divided, and instead base the exercise of that political authority on broad "civil" concerns upon which there is widespread interest *and* upon which public agreement is possible.

Further, we saw in preceding chapters that Locke, in his engagement with Proast, insisted that Proast not advance his case for the exercise of political authority in terms of "true religion", which, Locke said, in not being open to independent confirmation, was a plea that could equally be advanced by competing parties, with all the interminable disagreement that this involved. Instead, Locke was concerned (in his "civil perspective") that individuals only advance propositions on which public agreement was possible. This feature of the "civil perspective" again has its rough analogy in Rawls's political liberalism – not only Rawls's removal "from the political agenda the most divisive issues, serious contention about which must undermine the bases of social cooperation" (at note 39 above) but also Rawls's conception of "public reason":

> [O]ur exercise of political power is proper only when we sincerely believe that the reasons we would offer for our political actions ... are sufficient, and we also reasonably think that other citizens might also reasonably accept those reasons.... A citizen engages in public reason ... when he or she deliberates within a framework of what he or she sincerely regards as the most reasonable political conception of justice, a conception that expresses political values that others, as free and equal citizens might also reasonably be expected reasonably to endorse.[40]

In this way, by engaging in such strategies, Locke and Rawls seek to ensure that the exercise of political authority is based on principles sufficiently broad, and of sufficient common interest, that they are capable of eliciting the widest possible consent among individuals otherwise divided in their most fundamental commitments. Each therefore seeks to advance similar strategies, in response to similar circumstances, to secure common political agreement, and therefore civil peace, consistent with the liberty of individuals, in a context of deep doctrinal diversity.

Timothy Stanton, of the University of York, once accused me of being unable to "contemplate the possibility that Locke thought in anything but the secular liberal terms of a Rawls".[41] I think it would be more accurate to describe my position as one which insists that it is Rawls, at least in the later phase of his philosophical development, who increasingly thought in the "political" terms of a Locke.[42] We saw that Rawls's earlier work in *A Theory of Justice* was self-consciously Kantian in its orientation.[43] But it is Rawls's conception of a "political liberalism", whose starting point, we saw, was Rawls's recognition of the irreducible pluralism of contemporary liberal democratic societies, which moves Rawls far closer to Locke, since Locke too was confronted with this same problem of ensuring both political agreement, and political stability, between individuals fundamentally divided in their deepest commitments. We have seen above that some of the strategies Locke adopted to secure political agreement and stability in this context have their rough analogy in Rawls's "political liberalism" some three hundred years later.

Notes

1. My proposition that Locke retains his relevance because of his seminal role in the development of the liberal tradition is at variance to Ian Harris who, by emphasizing the theological dimension of Locke's political philosophy, centred in natural law, seeks to distance Locke from the liberal tradition, and John Dunn who, on the same basis, seeks to deny Locke's contemporary relevance altogether. See Harris 1995: 327–8; 2013: 87, 88, 90, 100, 101, 104; Dunn 1969: x–xi; 1990: 12, 2003: 37. For my criticism of Dunn and Harris, see, respectively, Tate 2013 and Tate 2015. Although Dunn denies relevance to those aspects of Locke's political philosophy which depend on theological assumptions, he believes that Locke's political philosophy retains its relevance when it focuses on "the nature of politics as a purely human activity", an activity wherein "God has since gone off the air" (Dunn 1990: 13. See also ibid.: 14, 21, 22, 25).
2. See Ch. 6 (note 47). See also Ch. 6 (notes 45, 46 and 53).
3. See Ch. 7 ("Non-Neutral Principles" and "Geneva and the Indies").
4. Locke 1993: 401–2. On the two hypothetical churches in Constantinople, see Ch. 9 (notes 70 and 71).
5. See Ch. 6 (note 90).
6. Locke 1963: 419. See also ibid.: 419–20; Ch. 7 (note 34).
7. For Proast's scepticism of type (2), see Ch. 9 (note 4). On Locke's denials, see ch. 9 (note 8).
8. See Ch. 7 (note 34).
9. Locke 1963: 419–20.
10. See Ch. 1 (notes 33 and 47).
11. On the "care" of each man's "salvation" belonging "only to himself", see Ch. 1 (note 25). See also Ch. 1 (notes 29 and 40), Ch. 5 (notes 55 and 56), Ch. 6 (note 86), Ch. 7 (note 39) and Ch. 8 (note 49). On individual debate, exhortation and admonishment, see Ch. 1 (notes 28–30, 34) and Ch. 2 (note 38). On the absence of the use of force, see Ch. 1 (notes 30, 31, 34, 36, 49, 50). On Locke's "privatization" strategy, see the concluding part of Ch. 9 ("Locke and Scepticism II").
12. On Locke's references to "private", see Ch. 7 (notes 88 and 89). On civil peace, see Ch. 9 (note 59).
13. On religion being left to the conscience, and free choice, of individuals, see Ch. 1 (notes 25, 29 and 40), Ch. 5 (notes 55 and 56), Ch. 6 (note 86), Ch. 7 (notes 39 and 91), and Ch. 8 (note 49).
14. Proast 1999: 85. As we have seen, it would seem that Waldron, like Proast, sees nothing at fault with such a response, and its explicit assumption of religious "truth" (see Ch. 7 note 55).
15. See Ch. 7 ("Begging the Question").
16. See Ch. 6 (note 47). See also Ch. 6 (notes 45, 46 and 53).
17. Tuckness 2009: 36.
18. See Ch. 1 (notes 35 and 76). For Locke's other differences from contemporary toleration theorists see Ch. 4 (notes 28–30).
19. See Ch. 4 (note 28).
20. See Ch. 7 (note 48).
21. See Heyd 2008: 175; Gray 2000: 323–5. See also Ch. 4 (notes 28 and 30).
22. Indeed, Rawls declares this to be his aim on the opening page of *A Theory of Justice* – see Rawls 1972: 3.
23. In *A Theory of Justice*, Rawls states: "What I have attempted to do is to generalize and carry to a higher order of abstraction the traditional theory of the social contract as represented by Locke, Rousseau and Kant" (ibid.: viii). However it is Kant, rather than Locke, with whom Rawls, in this period, most

identifies, and perceives as providing his most important philosophical antecedents. Rawls explicitly links his position in *A Theory of Justice* to Kant when, referring to a key aspect of his theory, he states "[t]he notion of the veil of ignorance is implicit, I think, in Kant's ethics" (ibid.: 140–1). See also note 24 below.

24 Indeed, Rawls admits as much when he states, "[t]he original position may be viewed, then, as a procedural interpretation of Kant's conception of autonomy and the categorical imperative" (ibid.: 256).
25 Ibid.: 587.
26 Rawls 1980: 518–19. See Rawls 2005a: 13–14, 100–1, 150–1.
27 Ibid.: xv, 13. My addition.
28 See ibid.: xvi–xviii, xxv, xxxix, 10, 133.
29 See note 23 above and Rawls's discussion of "overlapping consensus" at note 30 below.
30 As Rawls puts it:

> Since there is no reasonable religious, philosophical, or moral doctrines affirmed by all citizens, the conception of justice affirmed in a well-ordered democratic society must be a conception limited to what I shall call "the domain of the political" and its values.
>
> (Ibid.: 38)

The "political" involves a narrowing of those matters subject to public agreement and justification (see notes 36–9 below). Concerning the means of justification itself, as a basis for public agreement, Rawls points to the following process, in relation to the political principles of justice, perceiving these as being justified in two distinct ways. He writes that the political principles of justice are affirmed both as a "freestanding view" (ibid.: 10, 12, 38–40) and in terms of an "overlapping consensus" of individuals' comprehensive (and "reasonable") moral, religious and philosophical doctrines, where each doctrine affirms the principles of justice according to its own point of view (ibid.: xvi, xviii, xix, 15, 36, 38–9, 65–6). Rawls tells us that only if principles of justice are able to elicit such an "overlapping consensus" will they have sufficient stability to maintain their authority within civil society over time (ibid.: 15, 36, 65–6, 126, 140–1).

31 Rawls rejects the possibility of political justification arising from broad, comprehensive doctrines, precisely due to this lack of unanimity among individuals which he believes characterizes contemporary liberal democratic polities:

> Religious and philosophical doctrines express views of the world and of our life with one another, severally and collectively, as a whole. Our individual and associative points of view, intellectual affinities, and affective attachments, are too diverse, especially in a free society, to enable those doctrines to serve as the basis of lasting and reasoned political agreement.... These remarks lead to a ... general fact stated thus: that many of our most important judgments are made under conditions where it is not to be expected that conscientious persons with full powers of reason, even after free discussion, will all arrive at the same conclusion.
>
> (Rawls 2005a: 58)

32 Ibid.: xvi–xvii.
33 Ibid.: xxviii.
34 Ibid.: xviii.
35 For Rawls, see note 32 above. On Locke's claim that diversity "cannot be avoided", see Ch. 4 (note 2).
36 Rawls's political liberalism therefore reserves judgment on substantive questions concerning these comprehensive doctrines, such as their "truth" or "justice" (Rawls 2005a: 94, 116, 126–7, 153). Political liberalism is only concerned that

these comprehensive doctrines, existing within civil society, and therefore subject to political principles of justice, are "reasonable". Comprehensive doctrines are considered "reasonable" if they do not "reject the essentials of a democratic regime" (ibid.: xvi. See also ibid.: xlii, 36–7, 58–62, 63–4, 243, 394–5). They are declared "unreasonable" if they "reject one or more democratic freedoms" (ibid.: 64n. See also ibid.: 243).

37 Ibid.: 114.
38 Ibid.: xxviii.
39 Ibid.: 157.
40 Rawls 2005b: 446–7, 450. See also Ch. 9 (note 25).
41 Stanton 2012: 233.
42 In this respect I have sought to show how Jeremy Waldron is mistaken in his attempt to present Rawls as a radical contrast to Locke in matters of liberalism – see Tate 2013: 155–6.
43 See notes 23 and 24 above.

References

Dunn, J. (1969) *The Political Thought of John Locke*. Cambridge: Cambridge University Press.

Dunn, J. (1990) "What is Living and What is Dead in the Political Theory of John Locke?". In: J. Dunn *Interpreting Political Responsibility. Essays 1981–1989*. Cambridge: Polity Press, pp. 9–25.

Dunn, J. (2003) *Locke. A Very Short Introduction*. Oxford: Oxford University Press.

Gray, J. (2000) "Pluralism and Toleration in Contemporary Political Philosophy", *Political Studies*, 48 (2): 323–3.

Harris, I. (1995) *The Mind of John Locke. A Study of Political Theory in its Intellectual Setting*. Cambridge: Cambridge University Press.

Harris, I. (2013) "John Locke and Natural Law: Free Worship and Toleration". In: J. Parkin and T. Stanton (eds) *Natural Law and Toleration in the Early Enlightenment*. Oxford: Oxford University Press, pp. 60–105.

Heyd, D. (2008) "Is Toleration a Political Virtue?". In: M. S. Williams and J. Waldron (eds) *Toleration and its Limits*. New York: New York University Press, pp. 171–94.

Locke, J. (1963) "A Third Letter for Toleration". In: J. Locke *The Works of John Locke*. Vol. VI. Aalen: Scientia Verlag, pp. 141–546.

Locke J. (1993) "A Letter Concerning Toleration". In: J. Locke *Political Writings*. D. Wootton (ed.). London: Penguin, pp. 390–436.

Proast, J. (1999) "A Third Letter Concerning Toleration: In Defense of the Argument of the Letter Concerning Toleration, Briefly Consider'd and Answer'd". In: M. Goldie (ed.) *The Reception of Locke's Politics, Vol. 5. The Church, Dissent and Religious Toleration 1689–1773*. London: Pickering and Chatto, pp. 41–116.

Rawls, J. (1972) *A Theory of Justice*. Oxford: Oxford University Press.

Rawls, J. (1980) "Kantian Constructivism in Moral Theory", *The Journal of Philosophy*, 77 (9): 515–72.

Rawls, J. (2005a) *Political Liberalism*. Rev. ed. New York: Columbia University Press.

Rawls, J. (2005b) "The Idea of Public Reason Revisited". In: J. Rawls *Political Liberalism*. Rev. ed. New York: Columbia University Press, pp. 437–90.

Stanton, T. (2012) "On (Mis)Interpreting Locke: A Reply to Tate", *Political Theory*, 40 (2): 229–36.
Tate, J. W. (2013) "Dividing Locke from God: The Limits of Theology in Locke's Political Philosophy", *Philosophy and Social Criticism*, 39 (2): 133–64.
Tate, J. W. (2015) "Locke, Toleration and Natural Law: A Reassessment", *European Journal of Political Theory*, published on the journal's "early view" website in "Online First" on 8 November 2015. DOI: 10.1177/1474885115609739. Available at: http://ept.sagepub.com/content/early/2015/11/04/1474885115609739.abstract.
Tuckness, A. (2009) *Locke and the Legislative Point of View: Toleration, Contested Principles and the Law*. Princeton, NJ: Princeton University Press.

11 Conclusion

In the development of his ideas on toleration, and in his debate with Jonas Proast, John Locke advanced principles for dealing with difference and diversity which, as the preceding chapter shows, were profoundly influential for at least one form of contemporary liberalism. Within this context, Locke upheld principles of liberty in which individuals were to be their own judge in matters of religion. Proast, by contrast, perceived "true religion", and the eternal salvation which, he believed, was dependent upon it, as so important that he did not think it acceptable to leave individuals "to their own Consciences" in such matters. Rather, he insisted, they ought to be subject to "Penalties", imposed by the magistrate, if their beliefs were at odds with those considered necessary for their salvation. Not only did Proast believe this to be in the "true Interest" of each individual, he went further and argued that the "Commonwealth" itself benefited from such a "Method":

> And that those who cannot otherwise be brought to [the "true religion"] should be a little *disturbed and diseas'd* to bring them to it, I take to be the Interest not onely of those particular persons who by this means may be brought into the way of Salvation, but of the *Commonwealth* likewise, upon these two accounts. 1. Because the true Religion, which this Method propagates, makes good Men; and good Men are always the best Subjects, or Members of a Commonwealth.... And 2. Because this Care in any Commonwealth, of God's Honour and Men's Salvation, entitles it to his special protection and blessing. So that where this Method is used, it proves both a *Spiritual* and a *Civil Benefit* to the *Commonwealth*.[1]

Locke's Christianity was just as sincere as Proast's. But, on such matters, he arrived at entirely contrary conclusions to those above. We saw that Locke defended his ideal of toleration on both normative and practical grounds, each referring, respectively, to an imperative of individual liberty (to which all adult individuals of sound mind were equally entitled) and an imperative of effective state governance and civil peace. We also saw that Locke balanced imperative against the other in different ways throughout his intellectual career as he sought to maintain each of these normative and practical commitments.

In this respect, Locke's priorities were very different from those of Proast. Although Locke, like any sincere Christian, was concerned with the salvation of individual souls, his commitment to his normative and practical imperatives (as well as his ability to overcome what we have called the "moral challenge of toleration") meant that, unlike Proast, he was willing to leave such matters of religious truth and salvation to individuals' conscience alone, insisting that the magistrate adopt a "civil perspective" on such matters, treating all such concerns as "things indifferent", and subject to political authority only insofar as they impacted on those civil matters for which the magistrate alone possessed authority.

The American philosopher, Thomas Nagel, declared in 1987 that "[t]he defence of liberalism requires that a limit somehow be drawn to appeals to *the truth* in political argument".[2] We saw that it was precisely these limits (particularly when it came to religion) which defined Locke's "civil perspective", Locke declaring that "the business of laws is not to provide for the truth of opinions, but for the safety and security of the commonwealth, and of every particular man's goods and person".[3] In this respect, although Locke was by no means the first European to defend liberty of conscience on matters of religion, we have seen that the manner in which he did so was a seminal influence upon later developments within the liberal tradition.[4]

Locke and Proast engaged with each other on the subject of toleration over three hundred years ago. Yet we have seen that many of the issues salient within their debate are still of perennial concern to us now. This is because the irreducible disagreement and diversity between individuals that each confronted in their own time has not diminished in our own day. In the England that Locke knew, individuals were willing to kill, and to die, in the name of religion. Locke was fully aware of this, and from the time of the *Two Tracts on Government* onwards, was concerned to find a means to ensure civil peace in the midst of such ultimate commitments, thereby avoiding such violence. We see today that the same ultimate commitments manifest themselves, often inside liberal democracies themselves, whether above the skyline of New York, or on the streets of Paris, Amsterdam, Copenhagen, Garland in Texas, or South-West London. The *Charlie Hebdo* shooting, with which this book began, is only one of a number of recent tragic examples where the religious commitments of some individuals within liberal democracies have culminated in bloodshed and murder. So long as such individuals within these polities remain willing to interpret the imperatives of their faith in this way, we can only hope that Locke, and the liberalism he helped to inaugurate, will continue to be considered crucial not only to the ongoing engagement with these perennial problems but also to what we might hope will be their ongoing resolution.

Notes

1 Proast 1999: 96. My addition.
2 Nagel 1987: 227.
3 See Ch. 3 (note 71).
4 Clearly, as we have seen, such a view is at odds with some perspectives within contemporary Locke scholarship, which seek to separate Locke's legacy from contemporary liberalism. See Introduction (note 8) and Ch. 10 (note 1).

References

Proast, J. (1999) "A Third Letter Concerning Toleration: In Defense of the Argument of the Letter Concerning Toleration, Briefly Consider'd and Answer'd". In: M. Goldie (ed.) *The Reception of Locke's Politics. Vol. 5. The Church, Dissent and Religious Toleration, 1689–1773*. London: Pickering & Chatto, pp. 41–116.
Nagel, T. (1987) "Moral Conflict and Political Legitimacy", *Philosophy and Public Affairs*, 16 (3): 215–40.

Index

Abrams, P. 49–51, 56–7, 69n9, 69n14, 69n16, 71n54, 121n32, 236
account of the state 118, 187; contractualist 122n71; functional 122n62; modal 118–19, 125, 183, 185–6, 188, 190, 218
alternative 176, 256; coercive 113; definition of the state 113; favourable 88; influences upon Locke 68; preferable 116, 178, 229; state policy 6, 112; viable 89, 134; view 65
Anabaptists 66, 99n71, 227
anana baptist 174, 226, 254
Anglican 12, 57, 148; authorities 53, 147, 163n53; church and churchmen 143, 146–8; circles 24, 163n51; clergyman 1, 8, 212; counter-revolution against James 162; divines 152; intolerance towards Dissenters 21; Low Church 160; outwardly conforming 65; persecution 149; sacraments 62
Anglicans 144–5, 175
animal sacrifice 31, 93; proscribed 30, 249n74
anti-liberal 108–9
appeal to God 206; Locke's 196, 206; Proast's 186–8, 190, 196, 206, 209–10, 213, 218
argument against toleration 75–6, 82, 222n48
argument for toleration 2, 9, 15, 35, 39, 47, 75, 78–80, 82, 89, 92, 95n24, 102, 111, 128–33, 135–6, 138, 140n25, 144, 154–5, 180, 197, 226, 229, 231–2, 236, 242, 249n75; advanced 190, 230; biblical 110; Christian 163n58; contingent 179; key 247n19; main line of 115–16, 119, 167, 225; normative 81, 93, 204; practical 90, 106; primary 127;

see also consent argument, rationality argument, truth argument
Arminian church 22; see also Remonstrant
Arminians 22, 99n71, 242
Ashcraft, R. 37, 44n89, 47, 57, 68, 72n86, 125, 139n2, 192n60
Ashley (A. A. Cooper) 21, 23, 37, 48, 61–8, 72n71, 72n78, 72n86; see also Cooper, Shaftesbury
atheism 94, 102, 227, 246n6, 246n8; heathenism 236
atheists 84, 90, 227; Locke's refusal to tolerate 93; proscription of 94, 95n9, 96n54, 98n69, 99n72, 161
authoritarian 3; competence of magistracy 51; political authoritarianism 61

Bagshaw, Edward 49–53, 55, 57, 69n9, 69n16, 227
Bauman, Z. 3
begging the question 158, 173–5, 255
Berlin, I. 97n65, 188–9, 193n90
Black Hole 67–8

Calvinist 22; foreign king 145
Calvinists 66, 97n68, 242
case for toleration 15, 81, 83, 111, 118, 133–4, 153, 161, 195, 205, 236–7, 243–4; advancing 225, 231; negative 116–17; non-biblical 155; practical 82; underwriting 235; see also consent argument, rationality argument, toleration, truth argument
categorical distinctions 25, 71n70, 80, 92, 158, 235
Catholic 97n68, 162n9; persecution 150; persecution of Protestants 220n6; religion 97n59; Roman Church 69n16; see also popish, Roman

Catholicism 94, 97n59, 144, 146, 236; see also source of Catholicism's danger to state

Catholics 65–6, 73n101, 85–9, 93–4, 95n9, 96n34, 96n47, 97n59, 97n68, 101, 161, 175, 220n6; see also papists, Roman Catholics

choices 8, 49, 97n65; concerning fate of immortal soul 168; concerning salvation 131; free 255, 262n13; have to be made 13; individual 6, 31, 50, 128, 135, 160, 188, 210; of Man 208; meaningful array of 116–17; moral 240; other's 137–8, 184–5; rational 170; religious 130; voluntary 41n35, 94

Christ Church, Oxford 1, 48–9, 57, 65–6, 69n4, 69n16, 71n54

Christian 29, 51, 176; arguments for toleration 163n58; authority 146; commitments 218, 226, 241; credentials 233; duty 216; endorsements 116; evangelism 161; history 211–12, 215; liberty 149; Locke's view 237, 239; perspective 217; religion 129, 211–13, 215–16, 244; Scriptures 241, 248n68; sincere 127, 139n13, 206, 240–1, 267; texts 127; traditional view 237, 239; world 101, 149

Christianity 47, 97n61, 140n21, 233, 235–6; early years 215; history 212–13, 216; Locke's view of 234, 237, 266; moral challenge to 242; sincere 16, 173, 226

church 27–8, 41n31, 66, 103, 134, 145, 147, 168, 212, 227, 252; Arminian or Remonstrant 22; Christian 29; communion 209–10, 244; congregations 49–50; in Constantinople 242; contending parties 10, 15; doctrines 30, 53; established 12, 86, 102, 201; harmed 118; laws and customs 143; magistrate's 221n31; non-entitlement to confiscate property 41n31; no title to invade civil rights 239; official state 24; orthodox 174; party 221n36; penalties for religious beliefs 41n30, 41n34; politics 148; privileged access to truth 128; protective of 146; in the right 226, 254–5; Roman Catholic 69n16; of Rome 85; seeking to regulate civil matters 31; toleration 106; toleration refused 129; voluntary attendance 234, 248n57; see also Catholic, Presbyterian

church and state 1, 114; institutional separation 238; relative jurisdiction 31; separation of 13, 24, 28–30, 40n13, 94, 236–7, 239;

church, Anglican 12, 143, 146; politics 147; regime 148

Church of England 86–7, 202; conversion to 223n79; disestablishment 24; Dissenters 53, 144–5, 147; groups outside the bounds 85; Latitudinarian bishops 148; latitudinism 91; one true religion 161, 164n93, 173, 191n26, 198–200; outward conformity to 221n36; reformation 146; surplice 69n16

Churchill, Awnsham 22

civil concerns 5–6, 29–30, 36–7, 59, 137, 239, 249n74, 260

civil peace 4, 6, 9, 24–6, 32, 37, 79, 87, 89, 93, 109, 132, 212, 253, 256, 259, 267; concern for 10, 101; conducive to 255; consistent with 66, 91, 120n16, 152; contrary to the imperative of 81; doctrines contrary to 30; endorse 78; ensuring 7, 57, 71n70, 76–7, 84, 86, 94, 112, 131, 141n63, 251; essential to 103; in the interests of 117; Locke's commitment to 256; means to secure 39; practical commitment to 16, 252; practical imperative of 54, 83, 105, 266; securing 261; threat to 48, 55, 80, 82, 88, 90, 102, 215, 239; wider parameters 31

civil perspective 16, 174, 177, 251–6, 260–1, 267

clergymen 62; Anglican 1, 8, 212

coercion 41n30, 114, 117–18, 155, 159–60, 244; on behalf of true religion 156; conscience free from 112; exclusion of 247n33; of individuals 189; inefficient 111; justify 12, 242, 249n76; religious 133, 153; vulnerable to 121n48

coercive 27, 31, 51; alternative 113; force 114; imposition 234; means 53, 111, 154; persecution 116; religious discipline 146

Coffey, J. 162n16, 233

Cohen, A. J. 41n35, 43n76

commission 34, 126–7, 136, 139n5,

139n9, 156, 163n68, 184, 189, 205, 207–8, 210, 243
commitments 3–4, 9–11, 15–16, 66, 117, 207, 226, 252, 256, 267; alteration in 76; avowed 67; Christian 218, 241; to the Crown 145; to ecclesiastical liberty 65; fundamental 261; of government 26; intense 239; normative 177; personal 259; to religion 238; religious 171, 237; state 80; to toleration 212, 225, 242, 244; to universalization 192n47; wider 258
commonwealths 28–30, 35, 94, 98n69, 99n71, 137, 182–3, 205–10, 239, 243, 266–7
communion 174, 209, 244; with the magistrate 199
compact 35, 42n60, 44n85; level of 205; Locke's conception of 36–7, 105; origins of state 34, 114; process of 32–3, 42n53, 43n76, 60, 105, 120n21
conformity 17n21, 77, 79, 82–3, 92, 102, 108, 152; Church 134; enforced 88–9, 131; impose 40, 84; to magistrate's command 76, 78, 112; occasional 144; opportunistic 221n36; religious 1, 6, 71n70, 132, 197; state policy 86
consent 32–4, 42n52, 42n60, 43n76, 80, 94n10, 125, 127, 136–8, 168, 195, 204, 206–7, 222n54, 225, 258, 261; contractual process 105, 120n20, 183–5, 210; to government 187; individual 13, 31, 36, 39, 126, 186, 189, 208, 211; liberal notions 237; mutual 259; of the people 35, 37, 193n83; role in Locke's political philosophy 188, 209; tacit 33, 42n59, 141n63
consent argument 14–16, 18n46, 106, 114, 125, 131, 133, 136–8, 156, 160, 167, 181–6, 189, 190n3, 192n55, 193n80, 195–6, 204–10, 225–6, 240–4, 249n75
contract 32, 80, 95n10; individuals 114, 205; social 257, 262n23; *see also* compact
contractual 36, 126; model of authority 43n83; negotiations 210; process 32, 114, 122n62; process of consent 105, 120n20
contractualist account of the state 118, 122n71

contradictions 65, 98n69; Locke's 90; of opinions in religion 240
conversion 200–3; to the Church of England 223n79; to English magistrate's religion 198; to toleration 67; to true religion 173, 199, 221n24
convert 27; to magistrate's religion 203–4
Cooper, Anthony Ashley 21, 37, 48, 61
Cranston, M. 3, 40n1, 48, 62–3, 72n86, 72n97, 73n100, 161n2, 227, 231, 246n7

de Beer, E. 65
democratic regime 259, 263n36; society 258, 263n30; *see also* liberal democracies
Derrida, J. 107
Design *see* Proast's Design
designate 226, 228; modal definition 121n52
designated limits 37
designed 95n26, 138, 183, 199; to answer specific questions 10; for promoting true religion 198; to remove threats 102; Tuckness's procedure 256
differences 44n87, 51, 117, 132, 188, 229, 251–2, 258–9, 266; basic 75; categorical 13, 26; crucial 81; defining 240; implications of 119; important 215; key 39; in practice 71n70, 112; primary point of 125; in religion 91; under threat 116
disagreement 77, 82, 99n72, 258–60; capable of resolving 252; irreducible 267; limited to individual debate 255; Locke and Proast 150; religious 6; between rival religious adherents 90; source of public 254; space for 54
disobedience 39, 108
Dissenters 12, 21, 53, 62, 86, 88–9, 96n44, 96n59, 102, 106, 144–8, 152, 163n53, 172, 175, 201–4, 221n31, 222n42; *see also* non-conformism, non-conformist, non-conformity
diversity 101, 116–17, 180–1, 245, 266–7; doctrinal 261; inevitability of 192n60, 263n35; of opinions 160; persistence of 259; religious 6–7, 16, 48, 71n70, 78, 102, 111, 131, 154, 167, 220n18, 221n28, 240–1
Dunn, J. 2, 11, 15, 16n8, 17n17, 18n35, 68, 99n72, 122n74, 136, 153, 155–6, 190, 195, 206, 262n1
Dworkin, G. 175–7, 191n36, 192n47

E-type effects 115
English Civil Wars 6, 52, 90, 116; pre-Civil War 86
entitlements 85, 95n32; equal 80–1; fundamental 81; to liberty 80–1, 93
episcopal 62; church in Scotland 145
equal entitlement 4, 228; to advance their religion by force 229; to individual liberty 25, 32, 80–1, 93, 138, 189; to their natural rights of liberty 256
equality 4, 119, 229, 247n23; background 232; individual 32; natural 17n11; reciprocal 106–7, 256; *see also* liberty and equality
excommunication 31, 41n30; excommunicated kings 30, 129

false religion 8, 12, 157–8, 164n81, 171, 178–9, 199, 212, 215, 230–1, 241, 244–5
fanatics 85–9, 102; fanatical extremist 145
foundation(s) 26, 232, 246; of Church liberty 106; of consent argument 138; of justification 206; of all morality 93–4; theological 4–5, 17n17, 207; of toleration 239
foundational 3; commitments 4; documents 21
freedom of conscience 3, 57

Geneva 106, 176–9, 249n75
God 29, 36, 56, 178, 180–1, 186–7, 189, 206, 236, 246, 262n1; abomination in the eyes of 94; acceptable to 104, 135, 169; accountable to 95n14, 108; allegiance to 39; appeal to 188, 190, 209–10; authorized 223n72; belief or faith in 93, 132; children of 234; committed by 137; conception of 171; decreed 58; determined by 44n95, 207; dishonoured 66, 99n71; out of conscience to 60; praying to 90; prescribed by 127; religion of 212; set in place by 43n83, 208; will of 4, 17n13, 35, 37–8, 51, 215, 249n74; would not deceive 199; *see also* grace of God, worship of God
God appointed 103; force 126; Government 222n54
God as source 36; of political authority 211; stemming from 60, 71n69, 105, 210

God's 29, 187, 206, 216; Creatures 4–5, 25, 32, 38, 79; ends 208; favour 127, 238; Grace 219; Honour 266; omnipotence 222n54; power 213; purposes 98n69, 184, 209, 211
God's knowledge 140n22, 221n25; of existence of 129; of what is necessary 139n5
Goldie, M. 2, 11–12, 15, 16n8, 17n27, 18n35, 48, 53, 143–50, 152–3, 155–6, 159–61, 161n2, 162n9, 162n22, 163n50, 163n51, 163n53, 163n69, 164n85, 173, 190, 195, 206, 220n6, 232
got into a wrong Way 174, 196, 220
Gough, J. W. 44n95, 121n35
governance 6–7, 95n15; capacity for 37, 79; effective 79–80, 131, 141n63; excess of 9; impose limits on 80; practical imperative 105; *see also* state governance, effective
grace of God 15, 196, 213, 216; proposition 159, 217–20, 223n71, 223n72
Gray, J. 121n28

Harris, I. 17n17, 98n69, 99n71, 99n72, 248n57, 262n1
heretical 252
heretics 3, 30, 53, 85, 129
Heyd, D. 121n28
High Church faction 147; Tories 145
High Churchmen 145–8

illegitimate 115, 117; extension of the magistrate's authority 70n42; means 220
illegitimately 43n76; exercising power 34, 44n95
impiety 187–8, 216–20; cannot be said without 186, 213, 246
impinge 78; on civil concerns 58; for civil reasons 28; on individual liberty 188; on inner liberty of belief 152; liberty of conscience 60; limits on entitlement 27–8, 30–1, 34–5, 37, 44n95, 51; upon religion 135; unjustly 56
India 191n42
Indies 176–9, 191n42, 249n75
indirectly and at a distance 150–1, 153–4, 171–2, 190, 195–7, 225
individual conscience 50, 52, 56, 59, 120n8, 120n10, 120n16, 234; liberty of 55, 103; realm of 58, 76, 248n57; sphere of 254–5

individual liberty 5, 7, 9–10, 25–7, 42n61, 42n62, 59, 71n70, 76, 78, 80, 92–4, 117, 119, 122n74, 138, 209; account of 107; centred on 101; coercion of 189; commitments 4, 11, 15–16, 252; concerns 212, 251, 253; expression of 3, 211; greater 37; ideal of 93, 102; imperative 37, 55, 79–81, 93, 105, 109, 266; limits 50, 60; Locke's conception of 32; realm of 43n75, 135, 248n57; reconciled with political authority 136, 183, 188; respect due to 118; subject to 255
inequality 106–7, 256
influence 2, 65, 68–9, 85; of Ashley 67–8, 72n86; causal 155; on government policy 64; lines of 150; on Locke 48, 61–2; processes of 80; seminal 3, 7, 50, 267; of Waldron 11, 14, 101, 109, 164n85
interference: arbitrary 97n65; without 31, 106; see also non-interference
intrude on beliefs and practices 28, 30; on lives of individuals 25–7, 59, 118, 189; on men's souls 137, 189; on religion 132
intruding on religious practice 105, 137
intrusion government 43n76, 51; irrational 118; magistrate's 60, 240; state 131
Islam 233, 235–6

Jew 174, 226–7, 254
Jews 5, 17n17, 99n71, 212, 216
Judaism 233, 236
justification of toleration 4, 13, 16, 24–6, 132, 180, 243; normative 83, 106; overall 79

Kant, I. 97n65, 257, 261, 262n23, 263n24; proto-Kantian 92
Klibansky, R. 22, 24, 40n5
Kraynak, R. P. 71n70, 120n8

Laslett, P. 23–4, 44n89, 51, 61, 63–4, 69n4, 72n78, 125, 139n2, 246n7
Latitudinarian 147; bishops 148; tract 143
Latitudinarians 147
latitudinism 91
legal enforcement 37; force 122n56
legislate 50; legislation 144
legislative point of view 255–6; power 36
legitimacy 31–4, 117, 126, 136, 139n5, 139n9; claims to 37; of government 35, 222n54; of government authority 188; lacking 36; of magistrate's actions 98n69; of magistrate's authority 185, 187, 218; of means 127, 139n10; political 208, 211, 258; Proast's position 195, 240; of the state 39, 115, 118–19, 125; see also political legitimacy
legitimate 29, 34, 175, 177, 183, 232; end 139n10, 188; government authority 32; jurisdiction 31, 130, 190; magistrate's authority 182, 187; means 161; political authority 136; scope of state activity 117–18; use of force 113, 237
legitimate state authority 32; scope 114–15; use of 117, 125
legitimately 34, 137, 182; entitled 113, 115, 136, 138, 181, 183; exercising authority 211
liberal 3, 39, 68; direction 10; humanist 237–9; modern 236; theories of justice 111; tradition 1–2, 7, 16, 16n8, 21, 29, 50, 107–8, 118, 136, 251, 257, 262n1, 267; views 63, 260
liberal democracies 256, 258, 267; democratic polities 263n31; democratic societies 251, 258, 261
liberalism 16, 16n8, 63, 71n70, 117; contemporary 266, 268n4; defence of 267; political 251, 256–61, 263n36, 264n42
Liberals 3, 32
liberty 3, 25, 40n20, 43n80, 55, 60, 80–1, 90, 93, 97n65, 99n71, 102, 105, 117, 137, 152, 182, 202, 215; abuse of 54; commitment to 4, 16; for contention and persecution 91; defence of 108–9, 267; denied to children 42n61; to destroy self 234; entitlements to 71n70, 189; equal rights to 101, 138; imperative of 7, 9; inner or inward 76, 104; of judgement 27, 56; limits 99n74, 120n21; Locke's conception 193n90; made possible 94, 106, 113; natural 17n11, 32–3, 205; natural right 5, 26, 38, 79, 107, 256; normative role 15; oppressed 97n59; outward 53; politically possible 37; positive 188, 193n90; preservation of 31, 92; principle of 2; relation with governance 95n15; residual 118

liberty, ecclesiastical 65; Christian 149; Church 106
liberty and equality 32; individual 4–5, 32, 107, 119; natural rights to 32, 38; normative commitment to 16; norms of 17n11
liberty in religion 245, 248n57; to decide on religion 50; to express religious differences 55; of opinion and worship 68; outward rites of worship 103; in religious ceremonial 51
liberty of conscience 6, 12, 106–7, 234, 267; inward 51, 56–7, 60, 81, 92, 104
light of nature 235, 247n38
Locke, J. 1, 16, 16n7, 16n8, 17n11–17n27, 18n42, 22–3, 25–8, 30–9, 40n12, 40n20, 40n23, 41n30–41n35, 42n54, 43n72–43n83, 44n86, 44n87, 50, 52–5, 59, 62–3, 65–6, 69n4, 69n16, 70n20, 70n38, 71n54, 72n71, 72n98, 73n101, 77–81, 86, 90–1, 93–4, 95n26, 95n34, 96n55–96n65, 97n68, 97n69, 98n71, 99n74, 101–9, 112–13, 116, 118, 120n3, 120n7–120n10, 121n39, 121n44, 122n56, 122n69, 126–7, 131–2, 140n22, 140n33, 141n59, 141n63, 143–7, 151–3, 156–9, 163n58, 163n72, 164n83, 170, 173–4, 182, 186, 188–90, 191n42, 192n47, 192n59, 193n83, 195, 197, 200–4, 207, 211, 213, 216, 220n6, 221n24–21n36, 222n42–222n57, 233, 246n7, 246n9, 248n68, 249n75, 252, 255, 257–9, 262n23; biographer 48, 72n97, 120n8; close association with ruling authorities 40n1; exiled in Holland 47; ideas 8, 10–13; literature 15, 109; overcoming of traditional Christian view 237, 239; references to commission 163n68; scepticism 15n128, 140n21, 160–1, 164n81, 177, 225–9, 236–8, 246n8, 247n19, 248n52; scholars 2, 5, 17n17, 44n89, 67, 180, 190, 232; scholarship 64, 148, 268n4; transformation in attitude 48, 68, 75–6, 78, 84; transition 14, 60–1, 68–9, 75, 80, 136, 258; see also consent argument, rationality argument, truth argument
Locke, J. friendship 47, 61; closest 23, 72n78

Locke, J. politics 49; political exile 8, 21, 47, 57, 109; political philosophy 38–9, 262n1; political views 72n86; political writings 10, 17n27, 37, 53, 73n100
Locke, J. reassessment 76; normative 76, 80; practical 67, 76–8
Locke, J. religion 6; false 230; used for ulterior motives 70n36; true 139n16, 160, 164n93, 171–2, 178, 214, 231–2, 234–5, 245–6, 249n76, 253–4
Locke, J. religious belief 248n53; diversity 71n70, 221n28; persecution 111
Locke, J. right of resistance 17n23, 42n57, 79, 120n23; to government 7, 42n57, 79, 81, 93, 94n8, 95n14, 107, 120n23, 121n32; to state persecution 164n89
Locke, J. shift of position 57–8, 61, 67, 75–6, 78, 80, 84, 95n15; qualitative 59–60, 71n70
Locke, J. toleration 6–9, 48; conception of 1, 3, 10, 34, 41n35, 43n76, 107, 189, 236, 256; position on 14, 67, 76, 78, 80, 84, 102, 117; views on 61, 65, 68, 75
Locke, J. writings 7–9, 12, 37, 64, 99n72; concealed authorship 23–4; early politics 49; later 44n87, 55, 59–60; natural law 69n14; political 10, 17n27, 53, 73n100
Locke–Proast 14; debate 1, 11, 15, 18n35, 143–4, 148–9, 153–6, 159–60, 163n68, 167, 190, 233; engagement 2, 10, 85, 114, 127, 196, 232
Locke's *A Letter Concerning Toleration* 1–2, 8–9, 11, 13–14, 21–2, 24, 28–9, 36, 44n90, 47–8, 55, 60, 70n36, 71n69, 73n101, 79, 84, 90, 93, 97n61, 99n71, 109–10, 125, 127, 130, 136, 143–5, 153, 160, 167, 172, 182, 188, 190, 192n47, 192n60, 207, 211, 256; first 149–50, 177, 180, 195, 205–6, 216, 228, 238, 242, 244, 249n74, 252; second 243, 246n8, 254; third 149, 164n83, 210, 253–4; normative discourse 102–5, 108; practical discourse 101–2
Locke's *An Essay Concerning Human Understanding* 47, 65, 129, 237
Locke's *An Essay Concerning Toleration* 3–4, 6, 8–9, 12–14, 24,

Index 275

29, 35, 39, 40n12, 48, 57, 61–4, 66–8, 72n101, 75–6, 79–81, 85, 95n26, 96n56, 97n59, 97n68, 101–2, 104, 108, 120n8, 140n18, 140n34, 160, 189, 203, 221n28
Locke's conception of toleration 3, 6, 8–10, 34, 41n35, 42n52, 43n76, 189, 236, 256; commitment to 4, 16, 212, 225–6, 242, 244; denial of 94, 97n68; denial to Catholics 85; early rejection (denial) 50, 53, 85, 94, 97n68, 101; normative argument 78–81; three considerations 15–16, 110, 125, 167–8, 206
Locke's *Epistola de Tolerantia* 21–3, 40n5, 47
Locke's letters 68, 110, 119, 121n39, 130, 144–5, 147, 167–8, 182, 207; letter to Boyle 72n97; letter to Limborch 149–50; letter to Stubbe 66–7, 73n100, 73n103
Locke's political philosophy 2–8, 11, 17n17, 33, 38–9, 42n52, 44n89, 44n95, 80–1, 93–4, 105, 111, 114, 119, 122n62, 125, 136, 182, 193n90, 195, 207, 251–2, 255, 262n1; broader 31; wider 1314
Locke's *Sacerdos* 120n8
Locke's *Two Tracts on Government* 7–11, 13–14, 16, 17n21, 35–7, 41n36, 41n39, 43n75, 43n80, 48–9, 51–61, 66–8, 70n42, 71n69, 71n70, 72n97, 75–8, 80–4, 87–93, 95n15, 97n61, 101–5, 108, 111, 120n7, 120n10, 120n16, 121n44, 121n48, 121n50, 125, 132, 135–6, 152, 181, 197, 212, 215, 220n6, 223n89, 234, 251, 259, 267
Locke's *Two Treatises of Government* 4, 7, 12, 18n36, 23–5, 36, 42n61, 44n85, 44n89, 51, 60, 63–4, 79, 81, 93, 105
Low Church Anglican 160; factions 147
Luther 2–3; Lutheran 174, 226–7, 254; Lutherans 66

M-type means 115
Macaulay, T. B. 2, 162n16
MacIntyre, A. 237
Macpherson, C. B. 42n60
magistrate 16, 131, 144, 171–2, 176, 181, 185, 193n80, 198, 201, 218; accountable to God 95n14; assistance 216; capable of enforcing policy 86; capacity to impose religious conformity 82; church 221n31; decree opposed by force of arms 51; imposing religious conformity 88; interfere with religion 12, 18n42; intrusion 240; limited in command 120n7; material capacity 77, 83; means at his disposal 122n56, 135, 183, 186–7; no commission to promote true religion 127, 243; no power to enforce religious worship 27, 103; not entitled to interfere 30, 59; opinion in religion 244; own interests 132; penalties 108; persecution 96n56; province 113; religion 152, 172–3, 189, 200, 202–4, 221n36; *see also* power of the magistrate
magistrate's authority 34, 60, 93, 97n69, 105, 144, 182, 185–90, 190n3, 223n89, 239–40, 243, 260; encouragement or constraint of 214; exercised for civil purposes 94; God as source 36, 187, 190; illegitimate extension of 70n42; individuals subject to 240; justification of 249n74; legitimacy 218; legitimate 183; limits on 59; scope of 127; sphere of 30
magistrate's command 56, 58, 76, 79–81, 92–3, 105, 132–3, 150, 152, 184; conformity to 55, 78, 84, 112; contrary to 60, 94n8; falling outside 43n75; legitimate scope of 183; limiting 59; limits on 43n84, 94; means to enforce 122n56; obedience to 70n20, 83; religion not enforceable by 255; religious conformity imposed 77; resistance in matters of religion 204; subject to 6, 44n87; subordination of religious expression to 101; things indifferent 103–4
magistrate's jurisdiction 97n69, 183; commission from individuals subject to 184; confined to civil concerns 36, 59, 138; exclusion of religion 205, 207; extent 182; final confirmation of 186; over religion 185
magistrate's use of force 84, 134, 169, 171–2, 181, 203, 214, 219–20; to advance religion 177–8, 180, 190, 229; indirect 152; presumed entitlement 177; public 254; in religious affairs 78, 151, 190, 206, 215–16, 218, 220

Mahometan 174, 226–7, 254
Mahometans 5, 17n17, 99n71
Marshall, J. 12, 17n26, 52, 65, 73n103, 97n68, 162n16
Mendus, S. 121n28, 122n69, 122n74, 122n77, 164n85
Mill, J. S. 3, 116–17, 122n69, 245; *On Liberty* 2, 188
Miller, J. 145, 162n16
Milton, J. R. 64, 70n29, 97n59
"modal" account 126, 139n10; of the state 118–19, 125, 183, 185–8, 190, 218

Nagel, T. 267
natural law 4–5, 69n14, 98n69, 103, 206, 248n57, 262n1; enforce 37, 120n21; God-given 210; identification with the will of God 17n13, 38; natural rights derived 17n15, 26, 38
natural right 17n15, 33, 40n21, 106, 108, 114, 210; to liberty 5, 25–6, 32, 38, 79, 107, 256
negligence 151, 154, 172, 196–200, 220n18
Nicholson, P. 11, 18n35, 40n12, 232, 247n20
non-biblical argument 110, 119, 154; case for toleration 155
non-Christian discourse 125
non-conformism 201
non-conformists 220n6; Protestant 86
non-conformity 203
non-interference 41n36; legally prescribed sphere 106
non-jurors 145
non-neutral principles 175, 252
normative 9, 15, 37, 76, 93, 101–2, 131, 177, 205, 251, 255; argument for toleration 78–81, 89, 92, 117, 135, 204; basis 256; commitment to individual liberty 11, 16, 252; concerns 4, 7, 212; content of the Letter 109; critique 195–6; discourse 84, 94, 108; grounds 71; ideals 5, 188; imperative of individual liberty 55, 105; justification of toleration 24–6, 106; level 75; limits 39; means 67; parallels 107; premise (iii) 82, 116; right of individuals 138; sources 38, 54; terms 425
normative and practical 9, 80, 83; commitments 267; defence of toleration 266; dimensions 7;
elements of Locke's discourse 75–6, 79, 94; imperatives 10–11, 13, 81, 109; judgments 37; justifications of toleration 24–6

obedience 6, 43n83, 52, 76, 169, 205; hierarchy of 105; obligations of 27, 32, 34, 42n57, 44n87, 51, 56, 70n20, 70n42; outward 56–7, 81, 83; passive 51; political 33; receive 31
obligations 31–2, 49, 51, 56, 85; discharge 122n62; highest 127, 233, 238; of obedience 27, 34, 42n57, 44n87, 70n20; of political obedience 33; source of 136; unconditional 52, 70n42
one true religion 153, 156–7, 163n72, 167, 172–3, 181, 191n26, 192n56, 228, 235, 246n9, 248n52
outcomes 5, 25, 39, 54, 58, 84, 204, 256; adverse 92; avoid 77; between liberty and governance 105; contrary 89, 120n10; deadly 222n42; detrimental 229; Grace of God 218; likely 82; of the Locke-Bagshaw dispute 57; reciprocal 178; state policy 131; undesirable 78; unlikely 90
outward conformity 58, 76, 78, 83–4, 93, 95n26, 135, 152, 202–3, 221n36; enforced 85; impose 77, 82, 134; to the magistrate's command 55, 112; policy of 92

papists 84–5, 95n9
penalties 157, 171–2, 190n3, 193n80, 196–8, 200–4, 217, 219, 221n24, 221n26; civil 41n30, 41n31, 107; of death 113; force of 133, 151, 170, 178; imposed on Catholics 86; purpose of 191n13
penalty of excommunication 31, 41n30; state 39; submission to 108
persecution 2–3, 21, 55, 62, 86, 89, 96n41, 108, 153; Anglican 149; authority for 12; Catholic 150, 220n6; of Dissent 145; excuse for 128; failure to achieve its ends 116; indictment of rationality 119; magistrate's 96n56; of non-conformists 220n6; popish 150; of Protestants 220n6; rational methods 14, 109; religious 47, 111, 133, 152; Romish 149–50; state 17n26, 91, 97n59, 102, 164n89; victims of 109

persecutors 11, 111; interests of 14, 101, 110, 115, 117, 119, 122n77; rationality 118; state 109
Perswasion 170, 174, 196, 211; third sort or degree 144, 157–8, 231, 247n17
pessimism 3; Locke's pessimistic view 215
pitfalls 148, 159; of the truth argument 131
pluralism 258; Protestant 146–7; reasonable 259–60; religious 65, 99n71, 116, 160
political legitimacy 32, 136, 208, 211, 258
political philosophy 260; Locke's 2–8, 11, 13–14, 17n17, 31, 33, 38–9, 42n52, 44n89, 44n95, 80–1, 93–4, 105, 111, 114, 119, 122n62, 125, 136, 182, 193n90, 195, 207, 251–2, 255, 262n1; of John Rawls 257
political power 2, 28, 33, 113, 182, 261
political thought 10–11; liberal 3; Locke's 14, 62
popish 150; party 62
Popkin, R. 140n21
Popple, W. 8, 21–2, 143
power of the magistrate 43n83, 51, 60, 66, 130, 170–1, 181–2, 185, 187, 196–7, 203
prejudice 41n34, 106, 151, 154, 162n16, 170, 172, 181, 184, 196, 205, 211, 222n48; no 243; without 214
prejudiced 196, 217
premise (i) 77–8, 82–5, 87–92, 96n56, 101–2, 120n16, 212
premise (ii) 77–8, 82–9, 92, 101–2, 112, 212
premise (iii) 76, 81–3, 89, 92–3, 95n9, 102, 106, 108, 116–17, 131, 138, 212
Presbyterian 174, 226–7, 254; church 12
Presbyterians 99n71, 146
privatization strategy 239, 254, 262n11
Proast, J. 1, 9–11, 16, 97n65, 99n71, 133, 140n17, 140n33, 143, 148–50, 159–61, 161n2, 162n5, 162n12, 163n50, 163n53, 164n83, 164n93, 175, 180, 182–3, 190n3, 191n8, 191n26, 192n47, 192n59, 193n80, 193n83, 193n89, 212, 214, 217, 220n3, 220n6, 220n18, 222n48, 223n97, 225–7, 231–3, 236–7, 248n63, 255, 260, 262n14, 267; accusations of scepticism 228–9, 246n8, 253, 262n7; claims 154, 168, 173; contradiction 196, 206, 216, 218; debate 2, 17n26, 85, 95n24, 126, 128, 139n5, 147, 155, 161, 235, 266; expulsion from the chaplaincy 162n22; insists 187, 197, 227; magistrate's use of force 78, 134, 151, 169, 171–2, 181, 191n9, 216, 218–20, 223n89, 254; outlook 146, 251; perspective 179, 241; position 15, 196, 240, 252; prevarication 221n24; proposition 152, 174, 176; rejects 178; response 207, 221n26; Restoration argument 153; serious and impartial examination 191n13, 198, 200–2, 221n25; statements 163n37, 208; third sort or degree of Perswasion 144, 157–8, 247n17; true interests 184–6; true religion 211, 222n67, 245–6, 247n20, 249n76; wickedness of men 223n78
Proast Agonistes 218
Proast and Locke 134, 144, 154, 156, 167, 207, 225; engagement 2, 8, 14, 110, 112, 114, 127, 129, 147, 149, 155, 177, 184, 196, 226, 232, 237, 245, 252, 260; response to Locke 170, 173, 178, 190, 216, 248n63, 255; response to Proast 11, 15, 133, 139n5, 153, 158, 174, 200, 204, 210, 228, 246
Proast's Appeal to God 186–8, 190, 206, 209–10, 213, 218
Proast's Design 168, 195–8, 200–2, 204
Proast's Method 157, 170, 172–3, 195–205, 214, 221n36, 223n79, 243, 266
Proast's Proportion 196–7
proportion 195–7, 200, 204, 212; duly proportioned 198, 201
proscribe(d) 5, 41n35, 121n28, 122n74; animal sacrifice 30, 249n74; atheists 94, 98n69, 99n72; religious practices 55, 80, 90, 96n54, 102
proscription 43n76, 55, 66, 91–2, 94, 95n9, 96n54, 98n69, 120n3
Protestant country 66; Dissenters 145; monarchs 144; non-conformists 86, 220n6; pluralism 146–7; sects 146
Protestantism 3
Protestants 65, 86, 220n6; see also Dissenters

278 *Index*

public 5, 53, 95n32, 96n41, 249n74, 251–6; agreement 174, 176, 233–4, 260–1, 263n30; association with Latitudinarians 147; authority 173, 175, 191n26; debate 145; disorder 50; food supplies 30–1; good 189; interest 28; justification 232–3; liberty 55, 90; life 257; made 62; order 118, 135; professions allowed 66; protest 69n16; reply 143; safety 12; sphere 239, 248n57; worshipping of God 41n31
punishment 84, 95n34, 173, 199–201, 203, 209, 254; of the erroneous 197, 253
punitive 53; authority 41n31; sanctions 53, 214

Quakers 99n71
qualitative 59–60; difference 182, 190; shift 71n70; transformation 76
quantitative increase 59–60; transformation 76
quarrels 54, 66; between High and Low Church factions 147; Locke's with Proast 236–7

Raphael, D. D. 41n35, 43n76, 121n28
rational 14, 97n65, 109, 118; choice 170; individuals 232; means 127, 197; persons 257; point of view 116; religious commitments of individuals 237; use of force 135
rationale 79, 202
rationality argument 14–16, 95n24, 110–13, 115, 117, 119, 121n45, 125, 132–5, 137–8, 140n25, 144, 154–6, 163n63, 167–8, 182–3, 186, 190, 204–5, 225–6, 242–5
Rawls, J. 16, 95n32, 232, 234, 251, 256–60, 262n22, 262n23, 263n24, 263n29, 263n30, 263n31, 263n35, 264n42; political liberalism 261, 263n36
realpolitik 31, 34, 37–8, 44n95, 88, 105
reciprocal conclusions 179; dialogue 235; equality 106–7, 256; outcome 178; requirements 233
reciprocity 232; communicative 235; criterion of 85–6, 95n32, 177, 192n45, 254
Reformation 2, 7, 29, 146, 234; English 116
religious 16; conflict 83; diversity 6–7, 48, 71n70, 78, 102, 111, 131, 154, 167, 180–1, 220n18, 221n28, 240–1; toleration 2, 22, 34, 58, 63, 65, 137, 143, 234
religious conformity 1, 71n70, 77, 132; arguments for 197; enforced 6, 131; imposed 87–9; outward 82–4
religious differences 4, 8, 101; of fanatics 87; open expression of 54–5, 76–7, 82–3, 89–91; privatization 254; propensity to produce conflict 92; removing the visible signs of 112; toleration of 78, 131
religious liberty 2–3, 6, 27, 40n20, 58, 108, 118; individual 25, 78
religious worship 60, 81, 85, 103, 248n57; benign consequences 96n55; necessary matters 59, 104; outward 9, 76, 80, 93; perfect and uncontrollable 79–80; things indifferent in 49–50, 57, 69n9
Remonstrant 40n1; church 22
Restoration 53, 63; argument 153; of Charles II 49, 52, 90, 146; England 57, 152; period 163n51; settlement 145, 148
restrain 39, 222n54; unrestrained 42n61
restraint 54, 77, 96n34, 193n90
Revolution of 1688 10, 14, 144–5, 147–8
rights 5, 30, 33, 85, 95n32, 106, 118, 256; Bill of Rights 144; civil 27–8, 31, 99n71, 239; defending 109; equal 101, 177; individual 10, 257; natural 17n15, 25–6, 32, 38, 79, 107–8, 114, 210; of other men 249n74; residual 122n74; *see also* criterion of reciprocity
Roman 106; Catholic 69n16, 97n68; Catholics 161

salvation of souls 29, 151–2, 167–8, 178, 182–3, 188, 195–201, 203, 211, 222n42, 233, 235, 240, 244, 252, 255
Sancroft, William 147
scepticism 2, 15, 18n35, 128–32, 164n81, 178–80, 228–9, 233, 235–6, 240–2, 246, 255; denying 230–1, 246n8, 247n19, 248n52, 253; Locke's 140n21, 160–1, 177, 192n55, 225–7, 232, 237–8; role of 11, 192n58
Schochet, G. J. 24

secular 132; argument for toleration 167; authorities 49; interests 240; liberal terms 261; outlook 236; pluralism 160; power 96n47; terms 98n69
secularization 237; of religious belief 236, 238; societal 16
separation 105; of church and state 13, 24, 28–31, 40n13, 94, 236–9
Shaftesbury, Earl of (Cooper, A. A.) 21, 48, 57, 61–3, 68, 72n71, 72n78, 72n86
Skinner, Q. 3, 10–13, 18n36, 150
source of Catholicism's danger to state 97n59; conflict 94; disorder 91; removed 83
Stanton, T. 16n8, 17n17, 42n52, 43n68, 98n69, 99n72, 136, 261
state 4, 12–13, 24, 27–31, 41n30, 87, 91, 97n59, 102, 109, 111–13, 115, 117–18, 126–7; action 154; commitments 80; demand for limitation of 53; English 16; European 2; interests 93; interference from 106; intervention 50; intrusion 131; leaders 7; legitimacy 119, 125; material capacity 77, 92; matters concerned 62; minister of 61; persecution 17, 164n89; power 37; purposes 98n69; regulation 239; religious diversity 6, 48; requirements 107; security 25, 55, 85; threat 86, 88, 96n56; toleration opposed 9; of war 39, 44n95;
state account 190, 218; contractualist 122n71; functional 122n62; modal 118, 125, 183, 185–8
state authority 6, 49–50, 58, 131, 190; threats to 102
state conformity 82; religious 83, 85
state defined 115–16; impossible to define 113–14;
state definition 114–15, 119, 121n55, 122n62, 125; functional 218; modal 117, 121n52
state governance 37; effective 4, 6–7, 9–10, 16, 24, 26, 31–2, 54–5, 76, 79–81, 83–5, 87, 90, 92–4, 101–2, 105, 109, 212
state of nature 4–5, 24, 26, 32–3, 37, 42n54, 107, 109, 120n21, 136, 184, 206; corrupt 210
state policy 55, 78, 83; alternative 112; of religious conformity 83, 85; of toleration 3–4, 27, 92, 113, 131; of toleration opposed 9

state religion in England 85; official church 24
state willing to use force 112; force sanctioned 214
Strauss, L. 139n13
subordination 45, 101, 219
suppress 96n56; suppressed 2; suppression 96n34

Tate, J. W. 17n17, 18n35, 18n46, 98n69, 99n72, 121n39, 121n45, 122n56, 122n62, 122n69, 122n77, 140n22, 140n29, 193n90, 247n22, 262n1, 264n42
theological assumptions 51, 130, 237, 262n1; concerns 5, 119, 132; context 11; dimension 262n1; foundations 4–5, 17n17, 207; framework 14; imperatives 98n69; justification 186; level 184, 196; matters 15; outlook 220; perspective 16, 255; proposition 159; reasons 215; sources 4, 246
three considerations for toleration 14–16, 48, 106, 110–11, 114, 125, 127, 134, 138, 150–1, 154–6, 167–8, 195, 206, 211, 225
toleration 2, 15, 26, 28, 41n36, 48, 50, 53, 64, 73n103, 82, 90, 103, 116, 121n28, 143, 162n9, 180, 190, 212, 221n28, 234, 240–1, 243, 251; Act of 1689 40n12, 144–8, 162n16; alternative 134; campaigned for 49; case against 176, 196, 215; case for 205; commitment to 244; contrary positions on 125; defence of 11, 71n70, 154, 168, 188–9, 246, 266; denominational exception 93; doctrine of 70n38; European debates 1, 7–8; to fanatics 87, 89; force inconsistent 150; institutional foundations of 239; justification of 4, 13, 16, 24–5, 79, 83, 106, 132; limits on 92, 94, 96n54; moral challenge of 233, 235, 242, 245, 267; necessary relationship with liberty 27, 78; necessity of 133; negative position on 102; non-biblical account of 119; opposition to 54; position on 76, 80, 84–5; preferable alternative 178; primary objection to 211; process of 6, 31; reason for 181; scepticism as basis for 226; source of 137; standard conception 43n76; supporter of 65; support for 213; theory of 156, 161, 195; to things

toleration *continued*
  indifferent 52; of those that differ 110; undermining 58, 222n67; universal 214; *see also* argument for toleration, Locke, J. toleration, three considerations for toleration
toleration advocacy 58, 63, 66, 88; advocates of 35, 180
toleration denied 86, 94, 97n68, 101, 242; to Catholics 85–6; refused 93, 129; repudiate 241
toleration of multiple religious groups 99n71; accorded to Catholics 97n68; of Dissenters 102, 145; of Jews 216; of pagans 99n71, 216; of Protestant sects 146;
toleration of religions 173, 214; religious differences 78; rival 229
toleration policy 25–7, 37, 49, 53, 59, 62, 67, 76, 80, 92, 111, 131, 151, 154, 240–1, 245, 256; state 3, 9, 27, 55, 91, 112–13, 131
toleration rights 106; justifying in terms of 106–8; universal right to 58, 76, 206
true religion 15, 91, 128, 137, 139n16, 146, 151, 156, 159, 163n53, 164n83, 164n93, 168–72, 175, 181, 187–8, 190n3, 191n26, 192n59, 202, 206, 210, 212–14, 218, 220n6, 221n24, 221n36, 222n67, 223n89, 226–8, 235, 244–6, 253–5, 260, 266; knowledge of 129–30, 144, 157–8, 160–1, 164n81, 173–4, 176–80, 189, 197, 200, 225, 229, 231–2, 237–8, 241–2, 247n20, 249n76; promoting 127, 1512, 167, 183, 188, 1956, 198-9, 201, 203, 211, 233, 240, 243, 252
truth argument 14–15, 125, 127–33, 137–8, 140n25, 156, 161, 167–9, 171, 174, 176–7, 179–80, 185, 189, 192n55, 192n58, 204, 225–6, 231, 240–4, 249n75
Tuckness, A. 11, 255–6
Tully, J. 21–2, 47

ultimate conditions of possibility 11, 15, 225–6, 242, 244
use of force 1, 87–8, 151, 169, 190, 206, 215–16, 218, 237; upon Dissenters 163n53; due proportion 198, 220n6; impervious to 111; incapable of regulating inner belief 112, 135; justification 156–7, 229, 231; magistrate's 78, 134, 171–2, 176, 181, 219–20; in matters of religion 152–4, 254–5; no biblical authority 216; none needed 213
use of force absent 239, 248n57, 255, 262n11; magistrate's 244, 254

van Limborch, Philip 21–3, 40n1, 40n5, 47, 149–50
Vernon, R. 11, 17n26, 18n35, 85, 122n74, 192n45, 232–3, 235–6, 247n22, 248n53, 248n69
violence 54, 56, 89, 91, 108, 245; avoiding 267; government restraint 222n54; outward 84; without 39
von Leyden, W. 10

Waldron, J. 2, 15, 17n17, 18n35, 73n101, 93, 97n68, 111, 113–18, 121n44, 121n45, 121n52, 121n55, 122n56, 122n62, 122n69, 122n77, 125, 129–30, 134–5, 140n25, 153, 156, 163n58, 163n69, 164n85, 167–8, 176, 182, 190, 191n42, 192n55, 195, 197, 204, 206, 218, 220, 249n75, 262n14, 264n42; interpretation of Locke's Letter 11, 14, 101, 108–10, 119, 121n39; Locke's rationality argument 154–5; modal account of the state 183; rejects Locke's line of reasoning 179; silly principle 180
Washington, G. 107
Whig 22; associate 23; direction 145; opposition to Charles II 21, 47; optimism 2
Whiggery 162n9
Whigs 144–5
Wolfson, A. 11, 18n35, 18n46, 236–9
Wootton, D. 11, 17n26, 62, 64, 73n100, 73n103
worship 8, 66, 87, 119; church 69; dissenting places 201; divine 58–9, 76, 106, 152, 199; of False Gods 213; form of 91; liberty of 68; matters of 105, 120n8; necessary to 60; outward 27, 103–4; places and times of 54; prescribed 137, 184–5; purity of 252–3; ways of 206
worshipper 103
worship of God 27, 41n31, 50, 97n68, 98n69, 103–4, 106, 248n57; by Dissenters 144; public 41n31